Myanmar

Myanmar

The Dynamics of an Evolving Polity

edited by

David I. Steinberg

BOULDER
LONDON

Published in the United States of America in 2015 by
Lynne Rienner Publishers, Inc.
1800 30th Street, Boulder, Colorado 80301
www.rienner.com

and in the United Kingdom by
Lynne Rienner Publishers, Inc.
3 Henrietta Street, Covent Garden, London WC2E 8LU

Library of Congress Cataloging-in-Publication Data
A Cataloging-in-Publication record for this book
is available from the Library of Congress.
ISBN: 978-1-62637-181-1

British Cataloguing in Publication Data
A Cataloguing in Publication record for this book
is available from the British Library.

Printed and bound in the United States of America

The paper used in this publication meets the requirements
of the American National Standard for Permanence of
Paper for Printed Library Materials Z39.48-1992.

5 4 3 2 1

Contents

Acknowledgments

Along with the contributors, I would like to acknowledge the support that has come from a variety of sources for this project. An international conference was organized in October 2013 to bring all of us together at the School of Advanced International Studies (SAIS), Johns Hopkins University. Funding for the conference was graciously provided by the Luce Foundation, the Asia Foundation, Chevron, Mitsubishi, Proctor & Gamble, and SAIS itself. We thank those organizations for their confidence and interest.

At a personal level, I benefited from the unstinting support of Karl Jackson and William Wise at SAIS, which was critical to the success of this effort. The stalwart assistance of Jacqueline Ganem at SAIS and of our heroic manipulators of the mysteries of grammar and the Internet above and beyond the call of duty—Amy Killian and Melissa Carlson, also at SAIS—is also greatly appreciated. Helena Kolenda and Li Ling of the Luce Foundation could not have been more helpful.

We would like to thank the two anonymous readers of the manuscript for their comments, as well as each other for comments and suggestions on our chapters. We are grateful for the assistance of the staff at Lynne Rienner Publishers, who worked with us throughout the publication process.

The authors have some two hundred collective years of Burma/Myanmar experience, and it is fitting that we as a group acknowledge the friendships and support of a myriad of Burmese individuals who have given their time and energies to assist each of us in learning about that complex set of societies that was and is Burma/Myanmar. We all are in their debt. Although too numerous to list here, they are part of this collective effort. As authors, each of us, of course, is responsible for our own contributions to this volume—one that intentionally lacks a uniform political agenda, and one that we hope will contribute to the dialogue on the future of Myanmar.

—David I. Steinberg

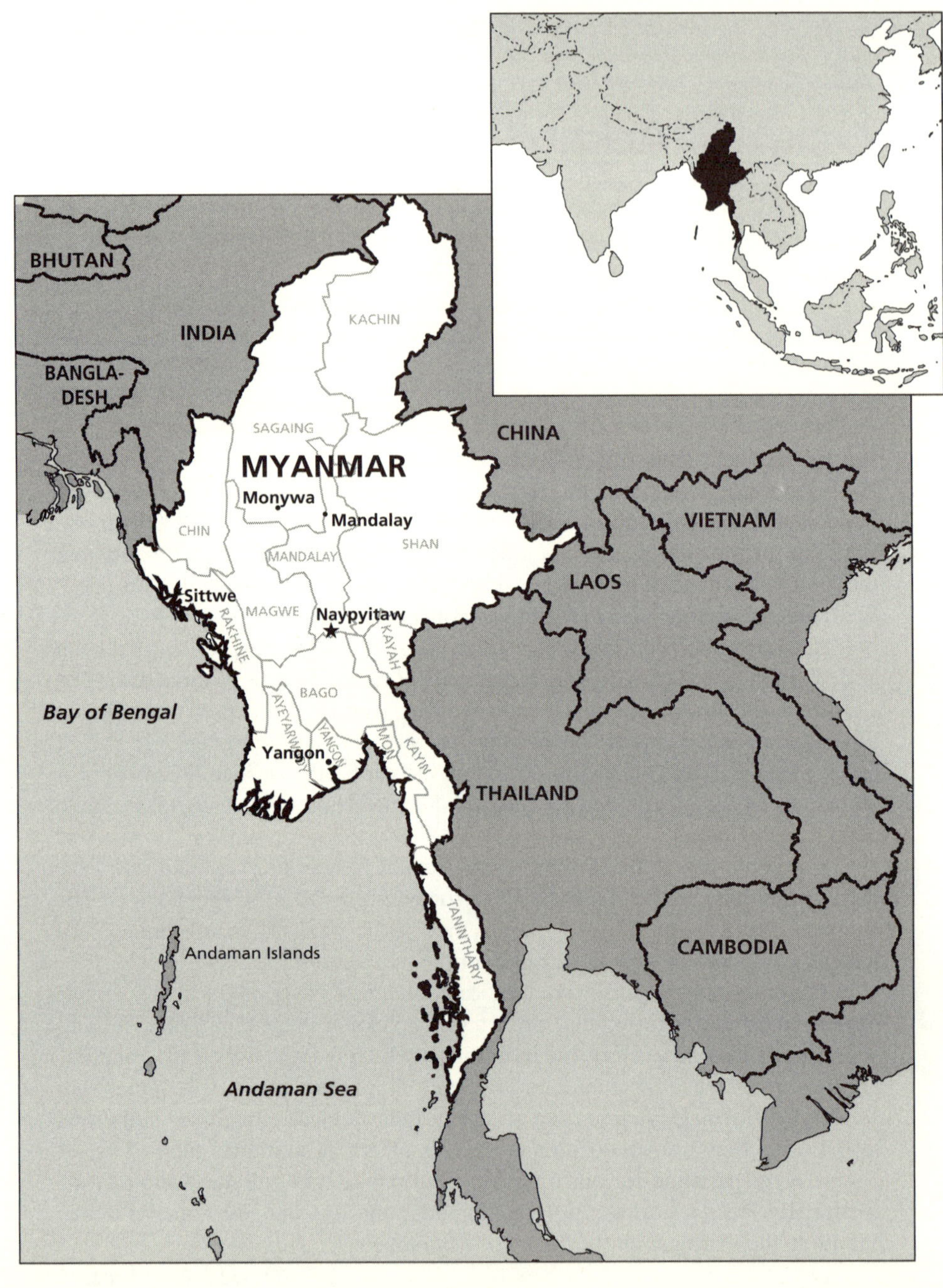
BHUTAN
INDIA
BANGLA-
DESH
CHINA
MYANMAR
KACHIN
SAGAING
Monywa
Mandalay
CHIN
SHAN
MANDALAY
Sittwe
MAGWE
Naypyitaw
RAKHINE
KAYAH
BAGO
AYEYARWADY
YANGON
MON
KAYIN
Yangon
VIETNAM
LAOS
THAILAND
CAMBODIA
Bay of Bengal
TANINTHARYI
Andaman Islands
Andaman Sea

1

Contemporary Myanmar: Setting the Stage

David I. Steinberg

In the darker days of the 1990s, a dissident, perceptive Burmese colonel privately summed up the military's dominant role in Myanmar. "The play is over," he said, "but the audience is forced to remain in their seats and the actors refuse the leave the stage." As trenchant and accurate as that characterization was at the time, and in spite of many dire predictions that the denouement of the tragedy that was Burma/Myanmar had no end in sight, a new era belatedly dawned in 2011. The audience no longer remains forcibly glued to their seats, although the actors may wish to continue to control the drama's action. More a type of experimental theater, audience participation has transformed the immediate scene with a cast expanded and the script blurred. Observers outside the theater anxiously watch, and the political drama critics are conflicted.

The audience could not exit the *tatmadaw*'s (armed forces') previous abject performance, and in some sense and for multiple reasons, the actors recognized that the script had to be at least partly rewritten, perhaps to continue to give themselves the starring roles, but with an expanded cast. Whether this will satisfy the audience or the internal and external critics remains unclear.[1] A final curtain is unknown, and even unscripted. Myanmar has undergone profound changes from which reversion to the old, military-authored drama is no longer completely possible. However, naively hopeful aspirations of the military's retirement to the barracks and that the tortuous road to modified democracy is open, clear, and inevitable are equally uncertain and indeed implausible. Beliefs that the drama will end as comedy, not tragedy, are widespread. But more likely, the play will simply continue, with crises and lulls, to no apparent final denouement, for realities and changing circumstances interdict the best-laid, scripted plans of states or nations, and especially those in the process of transition. Change and uncertainty are inevitable. "Happy endings, nice and tidy," as *The Threepenny Opera* reminds us, are only "learned in school."

The international euphoria over the "opening" to the West has led to effusive optimism, business and recreational tourism and exploration, rising prices, increasing foreign assistance, instant analyses, and ephemeral experts. Long prone to be a *tabula obscura* with few authoritative statistics not polluted by political whims or considerations, Myanmar has become more accessible, although accurate data are often still unavailable. Although access has become easier, many have been led to focus inadvertently on that society through ethnocentrically tinged lenses reflecting our own premises and hypotheses, most of which have remained untested. Most analysts lack the longitudinal knowledge, comparative experience, and disciplinary training to ponder the longer range issues facing that country—important because of its strategic location, size, diverse peoples and cultures, history, and potential.

Some important foreign groups and individuals have called for moderation, even skepticism, in acceptance of and assistance to a regime they regard as still suspect, having advocated "regime change" leading to a civilian-dominated government for some score of years. Others argue that, although the reforms are likely to be uneven and unsynchronized, support for positive changes in all fields will create expanded, vested interests in such changes, deterring the dangers of their being rescinded. Debate between these opinions is evident in the world's major capitals, with important policy implications. This volume will contribute to understanding some of the essential and basic issues involved in the future of Myanmar.

At this critical juncture in early 2014, a group of seasoned, expert observers of Myanmar from a variety of countries, multiple disciplines, and quite divergent viewpoints have written on what they regard as some of the important, continuing issues that Myanmar faces if it is to transition into a nation that uplifts the lives of its diverse peoples. These are considered opinions on more basic questions or problems that are unlikely to make the evening news or the latest tweets. They are, however, fundamental conundrums that the multiple societies that are Myanmar will have to face to achieve the goals that those diverse peoples have articulated for themselves. They are the issues of which foreign policy and business executives must be cognizant to be effective. This introduction provides the societal background leading to the political changes since 2011, the reform efforts, and a volume synopsis that will prove helpful to those internally and those externally involved in Myanmar policy affairs. It is addressed to serious observers of that society, and to those who wish to make comparative observations and studies of transitional states and their evolutionary issues. No attempt has been made here to enforce any analytical, political, or social framework onto this volume, as we have attempted to reflect the divergence of views that has been evident in modern studies of this important country.

On Names: Burma vs. Myanmar

No issue has been more confusing to the uninitiated, and more polarizing to those who are conversant with that society, than the name of the state. *Burma* was the Anglicized name of the country in the colonial period, and on independence in 1948, it was officially known as the *Union of Burma*. In Burmese, however, it was called *Myanmar Naingantaw*—"the Royal Country of Myanmar," a millennial-old term from classical inscriptions. The name of the state has changed several times: the Union of Burma, the Socialist Republic of the Union of Burma, the Union of Myanmar, and its present designation since 2011, the Republic of the Union of Myanmar.

In July 1989, the military junta, known as the State Law and Order Restoration Council (SLORC), changed the name to Myanmar. The United Nations (UN) adopted this designation, as did most countries. The Burmese opposition led by Aung San Suu Kyi, followed by a number of states—most conspicuously the United States—continued to use Burma because they believed the perpetrators of the changed name were not politically legitimate. The use of either term thus became a surrogate indicator of political persuasion. Here, without political intent, Myanmar is essentially used, but at the discretion of each author. Burma may be employed for the earlier period, and Burma/Myanmar for continuity. Citations remain as in the original. Some authors will use *Burmese* to designate a citizen of that state, the language, and as an adjective. Other names have been changed (see Appendix B). The majority ethnic *Burmans* are now call *Bamah*.

The Heritage of Authoritarian Rule

For two generations Burma/Myanmar had effectively been under military control. It was directly administered under martial law regimes (1962–1974, 1988–2011), and indirectly through the military's chosen channel of control—the Burma Socialist Programme Party (BSPP, 1974–1988). The military heritage in this country is, thus, exceptionally strong, and its national imprimatur has been one of the longest in the international modern era. Even in the civilian period from independence (1948–1962), military influence was profound; it saved the state from disintegration through political and ethnic rebellions and directly administered the country for eighteen months (1958–1960). There have been three coups d'état: a constitutional one in 1958 forced on a civilian administration to prevent a civilian civil war, the 1962 coup that was to enshrine military control perpetually and hold the fissiparous state together, and the coup of 18 September 1988 to shore up the previous, failed military-controlled government. Based on disdain of civilian politicians, whom the *tatmadaw* believed were corrupt, inefficient, lacking developmental skills or foresight, unpatriotic, and capable of sacrificing the unity of the state to special ethnic or economic interests, the military designed a set of systems that would ensure for perpetuity both its effective control over state power and its autonomy.[2]

That control was made manifest in 2008 in the formation of a new constitution—the third in the state's history. The first was in 1947 just prior to independence, and the second in 1974, which established a single-party totalitarian system based on an Eastern European model in the Cold War era. The newest constitution, under which the state now operates, ensures the leading role of the *tatmadaw* in the state, its autonomy, key cabinet positions, its ability to revert to military control in a crisis, prevention of criminal charges against any individual in previous administrations for actions taken in their official capacities, and 25 percent active duty military in all parliaments, national and local. It was passed by a clearly manipulated referendum in May 2008 (with 92.4 percent approval) and after a long (since 1993), heavily scripted, tortuous, and prolonged formation process of writing under severe restrictions. It was in response to the national elections of 1990 won by the opposition National League for Democracy (NLD) with 80 percent of the seats and 57 percent of the votes—an election the purposes of which are still debated but the results of which were ignored by the military administration.[3]

In 2004, the then head of state, President (General) Than Shwe, and his prime minister, General Khin Nyunt, declared a seven-point path to what was called "discipline-flourishing democracy." The government inaugurated on 30 March 2011 was the culmination of that process. Western governments were skeptical, having stressed the lack of human rights and the varied house arrest of the democracy icon Aung San Suu Kyi, who became a Nobel laureate in 1991 and who was extremely popular in many circles both inside the country and internationally. US policy for much of this period was "regime change"—honoring the results of the 1990 elections and returning government to civilian control after about half a century of military domination.

The totalitarian rule by junta from 1988, first by the SLORC until 1997 and then by the State Peace and Development Council (SPDC), resulted in authoritarian control (the socialist ideology of the BSPP had been abandoned), with extensive restrictions on civil rights, widespread human rights abuses, and a continuation of the unitary state. Successful attempts were made, however, to broker cease-fires with seventeen ethnic rebellions. These were respites from killing but far from peace treaties that have yet to be negotiated. The question of some fair, in some Burmese sense, distribution of power and resources among the majority Burman population and a variety of ethnic groups remains unresolved.

Public dissatisfaction over military administration prompted demonstrations following the 1988 coup—demonstrations that were brutally suppressed. Some 3,000 were said to have died in the failed people's revolution of 1988 and its suppression, although no definitive figure is yet possible. Sporadic unrest followed, including incipient riots by students that prompted the regime to close sporadically many educational institutions for long periods. Wholesale arrests of opposition figures or simply those identified as antistate were endemic, while Aung San Suu Kyi was placed under house arrest for much of the period. A major confrontation and resulting deaths with her followers at Depayin in Central Myanmar in 2003 prompted outrage and additional US sanctions that year, as did the Buddhist *sangha* (clergy) demonstrations in the fall of 2007. The *tatmadaw* has continuously evoked the specter of "chaos" as threatening their primary objective—the unity of the state and their continued political control.

Although in popular international parlance the Myanmar state was called isolated, this was inaccurate, as closer ties with the Chinese and improved relations with India and the Association of Southeast Asian Nations (ASEAN) occurred over this period. To the West, however, Myanmar (still referred to in the United States as Burma) was a pariah, thuggish state, and an "outpost of tyranny." Buoyed by an effective human rights lobby and expatriate Burmese activists, the previous stigma of an undesirable regime made positive modifications in Western policies toward that state difficult. The US administration under President Barack Obama effectively began to move US policy from "regime change" to what might be called "regime modification," officially known in the US Department of State as "pragmatic engagement"—high-level contacts but with the continuation of a complex set of sanctions.[4]

On the Cusp of Change

On 30 March 2011, a new government was inaugurated—the Republic of the Union of Myanmar. Called "quasi-civilian" by some official sources in the United States, it was highly reminiscent of the previous military administrations in terms of its personnel, most of whom were retired *tatmadaw* members. It was elected in grossly and blatantly manipulated elections in November 2010, which in turn had been based on a constitution that had obviously been fraudulently imposed by the military junta through a two-stage referendum in May 2008. Expectations among many Burmese and among most Western observers were skeptical at best, even dour. Although China commented favorably on the process, the United States and many Western nations decried what they described as a flawed, illegitimate government based on highly dubious premises.

If the senior government officials seemed overly familiar to many foreign analysts, the programs quickly announced were not. Whatever the accuracy of the claim of a "roadmap to democracy," internal and external observers were surprised by the extent and vigor with which that new administration pushed the reform process. The release of political prisoners seriatim; extensive relaxation of censorship; new freedoms for labor, the media, and for demonstrations; extensive and vigorous debates in the various *hluttaws* (parliaments); important economic and monetary reforms; formation of a human rights commission; an invitation to the Burmese diaspora to return; and foreign policy liberalization came with astonishing speed after a half-century of authoritarian, sclerotic military rule. President Thein Sein, former general and prime minister under the junta—the State Peace and Development Council (SPDC)—personally attended an antipoverty seminar where he heard, contrary to normal practice since the military coup of 1962, direct and severe criticisms of previous military rule. He met personally with opposition leader and Nobel laureate Aung San Suu Kyi, who had been released from house arrest immediately following the 2010 elections. She was later elected to the parliament in the by-elections of 1 April 2012, which in contrast to those of 2010 were free and fair. Some modus vivendi seemed to have been reached between the two, reassuring those in the West to whom she had become the world's democratic avatar.

These widespread reforms, ironically mandated by a government that many in the West regarded as illegitimate, were coupled with an important omission: the administration had wisely shelved the junta's previous, ill-conceived plan to castrate the dissident ethnic armed forces and militias under the "border guard forces" plan by integrating all of them into the *tatmadaw*. The most important ethnic armies, aggregating some 50,000 to 100,000 troops, refused to accept this plan, although some minor rebel battalions did (see Chapter 7). Instead, the administration began serious negotiations for new cease-fires with the major ethnic forces to formulate peace agreements. Ethnic issues, specifically the integration of the peripheral minority regions and peoples into a Burmese nation with an overarching national ethos, has been the single most important problem facing the state since its independence in 1948. The issue of a unitary or federal state has been, and remains, central to creating a national identity.[5] Never resolved, never even effectively addressed, the ethnic problem began to be negotiated seriously for the first time under the new government, and with some success, although a number of remaining and acute problems are yet to be resolved. Yet, vested interests within government and insurgencies may not wish peace to evolve that would threaten their goals, power, or economic rents.

Ethnic issues are intensely complicated by religion. The Burman (called *Bamah* by the present government) ethnic majority, the traditional rulers of what is now Myanmar, are distinctly Buddhist and number some two-thirds of the population, the remainder split among many large and smaller ethnic groups, generally inhabiting the porous, ethnically indistinct border regions.[6] Some have adopted Christianity, especially the Chin, Kachin, and a significant number of the Karen. The Rohingya, an important Muslim minority on the Bangladesh border, remain stateless. The government refuses to use the term *Rohingya,* referring to the group as *Bengali.*[7] Other Muslims are spread throughout the major cities and towns of the state. Although constitutional provisions and public statements call for respect for ethnic cultures, religions, and languages, this has been more cant than reality. President Thein Sein has repeatedly called for respect for all peoples and cultures, but the military's previous attempts at cultural "Myanmafication" have been evident for over two decades.

Myanmar's foreign policy also began to be transformed. The popular media had pictured Myanmar as a "client" state of China, and this seemed reinforced when in May 2011 President Thein Sein chose Beijing as his first official state visit. There he signed a Comprehensive Strategic Cooperative Partnership, a relationship never before proclaimed between those two states.[8] Yet the characterization of Myanmar cast inextricably in China's orbit proved to be wrong. In September 2011, President Thein Sein stopped Chinese construction of the US$3.6 billion Myitsone dam because of Myanmar popular opinion. Internally, anti-Chinese sentiment began to grow. Overtures to the United States had begun as early as March 2009 and culminated with the appointment of a special envoy and later ambassador to Myanmar (a post vacant since 1990) and the visits of Secretary of State Hillary Clinton in December 2011 and President Barack Obama in November 2012. The gloom in Beijing and the euphoria in Washington over the Obama administration's only foreign policy "success" in East Asia was probably premature on both accounts.

Myanmar exists in a context of regional importance. It chaired ASEAN in 2014 for the first time—a role that the United States had sought to deny Myanmar for a decade. Myanmar is essential in the Sino-Indian rivalry because of its littoral on the Bay of Bengal, its proximity to the disputed territory of Arunachal Pradesh occupied by India and claimed by China, the political fragility of numerous rebellions in Northeast India bordering Myanmar, its natural resources, and India's "look east" policy toward Southeast Asia. In the context of "rising China," Myanmar plays a role, at least as interpreted by the Chinese, in the US "pivot" to East Asia.[9] Japan views a strong Chinese presence in Myanmar as strengthening China at Japan's expense. At the same time, the Republic of Korea seeks to assure itself of Burmese markets and resources and to counter Japan's and North Korea's potentials there. Thailand, Burma's traditional enemy, remains the second largest investor in Myanmar, which supplies Thailand through a land and underwater gas pipeline with 25 percent of its electricity.

All these factors will come into focus through the lens of the planned 2015 general elections in Myanmar that will bring a new dynamic to internal politics and external relations. How these will be conducted; whether changes in the constitution will occur, and if so, what kinds of changes; how the peoples of Myanmar will view the results; and how foreign powers will react to these critical elections are all likely to be determining factors in the following five years before the next electoral cycle. This study, however, will look beyond the elections, and indeed beyond the next political cycle, to examine some of the more fundamental forces that have and will continue to affect that society.

Purpose and Structure

The purpose of this volume is to analyze beyond the immediate. The problems attendant on the 2015 elections and the events leading up to them have captured the attention of many foreign observers, but they are manifestations of more structural issues facing the society and its internal and external dilemmas; many go unrecognized even by those concerned with this important society. No single volume can encompass all the enduring, myriad questions that are likely to lie dormant in any tumultuous present.

This volume is divided into fourteen chapters, all of which intellectually are related, and divided into three groups: the political realm, issues of socioeconomic development, and international relations. It begins by analyzing the coercive forces that have played such critical roles since Burmese independence. It then moves to examine the relatively open legislative process that has been in effectual abeyance since 1962. Concepts of law and justice and the role of Buddhism form important chapters and question foreign characterizations of these issues in Myanmar. The volume proceeds to explore the economic plans and realities before moving into the issue of ethnic questions that have remained especially salient to the effectiveness of this complex polity. These are followed by consideration of the state in relation to China and the United States—two powers strongly influencing (positively or negatively) the future of Myanmar.

International concentration on the role of the military in Myanmar has been a natural consequence of *tatmadaw* rule in various guises since 1962. Yet the forces of coercion are more widespread, and as an ostensibly civilian or civilianized government has taken over since 2011, the expanded role of the police has become more evident. Although controlled by the Ministry of Home Affairs, which under the constitution must be led by a uniformed army officer, their role is broadened as the military, at least titularly, remains in the barracks. It also becomes more complex with the introduction of more freedoms for the individual. Andrew Selth examines the issues connected with these forces of coercion and their likely future roles in Myanmar society.

David Steinberg explores the continuing role of the military in Myanmar and examines the likely evolution of its predominant control in that society. He considers the control by the *tatmadaw* over all avenues of social mobility as unique in Asia—quite different from the military in Indonesia, Thailand, Vietnam, and South Korea, all of which have been dominated for various periods by their local militaries. This ensures a continuing prominence of the military unless other avenues are open to a broad spectrum of the peoples in that society. Manifestations of military prominence in the parliaments or cabinets are representative of a far more profound phenomenon and have important policy implications for domestic and foreign programming.

The reintroduction of the legislative process, in abeyance since 1988 and with some autonomy from the executive branch since 1962, has created a new dynamic which Renaud Egreteau examines. The formation of regional and state *hluttaws* (essentially provincial parliaments), a hitherto unknown element in the history of Burma/Myanmar, creates new opportunities for expressing and resolving local needs, so often ignored by the previous unitary state. The new tension between the executive and legislative branches of the government indicates the beginnings of a type of pluralism, a necessary but messy process. However, parliaments have to move beyond influencing policies to making policies—administrative, implementation, and intellectual jumps that are likely to take both time and rethinking of some of the dynamics of governance.

A standard ideological mantra among foreign observers of Myanmar is the need for the "Rule of Law," conceptually conceived in capital letters. Foreign aid organizations often regard this as a programmatic goal to which they will provide support. The issue of the role of law in Myanmar societies is far more complex than the simple concept of an independent judiciary, which is a state-articulated goal. In contrast to the Judeo-Christian, Greco-Roman traditions in the West that are relatively seamless, non-Western states, especially those that have undergone a fragmenting colonial experience built upon disparate customary and religious concepts, often have traditions in conflict with these supposedly "international norms." Elliott Prasse-Freeman considers the inherent tensions between Burmese customary concepts and practices and Western concepts of law and justice, and how even these foreign precepts could be used to subvert the very goals toward which the rule of law is devoted.

Matthew Walton examines the teachings, practices, and rhetoric of Buddhism and their impact on democratic thinking in Myanmar, as well as related issues that may inhibit pluralistic growth. These ideas are historically salient. The reemergence of an exclusionary Buddhist nationalism could undermine the integration of the extensive minority religious communities in the state, and communal relationships within the Burman areas and in the periphery. Yet some Burmese interpretations of Buddhism also offer resources for strengthening democratic practice in Myanmar. These ideas are also relevant. They could support the integration of the extensive minority religious communities in the state, and advance communal relationships within the Burman areas as well as on the periphery.

Economic planning has had a long but undistinguished history in Burma/Myanmar beginning in the early 1950s. The first major plan—covering the period 1953 to 1960—was designed with US assistance and was followed by a series of five-year plans under the socialist government of Ne Win and the authoritarian regime presided over by Than Shwe. These plans were so marred by political manipulation of data that in 1987 Ne Win himself complained that they were useless because of the intentional falsification of data. The past is not a necessary prelude, however. The government of President Thein Sein, assisted by a variety of external economic specialists and institutions, has produced a twenty-year plan that will address a variety of new economic and social challenges, as well as the legacy of past failures. Lex Rieffel in his chapter discusses these challenges, which will have a profound impact on Myanmar's economic prospects.

Although economic planning has been prevalent, major macroeconomic reforms have been recently instituted. While Myanmar's growth rate has markedly increased through extractive industries, the positive effects of economic reform have yet to filter down to the populace as a whole. Moe Thuzar and Tin Maung Maung Than examine the gap between macroeconomic and microeconomic indicators, as well as their effects on the population.

An enduring issue since independence has been the question of land rights and land ownership. For nationalistic reasons, the state has been the residual owner of all land since independence. This policy has resulted in economic disaster for farmers who have not been able to plant what they like or use land as collateral for credit. In the upland areas, traditional systems of land use have not been recognized by the state, a system that has enabled the seizure of land for other uses. Exploitative use of eminent domain by the state and its organs, including national and local *tatmadaw* units, have created intense resentment and led to attempts to resolve this continuing problem through legislation and other means. Christina Fink considers this issue that is of profound importance to the peasantry.

The "peace process," the contemporary vision of ensuring some form of acceptable majority-minority relationships, is shorthand for attempting to solve the most enduring problem facing the state—one that has existed from independence. This process seeks to create some equitable, in Myanmar terms, distribution of power and assets among the diverse peoples of that country. More a state than a nation with an overarching sense of national ethos necessary for multicultural societies, Myanmar now seeks to transform armed insurrections and fragile cease-fires into a national peace and to end the ethnic strife that has gripped the country since 1948. The civilian government of U Nu (1948 to 1962) never resolved the issue, and the military under General Ne Win and the subsequent *tatmadaw* rule of the SLORC and SPDC exacerbated the problems. The present apparent willingness to explore options and negotiate offers the most plausible opportunity for progress in over half a century. The ethnic issue is addressed through two chapters of this volume. Martin Smith analyzes the problem, while Ashley South considers the ramifications of the efforts. The problem is made more complex because of the history of foreign involvement, support, and sympathy for many of the rebellions and their adherents.

The popular portrayal of Myanmar as dependent on China, until its foreign policy shifted after 2011, was an overstatement and neglects the mutuality of the relationship. Yun Sun argues that the two decades between 1990 and 2011 represent a deviation from Myanmar's traditional, neutralist nonaligned foreign policy. Due to internal constraints and external isolation, Myanmar developed an overwhelming dependence on China for political and economic support. Confident in its advantaged position in the bilateral relations, China invested in a series of economic and strategic initiatives in Myanmar, which enhanced China's dependence on its neighbor. The two countries therefore formed an unbalanced, asymmetric mutual dependence. Myanmar's political reform and improvement of relations with the West largely freed the country from its previous dependence on China. This has resulted in an awkward position for China with economic and strategic investments at the mercy of the Myanmar government. China still enjoys influence and leverage in Myanmar, most importantly through its economic strength and ties with the border ethnic groups. In the foreseeable future, China will have to navigate a delicate balance between implicit coercion and explicit inducement to repair the damaged ties for optimal results.

As Sino-Burmese relations have been altered, so US-Burmese relations have shifted over the past several years. The various internal and external lobbying groups, including Burmese expatriates, with success across the political spectrum have affected what the US Department of State and the White House can politically recommend. Jürgen Haacke analyzes the forces that affected that shift and the internal pressures within the United States.

Two generations ago, Western observers described societies that seemed suspicious of foreigners, were quite different from the West, or were difficult of access, as "inscrutable." This was in reality a statement of the West's hubris, ignorance, and unwillingness to learn about those societies. Those days are happily over, but we often linger with misconceptions and apply our own sociopolitical and economic prejudices to other societies as policies are formulated. We have come a considerable way toward overcoming our conceptual mal-heritages, but we still must remain vigilant. This volume is an effort to explore some of the less obvious issues in our understanding of an important society. It is in part an effort to reexamine our premises and hypotheses about what Burma/Myanmar was and has become.

We will commit many sins of omission. Issues of space and financing prohibit extensive exploration of numerous other dilemmas that will determine the well-being of the people and the quality of governance. Our consolation is that as the interest in Myanmar has so vastly expanded, a large number of professional and casual observers, especially those inside that state, will continue to identify issues that it must address. So to our readers we apologize in advance for those questions that here remain unaddressed. In the concluding chapter, we will briefly recognize their importance, and in good, everlasting academic fashion, call for more research on these important problems.

Notes

1. A poll conducted in the spring of 2014 indicated that 88 percent of the people generally approved of what the government was doing and its direction, 76 percent felt that democracy was the better form of government, and 62 percent that democratic governance had improved. International Republican Institute, "Survey of Burma Public Opinion December 24, 2013–February 13, 2014" (Washington, DC). How representative that was, and given the mercurial nature of Myanmar politics, it may offer little in considering longer-range guidance for trends in that society.

2. It should be remembered that the 1958–1960 Burmese military government was regarded in Western political science circles as something of a third world model for effective, if authoritarian, administration. The social science literature during that Cold War period favored military regimes, in part because they were anticommunist.

3. The opposition, followed by the United States and the EU, claimed it was for a new parliament, but the junta insisted it was for a constitutional convention that would write a new constitution. In any case, the junta ignored the results and attempted to control the process of constitutional writing by declaring that any nongovernmental attempts to do so were illegal. The process may have been accelerated by the junta's concerns about political stability if they did not move expeditiously on the constitution after the so-called Saffron Revolution of the fall of 2007.

4. There is an extensive literature on this period from diverse vantage points.

5. See David I. Steinberg, "The Problem of Democracy in the Republic of the Union of Myanmar: Neither Nation-State nor State-Nation?" *Southeast Asian Affairs* (2012): 220–237.

6. A controversial comprehensive census was undertaken in March–April 2014, but the issue of ethnicity both conceptually and in numbers is unlikely to be resolved.

7. Derek Tomkin, "The 'Rohingya' Identity—British Experience in Arakan 1826–1948," *Network Myanmar* (9 April 2014).

8. For the text, see David I. Steinberg and Hongwei Fan, *Modern China-Myanmar Relations: Dilemmas of Mutual Dependence* (Copenhagen: NIAS, 2012), Appendix 5.

9. See David I. Steinberg, "China-Myanmar Managing Influence: The Mutual Dependencies of the 'Comprehensive Strategic Cooperative Partnership,'" in Evelyn Goh, ed., *Rising China* (forthcoming).

2

Myanmar's Coercive Apparatus: The Long Road to Reform

Andrew Selth

For more than half a century, whenever reference has been made to Myanmar's coercive apparatus, its army has usually sprung to mind. This is hardly surprising. The country has boasted the modern world's most durable military dictatorship and, since the abortive 1988 prodemocracy uprising, one of Southeast Asia's largest armed forces. However, there are two other branches of government that, in different ways and to different degrees, have helped the regime enforce its will over the Myanmar people and underpinned continued military rule. Since General Ne Win's coup d'état in 1962, the national police force has been overshadowed by the armed forces (*tatmadaw*), but in recent years it has begun to play a greater role in the maintenance of internal security. Attention has also been focused on Myanmar's main intelligence agencies which, despite fluctuating fortunes, have helped to protect the regime and promote its "national causes."[1]

Since President Thein Sein's reformist government was inaugurated, the *tatmadaw*, Myanmar Police Force (MPF), and intelligence community have adapted to the changing political landscape. Indeed, observers have been surprised at the way in which these feared institutions seem to have accepted the transition from direct military rule to what the constitution describes as a "genuine, disciplined multi-party democratic system."[2] Even so, questions have arisen over the extent to which they have genuinely embraced change and sought to reinvent themselves. Citing a raft of proposed reforms, particularly in the police force, most analysts are cautiously optimistic. The Western democracies have responded to the positive signs by renewing bilateral links and offering assistance. A number of developments since 2011, however, have shown that there are still serious problems in Myanmar and that a fundamental transformation of the state, and its coercive apparatus, remains a distant prospect.

To 2011 and Beyond

Since the inauguration of President Thein Sein, Myanmar has undergone a remarkable transformation, in appearance if not always in substance. The State Peace and Development Council (SPDC) did not intend to usher in a genuine democracy when it promulgated a new constitution in 2008, but since then there has been a dramatic increase in the number of political actors and a gradual diffusion of power within a multilayered system of government. State institutions are developing in ways probably unforeseen by the military regime. There has even been some scope for independent decisionmaking. Restrictions have been eased on political and economic activity, as well as on civil society. Hundreds of political prisoners have been released, among them Aung San Suu Kyi. In 2012, the National League for Democracy competed in by-elections that gave the party forty-three seats in the Union Parliament. Opinion is divided on the government's motives and ultimate goals, but most observers now accept that significant changes are taking place.

One reason for lingering skepticism is that much has also remained the same. Thein Sein's ambitious reform program is still in its early stages and faces formidable obstacles. Those legal and policy revisions that have already been made have yet to be fully or consistently implemented at the local level, particularly in those areas around the country's periphery that are dominated by the ethnic minorities. More to the point, according to an official US report on Myanmar during 2012:

> Significant human rights problems in the country persisted. . . . Government security forces were allegedly responsible for cases of extra-judicial killings, rape and torture. The government abused some prisoners and detainees, held some persons in harsh and life-threatening conditions, and failed to protect civilians in conflict zones. . . . The government generally did not take action to prosecute or punish those responsible for human rights abuses, with a few isolated exceptions. Abuses continued with impunity.[3]

Taken out of context, this statement gives the impression that, despite the momentous changes taking place in other spheres of government activity, Myanmar's coercive apparatus has remained unreconstructed, stubbornly clinging to the policies and practices of the past. Yet, in different ways and to different degrees, it too has been evolving.

The Armed Forces

For fifty years, the *tatmadaw* was the primary coercive arm of Myanmar's military regime. Troops were deployed not only to protect the country's frontiers, combat insurgents, and oppose narcotics warlords, but also to enforce the regime's edicts, maintain order, and crush civil unrest. To a large extent, it still performs these roles. It also continues to exercise a powerful influence over the government at all levels. However, over the past few years there have been important changes.

The 2008 constitution was written specifically to guarantee the *tatmadaw* a central place in national affairs, a position reaffirmed in 2013 by both the president and the armed forces commander-in-chief (CinC). According to law, the *tatmadaw* is an autonomous institution not subject to civilian control or oversight. It has the right to independently administer and adjudicate its own affairs, including the management of its personnel. It also has an exclusive right to set its own agenda with regard to military strategy and operations. There is some debate over the power of the CinC, relative to the president.[4] However, the key portfolios of defense, home affairs, and border affairs are filled by serving officers recommended by the CinC. Counting the deputy CinC, this gives him effective control over at least five of the eleven members of the powerful National Defense and Security Council (NDSC).[5] Also, as supreme commander of all "Defense Services," the CinC has ultimate control over the MPF, Border Guard Forces, other paramilitary organizations, and civil defense forces.

This is quite apart from the fact that almost all members of the government are former or serving military officers—including the president. Out of forty-six ministers at the union level, thirty-seven are from the armed forces, including five still on active service. Of the fourteen chief ministers of Myanmar's states and regions, all but one are retired servicemen.[6] At the parliamentary level, a quarter of all national, state, and regional assemblies are filled by serving military personnel. The majority Union Solidarity and Development Party consists largely of former servicemen and their supporters, and a large majority of senior civil service positions are filled by veterans.[7] This is not to deny the importance of Thein Sein's reform program and its impact on society. Nor can it be taken for granted that all ex-servicemen would automatically do the CinC's bidding. However, as Aung San Suu Kyi has acknowledged, in the current circumstances the *tatmadaw* remains the ultimate arbiter of power in Myanmar and a democratic system of government cannot be introduced without its agreement and cooperation.

In many respects, the internal workings of the *tatmadaw* remain a closed book. Even the most basic information is beyond reach. It is not known, for example, how large the armed forces are, although 350,000 is a popular estimate.[8] It is evident, however, that Commander-in-Chief Senior General Min Aung Hlaing has his own vision for their future.

In what seems to be an effort to create a smaller, better equipped, more professional, and more respected *tatmadaw*, the CinC has taken steps to strengthen its cohesion and unity.[9] He has removed a number of senior officers and posted others to new positions. He has trimmed the top-heavy command structure and replaced most regional military commanders.[10] There have been large-scale transfers of personnel to the MPF, and officer cadet intakes have been reduced. The CinC has introduced new training programs and revised others, while seeking to diversify the sources of the *tatmadaw*'s expertise. A major combined arms exercise was held in 2012, the first since 1995. There continue to be reports of arms upgrades and new weapons production programs.[11] There have been pay increases, and attempts have been made to exert greater control over the *tatmadaw*'s finances. A program is underway to demobilize child soldiers. Also, the CinC has spoken out against corruption and personal aggrandizement.

This reform program is still in its early stages and is encountering obstacles, both in structural and personnel terms. There are reportedly deep divisions within the *tatmadaw* over the loss of certain powers and privileges.[12] The armed forces also face problems of poor recruitment levels, low morale, and high desertion rates. There are concerns about an inflated junior officer corps, which threatens a promotions logjam.[13] In addition, the campaigns against the Kachin Independence Army (KIA), Shan State Army–South, and other armed ethnic groups have exposed deficiencies in leadership, tactics, training, and equipment. Confidence in the ability of the *tatmadaw* concurrently to pursue multiple counterinsurgency campaigns is low. Reports of human rights abuses against both combatants and noncombatants in Chin, Kachin, Shan, and Kayin (Karen) States have again raised questions over discipline, an issue that also arose in Rakhine (Arakan) State in 2012, when the army was called in to help quell widespread sectarian violence.

A revision of military doctrine to "suit the new political context" is reportedly under consideration.[14] Yet, doubts have been expressed over the *tatmadaw*'s ability to reach the levels of professionalism to which Min Aung Hlaing seems to aspire. For example, it has been suggested that in some military circles "professional" is equated with "mercenary."[15] Such an approach to soldiering is anathema to many officers, who see themselves as patriots charged with a historical responsibility to protect the country and safeguard the new constitution. This mindset envisages a continuing role for the armed forces in national politics.[16] At the same time, it has been claimed that:

> A serious internal problem for the Bama nationalists is that the tatmadaw's idealism, professionalism and patriotism have over the years been eroded by nepotism and corruption. The rapid expansion of the army and the officer corps has also diluted the tatmadaw's patriotic fervour. Today opportunism rather than professionalism motivate many young men to become officers. . . . Therefore, returning to a more disciplined system is not really practical.[17]

The CinC will also need to consider that, with the expansion of Myanmar's polity, economy, and civil society, a military career is no longer seen as the only way to obtain an education, technical skills, and social status.

Notwithstanding all these problems, the *tatmadaw* still commands substantial military power, which it can exercise in the event of any perceived threats to the union. These are usually seen in terms of the government's three "national causes," which emphasize unity, stability, and national sovereignty. Since 2011, the external threat to Myanmar has diminished, but Naypyitaw still faces a range of internal security problems. There is the potential for civil unrest once again to erupt over political, economic, or social issues. There are twenty-three Border Guard Force battalions and about a dozen People's Militia Force units, the reliability of which are suspect. There are also armed groups, which have resisted all efforts to be placed under government control. They include the estimated 30,000-strong United Wa State Army and the 20,000-strong KIA. There are several smaller groups waging guerrilla wars against the central government.[18] As long as these problems remain, there is little chance that the *tatmadaw* will return to the barracks.

For the time being, however, the government and armed forces seem to be in broad agreement about the way forward. The *tatmadaw* as an institution no longer runs day-to-day politics. While retaining certain privileges, it has let the government proceed with its reform program. It has gone from being a hegemonic player to a veto player.[19] For its part, the government seems content to let the armed forces manage their own affairs. Complications can arise when military and political factors coincide, as seems to have occurred over peace talks with the KIA, but so far they have been manageable.[20] It remains to be seen whether this level of accommodation continues as more radical reforms are proposed, particularly if they impinge on the *tatmada*w's role and entitlements. The 2015 elections will pose a major test. The military leadership will also need to decide whether or not to permit changes to the constitution, so that Aung San Suu Kyi can stand for the presidency despite the foreign citizenship of her immediate family. A positive decision cannot be taken for granted.

It is also worth noting that, under the provisions of the 2008 constitution, the *tatmadaw* has the legal means to return the country to full military control if deemed necessary. Given certain triggers, it could simply mount another coup. Some observers have put the likelihood of that happening over the next five years as high as 20 percent.[21] The *tatmadaw* is no longer the institution it once was, however, and there are significant constraints on action of that kind. There would inevitably be a strong reaction, both within the country and outside it. Even Myanmar's traditional friends are unlikely to welcome such a backward step, which could lead to precisely the kind of social "chaos" that the military leadership has tried to prevent. The generals would also need to weigh the benefits of such a move against the possibility that it could lead to a breakdown in military discipline. That has always been one of their greatest fears, and a reason for some of the measures taken by Myanmar's coercive apparatus over the past fifty years.

The Police Force

Even before Thein Sein came to office, an effort had been made to expand the police force's capabilities, improve its performance, and reform its culture. This initiative appears to have been driven mainly by Lieutenant General Khin Nyunt when he was SPDC secretary one and later prime minister. In 1994, he became chairman of the Committee for Reform of the People's Police Force (PPF) Management System (CRPPFMS), the aim of which was to conduct an assessment of the force, "promulgate laws, rules and regulations on PPF management and administration and make certain reforms in conformity with the changing situation."[22] In 1995, the PPF was renamed the Myanmar Police Force and a MPF Disciplinary Law was promulgated. In 1999, a new Code of Conduct was issued. Colonial-era manuals spelling out the duties, powers, and entitlements of all ranks were amended and reissued in 2000 and 2001.

At the same time, an attempt was made to introduce a "community-based policing" model. Booklets listing the Buddha's thirty-eight blessings, taken from the *Maha Mangala Sutta*, were distributed to police stations as guides to good behavior. In 2001, signs in both Myanmar and English were erected at police stations around the country asking, "May I help you?" A number of magazines were launched, aimed at boosting police morale and increasing public awareness of police functions. After Khin Nyunt was arrested by the SPDC in 2004, the reform program continued for a period under the stewardship of then-SPDC secretary two and later prime minister (now president) Lieutenant General Thein Sein. He was assisted by Brigadier General Khin Yi, the chief of police from 2002 to 2011. Not long after the 2007 Saffron Revolution, a comprehensive plan for the expansion and modernization of the MPF was endorsed by the military government.[23]

In 2014, the strength of the MPF was about 72,000, or around 120 officers per 100,000 people.[24] This figure had remained static for almost a decade, but the force was still larger and more powerful than it had been since the colonial era.[25] It included thirty-four battalions of paramilitary police able to mount rural counternarcotics campaigns, quell serious outbreaks of civil unrest, and help protect the country's porous borders. The details are unclear, but since then a major recruitment program has been launched to increase the MPF's size. Large-scale transfers are being made to the force from the *tatmadaw*.[26] A special effort is being made to boost the number of women, which currently stands at about 3.5 percent of the total.[27]

The aim is to expand to a national police force of 155,000 by 2018, or around 256 officers per 100,000 people.[28] This would put the MPF more in line with the forces of its regional neighbors and Western countries.

Naypyitaw is grappling with other challenges, with a view to creating a modern and professional force that commands greater respect. The MPF's headquarters is being upgraded, functional departments are being expanded and new ones created, internal coordination is being improved, and modern technology is being introduced. In some ways, the MPF's organizational structure now mirrors those of police forces in more developed countries. For example, a Department Against Transnational Crime was created in 2004. There is a new Financial Investigation Unit, and Maritime and Civil Aviation Police Departments.[29] A Tourist Police unit of around 300 officers has been formed in response to the dramatic increase in foreign visitors.[30] There have also been reports of a new cyber crime unit.[31] Efforts have been made to upgrade communications links between MPF headquarters in Naypyitaw, and state- and region-level MPF units. More police officers now carry personal radios or mobile phones.

In addition, officer selection standards have been raised and specialized instruction at all levels has increased. Loyalty to the central government is still valued highly and is reinforced by refresher courses designed to "keep patriotism alive."[32] At the same time, doctrine and training programs now focus on "democratic policing," which emphasizes accountability, transparency, and respect for human rights.[33] Aspects of the "community-based policing" model are being given renewed attention. MPF officers have been required to attend workshops on issues such as juvenile crime and human rights, and attendance at overseas training courses has increased.[34] There is also a greater focus on personal discipline, in an effort to reduce the level of corruption. For example, in 2011 several corrupt senior police officers were arrested at the instigation of the chief of police and the Bureau of Special Investigation (BSI). Steps have been taken to deal with other abuses, and more reforms have been promised.

One characteristic of the MPF that has not changed over the past 25 years is the police force's role as a strategic reserve. The CRPPFMS made it clear from its inception that Myanmar's police force was "a trained armed organization in addition to the country's regular armed forces to be able to safeguard the nation in emergency cases."[35] In this regard, the paramilitary arm has been singled out for special attention. In addition to pursuing its four stated objectives of "community peace and tranquility, the rule of law, prevention of drug menace and serving the interests of the people," the MPF is required to "discharge the duty of national security."[36] In official statements the MPF has long been referred to as the "younger brother" of the *tatmadaw*. This formula seems to have been invoked less often since 2011, but, as seen at annual Armed Forces Day parades, the MPF is still publicly embraced by the military leadership as an integral part of Myanmar's Defense Services.

The MPF still has a long way to go to achieve the "transformational changes" it desires.[37] However, it is increasingly being seen as a large, powerful, and influential institution that, in a more modern and civilianized form, has the potential to become a key instrument of state control under Thein Sein and his successors.[38]

The Intelligence Community

Little is known about developments in Myanmar's intelligence community since 2011. At one level, there are unmistakable signs of change but, once again, enough has remained the same for questions to be raised about the government's aims and influence.

As restrictions on political activity, freedom of speech, and freedom of association have been relaxed, so the level of overt oppression has diminished. Even organizations like Human Rights Watch have acknowledged that there has been a marked decline in the number of reported arrests, detentions, and cases of torture.[39] The MPF's Criminal Investigation Department (CID) seems to be spending most of its time on civil crimes, and the BSI appears to be focusing on corruption and economic crimes.[40] Despite the freer atmosphere prevailing throughout most of the country, however, old habits die hard. Community leaders, opposition political party members, and journalists still seem to be subject to surveillance.[41] Electronic eavesdropping and computer hacking by the authorities are believed to be widespread. By law, warrants to conduct searches and make arrests are required, but the Special Branch (SB) and the Office of the Chief of Military Security Affairs (OCMSA) continue to do both at will. The ability of both agencies to perform their functions appears to be highly variable, but most people in Myanmar still fear their power and reach.

Its size has probably increased, but in the absence of any official announcements, and new laws passed by the national parliament, it is assumed that the basic structure and roles of the intelligence community have broadly remained the same. In the new Myanmar, however, it might be expected that responsibility for the investigation of so-called political crimes would fall exclusively to the MPF, or to a dedicated civilian agency, as occurs in most democratic countries. That may yet occur, but these responsibilities still seem to be shared between the police and the armed forces. The SB tends to concentrate on the opposition political parties, dissent in the urban areas, and contacts between locals and foreigners, while the OCMSA appears to deal with the most serious cases and issues related to the ethnic communities.[42] As Thein Sein's reform program unfolds, however, relations between the two agencies could become more problematical.

Formally, the SB has responsibility for the collection and assessment of political intelligence. OCMSA is supposed to concern itself only with defense-related matters.[43] However, given the *tatmadaw*'s guardianship role and the power wielded by military intelligence agencies in the past, it is unlikely that the armed forces would give up its ability independently to monitor domestic developments. Not only do the generals distrust the civilian agencies, but the *tatmadaw* has always preferred to rely on its own resources when it comes to national security, a term with a wide meaning in Myanmar. This will doubtless remain the case while the military leadership perceives continuing threats to the country from exile organizations, political activists, armed ethnic groups, and others. There is thus the potential for continued duplication of functions, with the attendant jurisdictional disputes and jealousies over resources.

Since 2011, there have been rumors suggesting that renewed attention is being given to questions of oversight and coordination. For example, there are unconfirmed reports that Min Aung Hlaing has formed a new intelligence agency to investigate domestic security affairs.[44] It has been claimed that this body, known as the National Defence and Security Force, is about 200 strong and consists of members of all three armed services, the MPF, and BSI. The Ministry of Border Affairs is also said to be involved. According to the *Irrawaddy* magazine, the unit oversees all intelligence agencies and reports to both military and civilian authorities, at both the provincial and national levels.[45] Such reports have yet to be verified, but they may be related to claims that the government plans to reconstitute the National Intelligence Bureau (NIB) to provide a mechanism for the oversight and coordination of a "new security system" that will include an expanded surveillance network and a "data thief" hacking project.[46]

There are doubtless some in Myanmar who view the more open political environment with unease, if not concern, and thus deserving of close attention by official agencies. Certainly a coordinating body like the NIB seems justified. However, an entirely new security system seems unlikely. Whether or not there is a restructuring of the national intelligence apparatus, it will need a clearly defined mission that takes into account Thein Sein's reformist aims and the more liberal atmosphere now prevailing. That guidance currently seems to be missing. Also, a strong argument could be mounted for a rationalization and redistribution of intelligence duties. This would not only increase the level of cooperation between agencies and more effectively utilize their limited resources, but it would also provide a clearer delineation of their responsibilities, in particular the separation of military and civilian functions. This in turn could aid in the future oversight of intelligence operations by a genuinely elected civilian government.

A related issue is external intelligence collection and analysis. As Myanmar becomes more engaged with the outside world, and Naypyitaw deals more closely with its foreign counterparts, senior officials will need expert advice about other countries' positions and policies. In the past, such intelligence was provided mainly by the Ministry of Foreign Affairs.[47]

Operating from Myanmar's embassies, officials provided open source intelligence and analysis, in the manner of professional diplomats everywhere. *Tatmadaw* officers posted overseas, as defense attaches and intelligence agents, supplemented this advice with reports sent back through their own channels.[48] Myanmar's intelligence community also developed liaison relationships with foreign services. Yet the demand for data and assessments has doubtless increased under Thein Sein. This raises questions about whether the existing structures need to be strengthened or new ways found to provide the intelligence required for informed policy decisions.

These matters cannot be considered in isolation, but will have to form part of a much wider review of Myanmar's security environment and the state's coercive apparatus. As a Canadian parliamentary committee stated in 2013, "securing the rule of law in Burma will require the wholesale reform of the entire security apparatus in Burma."[49] The committee acknowledged that this would be a slow process and take considerable time, but it drew particular attention to "the urgent need to begin reforming the Burmese police forces" on the grounds that "a principled, effective, and accountable police force is a cornerstone of democracy."[50] It is still early, but there are signs that this is being done. If successful, the proposed reforms will see major changes not only in the role of the MPF and its relationship with the armed forces and intelligence community, but also with the civil population.

A New Police Role?

As Morris Janowitz once noted, "It is a basic assumption of the democratic model of civilian-military relations that civilian supremacy depends upon a sharp organizational separation between internal and external violence forces."[51] If the detachment of Indonesia's national police from the country's armed forces in 1999 is any guide, however, this is easier said than done. In that case, personal and professional rivalries led to tense relations between the two institutions. There were even gunfights over the distribution of off-budget revenues. The power balance in Myanmar is quite different, but the Indonesian example points to areas where there is the potential for disagreements between the *tatmadaw* and MPF over their respective roles and responsibilities, areas of jurisdiction, and budgetary allocations. These issues arose before the 1962 military coup and conceivably could do so again.

In administrative terms, the police force (including SB and the CID) falls under the home affairs minister. Under current constitutional arrangements, this position is reserved for a serving military officer recommended to the president by the CinC. Quite apart from the *tatmadaw*'s wish to retain the minister's ex officio positions in the cabinet and NDSC, the difficulty of amending the constitution without the *tatmadaw's* support means that the

MPF will effectively remain under military control for the foreseeable future. The same goes for the BSI, which is part of the same ministry. In addition, the chief of police is also the deputy minister for home affairs, and many other senior policemen are former military officers.[52] Should they be forced to pick sides, their primary loyalty, and that of ex-servicemen at more junior levels, would probably be to the *tatmadaw*.

Tensions between the armed forces and the police are bound to surface from time to time but, given the physical, legal, and psychological dominance of the *tatmadaw*, a direct and open confrontation between the two is very unlikely. If the MPF is to develop a distinctive civilian identity, however, its relationship with the *tatmadaw* will need to change. This will not be easy, as power and authority in Myanmar tend to be conceived as finite and limited. As David Steinberg has pointed out, alternative centers of influence are usually seen as threatening and likely to lead to instability.[53] There is the danger too that a more powerful and independent MPF will arouse jealousies in the armed forces and be seen as a competitor for status and resources. As the MPF expands, some in the *tatmadaw* could also become concerned that the police force will be seen by civilian politicians as a possible counterweight to the army.

If the MPF's institutional autonomy is to mean anything, much will have to change. The *tatmadaw* would have to accept that the police force is the national agency with primary responsibility for maintaining law and order. The military leadership will also need to recognize that the MPF is accountable to the public and not to the armed forces. There is a provision in the 2008 constitution that exempts members of the *tatmadaw* from civil jurisdiction, but military personnel must be subject to the same laws and restrictions on their behavior as other citizens. Until now, they have acted almost with impunity. Military bases have offered sanctuary from civil authority. Soldiers responsible for human rights abuses have rarely been charged or prosecuted. If the MPF is to perform its role fully, and the "rule of law" is to prevail in Myanmar, as advocated by both the government and opposition parties, then this situation cannot be permitted to continue.[54]

Also, if Thein Sein wants to civilianize the MPF and make it more independent, as befits a police force in a democracy, he will need to support efforts by the MPF to develop a separate identity and encourage its own esprit de corps. The MPF will have to open its senior ranks to career police officers. This should not only make the force less subject to military influence, but it would also improve morale by removing a persistent source of complaint from policemen resentful of servicemen being transferred into positions above them. At the same time, the current power structure in Myanmar will demand that the police force acknowledges the *tatmadaw*'s continuing influence and authority. The MPF's senior leadership will have to be on good terms with its armed forces counterpart, while finding a workable division of labor, not just legally but also in terms of practical cooperation and responses to internal security challenges.

Internal Security Challenges

There is no question that the *tatmadaw* will remain responsible for Myanmar's external defense. It will also continue to conduct military campaigns against insurgent groups that openly challenge Naypyitaw's rule, such as the KIA. This will require the collection and assessment of strategic, operational, and tactical intelligence, mainly within the country but also at times outside it. The MPF is sometimes directly involved in such campaigns, as occurs, for example, when insurgents attack rural police stations or when local police units are required to support counterinsurgency strategies involving the civil population. On those occasions, police duties can include manning roadblocks, protecting key infrastructure sites, and supporting village militias. Its function as a strategic reserve aside, however, the force usually has a noncombat role.

That said, it seems to be envisaged that the MPF will assume greater internal security responsibilities. The force already dominates the Central Committee for Drug Abuse Control and has taken the lead in efforts to combat narcotics trafficking. It has also played a role in frontier protection, in some areas as a member of the Border Control Force (NaSaKa).[55] With the abolition of the NaSaKa in 2013 and the creation of a new Border Guard Police department, the MPF's duties in this respect are likely to expand.[56] These days, there are more blue uniforms than green uniforms controlling rural checkpoints, patrolling city streets, protecting VIPs, providing security for government offices, and guarding diplomatic premises. Myanmar's specialist counterterrorist unit is drawn from the police force. In addition, the MPF takes the lead in quelling outbreaks of civil unrest, with the army only being called in to assist the "civil" power when the problem exceeds the police force's abilities to cope.

Naypyitaw is intent on building up the MPF's paramilitary capabilities, so that it can respond to major disturbances with modern antiriot control measures, rather than having to resort to the blunt instrument of the army. As revealed during the Saffron Revolution, there have been some advances in the training of the MPF's battalions since the 1988 uprising, when ill-equipped and ill-disciplined PPF paramilitary units known as Lon Htein were guilty of terrible abuses.[57] Some police battalions providing initial responses to outbreaks of civil unrest now wear special protective clothing and carry more-appropriate weapons. These offer nonlethal options ranging from baton charges, the use of tear gas and water cannon, to the firing of rubber bullets and small-caliber shotgun pellets. Modern equipment is still in short supply, but a new instruction manual is being compiled and a number of antiriot training programs are under way.[58]

Even if the battalions increase their capabilities, they will still face a conundrum. The MPF's responsibilities for crime prevention, the maintenance of law and order, and protection of the community place a premium on good relations with the public. Yet these roles are at odds with the military-style training and ethos of the police battalions, which are authorized to exercise violence up to and including lethal force. As seen in 2012, when tough tactics and military munitions were used to break up a protest near Letpadaung, the battalions are not yet imbued with the more restrained approach being held up as a model by Naypyitaw. In the Letpadaung incident, over twenty Buddhist monks were injured, prompting the government and MPF to make a rare public apology. If the police are to step in before the army, then they cannot act like the army. To do so undermines their civilian status and their standing with the population.

In performing these duties, the MPF must act—and be seen to act—impartially in restoring order and upholding the law. Yet this has rarely been the case. Not only has it acted as a strong arm of the government, but the force has often appeared to side with sectoral interests. During the civil unrest in Rakhine State in 2012, for example, MPF officers were clearly sympathetic to local Buddhists. Some reportedly joined in attacks against Rohingya Muslims.[59] The action taken near Letpadaung in 2012 was seen as another example of the police force backing government "cronies" and their business partners. After a series of riots in central Myanmar in 2013, the MPF was accused of allowing Buddhist mobs to attack Muslims and destroy their property. Such behavior not only damages the force's reputation, but also undermines the government's rhetoric about human rights and the rule of law.

The Question of Reform

For the current police reform program to have a significant impact, the MPF will need to undergo a profound change in its professional culture. There are a number of elements to such a change, including the force's view of its place in the new Myanmar, its attitude to both civil and military power, its understanding of conventional police roles and responsibilities, and its relations with the civil population. Reflecting the government's own top-down approach to reform, MPF headquarters has already issued a number of directives on such matters and implemented measures designed to encourage a different mindset in the force. However, these steps will only go so far in achieving the desired end. Real and lasting cultural change will require a tectonic shift of consciousness at the psychological and societal levels.

As Nick Cheesman has pointed out, ever since the colonial period, policing in Myanmar has been conceived as a regime service rather than a public service.[60] This has encouraged an authoritarian and hierarchical approach to law enforcement. The rights of individuals, if recognized at all, have been ignored or discounted. The adoption of democratic and community policing models will demand a more open and flexible structure in which individual officers and members of civil society can jointly identify problems and find mutually beneficial solutions. Emphasis is given to taking the initiative, rather than waiting for orders from higher up the command chain. Police officers are encouraged to question the effectiveness of ingrained practices and explore new ways of doing things. They are also urged to become familiar with their local neighborhoods and listen to their concerns.

While laudable, these ideas run counter to generations of police training and socialization. Arguably, some challenge traditional Myanmar culture, in which respect for personal status and official rank and submission to authority have important places.[61] In other Southeast Asian police forces that have embraced community policing models, the adoption of such an approach has encountered a range of problems. Old habits, fear of failure, and loyalty to one's superiors have invariably trumped personal initiative. Also, some proposed changes have been resisted by senior officers, who have seen them as undermining their own positions and threatening not only a breakdown in internal discipline but also an unacceptable loss of control over police operations and behavior. Attempts to introduce such progressive ideas into the MPF are likely to face at least equal levels of resistance.

It may be possible, however, to inculcate more of a service culture through education. New programs at training centers can increase levels of awareness about policing in democratic societies. Human rights are already being given a higher priority in MPF curricula. Special courses can raise leadership skills and encourage a more tolerant approach to public participation in political processes. Also, imaginative teaching methods can create a more productive learning atmosphere, in contrast to the rigid learning styles found in military-style institutions. Such lessons must be taught in a way that is relevant to the local political, social, and cultural context, but this approach can complement other initiatives by helping to change the force from below. Even so, it may take a generation before there are appreciable results, due in large part to the lack of public trust in the MPF as an institution.

Myanmar's police forces have never enjoyed the confidence of the civil population. Throughout modern history, officers have been seen as the servants of repressive and self-serving regimes that have cared little for the welfare and interests of the average citizen. As a result, the community's attitude has been one of fear and distrust. There have been exceptions, but the common image of the police has been of remote and poorly educated authority figures with low personal and professional standards.[62] During interrogations, violence seems to be routine. Broader concerns relate to the militaristic character of the force, its low level of institutional independence, its perceived ineffectiveness, and its collusion with a corrupt and inefficient justice system.[63] In these circumstances, it is little wonder that the public response to the MPF's past attempts at reform has been skepticism, if not disbelief.

Suspicions about the force are not helped by the ambiguous nature of some government decisions. For example, the large-scale transfers of military personnel to the MPF, in part to form new battalions of paramilitary police, is not seen as an attempt to "civilianize" the security forces, but a device to preserve the state's massive security apparatus by stealth. Some foreign observers are already speaking of a "green to blue" shift in coercive power.[64] Similarly, Naypyitaw's apparent reluctance to use army and police units to quell anti-Muslim unrest in central Myanmar in 2013 was not interpreted as incompetence, a lack of decisive leadership, or a fear of attracting international opprobrium, as occurred after the 2012 disturbances in Rakhine State. Instead, it was widely seen as support for, or at least complicity in, mob violence.

At times, the international community has appeared more sympathetic toward Thein Sein's attempts to respond to Myanmar's fiendishly complex challenges than the Myanmar population. Indeed, Naypyitaw's tentative steps toward a more democratic system and its efforts to restore Myanmar's international standing have attracted considerable interest abroad. Some of this attention has been directed at the state's coercive apparatus.

International Assistance

A striking aspect of Myanmar's reemergence as an international actor since 2011 has been the readiness of the Western democracies to renew or strengthen ties with its armed forces and police.[65] Before the advent of Thein Sein's reformist government, any relationship with the country's security forces was politically very difficult. Yet, several governments, international institutions, and private foundations have approached Myanmar with offers to help reform the security sector. These proposals have been enthusiastically welcomed by Naypyitaw and, albeit more cautiously, by Aung San Suu Kyi and other opposition figures. They have been condemned as premature and ill-advised by activists and human rights organizations, but it has been felt that foreign assistance can ameliorate the very problems about which Myanmar's critics are concerned.

Most of these initiatives have been expressed in principled terms, but broadly speaking they make up two separate, if related, sets of proposals. One is aimed at increasing the professionalism of the armed forces, reducing its political role, and encouraging it to observe internationally accepted norms of behavior. The other relates to the modernization and civilianization of the MPF. While the latter set is usually couched in vague terms, refers to the "rule of law" in Myanmar, and alludes to the reform of the country's judicial system, most offers seem to envisage direct aid to the MPF. The public rationale has invariably been that such approaches help develop bilateral relationships and exert a positive influence on the government by encouraging the reform process.

The United States has been interested in restoring ties with the *tatmadaw* since President Barack Obama came to office, something he hinted at during his visit to Myanmar in 2012.[66] Naypyitaw was invited in February 2013 to send two observers to Exercise Cobra Gold in Thailand. The State Department announced in April of that year that the United States was looking at ways to support "nascent military engagement" with Myanmar as a way of encouraging further political reforms.[67] Pentagon officials have referred to a "carefully calibrated" plan that includes Myanmar's cooperation in the search for the remains of 730 US military personnel missing since World War II.[68] *Tatmadaw* officers have already participated in events sponsored by the Asia-Pacific Centre for Security Studies in Hawaii, and the US Defense Institute for International Legal Studies is also engaged. Training places in the United States and a military-military dialogue or "partnership" have not been ruled out.[69]

Other countries have followed the US lead. During Thein Sein's 2013 visit to Canberra, the Australian government announced that it was restoring the resident defense attaché's position in Yangon,* which was closed in 1979. Former prime minister Julia Gillard said that this would permit engagement with the *tatmadaw* in areas like peacekeeping, humanitarian assistance, and disaster relief, as well as enhancing other forms of dialogue. Thein Sein also visited the UK in 2013, the same year the British government announced that it too was posting a defense attaché to Yangon. Myanmar was also offered training in human rights, the laws of armed conflict, and the accountability of democratic armed forces. Thirty senior *tat-*

---

*The capital of the state at independence (1948) was Rangoon (present population, some five million). The city's name was changed to Yangon in 1989. In October 2005, the newly built city of Naypyitaw, roughly 200 miles (320 kilometers) north of Yangon and close to the rail line between Yangon and Mandalay, was designated as the capital. Most foreign states, however, still maintain their embassies in Yangon.

madaw officers attended a tailored staff course in the UK in 2014.[70] An EU arms embargo remains in place, but Germany and France also appear to be considering posting resident defense attaché positions to Myanmar.

There has also been international interest in the reform of the police force.[71] Already UNICEF (United Nations Children's Fund) has helped the MPF prepare a guide to the treatment of children caught up in the criminal justice system. The UN Office on Drugs and Crime (UNODC) has provided police training, mainly in connection with transnational crimes. Myanmar's chief of police has told the International Bar Association that he would welcome advice on how best to implement civilian oversight procedures, and he has "expressed a particular interest in learning about good international practice in the matter of state security laws."[72] Likely with such initiatives in mind, Naypyitaw has asked the UNODC to conduct a comprehensive review of the MPF to identify issues requiring attention. This was not only to help formulate new reform programs, but also to assist in the coordination of future foreign assistance.[73] The report is due in mid-2014, but no public version has yet been released.

Some projects have already begun. For example, in 2013 the European Union posted two officers to Myanmar in response to a request from Naypyitaw for advice on crowd control and community policing.[74] Foreign training for the MPF in public order management was one of the recommendations made by Aung San Suu Kyi's commission in its report on the 2012 Letpadaung incident.[75] The UK sent a police expert to Myanmar in June 2013 to investigate options, and Naypyitaw later accepted an offer of training and other forms of assistance.[76] While Myanmar officials have always denigrated the colonial regime, including its police forces, both countries acknowledge that the MPF owes much to its British heritage and see this as the basis for cooperation in the future. Germany's Agency for International Cooperation is also interested in providing training in rights-based laws and practices.

The Australian Federal Police has maintained a liaison office in Yangon since 2000. Joint activities and courses have focused on combating transnational crime, but have included criminal intelligence training. Australia intends to maintain a high level of cooperation, taking advantage of Myanmar's current receptivity to closer bilateral ties.[77] For its part, the United States has lifted its embargo on Myanmar's attendance at the Bangkok-based International Law Enforcement Academy, and is considering aid to the police force. A US interagency "rule of law" mission visited Myanmar in early 2013, and Thein Sein, during his visit to Washington in June 2013, discussed US assistance to the MPF with President Obama. Forensic training for the CID is one possibility being considered.[78] Nongovernmental organizations like the US Institute of Peace are also looking at ways to help the MPF.

Where to from Here?

It has been suggested that the 2008 constitution is simply a political device behind which the *tatmadaw* can continue to run Myanmar, as was the 1974 charter. Whether or not that is true, the military leadership seems prepared to let the new government and parliament exercise their formal roles. While heavily constrained, both seem to be aiming for a more flexible and open system. Politics is no longer the exclusive domain of the armed forces.[79] A great deal depends, however, on the continued willingness of the *tatmadaw* to loosen its grip and allow the administration space to grow. Its attitude toward the amendment of the constitution will be critical. If the generals permit the evolution of a fairer and more open society, then the MPF can be expected to play a greater role in maintaining law and order, and safeguarding internal security. Indeed, such a step will be essential if Myanmar is to make an orderly transition to genuine and sustained democratic rule.

Given the optimism that has followed Thein Sein's inauguration and the subsequent relaxation of controls on Myanmar society, it is worth noting that in every country where major reform of the security sector has been attempted change has taken a long time. Inevitably, there will be setbacks, and some problems will be difficult to resolve. A few observers have suggested, for example, that the excessive use of force by the MPF at Letpadaung means that Thein Sein's reform program, and thus reform of the MPF, is stalling.[80] Certainly, that incident demonstrated that old ways of thinking have deep roots in Myanmar's security forces. Yet, it can be argued that the public apology and parliamentary inquiry that followed indicate that the government is aware of the need for change and is trying to be responsive to public concerns. It is also trying to demonstrate that the MPF is now being held accountable for its actions.

Also, the MPF seems prepared to acknowledge its weaknesses, within limits. Indeed, for all the criticisms leveled at the force over the years, the MPF has been well in front of the *tatmadaw* and intelligence community in its relative openness, stated willingness to embrace change, and attempts to improve relations with the community. For example, the MPF publishes English-language material for foreign distribution, manages a comprehensive vernacular language website, and is on Facebook. It has advertised for a foreign public relations expert to help MPF officers handle media inquiries. The police force has led the way in developing relationships with international organizations such as the International Criminal Police Organization (INTERPOL) and Association of Southeast Asian Nations Police Organization (ASEANPOL), as well as friendly countries, to combat transnational crime. The armed forces and intelligence agencies have also developed international links, but they have been much more secretive and, it appears, more isolated.

For all that, the transformation of the MPF will ultimately depend on factors that are out of the force's direct control. These relate in large part to developments in Naypyitaw, the outcome of Thein Sein's reform program, and, in particular, the hesitant steps being taken toward a more democratic society. For, ultimately, the police force will reflect the government it serves and the political system in which it operates. As David Bayley has written, for all the talk of their independence, "police forces are the creatures of politics."[81] The new MPF will reflect the transitions taking place in Myanmar from a military dictatorship to a "disciplined democracy," and possibly beyond. Real and lasting change will depend on a civilianized political system, which permits the MPF to operate freely, according to internationally accepted standards, without interference from those wielding power.

It needs to be borne in mind too that the reform of Myanmar's coercive apparatus cannot occur in isolation from other institutions of state. As the president has stated, echoed by Aung San Suu Kyi, the benchmark for all public institutions must be the rule of law, administered fairly and impartially. There can be no further tolerance of a system that constantly alluded to such a regime, but enabled practices that contradicted it. For decades, the "rule of law" was conflated with "law and order," as defined by a ruthless and self-serving military government determined to control Myanmar's past, present, and future. A more modern and effective police force, for example, will soon be rendered impotent if Naypyitaw's proposed legal and judicial reforms are unsuccessful and prosecutors, judges, and prison governors fail in their responsibilities. There needs to be a clear break with the past, at all levels of the system.

Notes

1. Arguably, Myanmar's Prisons Department could be added to this category, but its role is outside the scope of this chapter.

2. *Constitution of the Republic of the Union of Myanmar (2008)* (Naypyitaw: Ministry of Information, 2008), 3.

3. Bureau of Democracy, Human Rights and Labor, "Burma," *Country Reports on Human Rights Practices for 2012* (Washington, DC: US State Department, 2013).

4. Compare, for example, Maung Aung Myoe, "The Soldier and the State: The Tatmadaw and Political Liberalization in Myanmar Since 2011," *South East Asia Research* 22, no. 2 (June 2014): 233–249, with Euro-Burma Office, "The *Tatmadaw*: Does the Government Control the *Tatmadaw*?" Euro-Burma Office Briefing Paper (Brussels: March 2013).

5. The military bloc in parliament chooses one of three vice presidents for consideration by a presidential college. Either as the president, or one of the two remaining vice presidents, this person would probably also support the CinC in the NDSC.

6. Maung Aung Myoe, "The Soldier and the State."

7. The UN has estimated that 89 percent of Myanmar's members of parliament have some affiliation to the former military regime. Also, about 80 percent of directors, deputy director-generals, and director-generals in the civil administration or line ministries are retired military officers. International Bar Association, "The Rule of Law in Myanmar: Challenges and Prospects: Report of the International Bar Association's Human Rights Institute (IBAHRI)" (London: International Bar Association, December 2012), 52–53, and Maung Aung Myoe, "The Soldier and the State."

8. Andrew Selth. "Known Knowns and Known Unknowns: Measuring Myanmar's Military Capabilities," *Contemporary Southeast Asia* 31, no. 2 (August 2009): 272–295.

9. Personal communication from Yangon, March 2013, and Maung Aung Myoe, "The Soldier and the State."

10. M. P. Callahan, "The Opening in Burma: The Generals Loosen Their Grip," *Journal of Democracy* 23, no. 4 (October 2012): 128.

11. Andrew Selth, "Burma and North Korea: Again? Still?" *The Interpreter*, 10 July 2013.

12. Joshua Kurlantzick, and D. T. Stewart, "Burma's Reforms and Regional Cooperation in East Asia" (New York: Carnegie Council for Ethics in International Affairs, Summer 2013).

13. Maung Aung Myoe, "The Soldier and the State."

14. Callahan, "The Opening in Burma," p. 128.

15. The word *professional* has been given different meanings by different Myanmar officials. While the president and CinC use the term in English, and seem to recognize its full implications, even they do not envisage a completely apolitical armed forces, at least not yet. In the local language, the connotations of *professional* are even less clear. Interview, Washington, DC, September 2013. See also Maung Aung Myoe, "The Soldier and the State."

16. Zin Linn, "Burma Army's Boss Calls for Stronger Armed Forces," *AsianCorrespondent.com*, 28 March 2013.

17. Euro-Burma Office, "Does the Government Control the *Tatmadaw*?"

18. According to Maung Aung Myoe, there are 100,000 armed troops under nearly 40 nonstate organizations in Myanmar. Maung Aung Myoe, "The Soldier and the State."

19. A. P. MacDonald, "The Tatmadaw's New Position in Myanmar Politics," *East Asia Forum*, 1 May 2013.

20. International Crisis Group, "A Tentative Peace in Myanmar's Kachin Conflict," *Asia Briefing* No. 140 (Brussels: International Crisis Group, 12 June 2013). One can also speculate about the apparent disjunction between the *tatmadaw*'s continuing links with North Korea and Thein Sein's repeated claims that such links have been severed. Selth, "Burma and North Korea: Again? Still?"

21. Kurlantzick and Stewart, "Burma's Reforms."

22. "Lt-Gen Khin Nyunt Accuses Police," *New Light of Myanmar*, 14 March 1994.

23. Interview, Naypyitaw, February 2013.

24. Personal communication from Yangon, March 2014.

25. Andrew Selth, *Burma's Armed Forces: Power Without Glory* (Norwalk, CT: EastBridge, 2002): 309. INTERPOL's website stated in 2012 that the MPF's strength was "more than 93,000 men and women," and some estimates have ranged as high as 110,000. These claims are currently difficult to sustain. INTERPOL, "Myanmar," at http://www.interpol.int/Member-countries/Asia-South-Pacific/Myanmar, September 2014.

26. For example, 4,000 men will be taken from the Myanmar Navy to help create the new Maritime Police and another 4,000 will be transferred from the Myanmar Air Force to establish the Civil Aviation Police. Interview, Naypyitaw, February 2013.

27. Personal communication from Yangon, March 2014.

28. Interview, Naypyitaw, February 2013.

29. "Marine Police Established in Myanmar," *Eleven Myanmar*, 9 August 2012.

30. In 2010, Myanmar hosted about 792,000 tourists. In 2012, there was over a million, with the number expected to be even higher in 2013. "Burma to Launch Tourist Police Force," *Irrawaddy*, 26 March 2013, and "New Police Force to Patrol Myanmar," *Wanderlust*, 4 April 2013.

31. "Myanmar Police to Receive Assistance in Setting Up Cyber-Crime Division," *Eleven*, 27 March 2013.

32. "Training Activities," Central Institute of Civil Service, Union Civil Service Board, Phaunggyi, at www.ucsb.gov.mm/about%20ucsb/Central%20Institute%20of%20Civil%20Service%20(Phaung%20Gyi)/details.asp?submenuid=33&id=502

33. "Speech Delivered by the Chief of Police at the 49th Anniversary of Myanmar Police Force," Ministry of Home Affairs, Myanmar Police Force, 1 October 2013.

34. A total of 1,752 trainees attended 24 local workshops for capacity building in 2013–2014 financial year, and 2,787 trainees were attending workshops in August 2013. In addition, 52 trainees had been sent to the United States, China, India, and Malaysia for international workshops. "Retired Police Officers Criticise Current Police Force," *Mizzima News*, 28 August 2013.

35. "Myanmar Police Urged to Implement Three Main Tasks," *Xinhua*, 20 June 1998, at www.burmalibrary.org/reg.burma/archives/199806/msg00343.html

36. "Myanmar (Burma): 41st Anniversary of Myanmar Police Force Observed," *Asia Africa Intelligence Wire*, 13 October 2005.

37. "Speech Delivered by the Chief of Police."

38. Andrew Selth, "Burma's Police Forces: Continuities and Contradictions," *Regional Outlook* No. 32 (Brisbane: Griffith Asia Institute, 2011).

39. "Old Problems Resurface on Myanmar's Road to Freedom," *The Nation*, 6 August 2013.

40. Interviews, Yangon and Mandalay, February 2013.

41. Todd Pittman, "In Myanmar, Internal Spy Network Lives On," *The Hindu*, 30 July 2013.

42. Immigration and Refugee Board of Canada Research Directorate, "Myanmar (Burma): Whether the Military Intelligence Force in Myanmar Has Been Fully or Partially Disbanded and Who Is Carrying Out Their Duties (2004–February 2008)" (Ottawa: Immigration and Refugee Board of Canada, 25 February 2008).

43. Interview, Naypyitaw, February 2013.

44. "Burma Forms New Intelligence Unit," *Irrawaddy*, 3 May 2011.

45. Wai Moe, "Tatmadaw Commanders Discuss Recent Ethnic Conflicts," *Irrawaddy*, 29 June 2011.

46. "Yangon: Regime Pours Funds into Army And Intelligence to Block Web Protests," *AsiaNews.it*, 3 September 2011. See also Aung Zaw, "Burmese Spy Reveals MI's Dirty Deeds," *Irrawaddy*, 24 April 2006.

47. Interview, Canberra, October 2013.

48. Andrew Selth, "Burma's Intelligence Apparatus," *Intelligence and National Security* 13, no. 4 (Winter 1998): 42–44, 54.

49. "Conflicting Realities: Reform, Repression and Human Rights in Burma," Report of the Standing Committee on Foreign Affairs and International Development, Subcommittee on International Human Rights, House of Commons, Canada, 41st Parliament, June 2013, 34–36.

50. Ibid.

51. Morris Janowitz, *The Military in the Political Development of New Nations: An Essay in Comparative Analysis* (Chicago: University of Chicago Press, 1964), 38.

52. It was estimated in early 2013 that about 10 percent of the MPF were former members of the armed forces (Interview, Naypyitaw, February 2013). However, some estimates have been as high as 30 percent. See "Burma: Junta Moves to Control Rift in Police, Former Soldiers Shed Uniforms," *BBC Monitoring International Reports,* 3 January 2002.

53. David Steinberg, *Turmoil in Burma: Contested Legitimacies in Myanmar* (Norwalk, CT: EastBridge, 2006), 37ff.

54. Andrew Selth, "Police Reform in Burma (Myanmar): Aims, Obstacles and Outcomes," *Regional Outlook* No. 44 (Brisbane: Griffith Asia Institute, 2013).

55. The literal translation of the title *Nezat detha luwinhmu Sitseye Kutkehmu tanachok* (usually abbreviated to NaSaKa) is "Border Area Immigration Scrutinization and Supervision Bureau."

56. Interview, Naypyitaw, February 2013. See also Hannah Hindstrom, "Burma Disbands Notorious NaSaKa Border Guard Force," *Democratic Voice of Burma*, 15 July 2013, at www.dvb.no/news/burma-disbands-notorious-nasaka-border-guard-force/29916.

57. Bertil Lintner, *Outrage: Burma's Struggle for Democracy* (London: White Lotus, 1990); and Andrew Selth, "Burma's 'Saffron Revolution' and the Limits of International Influence," *Australian Journal of International Affairs* 62, no. 3 (September 2008): 281–297.

58. "Myanmar Police Slow to Adjust to Unfamiliar Role of Peacekeepers," *The Japan Times*, 12 April 2013.

59. Human Rights Watch. *"The Government Could Have Stopped This": Sectarian Violence and Ensuing Abuses in Burma's Arakan State* (New York: Human Rights Watch, 2012).

60. Nick Cheesman, "Policing Burma." Unpublished background research paper no. 2 (Canberra: Australian National University, 24 February 2009).

61. See, for example, Swe Win, "Kristallnacht in Myanmar," *International Herald Tribune*, 29 March 2013.

62. Interviews, Yangon and Mandalay, February 2013. See also Bureau of Democracy, Human Rights and Labor, "Burma."

63. Asian Human Rights Commission, "Burma's Cheap Muscle" (Hong Kong, Asian Human Rights Commission, 13 March 2009).

64. Gwen Robinson, "The Contenders," *Foreign Policy*, 12 July 2013.

65. Andrew Selth, "West Reaches Out to Burma's Security Sector," *The Interpreter*, 26 July 2013.

66. Kim Jolliffe, "US Myanmar Eye Military Links," *Asia Times Online*, 26 June 2012, and Carlo Munoz, "US Opens Door to Military Ties with Burma," *The Hill*, 15 October 2012.

67. Erika Kinetz, "US to Boost Military, Trade Ties to Burma," *Irrawaddy*, 26 April 2013.

68. "US Begins 'Calibrated' Defense Engagement with Myanmar," *ZeeNews.Com*, 26 April 2013. See also Gwen Robinson, "EU and US Seek Closer Ties with Myanmar," *Financial Times*, 19 October 2012.

69. "US-Myanmar Military Engagement: A Step to Counter China?" *Daily Star*, 1 December 2012.

70. Jon Lunn, "Burma: Recent Political and Security Developments." House of Commons Library, Standard Note SN06474, 13 February 2014.

71. Andrew Selth, "Burma's Police: The Long Road to Reform," *The Interpreter*, 13 December 2012.

72. International Bar Association, "The Rule of Law in Myanmar," 30.

73. Interview, Yangon, February 2013.

74. Personal communication from Brussels, March 2013.

75. "Final Report of the Investigation Commission," 2013, unofficial translation in author's possession.

76. Gwen Robinson, "Britain Revives Links with Myanmar's Military Establishment," *Financial Times*, 6 June 2013.

77. Personal communications from AFP Media Office, Canberra, 7 and 19 August 2013. The AFP has denied press reports that it will join the EU in providing "anti-riot" training to the MPF. See, for example, "Myanmar to Beef Up Anti-riot Forces," *Global Times*, 4 July 2013.

78. "Myanmar Police to Study Abroad," *Eleven*, 28 November 2012.

79. A. P. Macdonald, "From Military Rule to Electoral Authoritarianism: The Reconfiguration of Power in Myanmar and Its Future," *Asian Affairs: An American Review* 40, no. 1 (2013): 24.

80. Parameswaran Ponnudurai, "Is Reform Stalling in Burma?" *Radio Free Asia*, 4 December 2010.

81. D. H. Bayley, "The Police and Political Change in Comparative Perspective," *Law and Society Review* 6, no. 1 (August 1971): 91–112.

3

The Persistence of Military Dominance

David I. Steinberg

The Burmese *tatmadaw* designed a system of governance under the 2008 constitution in which they planned to play the predominant role, protect the national interests of the state as they perceive them, and maintain autonomy from any future civilian leadership. Protecting this system has been a paramount concern as the military state was "transformed" into what its previous military leader, Senior General Than Shwe (who reigned from 1992 to 2011), called "discipline-flourishing democracy." It was, in essence, this assertion and protection of its principal interests that enabled the *tatmadaw* to formulate in 2011 a reform-minded administration that loosened strictures on its peoples. In some official circles in the United States, this is referred to as a "quasi-civilian" government.[1]

In spite of past repression, or indeed perhaps because of the reforms, it is unclear whether the pace and essence of change will satisfy the diverse peoples of that state because of their heightened expectations and intimations of hope. Among pragmatic foreign governments and observers, however, the evident progress in reforms and the widening of the space between the state and its peoples give hope for continuing positive changes. Foreign human rights observers recognize the limitations of the system that is in play in Myanmar and complain, as they do with the more rigid political systems of China, Vietnam, Laos, and Cambodia—and, of course, North Korea—that progress is uneven and fragile. As the Burmese people expect more, well-wishing foreigners are equally demanding of rapid, transformational change. Whether such changes are solidified, however, may depend on social forces beyond immediate laws or regulations.

Many Western observers have considered the role of the military in modern times as ideally subservient to civilian leadership and administration. This was also the position of the 1989 political platform of the National League for Democracy (NLD). These observers now hope for a quick and decisive translation of military hegemony into a civilian administration through elections in 2015 and amendments to the 2008 constitution, although earlier they had demanded the immediate military abdication of power and transfer to civilian opposition politicians—thus, regime change. Political soothsayers are split. Although now some call for instantaneous change to authoritative civilian control in the 2015 elections, others believe that there will be a gradual erosion of military unity and control as pluralism becomes more evident.[2] Some observers predict effective military control will continue in spite of the "civilianization" process:

> Praetorian practices imposed by the Tatmadaw and its clusters of allies are bound to prevail in the near future, despite a gradual civilianization of Burma's polity. . . . The very presence of the Army leadership in the top positions of all of Burma's decision and policymaking structures cannot be understood as an aberrant socio-historical construction of an irrelevant "parasite" or an exogenous force that has imposed its anachronistic rule to the Burmese contemporary scene. Quite the contrary, its praetorian dominance of Burma's state politics and global socio-economic scene—although far from being considered as legitimate domestically or internationally—is the logical result of decades of nationalist, anti-colonial and failed state and nation-building struggles. . . . Domestic, but also foreign and strategic policymaking, will therefore more or less remain in military hands in the coming years.[3]

The full spectrum of opinion on the immediate and future role of the military in Myanmar's governance is thus evident: return to the barracks and a subordinate presence (a Western and NLD preference), continued complete control even under "civilianization" (the praetorian argument), and a gradual attrition of military influence (the intermediate possibility).

Western political science literature is ripe with studies, too numerous to mention here, of civil-military relationships that trace the evolution of military to civilian control of state power in the modern West—the current international ideal.[4] Even in the rise of communist societies in the twentieth century, it was the party that was theoretically to be in command whatever the actual distribution of coercive authority. As one author wrote, it is remarkable that there are so few modern military regimes, rather than there are so many, since they have the material assets to seize control.[5] Yet civilian vs. military control is not an example of the dualism that seems to be a pervasive categorization of Western intellectual life. There is, rather, a spectrum of competing or complementary influences in civil-military relations that more accurately reflect reality.[6] The positive and negative influences of the military on development and modernizations have been the subject of an extensive literature, beyond this chapter's scope.[7]

It was not always thus. Some Western political scientists in the 1960s considered the failure of third-world civilian leaderships in a variety of states and concluded that the military was the future hope of these societies. Civilian leaders, they maintained, were often corrupt, ineffectual, unimaginative, factional, had no concept of development, and produced few positive results. The third-world military, in their view however, was problem-oriented, uncorrupt, disciplined, and had a positive vision for the future of their states. Because the Cold War was a dominant intellectual security concern at that time, these positive positions may have strongly been influenced because third-world military governments were essentially anticommunist. Ironically, the first Burmese military regime (the "caretaker government," 1958–1960) was held up as a model of good, if authoritarian, governance. Perhaps this was an accurate assessment because it set out on a restricted time schedule, forcing quick and decisive decisions, rather than the *tatmadaw* planning for perpetual power, as it did following the coup of 1962.[8]

In spite of intense pressure from the West, especially from the United States, for "regime change," the military was determined not to turn over authority to a civilian-led government. Although overcoming sporadic and bloody popular uprisings, and in the face of severe economic decline and deprivation, the *tatmadaw* has been able to hold on to power longer than any other military-led state in the modern world.[9] Through direct administration (1958–1960, 1962–1974, 1988–2011), and through less direct, but directed control through their formulated and led political party (the Burma Socialist Programme Party [BSPP], 1974–1988), the *tatmadaw* determined the course of state action. In the sixty-five years of Burmese independence, civilian control was maintained for only twelve years, and only at the state's inception in 1948. The military conducted three coups to assert or reassert its power: a "constitutional" one in 1958 to which the civilian government effectively had to agree, an almost bloodless one in 1962 that was designed to keep military control for the foreseeable future, and a bloody one in 1988 to shore up the previously failed military-led government. Since 1962, the *tatmadaw* has been determined to maintain its authority either directly or indirectly for an indefinite period, believing only it could hold the country together and advance its interests. According to Moshe Lissak, "this distortion [amalgamating concepts of nation and state] is manifest by an officer corps who consider themselves the exclusive embodiment of the will of the nation and view all other functional groups as expressing only partial and temporary interests."[10]

In the course of military domination, the avenues to achieve power have become constricted and subject to military control. Whatever its many defects, and they were palpable, the civilian administration of U Nu had relatively open paths to status and authority that were not completely restricted by either religion or ethnicity, if one played by Burman rules.[11] This has changed; the controls and restrictions in these paths influence the role and power of the *tatmadaw* today and will effectively determine its future in that series of complex societies that are called Myanmar. Thus, if one wishes to try to consider the past and anticipate the future roles of the military in

Myanmar, one must analyze the effective avenues to authority and how these have changed and/or been maintained, why they were attractive, how they might diminish, and thus the future of governance in Myanmar. This chapter attempts to start such a process of inquiry.

Social Mobility in Premilitary Burma

The Burman areas of the country were traditionally a mobile society at certain levels, but completely dependent on the whims of the centralized monarchy. It was spared the burden of India with its caste system that effectively enshrined social stasis. It lacked a procedural road to an established order of meritocracy as in China, where at least in theory one might rise through the bureaucracy through superior learning. Although the Burman village headmen, and an occasional woman, were hereditary, the advisers to the monarch, the governors, and other officials served subject to the king's pleasure. The Burmese never developed a consistent succession system for the monarchy.

The British destroyed the monarchy, instituting a hierarchical series of status roles, expanding over time, effectively based on access to modern education, with special emphasis on English language ability. The precolonial elites in Burman areas did not reappear, although in memory they may have continued.[12] In various minority regions, traditional rulers, such as the *sawbwas* (maharajas) in the Shan and Kayah States continued, and in other minority areas, chieftains were chosen by local custom.

There were five avenues of social mobility in Burma under the independent civilian government, four of which were effective in providing opportunities for heightened status, authority, and financial opportunities. These were education, the *sangha* (Buddhist monkhood), the political parties/mass organizations and civil society, and the military. The private sector was an anomaly.

Higher education was open to all, and although statistics are lacking, anecdotal evidence indicates that students, both male and female, including those from poor and rural areas, were able to attend the universities of Rangoon and Mandalay. Ethnic students were in evidence, and students of such groups celebrated ethnic "national" days. Professors had high status, and students were regarded as the incipient intelligentsia and nationalist leaders.

The *sangha*, whose ubiquitous role in education at the village level had diminished with the British introduction of both secular Burmese and English language educational tracks, had still maintained an established monastic educational system through university level. Thus, a poor boy could gain access to higher education and then, depending on choice, leave the monkhood without opprobrium, or continue as a monk, in either case with great respect in the local community.

Political parties, especially the Anti-Fascist People's Freedom League (AFPFL), the ruling compendium of a variety of political persuasions, were important avenues to political power and prestige, together with the quasi–civil society organizations they sponsored. These included peasant and workers' associations and other types of mass mobilization organizations, such as those for veterans. Autonomous civil society and professional associations were prominent in that period.

The military itself was an avenue engendering great respect and was constantly sought as an avenue of mobility.[13] The applicants for the officer corps exceeded positions; it was a career that carried considerable weight, considering that many of the founders of the Republic, including and especially Aung San, were regarded as from the military. In effect, the "best and the brightest" opted for a military career, a pattern that intensified after 1962. According to a Burma specialist,

> One of the factors that contributed to the consolidation of the NCO [noncommissioned officers] and officer corps as a distinct status group was that the military has been since independence, the most available channel of social mobility. The military has a considerable advantage, compared to other public institutions, in attracting the most qualified personnel in the country. One main reason for this is the prestige of the military profession.[14]

The private sector was something of a dilemma. The state was avowedly socialist, but of a moderate and democratic nature.[15] The state-owned enterprises (SOEs) were numerous, but there was no attempt to destroy the for-profit private sector. The impetus for socialism came not only because it was a fashionable international intellectual trend, but more importantly because the economy in the colonial era had essentially been under foreign control—the British, the Indians (all those from the subcontinent), and the Chinese. The economy was to be restored to Burman control through socialism; the strengthening of the SOEs was a primary means. In addition, to encourage Burmese entrepreneurship, import and export licenses were given to Burmese firms. Too often, however, those Burmese firms were simply fronts for Indian or Chinese entrepreneurs who controlled the businesses. The unavailability of institutional entrepreneurial credit hampered those Burmese who wished to engage in productive enterprises, with the result that much of the informally available credit was obtained through Chinese clan and linguistic associations, which of course increased the Chinese influence in the society. The Indian subcaste of *chettyars* had become in the colonial period the hated moneylenders in the rural sector.

Ethnic participation was evident both symbolically and in fact. The president, a position more symbolic than powerful as the prime minister was the political leader, was alternated among the major ethnic groups. The first was a Shan, the second a Burman, the third a Karen, and the fourth was to have been a Kachin, but the 1962 coup ended that parade. At the time of independence, the head of the military was a Karen. He was replaced by a Burman after the Karen insurrection that began in 1949 even though he was loyal to the Republic.[16] There were ethnic Indians and Muslims in the cabinet, and a Burmese Muslim in the higher echelons of education. Minorities occupied prominent positions not only in their respective states, but also in the central bureaucracy, in education, health, and in the military itself.

Although the constitution of 1947 that came into effect on independence in 1948 called for respect for minority rights and cultures, this was in fact restricted, even though in comparison to successor military governments it was more open. But the state curriculum was mandated from the center and instructed in Burmese; minority languages were not taught in the official curriculum, although English was included as a foreign language. A common curriculum and language of instruction was intended to create national unity, but in part resulted in minority dissatisfaction with Burmanization and assimilation.

Buddhism was critical, as it was the religion of some 89 percent of the total population, for not only were the majority Burmans almost exclusively Buddhist, but so were the Mons, Shans, Rakhine, Kayah, and significant portions of other ethnic groups, such as the Karen. Buddhism was not the state religion, however, although it was given special status. U Nu won the election of 1960, in part campaigning to make Buddhism the state religion against the advice of the military, who warned that if this occurred, the Kachin would go into revolt, which they soon did. Ne Win reversed that decision after the 1962 coup. In the civilian period, the leadership of the state, including the military, was reasonably diverse. Those avenues began to be restricted in the BSPP era under General (also variously President and BSPP Chair) Ne Win, and virtually disappeared under the post-1988 military governments—the State Law and Order Restoration Council (SLORC, 1988–1997) and the State Peace and Development Council (SPDC, 1997–2011).[17]

The Evolving Rigidity in Social Mobility Under Military Rule

The intention of the *tatmadaw* to play active roles in or control the political process has been transparent and has not deviated from that purpose. In the BSPP period, the objective was attained through direct and indirect mechanisms. In the 1988–2011 junta era, the goals have been consistent. The *tatmadaw* defense policy contains the following mission: "To train and develop a strong defence force which possess military, political, economic and administrative outlook in order to participate in the national political leadership role in the future state."[18]

Maung Aung Myoe, writing in 1999, concluded, "Within a period of eleven years [1988 to 1999], the *Tatmadaw* has laid down foundation for its continued dominance in Myanmar's political, social and economic future."[19] This dominance has been solidified in the national constitution of 2008 that came into force in 2011.[20] He goes on to suggest that "the *Tatmadaw* [sic] is an autonomous institution within the state with little or no civilian oversight. . . . Civilian on non-military apparatuses of the state could not say anything about the *Tatmadaw's* command structure, financial allocation and procurement to scrutinize military businesses. Besides, the government cannot interfere in the appointment and promotion of military personnel; technically speaking, it also covers police and other armed forces under different ministries."[21] Succeeding regimes tightened their social control.

As Selth has noted, before 1988 the *tatmadaw* was essentially a voluntary organization in spite of a universal draft law that was enacted (under an Israeli model, but never implemented) under the military caretaker government in 1959. Later, as military incompetence in governance became apparent, "at a more practical level, military service was seen as a way of acquiring privileges and benefits not readily available in Burmese society, and of learning technical skills which could be profitably exploited on return to civilian life."[22]

The Burma Socialist Programme Party Government (BSPP, 1962–1988)

The military after the coup of 1962 became the nexus of government, and indeed one might say the state. The BSPP was formed by General Ne Win from within the military. Although a civilian, U Chit Myaing, was used as the "philosophical" father of the regime and was the author of the eclectic and abstruse ideology that became its ideological basis, "The System of Correlation Between Man and His Environment," this ideology was essentially ignored and was never questioned in the meetings of the Revolutionary Council—the military who controlled the party and the state.[23]

As Yoshihiro Nakanishi has summarized, "Thus the BSPP was far from being an autonomous party organization. It was an adjunct of the military with *tatmadaw* officers forming the human framework of the party."[24] Of the seventeen members of the Revolutionary Council that came to power after the coup, all were military.[25] Of the members of the Central Executive Committee of the BSPP from 1971 through 1985, only one had a civilian background, the remainder were active duty or retired military. Military control was evident as well in the executive branch of government. Between 1974 and 1988, 94 percent of cabinet ministers were from the military, of whom 88 percent were from the army.[26] This is in marked contrast to the military governments that dominated portions of Thai politics. Under 1976–1979 Thai military governments, 25.5 percent were military, and under the 1979–1988 mixed civilian-military period, 23.1 percent were military.[27]

Ethnicity at senior political party levels had not yet been closed off. Of the second BSPP central committee members elected from its candidate members, nine were Burmans; two each were Shan, Kachin, Rakhine, and Mon; and one each from the Danu, PaO, Paduang, Po Karen, and Kayah groups.[28] Because the BSPP was a national party, minorities were included (as they were later with the Union Solidarity and Development Party, 2011 to the present), but their inclusion did not translate into effective decision-making capacity, which remained with the military.

The paucity of women in national life, which has been a focus of many in the human rights community the past four or so decades, was less a product of Burman society than it was of military domination. There were in the BSPP period as well as in the civilian era a small but significant number of women in the armed forces, although not at senior levels.[29] The complete domination of the military since 1962 has resulted in a diminution of women in prominent positions, although there has never been significant discrimination against women in the school system at any level. Women remain renowned in the arts, in education at the professorial level, in health care as doctors, and in the bureaucracy now up to ministerial level. They have always been a significant force in the economy.[30]

Since there was only one legal party, the BSPP, effectively an arm of the *tatmadaw*, and the economy for a period was rigidly socialist, avenues of mobility through the political process and through entrepreneurship were absent except when explicitly condoned by the military. An effective socialist economy ipso facto requires a competent bureaucracy to guide and administer it. But early after their coup, the military replaced the most effective bureaucracy that the country had ever produced: the Burma Civil Service. Retired and active duty military were recruited into the bureaucracy, where they often had more enthusiasm and loyalty than competence.

During the course of the BSPP period, the *tatmadaw* took two highly significant actions that further solidified its control. In 1980, after efforts by the civilian government had failed, the *sangha* were finally registered. That meant that the state controlled the hierarchy of the monkhood, its educational system, and that each monk had to have an identity card indicating his status and his superior. No longer could a criminal or a communist shave his head, put on robes, and thus be given social protection from interrogation and arrest. It seems unlikely, however, that centralized control extended to the relative autonomy and elevated place of the monk in his sociopolitical village setting. In 2013, there were 265,204 monks, 291,293 novices, and 45,353 nuns registered, perhaps 1 percent of the total population, and a substantially higher percentage of the adult-age male cohort.[31]

In 1982, the state passed the nationalities act, defining citizenship. To be a full citizen, and thus eligible for certain positions and appointments, one had to be a member of a recognized ethnic group in the country or be able to prove that one's ancestors had lived in Burma before 1823. The First Anglo-Burmese War started in 1824, when Indian troops came into the country and the British occupied Rakhine (Arakan) and Tenasserim, so this act was an effort to disenfranchise foreigners, especially the Indians and the Chinese. The Rohingya were not included as an internal ethnic group and remain stateless, a major problem that faces the government as this is written.

Social Mobility Under the Military SLORC and SPDC (1988–2011)

If the military under the BSPP narrowed social mobility into channels it could effectively control, the avenues became even more constricted under the SLORC and the SPDC even as theoretically three new routes to power and authority were opened: the private sector, civil society, and multiparty politics. Yet non-Burman ethnicity and non-Buddhist religion became hurdles that few could overcome to gain entry into the elite: the upper echelons of the military (colonel and above), and the cabinet and subcabinet.

The failure of socialism, explicitly recognized at the end of the BSPP period, resulting in the openings to indigenous private sector activity and foreign investment, should have expanded long-restricted access to power and prestige through this long-belittled avenue. Yet this also was severely restricted. As the SLORC gave civil society legal status in 1988, this was designed to control a growing phenomenon evident throughout Asia and indeed the world—to preempt its acquisition of political power.[32] There was, in addition, the much heralded espousal of the theoretical "multi-political party" system, resulting in the famed but ignored elections of May 1990 that were swept by the opposition NLD.[33] Higher education, long intellectually confined to socialist-related dogma, was freed from those rigors only to have other forms of censorship, equally severe, imposed. Demonstrations against the SLORC/SPDC meant that schools were shut down for long periods, but colleges and universities expanded in number, dropped in quality, and were physically moved to the periphery of cities to stop student demonstrations. "Distance learning" became an important state priority not only to expand educational opportunities, but also to prevent students from congregating. The result was more rigid control without ideological conformity. Burma/Myanmar had progressed from a totalitarian state, complete with ideology and political control, to an authoritarian one, the controls still extant but an ideology substituted by censorship of anything deemed to be antistate in nature.[34]

The resuscitation of the private sector theoretically should have been an important avenue for mobility for the indigenous population. Several factors prevented this from occurring. First was an absence of capital through the banking sector for the foundation or expansion of businesses. The record demonstrates that the state-authorized banks that could provide credit did so first to the SOEs and their joint venture partners from abroad. Capital available for the Burmese entrepreneur without carefully cultivated relations with military protectors was limited. Bank interest rates on savings were most often below inflation rates, thereby discouraging bank use. Further, the state lacked a neutral judicial arbitration system to settle business disputes. Other select sectors were controlled by the state (e.g., defense industries), but others were monopolized or strongly influenced by the two military-held *zaibatsu* (economic conglomerates) that had been separately incorporated and were not part of the public sector. The *zaibatsu* were instead the financial backbone of military units and retirees who were assured of profitable investments. The Myanmar Economics Holdings Corporation and the Myanmar Economic Corporation have extensive interests, employ hundreds of thousands of workers in a variety of fields, and play important roles in the economy.[35] They have many joint ventures with foreign firms; the most notorious has been with the Wanbao Mining Company, the Chinese firm in partnership with the Myanmar government on the controversial Letpadaung copper mine in central Myanmar.

To take advantage of the state's opening to the private sector required intimate access to the military leadership, which essentially meant that those who had already demonstrated mobility simply reinforced their capacities to increase their assets. Called by many foreign observers the "cronies," they were able to get the monopolies and contracts to expand their wealth. This, together with the illegal immigration of perhaps some two million Chinese who had access to credit from family, clans, and linguistic associations, Burmese entrepreneurship, except in very limited areas such as in the bazaars, was severely circumscribed.

Although civil society was allowed to register and function, procedures for doing so, for either internal advocacy nongovernmental organizations (NGOs) or international ones, were haphazardly enforced and over time became even more stringent. These organizations did not exist under the BSPP era, except for a few foreign ones founded prior to the formation of the state in 1948 (e.g., the Young Men's Christian Association [YMCA]). Of course, local community-based organizations (CBOs) flourished all along under the state radar system, but they were essentially apolitical and did not threaten the BSPP, which of course established its own "civil society" under its spreading umbrella.

In the SLORC/SPDC era, political advocacy groups (in distinction to political parties) could not register as NGOs. NGO functions were to pursue rural development, environmental improvements, religious affairs, education, social welfare, and other socially beneficial programs. The state, however, did form a wide variety of state-controlled civil groups intended to further state policies and to act as mass mobilization avenues to ensure political conformity, but also to deny the field to organizations that had the potential to form antistate activities. The most widespread and prominent of such organizations was the Union Solidarity and Development Association (USDA), which at its peak had some 24.5 million members, certainly over half the adult population. It later morphed into the Union Solidarity and Development Party (USDP). The USDP was the chosen instrument of the government in the November 2010 elections.[36]

Political parties were formally allowed, although registration regulations were stringent. The NLD especially was harassed, many of its members jailed for obscure infringements of dubious regulations, and the opening of branch offices throughout the country severely restricted.

At the same time under the SLORC/SPDC era, ethnic and religious conformity within the military reached peaks hitherto absent in previous administrations. In effect, the result of the half century of direct and indirect military control has been to narrow the avenues of social mobility and place them under the *tatmadaw* imprimatur. When this system was combined with the personalization of power in Burman society, a not uncommon trait in many states, it effectively gave those with the coercive power the ability, both institutionally and personally, to ensure that the political and economic assets of the ruling elite were protected.

Thus, if broadening the opportunities for increasing the population's access and avenues for enhanced status and authority and eventual democracy means reducing the monopolistic controls of the *tatmadaw*, then how might this be accomplished without social disruptions that would vitiate the potential for broad progress?

The issue is obviously complex and dependent on local forces, sometimes in the context of international pressures. One author analyzed the withdrawal of the military as dependent on "two sets of four variables, Set I: (1) personal interests of the military, (2) corporate interests of the military, (3) military ideology, (4) military cohesion. Set II: (1) configuration of the civilian sphere (strength of parties and civil society), (2) economic development, (3) internal security (e.g., secessionist movements), and (4) external security."[37]

Marco Bünte considers internal Myanmar factors as decisive. Yet the situation in Myanmar is likely to be more complex. Recruitment into the higher ranks of the military may be overwhelmingly important both because of the attractions of power and authority as well as dismal alternatives in other professions. The economic interests and institutions directly controlled by the military may, depending on the society and timing, have different effects: continuing or relinquishing controls. The corporate interests of the military also may work in opposite directions depending on the society. In one direction is encouragement to hold onto such economic assets and controls (and thus institutionalized military power) because of fears that any civilian leadership might deprive the military of those assets that can supplement their budgets, incomes, and rent-seeking through nonmilitary or state bureaucratic channels and so diminish dependence on state-authorized allocations. Alternatively, the opposite direction would involve shedding highly open economic assets so that there might be less civilian interference in military-dominated affairs. The role of the middle class is unclear. In the West, the rise of the middle class may have been an important element in the diminution of military dominance as military-controlled businesses undercut civilian opportunities for this group. How important that might be for Myanmar is unclear, as much of the future middle class may be the Chinese, who have access to the capital necessary for economic entrepreneurship.

How have other societies changed their monopolies of military control to ones more advantageous to their populations as a whole? It is obvious that this has happened and is undergoing transitions in a variety of states. Here we will explore aspects of four Asian transformations: South Korea, Thailand, Indonesia, and Vietnam.

Social Mobility and the Military in Asia—Some Comparisons

The Burmese, Thai, Indonesian, and Vietnamese militaries in East Asia have controlled extensive economic assets.[38] The question remains unanswered as to whether such control affected positively or negatively both development and civilian control. The issue of military economic assets is usually explored in terms of their fiscal extent. This is obviously important, but how such assets affect the motivation, ease, and avenues of social mobility in any of these states seems unexplored. How much control resulted in individual as opposed to corporate wealth, and its contribution to the development process, has yet to be adequately examined in the Asian context.

The coup by General Park Chung-hee in May 1961 ended a year of ineffectual, tumultuous liberal government in South Korea that in turn was a violent response to the autocratic rule of President Syngman Rhee, who had governed since independence in 1948. In spite of the complete upheaval and physical dislocation of South Korean society during the Korean War, the Japanese colonial occupation (1910–1945), and three years of US military control (1945–1948), on the event of that coup South Korea was remarkably socially stable. The traditional elite, the *yangban* (literally "two classes," but translated as "the gentry"), still maintained a high social position even if their legal status had long been abolished and their wealth diminished.

Avenues of mobility were still highly restricted in practice even though they were legally open. Although primary schools had been established in virtually every village cluster, high schools were only in the market towns and transportation to them rudimentary at best. There were only approximately 100,000 students in all of higher education, and they were essentially from "good family backgrounds"—the *yangban*. The professors were from the same group. The private sector was undeveloped, except for some few individuals who were able to acquire Japanese-controlled industries after 1946.

The military coup changed the equation. Since there was, and remains, a military draft, the military became an important avenue of mobility. At a blue-collar level, it taught the technological skills that the society needed to develop. Recruitment into the officer corps was a classless contest, and with the power and authority of the military from 1961 until 1987, the armed forces were a preferred avenue of advancement. Then, economic development was encouraged by President Park, as this was his only avenue for political legitimacy. Public and private investments in education provided the basis on which industry, trade, and higher education expanded.

The middle class expanded as education and the economy grew, and with this came increasingly vocal demands for political change and a substantive democratic government. The military-dominated government of President Chun Doo Hwan (1979–1988), who obtained office in 1979 under what the Korean courts called a "coup-like event" after President Park's assassination, was forced to agree to constitutional changes that opened the society.

Perhaps in large part because of the development of these and other nonmilitary alternative paths to success, the desirability of recruitment to the elite through military channels decreased, and the military retired quietly to their barracks in 1987. In international terms in the modern era, this was a remarkable transformation. Were other forces in play at this time? One could argue that international education, the development of civil society, and the role of the United States as a military shield all were involved to some degree, but it is my contention that these changes related to the military becoming subordinate to civilian control were caused, or greatly assisted, by the opening up of social mobility in that society.[39]

According to Lissak, "Thailand's modern political history is so closely bound up with the history of the interrelationships between the military establishment and the civilian administration that any discussion of current political affairs in Thailand that omits reference to the sociopolitical and professional profile of Thailand's armed forces becomes difficult and unrewarding."[40]

The Thai military has played a complex and critical role in Thai politics since 1932, when a coup eliminated the absolute power of the monarch.

Since then, the number of successful and unsuccessful coups against various civilian regimes is legion. The military has been a close supporter of the monarchy. The assets of the Thai military are extensive, including a banking system, television, and radio stations, and a variety of industries.[41] Yet there are significant differences between the roles of the military in both countries.

Thailand is far more hierarchical as a society than is Myanmar. The extended royal family is, of course, at its apex supported both by the military and by a *lèse majesté* law that insulates the family from criticism. Under the absolute monarchy, 87 percent of the military elite were from the royal family and there were no commoners. Between 1932 and 1958, of the 237 ministers in thirty-two cabinets, 34.5 percent were from the armed forces.[42] Although there are major peripheral problems in Thailand, such as the Muslim unrest in the south that has existed for decades, this has not prevented Thai Muslims from becoming chief-of-staff of the army or Thai foreign minister. Even though Buddhism is an essential attribute of the monarchy, it is not the essential determinate of mobility. As we have noted, the Thai military, even when they had complete control over the government, essentially operated through the civilian bureaucracy and administration. The Thai military did not control all the avenues of social mobility in that society.

As the Thai political system opened, and the legislative branch became more important, many generals and high-level military and police opted to obtain power through these nonmilitary channels through election to the legislature together with their business opportunities. Although another Thai coup has occurred, social mobility, even in as highly hierarchical a society as Thailand, will mitigate that issue over time. Thailand, according to one author, is a "prestige hierarchy," with the royal family and the ruling class, and uppermost in that class has been the military.[43]

The fall of President Suharto after the Asian financial crisis of 1997 and the rise of the elected presidency did not end the role of the military in Indonesia, which had been predicated on the concept of *dwifungsi*—dual functions (civil and military). In addition to large-scale military control at local levels, the economic assets of the Indonesian military are still extensive, even if they have been diminished under International Monetary Fund (IMF) prompting. Increasingly, as in Thailand, retired military are finding their way into politics at both the national and local levels. As the economy has expanded, as education has flourished, there are increasing opportunities for aspiring youth in realms beyond the military. As Michael Vitikiotis has argued, "more importantly, the military is still able to pursue private business interests to support its budget and therefore fund and influence political campaigns. . . . Perhaps the main reason the military stayed on the sidelines is because the army has become a principal source of civilian political leadership."[44]

Indonesia's military, the Tentara Nasional Indonesia (TNI), has flourished in the past with off-budget resources gained from a variety of economic enterprises. The net income was more than substantial, but essentially unknowable. Yet the government declared under Law 34 of 2004 that by 2009 this was to cease and full funding for the TNI was to be included in the state budget.[45] But "recall that the number of [military] business units was first announced as 219, then raised to 1,520, and then dropped to 356."[46] In spite of IMF prodding, the TNI still has expensive business connections. It seems evident that the Indonesian military has never completely controlled social mobility in that complex society.

The relationship of the Vietnam People's Army (VPA) to both the political and economic sectors in that country has been highly significant, although figures are not available on the recruitment and cross-professional ties between the two. Yet the VPA has been built into the economic development program both through their charge to contribute to national reconstruction and the provision of vocational education to its forces.[47] Although the VPA has been under internal pressures to rid itself of its commercial enterprises since 1991, in 1994 there were 330 army-run commercial enterprises, and in the following year 45 joint ventures with foreign firms. These firms had been reduced to 140 companies by 2007, but their annual turnover in 2009 was some US$3.2 billion in 10 remaining companies, including the highly lucrative telecoms and information technology fields. In 2008, Vietnam stopped divestiture of its economic assets.[48] It is unclear whether the VPA is the critical avenue for mobility in Vietnamese society, but the state, in the constitution, recognizes the importance of nonmilitary economic employment for retired soldiers and their families.

The Future of Social Mobility and the Role of the Military

Myanmar is unique in East Asia in its military's control over social mobility since the junta period (1988–2011). In no other East Asian state has the indigenous military so completely controlled the avenues to social mobility. Not even in other countries where the military has held profound economic assets or been critical in the political sphere has this been as true. The relation of this phenomenon to the future of that country is thus important both for predicting Myanmar's next incarnation and the military's future position, and for the role of foreign assistance.

How does social mobility relate to democracy, however defined? Is it necessary for a transition from an authoritarian or monarchical state to one in which the populace has a greater say on who will govern? If so, how fast does this change need to occur? Or rather, is it a product of a transformation of a state in which governance is already in the hands of its peoples? And, of course, who controls that mobility, however much it may exist?

Even more of a conundrum is the prejudice that we may bring as to what constitutes social mobility. Many might argue that in the United States mobility is essentially focused on money, for with it may come access to prestige, better education, health care, and to whatever powers that be. Yet one might also complain that this is an ethnocentric approach, for in other societies culture, language, education, religion, and regional or clan affiliations are important elements of the mobility process. This is not an anthropological examination, and we must leave these important but abstruse considerations to a later time. What is evident, however, is that if the *tatmadaw* in Myanmar were to assume a less prominent role, there would need to be attractive, alternative, nonmilitary routes for ambitious youth (and their families) to seek advancement in that society. That advancement need not be only in political power, but in any of a number of potentially prestigious fields. It will also involve a need to satisfy the whole population, not simply the Burman majority.

The mosaic that is Myanmar is composed of peoples who cross the ethnically irrational borders of that state, since each of the major groups has ethnic cousins across the frontiers and with whom they are in constant touch. As conditions for minorities in China, Thailand, and India change, so the invidious comparisons will be made against any Myanmar administration that has failed to include these peoples in whatever progress is possible in that society. The minorities, while fairly isolated until the past two or three years, will increasingly be comparing their status and prospects to those in other, neighboring societies. Thus, the physical and social periphery of the state needs to be included in the process of expanding opportunities. This effectively means the ceilings on ethnic and religious advancement are required to be lifted, both within the *tatmadaw* and in civilian life, and the means to implement such changes found for those peoples, as well as those for the majority Burman population.

One critical dilemma facing the *tatmadaw* is the primary importance in their view of national unity, and the means to ensure that this is not threatened. Myanmar is a state, but not a nation with an overarching ethos and identity.[49] This is clearly a military goal. Since independence, this goal has been sought through the development of a national educational curriculum in Burmese. Obviously, knowledge of Burmese is essential for both social mobility and national unity. But just as the Burmans have felt that their culture has been under siege, the ethnic groups have felt even more strongly that this was the case of their cultures. The cry for education in the official curriculum in local languages at some level and to some degree is widespread, recently in the parliament as well, but has been denied by all governments. In 2013, the state has begun to approve publications in some local languages, a welcome reform, but real adherence to the constitution on fostering indigenous cultures, rather than the Burmanization now so obvious, would be an important element of a new, cultural unity and of any real majority-minority peace and reconciliation.

The question that is often asked about Burma/Myanmar is how the military has been able to continue in effective control for over half a century. Various opinions have been proposed, but one that may have been overlooked is the apparent *tatmadaw* control over virtually all avenues of social mobility. It has not only been their monopoly on coercive power, however strong that has been, but also the fusion of social mobility into military and military-controlled routes to advancement that has created a lack of opportunity to acquire power on the part of many. Opportunities for power and gain spread indirectly to military families, support groups, and related entrepreneurs that make up a significant portion of the population.

Thus, the closed doors and glass ceilings so evident in Myanmar under the new Republic of the Union of Myanmar must, respectively, be opened and taken down for the *tatmadaw* to achieve its own goals. This is also in the interests of all foreign governments that have some security, economic, or moral interests in that country. Without such evolutional changes, violent ones are more likely with even greater deprivation to the diverse populace. A change in the constitution by 2015 to eliminate direct appointment of the officer corps (25 percent of seats by active-duty military) in all parliaments at all levels, or changes in the requirements for the president or vice presidents, will not effectively change the social role of the *tatmadaw*, however desirable that may be in democratic representational terms. These are simply symptoms of the major issue, and their elimination is not the solution to a continuing sociopolitical problem, but rather an amelioration of an immediate manifestation of a condition often regarded as detrimental to effective governance.[50] The military may agree to constitutional changes, but not if they impinge on what the *tatmadaw* regard as their fundamental interests.[51]

A senior official in Naypyitaw said that the military in the legislature was their "end game." The antipathy to civilians and politicians so long a dogma of the *tatmadaw*, he explained, would gradually be erased as they worked together in the legislature. Therefore, this civilian-military duality might be a good interim measure for future relations, he maintained.[52]

The corollary to the elimination of barriers for the populace is the development of diverse opportunities for the members of the military itself. The advantages, access, perks, and opportunities need to be more evenly distributed so that ambitious youth look to a broader array of opportunities. These opportunities need to come not only from graduating from one of the esteemed military educational institutions, but also from foreign-supported and English language internal graduate instruction. The members of the military also need post–active duty careers, and the legislatures of Myanmar at all levels could help provide such employment, as it would enhanced business opportunities. In Myanmar, military families have access to better educational and health facilities, so some national uplift of the social sector is required. In South Korea, foreign investors often hired retired military personnel who had the contacts through their military academy classmates and regimental comrades and who could speed business activities.

From 2000 to 2012, the Defense Services Academy produced a total of 22,983 officers, and including the graduates of the Officers' Candidate School brought the total to over 30,000. Because of the lack of promotional opportunities in the bloated officer ranks, the intake into the academy has been reduced.[53] The need to find appropriate positions for retired military within the armed forces is likely to be challenging. It seems, therefore, that the junta has planned that graduates of these institutions will staff what had been civilian bureaucratic positions in government. Although this provides nonmilitary opportunities for the officer corps (and reasonable assurances of loyalty), it also may significantly limit civilian recruitment into elements of the bureaucracy. The state may be preparing to introduce legislation prohibiting this pattern.

The relationship of the Myanmar police to the *tatmadaw* is one of some importance in terms of mobility. Anecdotal evidence points out that military officers are sometimes transferred to the police, and in 1962 the Union Military Police were incorporated into the army. The *tatmadaw* clearly has greater prestige and opportunities for advancement. The relationship between the police and the military, their recruitment policies, and their separate operational fields are issues that deserve singular attention.[54]

Changes must emanate from the government itself. There are signs that openings are occurring, and that the government is considering speeding the changes that it is making to achieve longer-range objectives. If censorship is completely lifted and if the universities begin the process of free inquiry, if civil society organizations offer chances for contributing to social and other forms of welfare, if the private sector is encouraged with competitive capital available across the social spectrum, and if the various legislatures at the provincial level in the state have a greater opportunity to contribute to local social change, then the country will be strengthened, the military will resume its important guardian functions, and its reputation will be restored, and history will record its contribution, overcoming a half-century of decay.

Myanmar is experiencing a plethora of foreign assistance and investment. Indeed, the valid argument is that the needs are ubiquitous and thus more aid will contribute to quicker, more positive change, but there are those who disagree that such assistance will be effective.[55] Both multilateral and bilateral donors, and those from private foundations, might well consider in their planning more than just support to democratic change, although such support—popular with donor constituencies—might be welcome if it is not viewed internally as an attempt to control internal sovereignty, a singular concern of the *tatmadaw* over the years. Important for the long term are efforts to open these avenues of mobility and encourage diverse opportunities for the present youth and future generation. Such a longer view and programming approach lacks the rigor of adhering to evaluative techniques in foreign assistance that call for attainable goals over relatively short periods. "Success," however defined, is unlikely to be attached to such efforts. Yet planning for the longer term may be equally important as improving lives and the immediate politicoeconomic systems. This approach is something that could contribute to democratic sustenance in that society as well as development of the well-being of the state as a whole. Although social mobility considered as a singular factor alone will not bring democracy, however defined, to any state, it presents important prospects for growth, stability, and pluralism—more than current conditions allow. The opportunities for social mobility throughout Myanmar society need encouragement both by the state itself and by foreign donors and observers.

Notes

1. See, for example, the Michael F. Martin, "U.S. Policy Towards Burma: Issues for the 113th Congress," Report R-43035 (Washington, DC: Congressional Research Service, 12 March 2013).

2. As an example of the latter position, see David I. Steinberg, "Moving Myanmar: The Future of Military Prominence," *Kyoto Journal of Southeast Asian Studies* 14 (September 2013).

3. Renaud Egreteau and Larry Jagan, *Soldiers and Diplomacy in Myanmar. Understanding the Foreign Relations of the Burmese Praetorian State* (Singapore: NUS Press, 2013).

4. For a discussion of the role of the military in Western literature and the praetorian and garrison state, see Egreteau and Jagan, *Soldiers and Diplomacy in Myanmar.*

5. See Samuel E. Finer, *The Man on Horseback: The Role of the Military in Politics* (Boulder, CO: Westview Press, 1988).

6. For a discussion in general and in the Myanmar context, see Marco Bünte, "Burma's Transition to Quasi-military Rule: From Rulers to Guardians." *Armed Forces and Society* (5 July 2013): 742–764.

7. For a discussion, see Moshe Lissak, *Military Roles in Modernization: Civil-Military Relations in Thailand and Burma* (London: Sage Publications, 1976). The Western stress on "professionalism" of the military has led to the Burmese reaction that such professionalism is, in effect, a mercenary attitude and is deplored.

8. For the military's positive assessment of its own performance, see Burma Director of Information, *Is Trust Vindicated? A Chronicle of a Trust, Striving, and Triumph. Being an Account of the Accomplishments of the Government of the Union of Burma, November 1, 1958–February 1, 1960* (Rangoon: Government of the Union of Burma, 1960).

9. In contrast to the Thai military, it has been far more cohesive, with the inter-

nal image of Burmese military leadership pictured as the "father," and the military as the "family."

10. Lissak, *Military Roles in Modernization*, 20.

11. In this chapter, *Burman* refers to the majority ethnic group (estimated at some 66 percent) of the state, almost all of whom are Buddhist and who control governance in that country.

12. See Thant Myint-U and the discussion of his family in *The River of Lost Footsteps* (New York: Farrar, Straus and Giroux, 2006). The Burman areas may have been unique in East Asia in that regard.

13. A former Burmese professor who received his Ph.D. from Harvard remarked that his Burmese students passed the oral examination for becoming officers because he had trained them to answer questions and participate as if they were in a Harvard graduate seminar (personal conversation).

14. Lissak, *Military Roles in Modernization*, 157. The Burmese military has continuously been involved in politics. Of the twenty-three key colonels in the "Caretaker" military government (1958–1960), twenty had been involved in preindependence politics.

15. That it was not sufficiently socialist in part prompted two communist rebellions: the "Red Flags" and the "White Flags" (the Burma Communist Party), the latter finally collapsing in 1989.

16. See General Smith Dun, "Memoirs of The Four Foot Colonel," *Southeast Asia Data Paper* No. 113 (Ithaca: Cornell University Southeast Asia Program Publications, 1980).

17. Just prior to World War II, the Burmese military was 12.3 percent Burman, 27.8 percent Karen, 22.6 percent Chin, and 22.9 percent Kachin.

18. Maung Aung Myoe, "Military Doctrine and Strategy in Myanmar: A Historical Perspective," Working Paper No. 339. (Canberra: Australian National University, Strategic and Defence Studies Centre, 1999).

19. Maung Aung Myoe, "The Tatamadaw in Myanmar Since 1988: An Interim Assessment." Working Paper No. 342 (Australian National University, Strategic and Defence Studies Centre, 1999).

20. *Constitution of the Republic of the Union of Myanmar, 2008.* Chapter 1 Basic Principles 6 (f) ". . . enabling the Defence Services to be able to participate in the National political leadership of the State." 20 (b) ". . . The Defence Services has the right to independently administer and adjudicate all affairs of the armed forces."

21. Maung Aung Myoe, "The Soldier and the State: The Tatmadaw and Political Liberalization in Myanmar Since 2011," paper presented at the Burma Update conference, Canberra, 2013.

22. Andrew Selth, *Burma's Armed Forces: Power Without Glory* (Norwalk, CT: EastBridge, 2002): 76–77.

23. For an extensive discussion of, and interview with, U Chit Myaing, see Yoshihiro Nakanishi, *Strong Soldiers, Failed Revolution: The State and the Military in Burma, 1962–88* (Singapore: National University of Singapore Press, 2013), Chapter 3.

24. Ibid., 112.

25. Ibid., 102.

26. Ibid., 138–140.

27. Ibid., 144.

28. Ibid., 128.

29. The *Guardian* newspaper, in a picture celebrating the military on 27 March 1963, showed a women's element of the military marching past in the annual parade. Women make up perhaps 2 percent of the military, and there may be one colonel

(medical corps) among the approximately 700 female officers (Andrew Selth, personal communication).

30. The first female ambassador was Aung San's widow, Aung San Suu Kyi's mother. In 2012, the first woman career foreign service ambassador was appointed. Lucian Pye, in his pioneering study of the Burmese, *Politics, Personality, and Nation Building* (New Haven, CT: Yale University Press, 1962), believed that the early in-family discipline applied to girls, and its absence in males at an early age, gave women distinctly more power. Further, customary law in Burma gave women rights far in advance of those in the West in the same period.

31. Myanmar Ministry of Information, personal correspondence.

32. Edict 6/88 of the SLORC. See Robert Taylor, *The State in Myanmar*. (Honolulu: University of Hawaii Press, 2012). This may have been model on a comparable Chinese law of 1987.

33. The elections were for a national constitutional convention that would write a new constitution, following which new elections would be held for a new government. But the NLD and the United States and others interpreted the election as if it were for a new government. A stalemate resulted with no group willing to compromise. Thus, US sanctions were for "regime change"—recognition of the new civilian government.

34. For a comparison of North Korea and Myanmar, see David I. Steinberg, "Transforming 'Outposts of Tyranny'? Lessons and Cautions," paper presented to the ASAN Institute in Seoul at a conference on Myanmar's Liberalization and North Korea, 26 March 2013. For a discussion of the imposition of the role of the military as a substitute ideology, see David I. Steinberg, *Turmoil in Burma: Contested Legitimacies in Myanmar* (Norwalk, CT: EastGate, 2006).

35. These firms did not report state support through facilities and military personnel in their audits and thus could virtually guarantee high rates of return on investments, as they were, at least indirectly, subsidized by the state. Personal interviews, Yangon. For an early study of these groups and the military in the economy, see David I. Steinberg, "Burma/Myanmar: The Role of the Military in the Economy," *Burma Economic Watch* (August 2005).

36. The military had become disillusioned with the BSPP and perhaps sought a different mass mobilization technique at the beginning, since the USDA was registered as a social organization not a political party, as was (obviously) the BSPP. This changed as the regime transformed the USDA into the USDP.

37. Bünte, "Burma's Transition to Quasi-military Rule."

38. See also Andrew Scobell, "Going Out of Business: Divesting the Commercial Interests of Asia's Socialist Soldiers," *Occasional Papers* No. 3 (Washington, DC: East-West Center, January 2000).

39. In 1987, the United States publicly told the Korean military that it would not countenance the army's interference in subduing the popular demonstrations that called for extensive reforms.

40. Lissak, *Military Roles in Modernization*, 73.

41. For an excellent analysis, see Paul Chambers, "Where Agency Meets Structure: Understanding Civil-Military Relations in Contemporary Thailand," *Asian Journal of Political Science* 19, no. 3 (December 2011): 290–304. This article deals with "structure and agency," but does not cover recruitment or social mobility.

42. Lissak, *Military Roles in Modernization,* 91, 97.

43. Ibid., 125.

44. Michael Vitikiotis, "Lessons for Cairo from Jakarta, Manila and Elsewhere." *International Herald Tribune* (9 July 2013).

45. The following is drawn from Lex Rieffel and Jaleswari Pramodhawardani,

Out of Business and on Budget. The Challenge of Military Financing in Indonesia (Washington, DC: The Brookings Institution, 2007).

46. Ibid., 72. "This does not include the Ministry of Defense's own foundations and affiliated business units."

47. This is largely drawn from Carlyle A. Thayer, "The Political Role of the Vietnam People's Army: Corporate Interests and Military Professionalism," paper presented to the annual Association for Asian Studies meeting, Toronto 15–18 March 2012.

48. Carlyle Thayer, personal communication.

49. See David I. Steinberg, "The Problem of Democracy in the Republic of the Union of Myanmar: Neither Nation-State Nor State-Nation," *Southeast Asian Affairs* (2012): 220–237.

50. In August 2013, of the ninety-three ministers and deputy ministers, fifty-one had military backgrounds. *Irrawaddy*, 26 July 2013.

51. Maung Aung Myoe, "The Soldier and the State."

52. Senior official in Naypyitaw, personal conversation.

53. Ibid.

54. See Andrew Selth's pending volume, *Burma's Police Forces: Society, State and Sovereignty*, forthcoming.

55. Serious questions have been raised about too much foreign assistance too quickly. See Lex Rieffel and James W. Fox, *Too Much, Too Soon? The Dilemma of Foreign Aid to Myanmar/Burma* (Arlington, VA: Nathan Associates, March 2013).

4

Emerging Patterns of Parliamentary Politics

Renaud Egreteau

Recent scholarship has confirmed that a rich civic culture and lively parliamentary debates are essential conditions for democratic consolidation.[1] In transitional contexts especially, parliaments[2] provide an essential arena for open debates, political competition, innovative lawmaking, and oversight of government activities in ways that were often unthinkable under previous authoritarian rules.[3] Scholars of legislative politics have differentiated three conventional types of legislatures, according to their legislative performance, the political system under which they are shaped, and their broader impact: (1) "policymaking parliaments," commonly observed in well-established democracies, where strong and autonomous legislatures have a decisive impact on the way laws and policies are made and checked; (2) "policy-influencing parliaments," usually in transitional contexts and/or semiauthoritarian polities, in which legislatures influence policies, yet with a less decisive sway over the still dominant executive power or the judiciary; and (3) "rubber-stamp" or inactive parliaments under autocratic regimes.[4]

After a widely shared initial skepticism, the reemergence of legislative politics in post–State Peace and Development Council (SPDC) Myanmar has received considerable praise since 2011.[5] Following the national elections held on 7 November 2010, a bicameral national parliament was convened. Framed by the 2008 constitution, it combines a Lower House (Pyithu Hluttaw, or House of Representatives, with 440 seats) with an Upper House (Amyotha Hluttaw, or House of Nationalities, with 224 seats). In both chambers, the *tatmadaw* have constitutionally secured one-fourth of the seats. When convened together, the two chambers form the Union Parliament (or Pyidaungsu Hluttaw), the highest legislative body of the post-SPDC polity. The 2010 elections also produced fourteen local legislative assemblies: seven in the Bama-dominated regions (region *hluttaws*) and seven in the ethnic-dominated states (state *hluttaws*).

Since the first parliamentary session convened in January 2011, the new legislative system has proved to be novel in many ways. New members of parliament (MPs) now debate publicly political issues once deemed taboo. Governmental policies are routinely challenged and parliamentarians often question bluntly executive power. Abuses of power by army officers in the countryside are routinely exposed in standing committees or during plenary sessions. Political prisoners have been released following amnesty laws discussed by MPs. Trade unions, demonstrations, and strikes have been legalized. Above all, a new breed of political and legislative practitioner has emerged in the country and now competes with the executive branch, the state bureaucracy, and the still-dominant armed forces. Yet many challenges remain.

Drawing on recent interviews of newly elected Burmese parliamentarians and political party leaders, this chapter identifies and examines the (re)emerging patterns of parliamentarian politics in post-SPDC Myanmar. Fieldwork was carried out in Naypyitaw and Yangon in February, May, and August 2013, while the sixth and seventh sessions of the national parliament were convened (January–March and June–August 2013, respectively). Through the examination of interviews and discussions collected among party leaders, Bama, and ethnic MPs, including the speaker of the Upper House, as well as observations I gathered while attending a plenary session at Pyidaungsu Hluttaw, I hope to make a fresh empirical contribution to our understanding of post-junta politics and the rediscovery of legislative processes and parliamentary practices in the country.

After offering background to elections and parliaments in postcolonial Myanmar, I investigate the initial functioning of the new assemblies crafted after the 2010 elections, with a particular focus on the two national houses. Halfway through the first post-SPDC legislature (2010–2015), a preliminary assessment is provided of the experience of the national parliament as a lawmaking body developing an increasing—and surprising—oversight of post-junta executive power. This chapter analyzes the way debates are carried out during regular sessions, identifies voting patterns of MPs, and looks at how parliamentarian behaviors have gradually been shaped. It also examines how civilian and military MPs interact and how nonelected military appointees perform in parliament.

The scholarship on parliament and democratization indicates that, after an initial phase of euphoric optimism, the odds are that postauthoritarian legislative assemblies move back to old-fashioned clientelist and patrimonial politics, while facing increasing institutional limitations and capacity challenges.[6] If history is any guide, the new Burmese legislature may soon suffer from these very same banes and progressively see its performance and policy impact thinning. This chapter identifies some of the constraints the parliament is currently facing and concludes with the necessity to look beyond the transition and find pathways to legitimate and institutionalize a body essential to democratization. Comparisons are examined on how newly formed parliaments elsewhere in the world have helped political pluralism grow in other postauthoritarian contexts and fostered or, on the contrary, slowed down democratization processes.

The Renaissance of the Legislature in Post-Junta Myanmar

A Background on Elections and Assemblies in Postcolonial Myanmar

Elections have seldom been held in Myanmar, but voting and the formation of lawmaking bodies are not unknown to the Burmese contemporary polity.[7] The British organized the first nationwide elections in 1922 to establish a provincial legislative assembly. Boycotts were already in the air, as Burmese nationalists fiercely debated whether to join a parliament shaped by, and for, the British colonial administration. At the dawn of independence, a constituent assembly was elected in April 1947 to give the country its first democratic constitution. Subsequently, relatively free and fair legislative elections were held in 1951–1952, 1956, and 1960, although voting was not held in areas plagued with armed rebellions. Scholars who have studied Myanmar's first postcolonial years have argued that the deep mistrust of civilian and legislative politics, which army leaders have long nurtured, chiefly stem from the factional anarchy, corruption, interethnic disputes, and unruly parliamentary scene observed during the 1950s.[8] A half century later, official army publications still commonly underscore the negative impact this decade had over the country's political developments, and how it forced the military into intervention.[9] "The *tatmadaw*," a commentator argued recently in the state-owned media, "due to traumatic experiences of the early parliamentary democracy period worries that the nation would be thrown into turmoil by bigoted egocentric politicians engaged in fierce power struggle."[10]

These turbulent postindependence years indeed propelled the Burmese armed forces into power in 1962. The coup ended Myanmar's early parliamentary democracy. The national parliament was dissolved, and elections suspended. The 1974 Constitution offered only a cosmetic commitment to parliamentary activities, creating a unicameral People's Assembly (Pyithu Hluttaw), whose members were to be appointed after regular national elections. But the votes were held under a single legitimate party system, dominated by the Burma Socialist Programme Party (BSPP, or Lanzin). Tightly controlled parliamentary elections were arranged in January 1974, January 1978, October 1981, and October 1985. The Pyithu Hluttaw was relegated to a mere rubber-stamp assembly under the sole authority of the party. "We had to be involved in parliamentary activities," recalls a former Rangoon University professor and current Union Solidarity and Development Party (USDP) member of parliament, "so we got some first experience of parliament 'socialist-style,'" but this was "under the single party rules and regulations."[11]

Following the coup d'état of 1988, the *tatmadaw* dissolved the legislature elected last in 1985 and abrogated the 1974 Constitution. But the newly formed junta, or State Law and Order Restoration Council (SLORC), soon promised the organization of multiparty elections to elect a new 492-member legislature and transfer power back to civilians as soon as law and order were restored. Elections were eventually held on 27 May 1990, the first free and fair ones in three decades. The most outspoken opposition force to the SLORC, the National League for Democracy (NLD), won nearly 60 percent of the votes, but the results were denied by the new military rulers. Instead, the SLORC proposed the convening of a constituent body, or National Convention, to draft a new constitutional text. However, only 99 members of the 702-member assembly formed in January 1993 happened to be MPs elected earlier in May 1990. Lambasted by transnational prodemocracy activists and Western politicians as a sham assembly under full military control, the National Convention convened twice, from 1993 to 1996 and from 2004 to 2007. Unveiled in September 2007, the new constitutional draft was then controversially approved by national referendum in May 2008.

Crafting a New Legislature After the 2010 Elections

Nationwide elections were held on 7 November 2010 to form the new bicameral Union parliament as well as fourteen local assemblies. Unlike the 1990 elections, the objective of the vote was this time unambiguous. This was to be the fifth step (out of seven) of the road map toward a "flourishing disciplined democracy" unveiled by the SPDC in 2003.[12] Many irregularities were denounced during the pre-electoral campaign and many frauds signaled during the voting day.[13] Moreover, the Union Election Commission (UEC, a eighteen-member body nominated by the SPDC in March 2010) had unilaterally rejected the applications of ten political parties out of forty-seven having applied for registration—in particular, the organizations representing some Kachin, Shan, and Rohingya ethnic groups. On its side, the NLD of Aung San Suu Kyi (still under house arrest during the elections) opted to boycott the elections. The party was therefore dissolved by the UEC in May 2010.

The results of the national and local elections were uniformly condemned as a sham by many independent observers and human rights organizations, at home and abroad.[14] The USDP, a political platform gathering retired technocrats, some prominent figures reportedly close to the SPDC, ex-army officers, and a few enigmatic business cronies, won a comfortable majority at the national legislature, with 76.5 percent of all seats contested (see Table 4.1). The National Unity Party (NUP), reminiscent of the old Ne Winian BSPP created in 1988, came second with 5.4 percent of the seats at the national level. Then followed the Shan Nationalities Democratic Party (SNDP) with 4.9 percent of the seats, the Rakhine Nationalities Development Party (RNDP) with 3 percent, the All Mon Region Democracy Party (AMRDP) and the National Democratic Force (NDF, mainly formed by NLD dissidents) with 1.4 percent each, and the Chin National Party (CNP) at 1 percent.

Table 4.1: Seat Composition of the Lower House (Pyithu Hluttaw), Upper House (Amyotha Hluttaw), and State and Region Houses After the 2010 Elections

	Pyithu Hluttaw	Amyotha Hluttaw	State and Region Hluttaws
USDP	259	129	495
Tatmadaw	110	56	222
NUP	12	5	46
SNDP	18	3	36
RNDP	9	7	19
AMRDP	3	4	9
NDF	8	4	4
CNP	2	2	5
PNO	3	1	6
CPP	2	4	6
PSDP	2	3	4
KSDDP	0	1	1
WDP	2	1	3
UDPKS	1	1	2
TPNP	1	1	4
DP-(M)	0	0	3
INDP	1	0	4
KPP	1	1	4
NDPD	0	0	2
KNP	0	0	2
88 Youths	0	0	1
LNDP	0	0	1
Independent	1	1	4
Vacant	5	0	0
Total	**440**	**224**	**883**

The utter dominance of the allegedly pro-regime USDP prompted strong criticism; some observers have even argued that a new form of electoral authoritarianism had emerged in the country.[15] In the local assemblies, though, the regional and ethnic parties fared quite well in the seven ethnic-dominated state *hluttaws* (save in Kayah State), while the USDP has won a majority of seats in all seven Bama-dominated regional parliaments.

Three months after the nationwide vote, the first regular session of the national parliament convened on 31 January 2011. It lasted for two months and was tasked to elect the two speakers of Pyithu Hluttaw and Amyotha Hluttaw and their deputies, as well as the president of the Union and the two vice presidents.[16] Oaths of office were also administered for all the 659 new members of parliament, whether elected or appointed by the armed forces leadership: one-fourth of the seats of each house were indeed constitutionally reserved for military officers.[17]

Table 4.2: Seat Composition of the Lower House (Pyithu Hluttaw) and Upper House (Amyotha Hluttaw) After the 2012 By-Elections

	Pyithu Hluttaw	Amyotha Hluttaw
USDP	222	124
Tatmadaw	110	56
NLD	37	4
NUP	12	5
SNDP	18	4
RNDP	9	7
AMRDP	3	4
NDF	8	4
CNP	2	2
PNO	3	1
CPP	2	4
PSDP	2	3
KSDDP	0	1
WDP	2	1
UDPKS	1	1
TPNP	1	1
INDP	1	0
KPP	1	1
Independent	1	1
Vacant	5	0
Total	**440**	**224**

The new legislature has logically drawn strong condemnation in its early days, but critics were dampened by the organization of surprisingly free and fair by-elections on 1 April 2012. Indeed, a year after the transition was de facto initiated by newly elected president Thein Sein, both the NLD and the new ruling elites in Naypyitaw opted for a conciliatory approach. In August 2011, Aung San Suu Kyi was brought to the national capital for a closed-door meeting with Thein Sein.[18] The NLD, after vigorously boycotting the 2010 elections, was authorized by the UEC to reregister in December 2011 as a legal political party. It was therefore allowed, and this time willing, to contest the crucial by-elections.[19] The latter were organized to fill up the seats vacated by MPs who, for the most part, had become regional chief ministers or joined Thein Sein's ministerial cabinet in April 2011.[20] The NLD overwhelmingly won 43 out of the 45 seats to become the second civilian political force in parliament after the dominant USDP.[21] It has become particularly strong in Pyithu Hluttaw, where it can now count on some 11 percent of the (civilian) seats and on the charisma of Aung San Suu Kyi who was elected as the representative of a rural constituency, Kawhmu, some 29 miles (40 kilometers) south of Yangon (see Table 4.2).

From Potential to Influence: The Early Legislative Process (2011–2013)

According to the 2008 Constitution, all elected assemblies should convene at least once a year (Articles 79, 126, and 174). The regularity and schedule of the plenary sessions depend upon the will of their respective speakers—although Amyotha Hluttaw arranges its regular session according to the schedule fixed by Pyithu Hluttaw, as stipulated by Article 151. The president of the Union may however call for an emergency session, as for instance during the communal violence that in May 2013 broke out in the town of Meiktila in central Myanmar.[22] In 2011, the first two regular sessions of the national legislature drew heavy criticism.[23] Many elected MPs, especially those outside the dominant USDP, were skeptical about the possibility of nurturing free and fair debates within the parliament walls. Exiled media even dubbed the newly formed institution the "15-minutes assembly"; the brevity of the debates was indeed striking.[24] The second session was dominated by questions formulated by MPs to President Thein Sein's government to obtain clarifications about new policy orientations and, judging by the replies they received, clarity was not always forthcoming. With much uncertainty, MPs were looking for guidance from the most charismatic and prominent figures in both chambers. All were slowly adjusting to the new legislative structures and processes.[25]

Subsequently, session after session, a sense of bold optimism emerged.

Questions began to be raised on topics once deemed too sensitive. MPs started to openly challenge the government's proposals for new legislation, asking for clarifications or simply rebuffing drafts prepared by cabinet ministers. Some proved audacious enough to publicly expose cases of corruption, abuses of power, and restriction of rights by local authorities or army officials in their own constituency.[26] Surprisingly progressive laws—although most were first drafted by the executive branch—were soon adopted, such as the Peaceful Gathering and Demonstration Law (December 2011), the Environmental Conservation Law (March 2012), and the Social Security Law (June 2012). The national legislature therefore began to receive increasing praise, especially from local media and civil society.[27]

The assertion of Thura Shwe Mann as speaker of Pyithu Hluttaw has certainly played a significant role in strengthening the credibility of the parliament since the ex-*tatmadaw* chief of staff was selected for this key position in January 2011.[28] His charisma and sway over a substantial majority of MPs—especially, but not only, ex-military officers and retired civil servants who joined the USDP—have shaped him into a pivotal figure.[29] This is in stark contrast with Khin Aung Myint, speaker of Amyotha Hluttaw, who appears more diplomatic and cautious in his parliamentary agenda, and above all far less ambitious.[30] Shwe Mann, labeled a few years back by US diplomats as a "dictator in waiting," has proved a shrewd politician. As speaker, he holds considerable power.[31] He convenes sessions, forms new parliamentary committees, nominates their members, presides over debates, and in fact, decides and supervises most legislative activities in Pyithu Hluttaw. Without previous parliamentary experience, he has played by the rules of the constitution and managed to assert himself as a startling coalition builder, offering astute openings toward both non-USDP parliamentarians and military appointees.[32]

Certainly, his idea is to not leave the post-SPDC reformist agenda only to Thein Sein, who was—according to current rumors in Myanmar—chosen as president of the Union in 2011.[33] Indeed, under Shwe Mann's aegis, Pyithu Hluttaw has proved particularly instrumental in the formulation of an array of social and economic reforms. The Amyotha Hluttaw has also debated several bills since 2011, but with a less decisive impact. Its members have indeed increasingly deplored their de facto subordination to the Lower House. Despite the constitutionally sanctioned equality between the two houses (as in the United States between the Senate and the House of Representatives), when both chambers are convened altogether (as Pyidaungsu Hluttaw) for a decisive vote following a disagreement, the members of Pyithu Hluttaw are more often in position to impose their initial choice, being more numerous (440 MPs against 224).[34]

Then Aung San Suu Kyi arrived. Once the iconic opposition leader and her NLD entered both houses after the by-elections held on 1 April 2012, the parliament's prestige emerged ostensibly redeemed. After much internal debate, her participation in the political system occurred after the disbanding of the junta in 2011 and has subsequently altered the perceptions people had about the new legislature that she chose to eventually join.[35] The NLD recognized a new political space for discussion and policy influence in the formation of the parliament. According to parliamentarians that I interviewed, in just less than two years the new legislature—although far from perfect—has proved it was in no way similar to the erstwhile tightly controlled National Convention, hence the volte-face of the NLD in 2012.

But parliaments are always a reflection of what their members are making of it. The ways MPs frame the politics of lawmaking and oversight, and behave during parliamentary debates, are essential to maintaining a vibrant and valued legislative institution.[36] Different types of Burmese MPs have emerged over the past two years. A few charismatic Bama and ethnic leaders as well as former high-ranking army officers obviously stride the parliamentary scene—the *politicos* defined by US scholar Raymond Hopkins.[37] They guide debates, influence voting, and routinely propose or discuss draft bills. Their unexpected activism has surely contributed to the bold optimism the national legislature has instilled over the past two years. Among them are a handful of ambitious henchmen, notably in the USDP (such as Maung Toe, Thein Zaw, and Tin Maung Oo) and a few ethnic parties, who are already preparing for the next elections in 2015.

There are also Burmese intellectuals, social activists, or prominent figures such as Aung San Suu Kyi, Win Htein, and Aung Kyi Nyunt who have long been committed to the public—and now their constituencies—and who act as "mobilizers" in the parliament, a second category of MPs identified by Hopkins. Yet the substantial majority of the Union Parliament is mostly made of backbenchers: retired bureaucrats, public servants, and "followers" not really versed in legislative processes; they merely act as a supporting cast, or Raymond Hopkins's "silent partners." Many have indeed been picked up by the old regime to fill up the ranks of the USDP just for the duration of the first transitional legislature and are expected to retire in 2015. They therefore do not generally participate in debates and wait for voting orders from the most iconic of their party leaders, a common pattern of Burmese politics. Some are die-hard technocrats and are therefore willing to pursue their duty toward their country, just "as they were told."[38]

Parliamentary practices and the complex mechanisms of the legislative process have thus been rediscovered over the past two years, though with much approximation and shortcomings. Standing parliamentary committees have been formed in both houses on issues both speakers wanted to delve into: Health Promotion, Judicial and Legal Affairs, National Races Affairs, Economic and Trade Development, or the Committee on Farmers, Workers and Youth Affairs, for instance. Aung San Suu Kyi was asked in August

2012 to chair the newly formed Rule of Law, Peace, and Stability Committee. As only four standing committees are envisioned in each chamber by the constitution, all others have to be framed ad hoc, according to the needs of the moment or the will and whims of the speakers.[39] Committees regularly gather to discuss drafts, especially when the parliament is not in session. MPs ask questions, reformulate drafts, argue about articles; they organize shuttles between the parliament and the government or between the two chambers, before debating bills again and voting during regular sessions. A new parliamentary life and working style has thus resurfaced in Naypyitaw.

Ethnic MPs take their multidimensional role very seriously. The Rakhine (RNDP) and Shans (SNDP) are the most active (being among the more numerous ethnic MPs in the national parliament), as to a lesser extent the Chins and Mons. Kayin (Karen), Naga, Palaung, and Wa MPs are more discreet—but this might be explained rather by their small number of seats and the lack of capacity and expertise in parliamentary affairs. The outmost focus of all ethnic MPs is federalism and the deepening of the devolution of power, and therefore an in-depth revision of the center/periphery relation framed in the current constitution. Most do not seem to bother with other contentious issues such as the military presence in parliament or Article 59f, which prevents potential presidential nominees from having foreign family linkages, including, incidentally, Aung San Suu Kyi.[40]

What is more, MPs from Amyotha Hluttaw seem the most enthusiastic about their new functions. They found the Upper House a better place for discussion and debates, including with military MPs appointed there. Unlike in Pyithu Hluttaw, where the big shots are Shwe Mann, Htay Oo, and Aung San Suu Kyi, among others, MPs in Amyotha Hluttaw are far less prominent figures. Most are technicians, retired civil servants, teachers, and lawyers; very few ex-soldiers or SPDC former officials stand there. Debates are more vibrant, open, less confrontational, and also occur beyond the parliament's walls: the guesthouse compound reserved for non-USDP parliamentarians in Naypyitaw is indeed a fascinating place to wander. There are discussions every evening, trainings are held there, as well as regular seminars organized around foreign experts.[41]

Interestingly, party lines are often blurred when voting is at stake. Initial observations indicate different degrees of party cohesion. In Pyithu Hluttaw, the 37 delegates of the NLD under the aegis of Aung San Suu Kyi appear for instance far more cohesive than the 222 MPs from the USDP.[42] The latter is such a collection of divergent vested interests that it can hardly offer a unified front. Factions have already emerged around a few energetic leaders such as Htay Oo, Aung Thaung, and Aung Thein Lin, and of course Shwe Mann. Voting behavior seems also quite unconventional, as I gathered from my interviews. The usual pattern of "ruling party versus opposition parties" does not appear to be systematically followed. Most MPs agree that, in fact, there is no real opposition, or rather that the opposition is the parliament itself, as a whole institution attempting to check the executive policies and activities. Besides, military MPs have vetoed proposals put forward by the USDP or the presidential cabinet, while the NLD and the USDP have frequently approved draft bills together. Ethnic parties have often aligned themselves with the few members of the National Democratic Front.[43] Military appointees have even adopted the general amnesty law proposed by an NDF-turned-independent MP from Yangon and openly supported by Shwe Mann in August 2011.[44] As Speaker of the Upper House Khin Aung Myint put it, "all nineteen political parties in the Parliament are gathered in one circle, . . . and all are, in essence, opposition parties [all together fulfilling] the aspiration and desires of the people."[45]

The Parliament in Search of Institutional Autonomy

Far from being the mere rubber-stamp body many thought it would become after the disbanding of the SPDC in 2011, the new national legislature has proved able to exercise significant oversight over the newly formed executive power. One can argue the Burmese parliament has thus entered the second classical type of legislative institution put forward by the scholarship, that is, a policy-influencing body positioning itself as a key institution arbitrating and checking decisions made by the executive branch.[46] Yet it remains an organization that is still in search of a legitimate autonomy, including vis-à-vis the armed forces, still unable to critically impact lawmaking processes, while facing scores of continuing political, bureaucratic, financial, and technical challenges.

There has nonetheless been a sense of bold optimism among Burmese parliamentary circles, foreign observers, as well as the Burmese civil society and electorate, that the new national assemblies can become a strong check on the once all-powerful executive power in Naypyitaw. One of the most prolific areas of research on legislative politics, the check-and-balance function of the legislature, has drawn increased attention from the newly elected Burmese parliamentarians. All MPs that I interacted with, including Speaker of the Upper House Khin Aung Myint, proudly and firstly insisted on being devoted to the check-and-balance core objective. Recent scholarship has examined how national assemblies in a wide range of different political systems, and throughout Asia in particular, have exercised oversight procedures and subsequently fostered democratization processes and government accountability.[47] Myanmar appears to have entered this new phase in which a new type of policy practitioner—parliamentarians—compete with ministers, bureaucrats, and party officials to see their profile raised.

An array of techniques exists to perform oversight of the executive; most are routinely used in parliamentary democracies. These techniques include the introduction of bills to oversee government activities, asking questions to cabinet ministers, debating government policies in assembly, or raising motions. A few active Burmese MPs have thus steadily reappropriated those techniques, with the usual hesitations and shortcomings observed among people neither initially trained as parliamentarians nor acquainted with open and frank public debates. Interestingly, MPs from all the nineteen political parties present in the national parliament since 2012, including the dominant USDP, have tentatively participated in the scrutiny of the executive power.[48] Over time, question-and-answer sessions have become particularly vibrant.

Cabinet ministers are often staunchly criticized by parliamentarians, and the draft proposals their ministries submit to the parliamentary houses have increasingly been debated, and often sent back for revision. While the old guard of the USDP frequently attempted to adopt draft bills proposed by their colleagues in the government without much discussion, a few MPs have repeatedly challenged these drafts. Most were supported by the two speakers, Shwe Mann and Khin Aung Myint, both eager to strengthen the visibility and credibility of the two houses they preside over. Both indeed generally allowed interruptions for clarifications and further debate on specific issues, if they felt MPs could learn more and be sharper in their review.

Members of parliament are now commonly investigating illegal land grabbing by local authorities and corruption cases of government officials. They cut ministry budgets and rebuff presidential decisions, up to the point of asserting themselves as the new opposition. In March 2012, the parliament refused to approve a budget proposal for the Human Rights Commission submitted by the government on the grounds that the formation of the commission had not conformed to the constitution.[49] In August 2012, it started a procedure to impeach all nine members of the Constitutional Tribunal, nominated by Thein Sein a year and a half before.[50] MPs from both the USDP and the NLD had indeed objected to a decision of the tribunal that denied parliamentary committees the status of Union-level bodies. Grippingly, Aung San Suu Kyi along with Shwe Mann spearheaded the opposition to the tribunal and the executive power that had nominated its members.[51] All of this is a positive indication that Burmese MPs perceive their new oversight role as critical.

Securing the insulation of a legislative branch from the once all-powerful executive power contributes to the institutionalization of parliaments and legislative processes. Yet, this is not sufficient to guarantee political stability and legislative performance at the same time. As Samuel Huntington once noted, "recurring patterns of behavior" are needed for political institutions (including legislative bodies) "to acquire [the needed] stability and value."[52] Postauthoritarian parliaments ought therefore to sharpen their organizational cohesiveness and boundedness, secure and implement their own internal regulations, increase the complexity of the legal and bureaucratic mechanisms, and more globally improve the capacity and the coherence of the whole lawmaking process, as well as the capacity of their main elected and nonelected actors, as the example of postcommunist legislatures showed in Eastern Europe.[53] On the contrary, local people's congresses in China have long illustrated how the lack of institutionalized mechanisms impedes the authority of bodies supposed to legislate.[54] In post-SPDC Myanmar, it will prove difficult to move beyond the mere check-and-balance credo in coming years, to forge an effective lawmaking body. After all, the constitution put the emphasis on the president and the wider executive, and about 80 percent of the bills drafted by both national houses since 2011 were initiated by the presidential cabinet.[55]

Military Behavior in the National Parliament[56]

According to the 2008 Constitution, Burmese army officers are specifically commissioned to all legislatives bodies formed after national and local elections, much echoing the presence the Indonesian armed forces had secured in parliaments until their withdrawal in 2004.[57] This policy of seat reservations for the *tatmadaw* has been heavily criticized by activists and prominent political figures ever since. In post-junta transitory regimes, armed forces commonly seek a constitutionally sanctioned executive and legislative influence. Through a legal presence in lawmaking bodies, they indeed aim to keep an eye on the legislative process and safeguard their own corporate interests, in addition to other channels of influence they may have captured in the state bureaucracy and other policymaking structures. In post-SPDC Myanmar, military appointees represent a quarter of each house of the national parliament, or 110 seats in Pyithu Hluttaw (Article 109b of the constitution), and 56 seats in Amyotha Hluttaw (Article 141b). In the fourteen local assemblies, the number of military delegates is to be equal to one-third of the total number of elected representatives—which as a matter of fact mathematically corresponds to a rough fourth of the assemblies as well (Article 161d). The *tatmadaw* therefore enjoys a total of 222 seats in all the state and region legislatures.

All military appointees are nominated by the commander-in-chief, at his full discretion. It was one of the last public decisions made by Senior-General Than Shwe on 20 January 2011, two months before his retirement.[58] Out of the 388 first-time military appointees, there were in 2011 only three army colonels in Pyithu Hluttaw, two colonels in Amyotha Hluttaw, while one colonel was leading each of the fourteen military delegations in the local assemblies—except in the Kayin State where a brigadier-general was posted.[59] All other military appointees were of lower ranks: army majors, captains, and navy lieutenant commanders. They always attend in uniform and therefore impressively paint the new legislatures in khaki.[60]

For many observers, the sole reason for military officers to sit in parliament is to ensure that the *tatmadaw* gets a nonnegotiable veto on any potential amendment to the constitution.[61] As the safeguard of the constitution is one of the major tasks assigned to the armed forces (Article 20f), military delegates must ensure that all reform proposals put forward by civilians are formulated according to the basic principles already enshrined in the main body of the constitution. A vote of more than 75 percent of all the legislators is then required to pass any amendment. With its 25 percent seat reservation, the *tatmadaw* can therefore effectively act as a "veto force."

Yet, the role that the military appointees can play in the reemerging Burmese parliamentary politics may grow more complex in coming years. Official army publications are particularly revealing in the matter. The *tatmadaw* has long distrusted the civilian sphere. Its ideologues have frequently accused politicians and parliamentarians of having drawn the country from one crisis to another since the 1950s.[62] As a consequence, the *tatmadaw* likes to position itself as the sole cohesive, dedicated, and disciplined state institution able to safeguard the unity of the nation and bring about political stability, including in legislative assemblies where factional rivalries and petty political infighting traditionally abound. In a recent interview, Khin Aung Myint, a former two-star general and current speaker of the Upper House, highlighted the role of "arbitrator" that the armed forces shall play in parliament.[63] The very presence of army officers in all the legislative bodies of the country, he stressed, ensures that no single political party dominates the new parliamentary scene—whichever this party is (USDP and NLD therefore included). In line with the image the *tatmadaw* has always attempted to project of itself, soldiers seek to moderate the political and legislative debates, balance potential feuds between the executive and legislative branches as well as between the two houses of the national parliament (which have equal powers according to the constitution), and above all remain politically "neutral."[64]

The political significance of the army representatives in the national parliament has already evolved since 2011. True, interviews of civilian MPs have revealed that most of their military colleagues have kept a low profile ever since the first parliamentary session was convened. None of them had initially been nominated to key committees.[65] Yet session after session, their presence has been felt in stronger ways. Military appointees have progressively showed skills at discussing draft proposals or asking other MPs and ministers for clarifications in both houses.[66] From 2012, they also have gradually been including themselves in all parliamentary committees, with representatives boasting voting powers as well as others just acting as observers.[67] They increasingly ask questions when committees convene in closed doors and make the *tatmadaw* views known to other MPs. Discussions between civilian and military MPs within the premises of the national assemblies in Naypyitaw have thus appeared far more forthcoming than initially expected.[68]

What is more, higher-ranking officers have joined the legislative assemblies after 2012. Three weeks after the election of Aung San Suu Kyi to the Lower House in April 2012, the substitution of fifty-nine majors and captains with as many brigadier-generals and colonels underscored an evident policy change from the military top brass.[69] The new army chief, General Min Aung Hlaing, obviously intended to raise the profile of the *tatmadaw* in the legislative branch.[70] Unlike his predecessor, Than Shwe, Min Aung Hlaing seems to believe senior officers have to project an image of responsibility and dedication to the public by standing in lawmaking civilian bodies and interacting with politicians for the good of the nation and its long-awaited democratization.[71] Special trainings are now provided to military delegates in parliament, and political science teachings are compulsory for cadets at the Defence Services Academy (DSA) based in Pyin U-Lwin (Maymyo), near Mandalay.[72]

Odds are therefore that the *tatmadaw* may still linger in all legislative assemblies in coming years.[73] This has been much criticized, inside and outside the country.[74] While there can be an effective civilian oversight of the military in nondemocratic regimes, a democracy cannot be consolidated without a full-fledged civilian supremacy over interventionist armed forces, claims the extensive scholarship on civil-military relations. Interestingly, most parties involved seem very much aware of the problems generated by the presence of nonelected military MPs in parliaments. The major state-owned newspaper frequently publishes editorials underscoring the need for a gradual withdrawal of military personnel from all local and national parliaments, albeit only at a later stage. Pro-army commentators often bring forward the Indonesian example. It was only in the early 1990s that the mandated presence of the Indonesian armed forces in the national parliament in Jakarta began to be seriously debated. Military appointees were eventually withdrawn from all Indonesian legislatures in 2004.[75] Even President Thein Sein, himself a former three-star general, does not seem averse to the idea of a military disengagement from the legislative institutions, in time.[76] Many elected representatives of ethnic and regional parties also consider this issue as a nonurgent one and wish not to confront a still powerful institution during the first post-SPDC legislature.[77]

Limits to Parliamentary Change: Old Habits in New Clothes

Despite a bold optimism, there is a long way to go before the national and local *hluttaws* become stable and functioning institutions that can gain autonomy, legitimacy, and credibility, and move beyond their primary oversight functions to produce innovative laws by themselves. Halfway through the first post-junta legislature (2013), it appears that all legislative bodies suffer from several impediments, besides the continuing presence of non-elected military representatives in their own ranks. Odds are that most of these problems may be exacerbated after 2015 unless addressed early on. Among them are an appalling lack of capacity; institutional constraints imposed by the constitution; a lack of legitimacy, which may be corrected once free-and-fair elections are held in 2015; the gradual reemergence of old-fashioned Burmese factional, personified and clientelist politics; and a deepening gap between national and local assemblies in terms of influence and prerogatives.

Lack of Capacity

Parliamentary effectiveness is usually guaranteed when the legislative bodies and their members (elected MPs as well as the bureaucracy, which remains in office election after election) have enough expertise and adequate capacity to perform the various parliamentary roles they are assigned. Obviously, when first gathered in their respective assemblies in 2011, the great majority of the newly elected Burmese MPs lacked competence and knowledge about legislative processes and oversight mechanisms. Whether schoolteachers, soldiers, or singers, very few had received appropriate training to draft, review, or analyze laws. From the beginning, the parliaments themselves (as institutions) did not enjoy the relevant human, organizational, and financial resources to carry out all the expected tasks. In spite of the construction of flashy new buildings in Naypyitaw, in particular, expectations for the functioning of revived legislative bodies were too great.[78]

Yet, officials were quite aware of this set of daunting challenges.[79] Consequently, the bureaucracy assigned to the parliament has progressively been expanded. Libraries have been created and now welcome donations of books and parliamentary reports from foreign parliaments. MPs, including military appointees, have received regular training on a wide range of topics including framing a national budget, drafting bills, formulating questions, and understanding decentralization. Gradually they learned the ropes of legislative process.[80] Broader funding has emerged also, especially thanks to Burmese businessmen—including cronies once lambasted for being too close to the military junta—who have started to financially support political parties and local MPs.[81] Above all, the international community has proved very willing to provide all-out support, although a much disordered one. Everyone wants to join the capacity-building process and assist the Burmese parliament in its rise. Australia, Japan, France, India, the United States, Germany, and the UN are now regularly delivering skills training to parliamentary staff and MPs, or are in the process of establishing close cooperation in the matter.[82] However, there is a long road ahead. Most MPs do not enjoy personal offices in the parliament buildings and Internet Wi-Fi access is erratic. Very few can boast well-trained parliamentarian assistants or secretaries; they stand alone to perform their legislative duties, waiting for inputs and suggestions from their respective party headquarters. Interpreters are lacking too. All discussions and writings in the parliament, including in local ones, are conducted in the Burmese language. Some ethnic MPs have difficulties in following the debates and thus cannot play a stronger role.[83]

Institutional Constraints

The performance of the new legislature is also constrained by various provisions in the main body of the constitution. If not revised or dropped, many can pose a considerable challenge to the credibility and long-term value of the post-SPDC parliamentary system and thwart the country's prospects for stability and democratization.[84] Among them stands the loosely guaranteed separation of power between the executive and the legislative branches. This is particularly evident in state and region *hluttaws* where chief ministers are nominated by the executive center regardless of the results of local elections, while elected legislators are not required to resign if they are appointed as cabinet ministers.[85] This was one of the core issues to be addressed by the joint parliamentary committee for the revision of the constitution whose formation was announced by Shwe Mann in July 2013.

Another serious institutional constraint is the existence of bodies that cannot be checked by the legislatures: a fully independent military institution (Article 20), the opaque thirteen-member National Defence and Security Council (Article 201), as well as the military officers whose nomination in assemblies or executive cabinets are unbridled (Articles 74, 109, and 141). Military appointees are indeed removed from their parliamentary seats on a very regular basis, without any civilian oversight. Besides, as observed in many other postcolonial societies, the constitution grants extraordinary emergency powers to both the executive (the president) and the armed forces (commander-in-chief of the *tatmadaw*). According to Article 40 and the full Chapter XI (Articles 410 to 432) they both may easily bypass the parliament and summarily restrict basic civil rights, although those are otherwise recognized (Articles 354 and 420).

Furthermore, the immunity clause, which safeguards army officers and former junta officials, most of them now members of both the post-SPDC executive and the parliament, against any form of civilian prosecution (Article 445), and the unchecked amnesty prerogatives of the president (Article 204) are also controversial measures impeding a more autonomous functioning of the legislative branch. Lastly, to be fully independent, the legislative bodies need the support of a strong and well-functioning judiciary system, sadly a long way from realization in Myanmar. All these institutional constraints can therefore potentially slow down every recent progress made by the parliament, unless an adequate constitutional reform is provided. The formation in July 2013 of a 109-member legislative committee to review the constitution was a good sign. But interviews of MPs nominated in this committee underscored how divided the parliamentarians were about which articles to revise in priority, and how to proceed. Most were in fact quite pessimistic about any in-depth review of the main body of the constitution.[86]

From Legislation to Legitimating, or the Current Lack of Inclusiveness

The first post-SPDC legislature (2010–2015) suffers from an obvious lack of legitimacy.[87] The 2010 elections were contentious, and the subsequently controversial results have not been fully laundered by the surprisingly free and fair by-elections held in April 2012. Many groups inside and outside the country continue to condemn the parliament, peppered with ex-generals and junta officials, as illegitimate. This perspective is despite the liberal legislation the parliament has adopted since 2011 and the entry of the iconic Aung San Suu Kyi. As the literature on postmilitary Brazil has for instance underlined, when the old ruling political class is still around after a transition it usually does not appear much willing to openly challenge its own vested interests in the new institutions it has helped shape, despite the euphoria nurtured by the initial political change.[88] What happened after the 2010 elections in Myanmar is a "conservative transition"; the former well-established political and military elites have managed to stay relevant in the new system that has emerged after the disbanding of the SPDC in March 2011. The core objective for ex-junta officials and their pretransition associates was indeed to remain close to the new power circles after 2011, but under different patterns.

Ex-authoritarians have therefore joined the flow of the post-junta institutional bodies and remain significantly influential there. They brought along their own political culture, elite practices, and clientelist behaviors—something very difficult to fundamentally, and rapidly, change. Many of them quite logically show weaker commitment to democratizing practices. Fresh, inclusive, free-and-fair elections are therefore needed to bestow a higher degree of legitimacy to the new parliament. If the first post-SPDC legislature can be construed as transitional, the second ought to be transformative in order to bring the necessary legitimating to an institution much in search of it. This will prove difficult. A few political movements still are considering boycotting the forthcoming national and local elections in 2015—for instance the SNLD and its charismatic leader Hkun Htun Oo.[89] Yet, the second (from 2015) and third (from 2020, probably) post-SPDC legislatures may provide new opportunities for social mobility for young and ambitious Burmese, especially those who do not belong to army circles (see Chapter 3). If the parliament proves resilient after 2015, prestigious political careers may be shaped and reshaped there, beyond the once-dominant military sphere or the oligarchy that has long offered access to only pathways to wealth, but not to power (*awza* in Burmese).

Bringing Back Old-Fashioned Burmese Politics

Scholars who have studied the impact of newly crafted legislative bodies on democratization processes have often highlighted a peculiar trend. After initial moments of optimism, postauthoritarian parliaments are often drawn back into old-fashioned factional politics and patronage. After one acclaimed legislature or two, when newly elected parliamentarians see their role strengthened in front of the executive branch, the latter tends to rapidly recover, grow stronger and better organized, particularly in (semi) presidential systems. At the same time, one can observe the gradual reemergence of paternalistic politics in postauthoritarian legislative assemblies, where patrimonial political culture and corruption tend to resurface. This was observed for instance in postcommunist Ukraine and Russia in the 1990s,[90] in the Philippines' senate and congress under Joseph Estrada at the turn of the century,[91] and in Indonesia in the early 2000s.[92]

From the initial transition, parliaments soon transform themselves into arenas of contention between old and new rivals who have found new political spaces for influence and power grabbing. Personal rivalries, traditional elite struggles, and patrimonial political culture soon rematerialize there. Clientelism appears to play a significant role in the process of decline of political institutions, especially parliaments. The latter commonly lose credibility and value after transitional moments when MPs, who often were already members of the old regime, tend to vie for personal power rather than focus on their legislative duties. The assemblies serve as springboards for influence and prestige. This is the unruly and divisive civilian scene, which the armed forces commonly revile and which force the latter into recurrent political intervention, claims the literature on praetorianism.[93]

A clear propensity to personified power in Myanmar has long been underlined by a focused academia. The failure of institutionalization and the dominance of a few personalities have long been described as salient and essential features of the postcolonial Burmese political culture.[94] Burmese follow leaders, not institutions. In the current post-SPDC context, not much has changed, and it is hard to envision a striking evolution in coming years. Decisions are still made on the stately avenues of Naypyitaw, policies are formulated at the top (wherever this political center revolves), and competing visions of the future of the country are proposed by only a handful of charismatic leaders, whom scores of Burmese individuals are willing to follow. Elite and paternalistic top-down processes are commonplace. In the rising post-SPDC legislature, as it grows more open, these processes are gradually being shaped according to the charisma of only a few outspoken MPs.

Despite a tentative rejuvenation envisioned during its first national congress in March 2013, the NLD remains an electoral machine built around a sole iconic leader. On its side, the USDP appears increasingly structured around a few powerful factions led by energetic and ambitious leaders who want to move away from the traditional and once all-powerful military circles. Ethnic leaders have also increased their visibility through their parliamentary dynamism, after years, if not decades, of underground prodemocracy activism. Rivalries are increasingly fueled by personal ambitions. The prospects of new elections in 2015 may well exacerbate political struggles and infighting within the walls of the new assemblies, interviews revealed. Many commentators have highlighted the lingering competition between Shwe Mann and the executive power, President Thein Sein in particular.[95] But the rivalry between Aung San Suu Kyi and Shwe Mann himself, both having mounted bids for the next presidential nomination, is now emerging more vividly.[96] Elite and paternalistic legislative politics might find their ways to the Burmese parliament as they did in the 1950s, therefore visibly diminishing the credibility of the legislative bodies.

Local Parliaments in Slow Motion

Lastly, not much is happening beyond Naypyitaw. Among the fourteen region and state *hluttaws*, only four seem relatively active, regularly convene, and have so far adopted significant legislation on social, economic, and technical local matters: the region *hluttaws* of Yangon, Mandalay, Bago, and Ayeryarwaddy (Irrawaddy).[97] All four are in Bama-dominated regions. Other state *hluttaws* in ethnic areas also seem to be functioning, but with far less vibrancy, especially the Kayah and Kayin *hluttaws,* which fall under quasi full control of the USDP and the armed forces. The Rakhine *hluttaw*—the only local assembly where the USDP has not won a majority in 2010, yet has secured the key positions of speaker, deputy speaker, and chief minister—has held many question-and-answer sessions about the communal violence between Buddhist and Muslim communities in 2012 and 2013 as well as the local impact of the exploitation of the Shwe Gas offshore project and the construction of a Chinese oil and gas pipeline from the port city of

Kyaukphyu, along the Rakhine coast, to Yunnan. But for a critical legislation to be passed, leaders from the most prominent Rakhine party (RNDP) reckoned that the national parliament has to be involved.[98]

On their side, local MPs from the Kachin and Shan *hluttaws* deplored being marginalized and prevented during regular session from addressing the dramatic armed conflict that still lingers between the Burmese armed forces and the Kachin Independence Army in northern Myanmar.[99] On a positive side, the Chin *hluttaw* has pushed for the withdrawal of expensive permits long imposed by the central government on domestic and foreign visitors visiting the Chin State—and recently gained satisfaction.[100] Many ethnic party leaders have thus expressed hopes. If adequately revised, the constitution might offer new opportunities for ethnic nationalities through a greater devolution of power. Shan, Rakhine, Mon, and Chin MPs see more potential for state *hluttaws*, in particular if the next elections scheduled for 2015 are to be free and fair. As the resolution of the ethnic conundrum is one of the keys to long-term stability in the country, securing a broader autonomy and asserting the credibility of local parliaments will be critical after 2015.

But on the whole, most local parliaments are currently facing too many obstacles to be considered as autonomous assemblies. They often fall under the sole authority of the local government and chief minister, directly nominated by the president of the Union. At the local level, the separation of powers between the executive and legislative branches is far from being guaranteed. Many local ministers have still not resigned from their parliamentary seats, consequently combining executive powers and legislative functions. As for the national parliament, the convening of regular sessions in local assemblies much depends on their respective speaker, and subsequently his (there has been no "her" so far) own personality and the agenda of the dominant political party, the USDP.

Military appointees are also present in local parliaments, where they usually remain discreet. It seems, however, that on noncritical matters (as a matter of fact, local assemblies typically debate on noncritical issues, leaving key matters to be discussed in the national parliament) they can enjoy more room to maneuver. They are sometimes even encouraged to vote according to their own judgment—a surprising freedom of choice for young mid-ranking officers. This is again in line with the image of responsible army officers, much dedicated to the public, which the *tatmadaw* propaganda wants to project. An anecdote can sometimes be particularly revealing: in early 2013, a local MP from the Democratic Party (Myanmar) recalled how she offered flowers to the four army majors who voted in favor of her draft bill on licensing pedicabs at the Yangon regional *hluttaw*.[101] The four majors had stood in a surprising opposition with their other twenty-seven colleagues in uniform.

Looking Beyond the Transitional Moment: A Comparative View

In transitional periods, the significance of newly formed legislatures increases considerably. However, after a first transitional legislature, political forces commonly realign, executive bodies grow stronger under the aegis of charismatic leaders, and parliaments lacking sufficient capacity are often drawn back into paralyzing patrimonial politics. In many countries in postcolonial Africa for instance, parliaments have remained weak even several years—if not decades—after a transition to democracy; and this despite the return to multiparty politics, regular nationwide elections, and even the alternation of power between political foes, as underlined by Africa-watcher Joel Barkan.[102] In postmilitary Kenya, Benin, and Nigeria, for example, MPs have, legislature after legislature, proved far more concerned with rent-seeking and with whatever they can grant themselves while in office, than with their legislative performance and obligations.[103] But with the positive impact of an increasingly free African press and the development of an autonomous civil society, scandals and bad behaviors are routinely exposed and MPs frequently voted out after just one mandate. However, a high turnover of MPs from one election to the next erodes the capacity of elected legislative bodies.

Furthermore, as Cristina Chiva noted using various case studies in postsocialist Eastern Europe, the institutionalization of postauthoritarian parliaments is essential to consolidating their policy-influencing, and then policymaking, power.[104] For this institutionalization to emerge, three prerequisites appear critical. First, and Chiva agrees with Barkan, a core group of experienced and dedicated MPs regularly returning to legislative office (and each time with more professional tools at hand) is needed. If not, instability and amateurism prevail. In Myanmar, all MPs had to learn their job from scratch when they joined the national and local parliaments after the 2010 elections. What is more worrying is that a substantial number of them seem unwilling to compete for the 2015 elections, as interviews have indicated. Newcomers might again pepper the second post-SPDC legislature, and therefore impede progress, professionalization, and the overall institutionalization of the *hluttaws*.

Second, party discipline and cohesion should be observed by MPs when campaigning for elections, and then drafting laws, debating, and voting in parliaments.[105] When parliamentarians frequently change their party affiliation, jump from one political force to another or become independent and draft bills and vote in isolation, instability prevails in assemblies. Weakened and unruly political parties can neither implement their policy agendas nor offer a cohesive voice in parliament. In a Burmese society structured by patron/client relationships, loyalties have long been personal, and not based on party lines. Burmese politicians have long proved they were not always willing to enforce party discipline. Splinter groups abound; party dissidents are legion, in Bama and ethnic movements alike. Observers of the Asian contemporary political scene would also inevitably stress the regular fights breaking out in the parliament of postauthoritarian Taiwan, the common mass brawls involving South Korean MPs, and the salience of nepotism practices in the assemblies in the Philippines, Bangladesh, and Indonesia. Parliaments often lose public legitimacy when they revert to old-fashioned paternalistic struggles across party lines.

Third, parliamentary committees need to be developed and strengthened in assemblies as they form the core of every autonomous legislative process.[106] But many Burmese MPs I have interviewed have complained they were part of too many committees at the same time and were not prepared to cope with all the daily meetings and discussion groups. Moreover, many have been asked to move from one committee to another every twelve months, an incentive for mobility. As a consequence, they discover a new area of research and analysis on which they have to give their opinion and vote every year. Yet, this is where the Burmese *hluttaws* have the better chance to strengthen their capacity in the short term—in particular, thanks to the emerging international assistance on these matters. This is their best chance to move beyond policy-influencing into the realm of policy-making, and to develop autonomous lawmaking functions in tandem with the scrutiny and oversight activities in which policy-influencing bodies always first devote themselves.[107]

Concluding Remarks

Since the disbanding of the SPDC in 2011, parliamentary debates and legislative processes have been revived in a country long deprived of any valued lawmaking institutions and mechanisms. Lively and quite open public debates are surprisingly being allowed in the parliaments crafted after the controversial 2010 elections. Burmese journalists, barred from the first plenary session in January 2011, are now covering discussions and interviewing MPs on a daily basis. Burmese pupils are visiting the parliament buildings with their teachers, peasants are invited to meet their MPs, foreign observers can hang out in the impressively wide corridors of the national *hluttaws* and chat with military representatives in uniform, while party leaders can observe their own MPs voting and debating during regular sessions. *Hluttaw* discussions are now on television. The first two years of the first post-SPDC legislature have thus provided many reasons for optimism. Newly elected parliaments can sometimes act as obstructionist bodies stoutly defending the interests of the old ruling class (who often managed to pepper the new assemblies) and therefore resisting the transition. But more generally, in the first years of their existence, they foster pluralism and allow political participation to expand. It is only later that they tend to move back to old-fashioned factionalism and egotist power games, and fall again under a strengthened executive branch.

What would it take for Myanmar's new legislative bodies to keep the post-2011 momentum and avoid the usual trap and decline transitional parliaments commonly face? It is difficult to envision a country not looking back toward its first democratic experiment, before the 1962 coup. Lessons from this period have, however, been much rewritten since, if not forgotten. The 1950s are now too often caricatured as a vibrant and ideal experimentation in postcolonial democracy. The impact of factionalism, clientelism, and centrifugal personified politics is often downplayed, but not by the propaganda of the still-dominant *tatmadaw*. Adequate representation and a broader inclusiveness for the next by-elections in 2014 (subsequently cancelled) and the national elections in 2015 would be a start. The legislative branch also needs a core group of experienced parliamentarians and bureaucrats remaining in office, from one election to the next. Constitutional reforms should also be engaged to strengthen the mandate of the legislature: more devolution of power for the decentralized states and regions and more autonomy for the local *hluttaws*; consolidated mechanisms for the scrutiny of the central executive's activities, including the defense services and its appointed representatives; and more transparency in standing parliamentary committees as well as in ministries where bureaucrats prepare drafts alone. Better party cohesion and discipline are needed if the legislature aims for long-term stability, and therefore credibility. In all, raising the performance and strengthening the institutionalization of the legislative branch is essential in a postauthoritarian society where the executive branch traditionally tends to concentrate power and influence. Otherwise, the *hluttaws* may remain bogged down in a staunch opposition to the powerful presidential office without being in a position to move beyond power games and become a body that makes policy.

Notes

1. Arend Lijphart, *Patterns of Democracy: Government and Performance in Thirty-Six Countries,* 2nd edition (New Haven, CT: Yale University Press, 2012).

2. The terms *parliament, legislature,* and *legislative assembly* or *legislative body* will hereafter be used interchangeably. In Burmese language, though, the conventional term is *hluttaw,* or parliament.

3. See, for instance, in different contexts and across continents: Thomas F. Remington, ed., *Parliaments in Transition: The New Legislative Politics in the Former USSR and Eastern Europe* (Boulder, CO: Westview Press, 1994); Jürgen Rüland, C. Jurgenmeyer, M. H. Nelson, and P. Ziegenhain, *Parliaments and Political Change in Asia* (Singapore: ISEAS Publications, 2005); and Joel D. Barkan, *Legislative Power in Emerging African Democracies* (Boulder, CO: Lynne Rienner, 2009).

4. In particular: Michael L. Mezey, "The Functions of Legislatures in the Third World," *Legislative Studies Quarterly* 8, no. 4 (1983): 511–550; Philip Norton, ed.,

Legislatures (Oxford: Oxford University Press, 1990); and David M. Olson, *Democratic Legislative Institutions: A Comparative View* (Armonk, NY: M. E. Sharpe, 1994).

5. For instance, in the international media: Jason Szep, "In Myanmar, a 'Sham' Parliament Stirs to Life," Reuters, 26 January 2012; "Myanmar's Parliament: Power Grab," *The Economist*, 3 November 2012; Tom Kean, "Burma's Biggest Win: Its Legislature," *The Diplomat,* 1 February 2013.

6. Thailand and the Philippines offer a good example. During the 1990s and early 2000s, the rise of populist leaders led to a sudden decline of the Senate in Manila and the National Assembly in Bangkok; see Rüland et al., *Parliaments and Political Change in Asia*, 246–247.

7. Robert H. Taylor, "Elections in Burma/Myanmar: For Whom and Why?" in Robert H. Taylor, ed., *The Politics of Elections in Southeast Asia* (Washington, DC: Woodrow Wilson Center Press, 1996), 164–183.

8. Mary P. Callahan, "On Time Warps and Warped Time: Lessons from Burma's Democratic Era," in Robert Rotberg, ed., *Burma: Prospects for a Democratic Future* (Washington, DC: Brookings Institution Press, 1998), 49–67.

9. Mya Win, *Tatmadaw's Traditional Role in National Politics* (Yangon: News and Periodicals Enterprises, 1992), 20–21.

10. *The New Light of Myanmar*, March 27, 2012, 8.

11. Interview with author, Naypyitaw, August 2013.

12. International Crisis Group (ICG), "Myanmar's Post-Election Landscape," *Asia Briefing* No. 118 (2011); and Tin Maung Maung Than, "Myanmar's 2010 Elections: Continuity and Change" *Southeast Asian Affairs* (2011): 190–207.

13. Richard Horsey, "Outcome of the Myanmar Elections," Conflict Prevention and Peace Forum Briefing (New York: SSRC, 17 November 2010).

14. International Crisis Group, "Myanmar's Post-Election Landscape," *Asia Briefing* No. 118 (Brussels: ICG, 2011); and Neil A. Englehart, "Two Cheers for Burma's Rigged Elections," *Asian Survey* 52, no. 4 (2012): 666–686.

15. Adam P. Macdonald, "From Military Rule to Electoral Authoritarianism: The Reconfiguration of Power in Myanmar and Its Future," *Asian Affairs: An American Review* 40, no. 1 (2013): 20–36.

16. "First Parliament Sessions Conclude in Nay Pyi Taw," *Myanmar Times,* 28 March–3 April 2011.

17. Richard Horsey, "The Initial Functioning of Myanmar Legislatures," Conflict Prevention and Peace Forum Briefing (New York: SSRC, 17 May 2011). For a profile of all MPs from both chambers, see *The Parliaments of Myanmar* (Yangon: MCM BOOK Publishing, 2013).

18. Larry Jagan, "What Thein Sein Promised Suu Kyi," *Asia Times*, 30 September 2011.

19. David I. Steinberg, "The Significance of Burma/Myanmar's By-Elections," *Asia-Pacific Bulletin* No. 156 (Washington, DC: East-West Center, 2012).

20. Three seats were also available in the Kachin State, but elections were postponed in March 2012 due to the continuing conflict between the Burmese armed forces and the Kachin Independence Army (KIA).

21. "By-Elections in Myanmar: The Lady of All Landslides," *The Economist*, 7 April 2012.

22. "MPs Extend Meiktila Curfew Order for 60 Days," *Myanmar Times*, 27 May 2013.

23. The seventh regular session, which was convened in June 2013, ended two months later in August. The tenth and latest parliamentary session started in May

2014. The first session was convened from January to March 2011, the second from August to November 2011, the third from January to May 2012, the fourth from July to September 2012, the fifth from October to November 2012, and the sixth from January to March 2013.

24. Wai Moe, "Burma's 15-Minute Parliament," *Irrawaddy*, 22 February 2011; "Myanmar's Sham Legislature," *The Economist*, 27 January 2011.

25. "Signs of Progress, but Questions Remain," *Myanmar Times,* 18–24 July 2011.

26. "Burma Old Guard Adapts to New Life as Lawmakers," *Bangkok Post,* 18 January 2012, and Soe Than Lynn, "The *Hluttaws* Flexes Its Muscles," *Myanmar Times,* 21–27 May 2012.

27. Thomas Kean, "Myanmar's Parliament: From Scorn to Significance," in Nick Cheesman, Nicholas Farrelly, and Trevor Wilson, eds., *Debating Democratisation in Myanmar* (Singapore: ISEAS Publications, 2014), 43–74.

28. Soe Than Lynn, "Man of the House," *Myanmar Times*, 21–27 November 2011.

29. Interviews I recently conducted with ethnic and Muslim MPs have highlighted the respect and even admiration many MPs beyond the USDP have developed toward Shwe Mann.

30. Interview with author, Naypyitaw, 15 August 2013. Khin Aung Myint aims to retire in 2015, while Shwe Mann has already mounted a bid for the 2015 presidential nomination.

31. According to the constitution, during the five-year legislature the chairmanship of Pyidaungsu Hluttaw is alternatively shared by, first, the speaker of the Upper House, and then the speaker of the Lower House—for thirty months each. U Khin Aung Myint was therefore speaker of Pyidaungsu Hluttaw from January 2011 to July 2013, and Shwe Mann took over on 1 August 2013. Interestingly Shwe Mann has been active even before he became Pyidaungsu Hluttaw speaker.

32. Thomas Kean, "Burma's Biggest Win: Its Legislature," *The Diplomat,* 1 February 2013.

33. International Crisis Group, "Reform in Myanmar: One Year On," *Asia Briefing* No. 136 (Brussels: ICG, 2012).

34. As revealed by many discussions I had with Amyotha Hluttaw MPs from different political parties and backgrounds, Naypyitaw and Yangon (February, May, and August 2013).

35. Tin Maung Maung Than, "Myanmar's 2012 By-Elections: Return of NLD," *Southeast Asian Affairs* (2013): 204–219.

36. See the seminal work on parliamentary behaviors, Raymond F. Hopkins, "The Role of the M.P. in Tanzania," *American Political Science Review* 64, no. 3 (1970): 754–771.

37. Ibid., 759.

38. Interview with a seventy-two-year-old retired university professor, now representing the USDP at Pyithu Hluttaw, Naypyitaw, August 2013.

39. Bill Committee, Hluttaw Rights Committee, Public Accounts Committee and Government's Guarantees, Pledges and Undertaking Vetting Committee (art. 115a and 147a). A defense and security committee may be required to meet, according to the constitution, but this has to be decided upon by the commander-in-chief of the army.

40. Interviews with MPs from the CPP, SNDP, AMRDP, and RNDP in Naypyitaw, February and August 2013.

41. Personal observations, February and August 2013.

42. Interview with NLD MPs, Yangon, May 2013.

43. Interview with two NDF elected members from Pyithu Hluttaw and Amyotha Hluttaw, Naypyitaw (15 February 2013) and Yangon (28 May 2013).

44. *The New Light of Myanmar*, 26 August 2011, 9, and *The New Light of Myanmar*, 27 August 2011, 7.

45. Interview with author, Naypyitaw, 15 August 2013.

46. Mezey, "Functions of Legislatures," and Norton, *Legislatures*.

47. Rüland et al., *Parliaments and Political Change in Asia*; Taiabur Rahman, *Parliamentary Control and Government Accountability in South Asia: A Comparative Analysis of Bangladesh, India and Sri Lanka* (London: Routledge, 2008); and Patrick Ziegenhain, *The Indonesian Parliament and Democratization* (Singapore: ISEAS Publications, 2008).

48. USDP leaders too like to claim they are therefore not a "ruling party" and that there is no opposition in parliament: author's interview with two USDP MPs (Pyithu Hluttaw), Naypyitaw, August 2013.

49. Soe Than Lynn, "*Hluttaw* Refuses Human Rights Body Budget," *Myanmar Times,* 26 March–1 April 2012.

50. In February 2011, their nomination was approved by the parliament without discussion: "Parliament Impeaches Constitutional Tribunal Judges," AFP, 7 September 2012.

51. Dominic J. Nardi, "After Impeachment, a Balancing Act," *Myanmar Times*, 1 October 2012. All members resigned and were replaced six months later. Win Naung Toe, "Burma MPs Nominate Constitutional Court Chief," *Radio Free Asia*, 21 February 2013.

52. Samuel P. Huntington, "Political Development and Political Decay," *World Politics* 17, no. 3 (1965): 394.

53. Cristina Chiva, "The Institutionalisation of Post-communist Parliaments: Hungary and Romania in Comparative Perspective," *Parliamentary Affairs* 60, no. 2 (2007): 187–211.

54. Kevin J. O'Brien and Laura M. Luehrmann, "Institutionalizing Chinese Legislatures: Trade-Offs Between Autonomy and Capacity," *Legislative Studies Quarterly* 23, no. 1 (1998): 91–108.

55. Interview with a USDP member of Pyithu Hluttaw's Bill Committee, Naypyitaw, August 2013.

56. This section draws on Renaud Egreteau, "Patterns of Military Behavior in Myanmar's New Legislature," *Asia Pacific Bulletin* No. 233 (Washington, DC: East-West Center, 24 September 2013).

57. See, for instance, Marcus Mietzner, "The Political Marginalization of the Military in Indonesia," in Marcus Mietzner, ed., *The Political Resurgence of the Military in Southeast Asia*: *Conflict and Leadership* (London: Routledge, 2011), 126–147.

58. *The New Light of Myanmar*, 21 January 2011, 9.

59. He would thereafter be nominated chief minister of the Kayin State.

60. Especially as they seat all together in the same block of the assembly in Pyidaungsu Hluttaw, Pyithu Hluttaw, and Amyotha Hluttaw.

61. International Center for Transitional Justice, *Impunity Prolonged: Burma and Its 2008 Constitution* (New York: ICTJ, 2009).

62. Win, *Tatmadaw's Traditional Role in National Politics,* and Min Maung Maung, *The Tatmadaw and Its Leadership Role in National Politics* (Yangon: News and Periodicals Enterprises, 1993).

63. Interview with author, Naypyitaw, August 2013.

64. Army ideologues have long insisted on the need for the *tatmadaw* to remain "eternally" involved in crucial "national politics" but to avoid unruly and divisive "party politics" and partisan struggle, Win, *Tatmadaw's Traditional Role in National Politics,* 5–7.

65. *The New Light of Myanmar*, 4 March 2011, 8–10.

66. "Burma Old Guard Adapt to New Life as Lawmakers," *Bangkok Post,* 18 January 2012.

67. An observer role that civilian MPs cannot enjoy. Interviews with the respective secretaries of the Rights Committee and Public Accounts Committee (both are USDP MPs from Pyithu Hluttaw), Naypyitaw, 15 August 2013.

68. International Crisis Group, "Reform in Myanmar: One Year On," 10. Civilian MPs reside in a separate compound in Naypyitaw and therefore cannot freely mingle outside the parliament or during special events with military delegates, who go back to their barracks after each working day.

69. *The New Light of Myanmar*, 23 April 2012, 1, and Andrew R. C. Marshall, "Myanmar's Military Moves amid Suu Kyi No-Show," Reuters, 25 April 2012. See also the analysis in Min Zin, "Military Maneuvers (in Burma's Parliament)," *Foreign Policy*, 30 April 2012.

70. Mary P. Callahan, "The Opening in Burma: The Generals Loosen Their Grip," *Journal of Democracy* 23, no. 4 (2012): 128.

71. Aung Hla Tun, "Myanmar's General Lauds Army Democratic Role," Reuters, 27 March 2013.

72. Sandar Lwin, "In Hluttaws, More Green Shoots," *Myanmar Times,* 2–8 January 2012.

73. Renaud Egreteau, "Soldiers as Lawmakers? Assessing the Legislative Role of the Burmese Armed Forces in Post-junta Myanmar," in Renaud Egreteau and François Robinne, eds., *Burma/Myanmar: A Country in Transition* (Singapore: NUS Press, forthcoming 2015).

74. Ba Kaung, "Opposition MPs Take Aim at Army Influence," *Irrawaddy,* 15 February 2012, and ASEAN Inter-Parliamentary Myanmar Caucus, "Myanmar Military Remains an Obstacle to Progress," 13 December 2012.

75. Ziegenhain, *Indonesian Parliament and Democratization*; Marcus Mietzner, "Political Marginalization of the Military"; Jürgen Rüland and Maria-Gabriela Manea, "The Legislature and Military Reform in Indonesia," in Jürgen Rüland Maria-Gabriela Manea, and Hans Born, eds., *The Politics of Military Reform: Experiences from Indonesia and Nigeria* (Heidelberg: Springer-Verlag, 2013), 123–145.

76. Bill Keller, "A Conversation with President U Thein Sein of Myanmar," *New York Times,* 30 September 2012.

77. Interviews with MPs from the Kayin People's Party (KPP), the Shan Nationalities Democratic Party (SNDP), the Chin Progressive Party (CPP), and the Rakhine Nationalities Development Party (RNDP), Yangon and Naypyitaw, May and August 2013.

78. Robert H. Taylor, "Myanmar in 2012: *Mhyaw ta lin lin* or Great Expectations," *Southeast Asian Affairs* (2013): 189–203.

79. Interview with Khin Aung Myint, speaker of the Upper House, Naypyitaw, 15 August 2013.

80. Kean, "Myanmar's Parliament."

81. "Myanmar's Suu Kyi Defends 'Crony' Donations," AFP, 18 January 2013.

82. However, the international community walks on eggshells on this matter. Indeed, Article 121g of the 2008 constitution prevents any active or would-be

Burmese MP from receiving funding or any kind of material support from foreign organizations and/or governments.

83. As indicated by discussions that I had with a few ethnic MPs from different backgrounds, Naypyitaw and Yangon (February, May, and August 2013).

84. International Center for Transitional Justice, *Impunity Prolonged.*

85. Marte Nilsen and Stein Tønnesson, *Can Myanmar's 2008 Constitution Be Made to Satisfy Ethnic Aspirations?* Policy Brief No. 11 (Oslo: Peace Research Institute Oslo, 2012).

86. Discussions with author, Naypyitaw, August 2013.

87. On legitimacies in a Burmese postcolonial context, see David I. Steinberg, *Turmoil in Burma: Contested Legitimacies in Myanmar* (Norwalk: EastBridge, 2006).

88. Timothy J. Power, "Elites and Institutions in Conservative Transitions to Democracy: Ex-Authoritarians in the Brazilian National Congress," *Studies in Comparative International Development* 31, no. 3 (1996): 56–84; Scott W. Desposato, "Legislative Politics in Authoritarian Brazil," *Legislative Studies Quarterly* 26, no. 2 (2001): 287–317.

89. Interview with Hkun Htun Oo, Yangon, June 2013. The SNLD was dissolved in 2010 for failing to register with the Union Election Commission.

90. Thomas F. Remington, ed., *Parliaments in Transition: The New Legislative Politics in the Former USSR and Eastern Europe* (Boulder, CO: Westview Press, 1994); Timothy J. Colton, "The Constituency Nexus in the Russian and Other Post-Soviet Parliaments," in Jeffrey W. Hahn, ed., *Democratization in Russia: The Development of Legislative Institutions* (Armonk, NY: M. E. Sharpe, 1996), 49–82.

91. Rüland et al., *Parliaments and Political Change in Asia.*

92. Stephen Sherlock, *Struggling to Change: The Indonesian Parliament in an Era of Reformasi* (Canberra: Center for Democratic Institutions, 2003); and Ziegenhain, *Indonesian Parliament and Democratization.*

93. Renaud Egreteau, "The Continuing Political Salience of the Military in Post-junta Myanmar," in Nick Cheesman, Nicholas Farrelly, and Trevor Wilson, eds., *Debating Democratisation in Myanmar* (Singapore: ISEAS Publications, 2014): 259–284

94. Steinberg, *Turmoil in Burma.*

95. Kyaw Yin Hlaing, "Understanding Recent Political Changes in Myanmar," *Contemporary Southeast Asia* 34, no. 2 (2012): 205.

96. Gwen Robinson, "The Contenders," *Foreign Policy*, 12 July 2013.

97. Interviews with leaders from political parties having representatives in regional parliaments (Yangon and Naypyitaw, February–August 2013).

98. Interview with an Amyotha Hluttaw MP from the Rakhine Nationalities Development Party (RNDP), Naypyitaw, August 2013.

99. Interview with a Pyithu Hluttaw MP from the Shan Nationalities Democratic Party (SNDP), Naypyitaw, August 2013.

100. Interview with an Amyotha Hluttaw MP from the Chin Progressive Party (CPP), Naypyitaw, August 2013.

101. Interview, Yangon, May 2013.

102. Joel D. Barkan, "African Legislatures and the Third Waves of Democratization," in Joel D. Barkan, ed., *Legislative Power in Emerging African Democracies* (Boulder CO: Lynne Rienner, 2009), 2.

103. Ibid., 18.

104. Chiva, "The Institutionalisation of Post-communist Parliaments," 201–202.

105. Ibid., 203–204.

106. Ibid., 205–206.

107. M. Steven Fish, "Stronger Legislatures, Stronger Democracies," *Journal of Democracy* 17, no. 1 (2006): 5–20; David Arter, "Introduction: Comparing the Legislative Performance of Legislatures," *The Journal of Legislative Studies* 12, no. 3/4 (2006): 245–257.

5

Conceptions of Justice and the Rule of Law

Elliott Prasse-Freeman

After half a century of military rule, Burma's legal system exists as an exploitative institution designed to maintain order, police politics, and extract resources from those swept up in it.[1] As a result, it is a sphere that Burmese subjects take pains to avoid. This does not mean, however, that subjects do not make justice claims or seek redress, but rather that (1) these occur in "informal" spheres and (2) the modes for redress and conceptions of justice may not be coincident with Western liberal conceptions that are increasingly taken as universal.[2] Little scholarly work has been done on these respective domains.[3] Thus, drawing on introductory fieldwork, this chapter attempts to sketch some of the contours of the Burmese justice universe and some of the methods by which lived conceptions of justice in Burma may become perceptible. Specifically, this means attending to the idioms through which claims are made, the political values that are transmitted, and the kinds of potentially justiciable claims that are elided. Much of this chapter must be speculative at this stage and is designed to advance a number of hypotheses, some of which may be rejected or advanced by others' future research. Speculations will focus on two spheres, the first more architectural (defining how the system looks) and the second more conceptual (discussing its concepts and their consequences). Specifically this includes:

- How do certain extra-legal social institutions prevent certain individuals from accessing formal justice?
- How do these institutions construct certain individuals as subjects without legitimate or actionable claims to justice—in other words, which subjects have the opportunity to have "rights" and which do not?
- How are moral economies constructed in which certain events—forced labor, for instance—are not seen as per se unjust?

In order to convey some of the realities of this universe and the values that animate it, I will convey findings from introductory fieldwork with lawyers and legal aid professionals working in Yangon. These professionals daily play an intermediary role—as they mediate between the global cosmopolitan regime of international legal norms on one hand, and their clients and the Burmese courts on the other. Given this, they stand as particularly capable of reflecting on and providing insight into the disjunctures in thought that exist between the two spheres. Such thoughts might be missed by others too deeply enmeshed in a particular life context.

This Burmese informal justice universe will be mapped with an eye to those Western liberal conceptions of justice indexed above, ones that are only relevant because an explosion of discourse surrounding the so-called rule of law (RoL) has emerged in discussions about Burma's potential political transition. For these RoL endorsers (including Aung San Suu Kyi and a cadre of international rights activists), RoL is being utilized both as a substitute for substantive politics and a way to avoid engaging the informal system. Indeed, "bringing the rule of law to Burma" seems to mean simply transplanting the Western liberal tradition: formal checks and balances through judicial review, institutions that ensure (ill-defined material articulations of) human rights, and so on.[4] While transplanting formal mechanisms prima facie provides the opportunity to infuse those procedural institutions with values and politics that will speak to issues, such as resource allocation and conflicting normative values, that matter to normal people, the proponents do not seem to entertain this opportunity. Instead they seem to de facto endorse the *substantive* values that attend the Anglo-American rule of law ideology and that are tied up in the RoL procedural forms. Not only is this troubling given the way such a rule of law privileges, for instance, narrow property rights over collective values (the institution of which may entrench inequality), but it may also build a system that remains irrelevant for many Burmese.[5] Indeed, a system that formalizes these foreign conceptions of procedural and substantive justice may not "pull in" individuals currently avoiding the formal system. Moreover, it may alienate those who see in it the hypocrisy or blindness of a formal success but a material failure—an inability or unwillingness to deliver on the promise of justice.[6]

This chapter will conclude by reflecting on the collective desire for the rule of law,[7] and will present it as both a demand for an end to impunity (and hence an index for a more complete—but as yet unrealized—public discussion of political justice), but also as an impulse to safety during a time of deep social uncertainty.

Burma's Informal Justice System

Toward Research on Lived Conceptions of Justice in Burma

For most of the military period, Burma's legal system remained largely opaque—to external observers and those caught within it alike—given the insularity of the regime and the legal system's arbitrariness. That said, a number of Burma scholars have been chipping away at that opacity, using court texts and interviews with lawyers to map the physics of the system. This work fills in a sizeable blind spot in Burma studies, illustrating what "law" actually looked and felt like under the military regime's despotic political rule. Among many critical points, one of the most essential is that this work allows us to see that there was a legal system at all, one that heard cases, dispensed judicial decisions, allocated punishments, accepted appeals, and so on. To a certain extent, it is hard to imagine otherwise—the mechanistic nature of bureaucracy, however attenuated by extrasystemic political demands, meant that policemen continued to arrest, judges continued to adjudicate, lawyers continued to defend the accused. And yet, the general avoidance of the legal realm by mainstream discourse and most scholarship may have sent the symbolic message that there was nothing here worth exploring: only despotism and abuse obtained.[8]

While the arbitrary exercise of unrestrained power certainly predominated in Burma's legal system, recent research illustrates the particular ways the respective functions (police, defense/prosecution, adjudication) have become distorted from the ideal-typical image of how a system of "law and order" is supposed to work—wherein laws describe rules to be followed and punishments for their violation—in general or in Burma. These works show how politically generated conviction quotas imposed from above compelled judges and lawyers to conspire to search for and create criminals, how many forms of politics (speech, assembly) themselves were criminalized, and how elites used the courts for petty vendettas. Various documents explored by these scholars (cases, interviews, internal legal commentaries authored by apex courts) present not only the rationalizations and justifications for decisions, but provide insight into the undergirding logics that animated both them and the political regime behind them. For instance, Myint Zan shows how the bar has been continually deprofessionalized as the importance of actual legal knowledge was obviated within the context of an increasingly politicized system.[9] Andrew Selth's research on Burma's police force outlines the connection of that institution with the military, and hence its central role as a frontline coercive apparatus.[10] Nick Cheesman's thorough research, achieved through the translation and analysis of hundreds of court logs, demonstrates how market and political logics have conflated within the formal legal system to create a dangerous zone that average Burmese attempt to avoid.[11] To wit, Cheesman's pathbreaking work shows how the executive branch has imposed political imperatives on the legal system, dictating that courts maintain the *perception* of order. This has created incentives for judges and lawyers to conspire against defendants, both by punishing political activists with extreme prejudice and by generally keeping conviction rates high to signal a commitment to "law and order." However, because these imperatives are political, and so in nonpolitically adversarial cases only the aggregate percentage of convictions have really mattered, actors are able to insinuate market logics into the system, making conviction and sentencing functions of the availability of extractable resources (through bribes and favors).

Taking these accounts as a whole, Burmese formal justice looks increasingly nightmarish. But the question then becomes the following: What is at stake in all this? Isn't this merely part of the old system that is being swept away by political transition? Perhaps not. First, as protesters continually arrested can attest, it is unclear that things have qualitatively changed.[12] More importantly for this chapter, even if the legal system were to be fully "reformed" (in line, let us say, with international standards of political liberalism), the vestiges and legacies of this system may be long-lasting. I say *may* be long-lasting because there is simply little known about the effects of this legal system (and the broader political system out of which it emerged) on the polity's collective (if diffuse) conceptions of justice.

Two sets of questions emerge from this line of inquiry. Logistically, if the law was something to avoid, how present was it in the daily lives of Burmese during the military period? Given the generally blunt and even obtuse nature of control under the military state, was the law avoidable?[13] Rather than a predator descending on subjects to police every move, was it more of a metaphorical Venus fly trap, a reactive and receptive institution that subjects could fly around if they could deploy effective strategies to that end?[14] Determining the strategies for circumventing the courts encourages seeing the "formal" and "informal" legal domains as both consubstantial but also distinct; tracing the "politics of passage" that leads to someone ending up in the courts can tell us a great deal about the way justice, conflict resolution, and moral economies function on the ground.

This is an argument for understanding "access to justice" in a more nuanced way, in which actually accessing justice can mean avoiding *in*justice, by way of avoiding the courts. Barriers to the formal justice sphere hence can be recoded as protections against it; actors can have access to barriers that allow them to be rerouted away from police and courts. The question is whether outside of the courts they are able to access material justice.

Such an inquiry can also inform existing and forthcoming external interventions. The current assumption in the outpouring of funding and focus for rule of law projects and programs is that the RoL will simply and smoothly "fix" the sclerotic and rapacious legal sector, pulling in justice consumers, hence rationalizing Burma's legal system.[15] But this assumes an image of Burma's current "universe of justiciable events"—interactions in which one or more parties may have a reason to seek some sort of redress facilitated at least in part by a third party—that is generally coincident with the cases that are heard in Burma's respective courts (the formal universe). To the extent that there is a gap between the formal and informal domains, these reform projects believe it exists because citizens are not demanding justice from formal mechanisms that are in place. Further, they believe that people are not making such demands because they do not find courts efficient, just, accessible, legible, and so on, but rather exploitative, capricious, usurious, and to be avoided.

Such assumptions may obscure the size and composition of this entire universe of justiciable events. Reform projects seem to often underappreciate the fact that if the formal system is transformed into something that people might objectively want to utilize, other distortions still can exist to prevent people from attaining something that they might call justice, or at the very least, improved life outcomes and opportunities. In other words, the cases heard by Burmese courts may continue to only occupy a minute and sociologically relatively insignificant percentage of the entire universe of justiciable events.

Building on this is the second line of inquiry, the conceptual one. If courts were or are avoidable, what concepts of positive justice were fashioned and implemented in the informal sphere during the military period? Were the logics of the courts merely duplicated in the informal settings?[16] Or were alternative forms of justice articulated and performed in opposition to, or independent of, the "unjust justice" of the formal sector? The following subsections will present early research (conducted by the author and other legal aid nongovernmental organizations [NGOs] working in Burma) that helps map these issues in turn.[17]

"Access to Justice" Barriers

One of the most striking findings encountered while talking with defense lawyers at two different legal aid NGOs during 2013 fieldwork was how rarely the lawyers won cases for their clients. I had expected a low percentage, but the actual reported numbers were shocking: some defense lawyers had never won cases; others had only a handful of acquittals. Said one lawyer, "Our only hope in representing the cases is to reduce the sentence because we know the [client] will always be convicted." Another lawyer, laughing ruefully, described herself as a broker and a purveyor of "bribery advice." Continuing, she described the different tactics involved and issues that must be considered:

> The point of the lawyer is to serve as a broker between the defendant and the judge. The defendant doesn't know who to go to. If the party is the state it is very easy to give bribes to the judge and the prosecutor. But for example in a rape case where there is a victim, it is difficult for the defendant to pay . . . [as] the victims will not negotiate. . . . If the defendant has a large criminal record the judge will not dare to take a bribe to reduce. Political cases are off limits. Sometimes if there is publicity in the media, they cannot acquit.[18]

Rather than knowing anything about the substantive law—they told me that such details were largely irrelevant—the lawyers become masters in everything *around* it, advising on a host of tactics. To their clients, they suggest which character witnesses are the most sympathetic to a judge, and coach the accused on how to make their final appeals. Defense lawyers talk directly with the prosecutor and make pleas for leniency. Because they know the levers of power and because they can access key figures, they often deliver the bribes to the various parties involved. In situations in which the reduction of a sentence appears impossible (because perhaps the complainant appears richer than the defendant), lawyers will often suggest that defendants keep what money they have so they can later bribe prison guards for better treatment.

Setting aside for now the potential lines of inquiry into how this behavior influences clients' conceptions of real, accessible justice, a number of immediate logistical questions are suggested by the operations in the courts. For instance, while market logics within the legal process become apparent, this is certainly not a pure market where justice simply goes to the highest bidder. Rather, cases almost always end in conviction. Even if the accused effectively negotiates a release, they are often convicted and sentenced to time served, something that Cheesman documents extensively and reports as termed "sentence-release" by Burmese lawyers.[19] Mass conviction can be partially explained by the combination of political-economic incentives and political pressures shaping a judge's decisionmaking opportunities, but there seemed something beyond these variables. Indeed, the lawyers described how judges "always assume defendants are guilty." I became interested in what shaped that perception. Further questioning about how a person made it into the court—what processes she has to navigate to avoid it—made me speculate on the judge's propensity to convict. In looking closely at how a conflict becomes a case, it appears that much work is done to siphon off the innocent, or rather the unconvictable, as defendants flow into courts. Indeed, there appear to be quasi-formal gatekeepers that act as sieves, preventing or facilitating access to courts. Whether the judge realizes it or not, it appears that significant "legal" work has been conducted prior to adjudication. By the time the body reaches the court, the accused has already been deemed eminently condemnable.

What does this politics of passage look like? A useful place to start is with the figure of the ward administrator, long an implicit part of the state apparatus and recently made an elected position, with regulations enumerated by the 2012 Ward Administrators Act. The ward administrator (WA) occupies a quasi-formal legal position in Burma, being generally tasked to oversee informal governance systems (in the figures of the 100-household head and the 10-household head) at the village and village tract levels, respectively. An informal survey conducted by a Yangon-based legal aid organization has determined that the WA was regularly reported as the most important government figure in the lives of those surveyed.[20] This importance varies with location (in urban areas WAs appear to be less important), but it warrants mentioning that the WA's importance appears to cut both ways. Because the WA *purchases* his position (despite the formal election, legal aid professionals relay that the winner is the one who pays approximately US$2,000 to the township administrator for the opportunity to rule), the WA exists to extract bribes and charge for services so as to make a return on his investment. In this regard, the WA stands as a liminal figure—occasionally an extracting force, occasionally a potential (if inadequate) resource for avoiding the clutches of the courts and police.[21]

As the position pertains to formal justice, the WA brings this liminality to bear by preventing interactions between citizens and formal juridical and police institutions.[22] In so doing, the WA is a quasi-legal figure acting both with and against the formal law—"against" in the sense that the WA prevents the abuse that the law does to the accused, and "with" the law in the sense that his role stabilizes the whole system.

In this role, it is noteworthy that respondents reported that WAs "never use the law to solve the problem. They solve the problem socially, and they make some settlement. If one of the parties is not satisfied, then you have to go through the courts."[23] According to others, WAs themselves highlight the fact that they know little of the law itself. Rather, they see their task as that of solving conflict and reducing collective social embarrassment. The Burmese expression "Don't make one shame into two shames" (*tiq sheq ga nay niq sheq ma pyit say neh*) encapsulates this ethic and was mentioned by the legal aid project workers as a sentiment they found in these interactions.

All this said, there are significant limits to the scale and scope of the potential interventions of WAs. According to lawyers and legal aid professionals, the ability of the WA to prevent an incident from becoming a case depends on the type of infraction. A paralegal at a different legal-aid group illustrated this point as follows: "For a drug case you have no chance. The WA and the police pass the [arrested] IDU through to the courts. But if a CSW [commercial sex worker] is arrested, they will first be sent to the [WA], and at that point [our] paralegal can intervene to help prevent it from going into the courts."[24]

This limitation on the WA suggests that only certain kinds of "criminals" make it through to the courts: those who commit a certain kind of offense or those who are too poor (or without immediately mobilizable networks necessary) to pay the appropriate bribe. It also suggests that there is a significant world of conflict resolution and avoidance that is occurring through and below the WA. Research can further explore the idioms or concepts used in this domain, perhaps using this as the base, both in terms of values and institutions, for legal reform. The following subsections elaborate on some methods for teasing out those values and how they relate to those who might have reason to claim redress.

Conceptions of Legitimate Claimants to Justice and Different Conceptions of Justice Itself

"Where do people go when there is a dispute?" is a common question posed by legal reform projects seeking to understand how people seek justice.[25] However, it also works to limit the universe of justiciable claims to that of situations in which there is a dispute. Yet often in a situation that might be deemed justiciable—where one party (an individual or system) may be seen as exploiting another—the exploited party does not muster opposition or a claim to redress. The "violated actor" (in quotes because the conception of victim is itself what is at stake) may perceive such treatment as unjust or undesirable, but may assess that there are no manifest channels for raising the issue to the level of dispute. Or channels may exist, but the actor for whatever reason disqualifies himself as capable of standing as a legitimate disputant. Finally, it is possible the abused may not believe that an injustice has occurred—that the moral system of the particular community deems these interactions as acceptable rather than as violations.

One of the most relevant idioms here is that of *rights,* and the way that many Burmese experience power has meant that rights are, as a political concept, always contingent and contested rather than durable and guaranteed.[26] This is in contrast to the Western liberal concept that holds that rights mediate the contractual relationship between citizen and state such that when subjects "choose" to relinquish "some" liberty in exchange for security, the state cannot wholly violate that liberty.[27] Many Burmese subjects do not have such a conception of a transcendent right, a right that could exist outside of the context of realizing it. Rather, early fieldwork suggests that in Burma the respective Western concepts of *rights* and *opportunities* blur together, and tend to index an appeal to power rather than a demand for a restoration of what one already "has."

What would it mean for *right* to be inseparable from *opportunity*? It might say something about the realities of power and the modes for "legitimating" (if that can even be thought of as the correct word) that power. While there is not space here to explore the *longue durée* of power in

Burma, scholars have long described precolonial Burmese kings as presenting their power as "self-justifying."[28] Burmese legal scholar Myint Zan sketches the history of how power articulated itself in Burma's legal system, showing how Burmese kings traditionally governed subjects based on divine authority, creating a system of natural law borrowing from Buddhist cosmology and traditional authority rather than on the rights of the governed.[29] Such a system appears similar to forms of power tracked by Benedict Anderson and Clifford Geertz in Java and Bali, respectively, wherein power was substantiated in its performance, and hence legitimated itself through its very existence.[30]

Where Myint Zan, Geertz, and Anderson look at this power apparatus from the inside, James Scott looks at it from the outside, reading court documents not as texts that describe reality, but rather as descriptions of what kings *would have liked* to have been true.[31] Buttressing this revisionist view, Burmese jurist E Maung points to a number of historical cases in which kings themselves deferred to rules that existed outside of their own desires, caprices, and whims. Many of these rules were inscribed in *dhammathat*, something that Burmese legal scholar Andrew Huxley describes as falling somewhere between law report and legislation,[32] and which he endorses as evidence that the king was not wholly sovereign but constrained by law. Huxley highlights how "a dhammasat [sic[33]] written just after King Badon (1781–1819) came to the throne … was written specifically to instruct the new king in the rights and duties of kingship."[34] However, just as a king's chronicles overstate the power of the king, dhammathats can equally understate it. Moreover, just because kings delegated *some* of their tasks does not mean that their sovereignty was in any way constrained; abdication could have been done for convenience, a version of control that has long characterized feudal regimes.[35] As Maung Maung Gyi argues, "From the historical accounts it will be seen that precept and practices never do tally and it would be folly to interpret the behavior of the king from the ten moral precepts that he was bound morally to follow."[36] Of course, Maung Maung Gyi substantiates his claims by invoking suspect sources: the historical record, written after all by elites; he notes that a Burmese word for history (*yazawin*) means "chronicle of kings." But the ultimate point is that power presented itself as limitless and without need of sanction by logics external to it, a fact that became sociologically real. For instance, Matthew Walton, scholar of politics and Buddhism in Burma, points out how fear of the king, and the figure's metonymic association with uncontainable blights such as disease, flood, and fire, is reperformed every day in Burma: "The Lawkaniti, a Burmese collection of folk wisdom lists kings as one of the 'five enemies,' along with water, fire, thieves and disease. Many Burmese Buddhists still pray for protection from these 'enemies' as part of their daily practice."[37]

In this context, it is not surprising to see to the legal domain drained of autonomous power. In a different article, Myint Zan highlights a brief moment during the constitutional period (1947–1962) where judicial independence[38] may have internalized in elites the idea of "rights," but this conceptualization did not diffuse into general society.[39] Since the military government's installation in 1962 through the present day when some reforms may be occurring, Myint Zan shows how substantive legal ideas have been effectively removed from legal education. This produces lawyers with little sense of "the law" as a domain of professional or expert knowledge, let alone as a sphere of rule-making power that exists autonomously (i.e., separated from the state's ability to arrogate the ability to act in the exception).[40] Across this history, the common denominator is the absence of "rights."

This does not mean laws did not exist in Burma. Laws were simply instantiated and effected by fields of governance (from dynastic kings to various iterations of military regimes) in ways that crafted a normative political relationship between governor and governed that deviated from that of the Western liberal tradition's normative imaginary about itself. The law delineated actions that were forbidden without creating any reciprocal "rights" allowing subjects to make claims against the state.[41] David Steinberg has argued that "law is not a protection of rights but rather an arbitrary set of regulations promulgated to support the state establishment and to prevent dissidence."[42] Even when the state's law articulated privileges or opportunities that citizens may have enjoyed, these were not absolutes designated by any compact (either de jure or de facto), and hence could be violated at any time. Everyone was aware of this and as a result a "right" literally only existed as an opportunity, with all the contingency that that latter word implies. The "contract" written between the governed and the state was always contextual and contested. It was subject to one's ability to marshal other resources (symbolic, material, social), subject to luck or contingency, and subject to the conflation of variables (state agent whim or risk profile, the extant political conditions in the country, etc.) that may remain opaque to those on both sides of the interaction. What mediates the relationship is not "rights," argues Burmese scholar Ko Ko Thett, "it is Burmese cultural institutions (a set of norms and practices) that ease the encounters."[43] When decisions were made, because they did not require explanation or justification, any information flowing through the feedback loop was blurred, made translucent rather than transparent. As a Burmese informant puts it, "We have to go back and see [that] the basic word [for right is] *khwint*, which is ideally subject to permission/approval/consent of the other parties or circumstances."[44]

Observe how this plays out in daily sociopolitical practice. For instance, a member of one of the wealthiest real estate and business families in Burma told a group of visitors learning about Burma's political economy that there are rights and that: "The rule of law is actually fine."[45] He went on to argue that "there has never been a legal judgment against us that is unjust." These actors capitalize on their position of social privilege while thinking that such leveraging is a simple exercising of rights, a fact that comes through when contrasted with experiences of those *without* billions of kyat at their disposal. For instance, an NGO worker holding a workshop on rights related to me a story about such relative power relations. When she asked the participating non–upper class Burmese whether they, hypothetically, would still own their house if their vindictive in-laws kicked them out of it, most responded that they would still have a "right" to it. However, when asked about the status of ownership if the government kicked them out, the answer was quite different. In this case many did not use *akwint-a-yeh* (the common word for "right") to describe their claims. It of course did not cease to be immoral or unjust that they were expropriated, and Burmese are in the process of employing a number of creative protest and negotiation strategies to reattain land and property currently being lost to the military and its cronies.[46] It just ceased to be a right.

And yet, negotiation strategies such as these can be mischaracterized as rights claims by external observers, something that may signify the difference in political ontology between liberal political logics and the different understanding deployed by many Burmese. For instance, researcher Jill Davison has outlined many of these negotiations, but labeled them "rights" claims, perhaps because there is a reflexive tendency on the part of Western political analysts to assume any protest is a "rights" claim.[47] Indeed, when Davison writes that "villagers attempt to prevent displacement or secure some form of tangible redress through informal rights-claiming strategies like negotiation, non-compliance, complaint and open protest," what is obvious is the incongruence between tactics and her description of them. None of those tactics is actually a *rights* claim, which we could rather imagine as the ability to say "no" to land confiscation or at the very least a "right" to (1) get specific compensation, (2) appeal for independent arbitration, or (3) enact some mechanism that seems to transcend, or exist independently of, the specific interaction.[48] Nick Cheesman makes a similar move in his thesis. When he records speech that challenges the regime, he paints the claims in rights terminology, even though there are no explicit mentions of rights, and very little can be found of implicit rights either. Indeed, the norms that actors assert are of course potentially multiplicitous.[49] When scholars only recognize "rights" claims as existing in that contesting space, they foreclose on other meanings. It is certainly possible to think of a host of types of claims that can be marshaled in that adversarial position and that do not require or rely on rights. For example, the responsibility of the state and the good conduct of divine kings are conceptions of justice that can be mobilized without rights.

Ultimately, those under or fleeing the state for decades have a different experience with power, and hence different understandings of words that describe it. The subaltern cannot afford to think of these two words—rights and opportunities—as being always different. Many Burmese people make claims and aspirations—as all people often will—but they may have no illusions about any grounding in a transcendent regime that somehow exists despite the fact that it manifestly does not deliver what it claims to guarantee.[50]

Conversations with lawyers help illustrate the way this concept functions. For instance, lawyers rarely used rights language when appealing for their clients. This in itself does not necessarily signify anything; the lawyers could simply be deemphasizing something they believe in (rights) in favor of idioms they believe would work on police or judges. For instance, lawyers described the need to appeal to the pity of the leader, or to make subtle, but never direct, references to how a good leader has a certain responsibility to uphold vis-à-vis subjects. These lawyers also reference how the goals of the government ("to a more peaceful and developed nation") can be achieved by treating people in certain better ways.

Rather, it is the particular *way* that rights were discussed that signifies a different meaning in the concept. The intermediary status mentioned earlier is again relevant here. On one hand, lawyers were able to report how their clients did not only not know their rights—in other words knowledge of the law—but did not have a concept of rights themselves. On the other hand, lawyers themselves seemed to engage the perilous nature of rights in the Burmese context. One lawyer, when describing how she works for the rights of her clients, mentioned that without her organization's intervention, those rights would simply not exist. It is here we see quite clearly the radical immanence and contingency of the rights concept in some Burmese political contexts: rights did not exist until they did, and if resources were withdrawn to buttress them, they would disappear again.

It is in this context that an ethnographic anecdote is worth relaying. An international lawyer was brought to Yangon to give a training on a key legal concept to a number of lawyers and legal aid professionals. The trainer ultimately argued that Burma should sign a certain international legal statute, as it would provide the lawyers leverage and legitimacy in their arguments against particular state practices inconsistent with this statute. After some murmuring from the audience, a Burmese lawyer raised his hand and ventured that the signing of international laws is not really the issue, for Burma has lots of laws that are sufficient, they are just not respected. The trainer maintained that signing the law would give an extra impetus for the government to respect it. The training moved on to the next topic.

The point here is not that the trainer was completely incapable of understanding the Burmese context. Further, the point is also not that the

Burmese lawyers completely rejected the specific advice, and certainly not the entire training. Many of them actually expressed how they found the trainings invaluable and, while many did not precisely explain why, it seemed that knowledge of standards forged by "the international" were seen as an essential touchstone for putting the Burmese context into critical relief and for contemplating the proper role of law. What does come through from this interaction between trainer and Burmese lawyers is that the former seemed to assume that *knowing* the law and thinking that a right flows from the law are coincident, but the lawyers reflected the Burmese political reality that seems to perceive a gap between them and cannot take advantage of that gap.[51] In other words, the law making a declaration and the concept of being an actor who can access the opportunity that the law guarantees in that declaration are not the same. One must qualify, or must get lucky, perhaps, in order to be protected rather than assaulted by the law.

Exploring Who Has the Opportunity to Have Rights, and Why

The task then becomes to identify who qualifies, who gets lucky? Classic critical legal work from respective Marxist political economy, critical race, and feminist perspectives have identified respective class, racial, religious, and gender variables as predicting differentially degraded access to justice outcomes.[52] While all these likely hold in Myanmar, and need to be explored, inadequate access to justice may not be a simple one-to-one function of those (or other) relevant positions. Different conceptions of justice as well as diverging conceptions of the role of various actors (courts, administrators, local leaders, etc.) in facilitating that justice are all relevant here. Access may be denied for other reasons. First, current understandings of justice may disqualify certain populations as legitimate justice claimants. Second, systems may not perceive as "justiciable events" certain interactions that other legal systems might see as such as a matter of course.[53]

Taking the issue of claimants first, beginning with "dispute" (as outlined previously in the question "Where do people go when there is a dispute?") may effectively restrict the universe to those with equal standing to actually dispute one another. A methodological way around this would be to develop a set of questions about hypothetical wrongs: your in-laws steal your land, versus your neighbors steal your land, versus the state steals your land, and see how different groups of people respond to it. Do they see each as wrong? Do they see each as justiciable? If so, where would they go for some sort of rectification?

Moreover, examining the lawyers' cases allows us to perceive not only how courts function but what kind of claims are considered legitimate or worthy of the justice system or the state itself. The interviews identified property (loans, land), family law, public order (gambling, drunkenness), and assault as legitimate claims. In such cases, citizens are conflicting with other citizens. But in the universe of issues that bother people, all of these seem relatively mild. Health, education, the struggle to survive are all absent from these discussions, which suggests that either (1) people do not see these issues as pertaining to the law or (2) they do not see the discussion of law as bringing in issues of the state, but only see it as pertaining to interpersonal issues. Early research has only begun to touch on these issues. One respondent replied, "If the state steals your land, then you cannot rely on the court. You will only become the defendant."

Finally there is the question of what mechanisms have created moral economies that prevent certain events from entering the justiciable universe? For instance, forced labor may be perceived by both those insisting upon it and those participating in it as a necessary and mutually beneficial method for mobilizing collective resources (labor) to attain collective goods (roads, for instance) or even individual/collective karmic benefits.[54] From these methods, laborers ultimately benefit. Within this structure, actors still assert moral claims, for instance, opposing the fact that some participants may be disqualified from forced labor (monks) while others (Christian pastors) are not.[55]

As one interviewee put it, "Not everything should go to court . . . [people] should resolve many matters socially, not legally, so that their time and money is spared."[56] This suggests that courts are costly, an access-to-justice barrier as outlined previously. However, it also suggests a different perspective on law and conflict resolution—that some sort of "social" redress (and it remains to be seen what this word *social* signifies or how it works) can lead to better outcomes. Research can ascertain whether these social mechanisms are providing justice that is satisfactory to the least empowered of the community members and work to improve those systems where they are lacking.

Ways Forward

This does not mean that certain Burmese are doomed to always believe that forced labor is acceptable, if not desirable, policy, or that rights as such do not exist (although, in the case of rights, the Burmese might be better off with their current ontology). Instead, the early point is that if the formal legal system is reformed but does not connect with these diverging conceptualizations to both substantive and procedural conceptions of justice, which are currently extant, then even people who might otherwise benefit from the formal domain, and who are not otherwise prevented from it, may not seek it out. More importantly, if institutions are declared "reformed" and yet do not address the structural impediments that prevent average Burmese actors from achieving what they consider to be justice, they may view these reforms as hypocrisy or callous dismissal of their realities. The way the Letpadaung protesters in Sagaing Region resoundingly rejected an empty rule of law, even when it came from the long-revered Aung San Suu Kyi,[57] demonstrates that Burmese may not be fooled by the new common sense. Against such an RoL divorced from daily political struggle, they may be even more receptive to movements expressing alternative forms of redress. It is certainly reasonable to surmise that the current flourishing of exclusionary and violent sectarian political movements in Burma could be buttressed by tepid elitist reform.[58]

These outcomes certainly are not inevitable. Rather than focusing all resources on the formal sector—as law reform projects tend to pursue their own versions of justice—law reform projects may deem what justice mechanisms people are using instead of the formal system. These projects can then work to improve those actually functioning systems to bridge the formal with the informal.[59] The next section will turn to the ideology of rule of law—and the constellation of institutions that its proponents create to effect it—that may prevent such a proportionate consideration of the informal sector of Burmese law.

Rule of Law Police

Burma's legal and political spheres have long been sites of arbitrary intervention.[60] Burmese yearn for a system that attempts to adjudicate conflicts fairly, and the phrase "rule of law" has become a signifier for invoking that desire. In fact, a deeper historical study could likely profitably trace how "rule of law" has been used across the decades to index a long-standing anxiety about arbitrary exercise of power in Burma.[61]

But invoking the rule of law and creating a system that responds to the particular needs of Burmese citizens are not necessarily the same project. Moreover, it is possible that the first could militate against the second. It is here that the RoL must be deconstructed, so that we can explore what effects it has when deployed as such, and whether, as designed now, RoL interventions can take the informal sector seriously.

What Is the Rule of Law?

When Aung San Suu Kyi came to Yale University in late 2013 to speak and ask the university to assist in Burma's transition period, she spoke the phrase "rule of law" over thirty times. She presented the concept as already-decided: every time rule of law was mentioned it was prefixed with the definite article *the.* Hence, rather than saying, for instance, that "we need to develop *a* Burmese rule of law," Aung San Suu Kyi invoked rule of law as a universal standard that exists not "in the West" as it were, but rather simply "out there" for every political-legal tradition to draw upon: "we need the rule of law," she said again and again. Perhaps because she assumed the issue already decided, Aung San Suu Kyi never paused to clarify what particular values animate the rule of law; while she added once that laws had to be "just," she did not define the substance of that justice, implicitly asserting that all Burmese (or even all humans) share, or should share, a common understanding of the values that should regulate conflict between people and groups. Such lack of clarity regarding such details has attended all of her discussions of RoL that I have surveyed, something that is not unique to Aung San Suu Kyi. As legal theorist Brian Tamanaha puts it, "The rule of law . . . stands in the peculiar state of being *the* preeminent legitimating political ideal in the world today, without agreement upon precisely what it means."[62]

What, then, is the rule of law? Is it an outcome, or a process? Is it a universal standard of conduct or is it highly specific to given political formations? How to even define it? A central debate over its meaning has been waged between what could be respectively called proceduralists and substantivists.[63] The former distill the rule of law into a framework of basic procedural conditions in which the law is sovereign, is knowable by subjects, and treats those subject to it equally. In such a conception, the RoL provides a platform for many different substantive legal regimes—from the republican to the authoritarian. The substantivists for their part reject such a "thin" conception, insisting on an additional substantive dimension running through and animating the procedural infrastructure of the law: the justness invoked by Aung San Suu Kyi. Tamanaha argues that while theorists find the latter version more vexed and often agree only on the former, this is not the case for its understanding in policy circles and in general common sense understanding: "While formal legality is the dominant understanding of the rule of law among legal theorists, this thick substantive rule of law, which includes formal legality, individual rights, and democracy, likely approximates the common sense of the rule of law within Western societies (assuming a common understanding exists)."[64] Because I am interested in the effective version of RoL being deployed in Burma, I will use this latter version (as it tends to be the dominant one exported abroad, as will be seen later in this chapter).

But are the distinctions between thick and thin meaningful? Political philosopher Jürgen Habermas argues that they are—that law can be assessed as "neutral" in procedural ways in societies that can nonetheless never agree on values: "The neutrality of the law vis-a-vis internal ethical differentiations stems from the fact that in complex societies the citizenry as a whole can no longer be held together by a substantive consensus on values but only by a consensus on the procedures for the legitimate enactment of laws and the legitimate exercise of power."[65] But by this Habermas denies the fact that conceptions of "justice" are immanent to the processes themselves. Let us explore "equality before the law," a fundamental "rule of law" tenet. While it appears straightforward, the idea is open for significant interpretation, interpretation so broad as to allow the tenet to attach to radically different political systems. For instance, the US legal system in practice implicitly asserts that governing a legal services by market logic—wherein poor US citizens are afforded only overburdened public defenders while the wealthy can utilize their resources to purchase expertise of many kinds—does not violate equality before the law.[66] The system draws upon an ideological commitment to a strain of political libertarianism that privileges "liberty" (the freedom to purchase unequal access to justice) over "equality" (wherein an adversarial system is only fair if there is a level playing field for the adversaries to contest each other).[67] Alternative systems, on the other hand, present such differential access as inimical to justice, and hence restrict such marketization.[68] The outcomes of the US system have led analysts to argue that such discrepancies are responsible for those 98 percent of legal cases ending in a plea bargain, as under-resourced defendants, fearing the outcome of a trial in which they face a better-resourced state, avoid the stacked game.[69] These analysts question the equality both in terms of procedures and outcomes of such a system. By treating all of its citizens equally under a grossly unequal system, this rule of law reinforces brutal inequality.[70]

The point is that procedures are inevitably informed by the society's visions of justice or normative conceptions of the good—or, rather, what outcomes are rendered acceptable and normal. When the jurisprudential processes themselves convey those conceptions, any distinction between "thick" and "thin" RoL becomes blurry to the point of collapse.

Hence, even if RoL activists formally establish checks and balances, officially codify "human rights," provide mechanisms for judicial review in Burma, and somehow animate these concepts so that they affect sociological reality there, these institutions still have to be invested with specific political meanings. Without such political intervention, the RoL can merely serve the existing vested interests. As British colonial officer John Furnivall said in 1948 about the colonial-era regime, "The rule of law becomes, in effect, the rule of economic law."[71] Furnivall went on to argue that the rule of law "naturally expedites the disintegration of the customary social structure."[72] Legal scholar David Kennedy reminds us that this is still true today, stating that

> the idea that building "the rule of law" might itself be a development strategy encourages the hope that choosing law in general could substitute for all the perplexing political and economic choices that have been at the center of development policy for half a century. The politics of allocation is submerged. Although a legal regime offers an arena to contest those choices, it cannot substitute for them.[73]

The International Rule of Law Machine

Yet, warnings about the potentially silencing or obfuscating content of the RoL remain, as is said, somewhat academic. The global RoL advocate Thomas Carothers elides them entirely, asserting that the RoL indexes a system that ensures access to universal human rights values: "The rule of law can be defined as a system in which the laws are public knowledge, are clear in meaning, and apply equally to everyone. They enshrine and uphold the political and civil liberties that have gained status as universal human rights over the last half-century."[74] This universality has allowed the RoL to achieve a postideological status:

> For . . . political, economic, and social [reasons] Western policy makers and commentators have seized on the rule-of-law as an elixir for countries in transition. It promises to remove all the chief obstacles on the path to democracy and market economics. Its universal quality adds to its appeal. Despite the close ties of the rule of law to democracy and capitalism, it stands apart as a nonideological, even technical, solution. In many countries, people still argue over the appropriateness of various models of democracy or capitalism. But hardly anyone these days will admit to being against the idea of law.[75]

Carothers is part of a second generation movement in RoL that now sees the importance of embedding political liberal values along with the formal reforms. RoL promoter Rachel Kleinfeld enumerates the distinction:

> So, for instance, a first-generation contractor might work with local educators to develop a curriculum for a magistrates' school to make it look like a Western judicial curriculum. A second-generation contractor would work to create a curriculum that is focused on helping judges see their role as an independent check on the power of parliament and the president or prime minister, giving them the skills to be both trained judges and upholders of a more balanced power structure.[76]

Any meaningful distinction between the two generations is difficult to ascertain; if there is any difference it seems to be merely tactical: whereas the initial strategy was communicated in dogmatic and univocal ways, the new strategy devotes time to enrolling recipients into the logics of liberalism.

Returning to Burma, a question is whether in the face of this RoL machine, the meanings of RoL can be expanded and adapted to the needs of this particular polity and political economy. A lack of consideration can be at least partially attributed to the "some reform is better than the system we have" theory of transition, in which Burma reformers seem ready to transplant externally generated solutions because these solutions appear (at first glance) to be vastly superior to the current system. But without considering what precepts of justice are being (sometimes silently) inscribed in the new system, Burma risks naturalizing rather than transforming existing structures of domination and exclusion.[77] RoL will have to be made real to people in Myanmar given their own particular experiences, values, and visions for the future.

Conclusion: Rule of Law as Police Against Rule of Law from Below

Rule of law ideology as conceived and currently utilized may end up operating in Burma as a way of reinscribing social control after despotism, a way of creating a new regime of regulation—what philosopher Jacques Ranciere calls "the police"—that not only contains unruly politics but forecloses on the plurality of heterogeneous and irreconcilable claims that could be performed through such politics.[78] Ranciere stresses that police is not a repressive form of silencing, but rather a creation of a condition of impossibility for political contention (which he calls dissensus). Aung San Suu Kyi's use of rule of law regarding violence in Arakan State and protests in Sagaing Region stand as the exemplars: she has used RoL to deflect, contest, and combat collective political and moral action by recodifying the conflicts as issues redounding upon administrative legal reforms. This utilization of RoL compels us to perceive RoL and politics as adversarial and opposed. RoL appears poised to become part of a diffuse and nebulous regime of control that entrenches extant hierarchies and justifies the status quo against social movements working for particular local conceptions of justice that bring alternative and even transformative demands.

Indeed, RoL tells the people, in essence, that there is a certain perfect and prescribed way to do things that can come readily packaged from the outside, and that hence the role for the people in politics is as silent partner. Rule of law here is the method of effectively containing unruly politics, as clean, quiet, tranquil, and disciplined (the ever-present *sii-gaan*—the discipline in Myanmar's "disciplined democracy").[79] What is underestimated is the extent to which *breaking* the law is necessary to change a society, the way they might miss the fact that law can get in the way of justice. Increasingly scholars are looking at the way justice social movements are actually nomothetic—or generative of law; these researchers argue that law *only* bends toward justice if there are people in the streets violating earlier instantiations of it.[80] This may help explain why postcolonial states with de jure progressive legal regimes do not realize those rights in practice; these laws remain a dead letter when they are not compelled into existence by social movement action.[81]

We must ask, then, what is the appeal to the discipline within rule of law? After enduring a regime that thrived on illegibility, inconsistency, and plausible deniability, is the search for the rule of law a search for the safety of stability? Such a framing suggests that Burma's ongoing political transition will be framed by this battle within a schizophrenic Burmese polity: the need for legibility against the desire for uncaptured politics; the need for organization and hierarchy against the desire for a horizontal and hence unpredictable polity; the need to maintain the unity of the nation against the desire to experiment with more inclusive forms of belonging; the need to keep the country stable (during this unpredictable time) versus the desire to transform it now (because during transitions is the only time that such fundamental changes can occur). This is not meant to pit regressive and reactionary molar forces against the anarchic and progressive molecular ones. It seems instead that both sides of the equation are necessary.

Aung San Suu Kyi herself is an exemplar of this internal division. At times she polices politics and follows the dogmatic global rights ideology. At other times she engages the politics of daily struggle. In a 2012 speech at Harvard University's Kennedy School of Government, Aung San Suu Kyi discussed Burma's changes through the optic of the challenges that villagers face, and mentioned that political attitudes were malleable and shifting.[82] Moreover, in a 2013 speech at the East-West Center in Hawaii, Aung San Suu Kyi demonstrated that the constitution might not be her ultimate goal.[83] While she remained vague, this implies that Aung San Suu Kyi is leaving space for real politics. This vagueness suggests that she and other democrats in Myanmar are attempting to find their way in a new political landscape.

In this vein, Cheesman quotes activist farmers who make sure they contrast RoL in its hegemonic form with one that is attuned to justice. He writes,

> a 2011 complaint by over forty cultivators against land confiscation is signed off as "farmers together seeking implementation of just rule of law." Their rule of law is not the rule of law of the police state: it is the rule of law based on an explicit claim to justice. It implicitly challenges the rule-of-law as law-and-order idea by distinguishing it from the rule of law with justice that the farmers seek.[84]

Here justice (the political) is inserted into the rule of law (the organized framework). The rule of law is *opened* by the farmers' intervention—there is necessarily more discussion to come after such statements, as farmers and those who hear them are now compelled to think through their (potentially contrasting) senses of justice, including how they can be generalized to others and how they can interface with the rule of law as a codified system. The continuation of this debate, rather than the cessation of it through the current RoL discourse, may be central to the Burmese truly directing their political transition.

Notes

1. See scholar Nick Cheesman's Ph.D. dissertation for groundbreaking work on the internal logics of this system: "The Politics of Law and Order in Myanmar" (Canberra: Australian National University, June 2012).

2. While it is admittedly impossible to identify a single definition of liberalism, as it contains many strains, I mean by it the political ontology founded on a self-contained, self-reflective, rights-bearing subject, and deployed in a global regime of rhetoric, political interventions, and biopolitical noninterventions (along the lines of the Rule of Law programs being witnessed now in Burma). For an elaboration of this imagined subject and the regime in which it fits, see Elizabeth Povinelli, *Economies of Abandonment: Social Belonging and Endurance in Late Liberalism* (Durham, NC: Duke, 2011).

3. See Ardeth Maung Thawnghmung, *Behind the Teak Curtain: Authoritarianism, Agricultural Policies and Political Legitimacy in Rural Burma/Myanmar* (London: Kegan Paul, 2004) for a rare example.

4. For an exemplar of this rationale, see Ellen Wiles, "In Defence of the Rule of Law," *Democratic Voice of Burma*, 20 March 2013, and for programming seeking to implement it, see Colette Rausch, Susan Hayward, Leanne McKay, and Kay Spencer, "USIP Burma/Myanmar Rule of Law Trip Report," US Institute of Peace Rule of Law Center, June 2013.

5. Ugo Mattei and Laura Nader, *Plunder: When the Rule of Law Is Illegal* (Malden, MA: Blackwell, 2008).

6. Although, as Richard Horsey's work with the International Labour Organization (ILO) shows, formal reforms can lead to substantive changes. Richard Horsey, *Ending Forced Labour in Myanmar: Engaging a Pariah Regime* (Hoboken, NJ: Taylor & Francis, 2011); see also Matt Shissler, "Changing Dynamics of Forced Labour: The International Labour Organization and Local Responses to Abuse in Eastern Myanmar," Masters dissertation (Oxford: Oxford University, 2013). These are empirical questions, which must consider the relevant political-economic factors influencing the likelihood of formal reform to effect better real outcomes. For instance, the entrenched collusion between economic and political elites and the rising value of land are rendering current land-grab victims unable to gain redress in court; more often they end up becoming the defendants, indicted on unlawfully congregating or defaming the state. See Asian Human Rights Commission, "Burma/Myanmar: Courts, Cops, Cronies—The Three C's Driving Farmers to Ruin, and Jail" (Hong Kong: Asian Human Rights Commission, 13 May 2014).

7. Although it is impossible to make a dispositive assertion as to how collectively shared is the endorsement of Rule of Law, this author's ongoing research on grassroots movements against landgrabs—movements that cut across class, ethnic group, and area of the country—has found that most utilize Rule of Law discourse as part of their oppositional protest repertoires. See Elliott Prasse-Freeman, "Grassroots Protest Movements and Mutating Conceptions of 'the Political' in an Evolving Burma," in Renaud Egreteau and Franciois Robbine, eds., *Contemporary Burma: What National Reconstruction?* (Bangkok: Research Institute on Contemporary Southeast Asia [IRASEC], forthcoming).

8. The caveat being that it was admittedly difficult to study this topic.

9. Myint Zan, "Judicial Independence in Burma: No March Backwards Towards the Past," *Asian-Pacific Law & Policy Journal* 1, no. 5 (2000); Myint Zan, "Legal Education in Burma Since the 1960s," *The Journal of Burma Studies* no. 12 (2008): 63–107.

10. Chapter 2 of this volume.

11. Besides his dissertation, see also Nick Cheesman, "Thin Rule of Law or Un-Rule of Law in Myanmar?" *Pacific Affairs* 82, no. 4 (Winter 2009/2010): 597–613.

12. As of mid-2014, a perverse cycle of protest and arrest continues to punctuate Burmese news reports: see, for instance, Khin Min Zaw, "Protesters Arrested After Appealing for Latpadaung Activist's Release," *Democratic Voice of Burma*, 17 February 2014; Paing SXoe, "Three Farmers Sentenced to Three Years for Plough Protest in Sagaing," *Democratic Voice of Burma*, July 2014; and Mamg Mya Nadi, "Tavoy Farmers Jailed for 'Disturbing' Officials," *Democratic Voice of Burma*, 17 July 2014.

13. Elliott Prasse-Freeman, "Power, Civil Society, and an Inchoate Politics of the Daily in Burma/Myanmar," *Journal of Asian Studies* 71, no. 2 (May 2012): 372–397.

14. I use *subject* rather than *citizen* here to highlight the fact that many individuals who are functionally Burmese—live in the country, speak the language, participate in Burmese modes of dress and commensality—are nonetheless denied citizenship.

15. USAID has devoted US$5–7 million to rule of law programs from 2013 to 2017; UNDP has announced an Access to Justice program. Japan, Australian, and UK aid organizations (JICA, AUSAID, and DFID, respectively) are also reportedly working on similar programs.

16. While it is beyond the scope of this chapter, future inquiries may explore whether religious figures (monks, imams, pastors, etc.) and logistics play roles in conflict resolution.

17. I am currently doing participant observation fieldwork with a legal aid NGO in Yangon that works explicitly on access to justice and legal reform. Many of the early conclusions here have been derived from its work and from my own research through their networks. Due to the continuing sensitivities of legal aid work in Burma, the organization will remain anonymous here.

18. Interviews, Yangon, July 2013.

19. Cheesman, "The Politics of Law and Order," 175.

20. I accessed this internal report July 2013 and discussed its findings with the research team.

21. These figures appear to operate in similar fashion to the *daik* and *myo* authorities who acted as intermediaries between villagers and the British during the colonial period. See Robert Taylor, *The State of Myanmar* (London: Hurst, 2009), 16–17. But whereas those roles were based on political-economic power, the ward administrator was often described by informants as a more entrepreneurial figure. I thank an anonymous reviewer for identifying this connection.

22. It is not just courts that are potentially unjust and dangerous, but police also are nearly always exploitative, and since one must go through the police in order to access courts, the WA prevents potential exploitation from both of those institutions. If this is the case, law reform will not be particularly effective without police reform as well.

23. Interview with legal-aid worker, August 2013.

24. IDU and CSW are acronyms used by Burmese-speaking paralegals to describe intravenous drug users and commercial sex workers, respectively.

25. This question framed the survey form of one legal-aid NGO I worked with.

26. While space constraints here prevent the thorough exploration that it deserves from being achieved, I would like to use this section to introduce and sketch the contours of the diverging conception of rights in Burma.

27. There is an extensive literature on "rights"; for one of the most famous defenses of them in their dominant liberal conception, see Ronald Dworkin, *Taking Rights Seriously* (Cambridge: Harvard University Press, 1977–1978).

28. For a review of this literature, see Matthew J. Walton, "Politics in the Moral Universe: Burmese Buddhist Political Thought," Ph.D. dissertation (Seattle: Department of Political Science, University of Washington, 2012), especially chapter 2, "Burmese Buddhist Perspectives on the Nature of Politics."

29. Myint Zan, "Position of Power and Notions of Empowerment: Comparing the Views of Lee Kuan Yew and Aung San Suu Kyi on Human Rights and Democratic Governance," *Newcastle Law Review* 2, no. 1 (1997): 49–69.

30. Benedict Anderson, "The Javanese Idea of Power," in *Language and Power: Exploring Political Cultures in Indonesia* (Ithaca: Cornell University Press, 1990); Clifford Geertz, *Negara: The Theatre State in Nineteenth-Century Bali* (Princeton, NJ: Princeton University Press, 1980).

31. James C. Scott, *The Art of Not Being Governed* (New Haven, CT: Yale University Press, 2009), chapter 4.

32. Andrew Huxley, "Burma: It Works, but Is It Law?" *Journal of Family Law,* Vol. 27 (1988–1989): 23.

33. *Dhammasat* is another transliteration from the Pali of the same word labeled *dhammathat* here.

34. Andrew Huxley, "Pre-colonial Burmese Law: Conical Hat and Shoulder Bag," *International Institute for Asian Studies Newsletter,* no. 25 (2001), www.iias.nl/iiasn/25/theme/25T7.html.

35. See Michael Mann, "Autonomous Power of the State: Its Origins, Mechanisms, and Results," *European Journal of Sociology* 25 (1984).

36. Maung Maung Gyi. *Burmese Political Values: The Socio-Political Roots of Authoritarianism* (New York: Praeger, 1983), 21.

37. Walton, "Politics in the Moral Universe," 72–73.

38. Myint Zan, "Judicial Independence in Burma."

39. While Nick Cheesman asserts that rights conceptualizations took hold during this same period, he is never able to demonstrate that these ideas existed outside of a narrow swathe of elites, or how democratic life actually incorporated rights orientations. For an elaboration of the counterargument (that the constitutional state and its rights frameworks may not have penetrated average village life), see Prasse-Freeman, "Power, Civil Society, and an Inchoate Politics."

40. Myint Zan, "Legal Education in Burma."

41. As opposed to the West's "rights without responsibilities," Burmese have "responsibilities without rights."

42. David Steinberg, *Burma: the State of Myanmar* (Washington, DC: Georgetown University Press, 2001), 41.

43. E-mail, 20 November 2011.

44. E-mail interview, 19 November 2011

45. Conversation occurred 8 January 2013.

46. See Elliott Prasse-Freeman, "Grassroots Protest Movements."

47. Jill Davison, "Rights-Claiming in a Rule of Law Vacuum," *Democratic Voice of Burma,* 11 March 2013.

48. Philosopher Jacques Ranciere has outlined how actors perform into being the rights that they do not have (see Jacques Ranciere, "Who Is the Subject of the Rights of Man?" *South Atlantic Quarterly* 103, no 2/3 [Spring/Summer 2004]: 297–310). and is useful for theorizing the way that rupturing political acts lead to new conceptions of rights. But his work is specifically located in the West, and it is common for activists influenced by this tradition to hence see the actions of those com-

ing from other political traditions to be essentially making similar moves: that these are protoliberals in the villages of upland Burma demanding the rights they do not have. But claiming rights as rights can only exist if actors are appealing to a field that recognizes rights as such. Absent such a context, different demands are being made. Partha Chatterjee's anthropology of subaltern demands makes it clear that often actors are pleading for exceptions that are not codified as durable or permanent—which are not rights—and hence that continue to be left open to erosion or sudden elimination. See Partha Chatterjee, *Politics of the Governed* (New York: Columbia University Press, 2004).

49. Cheesman, "The Politics of Law and Order," 209.

50. I am indebted to the research by James C. Scott and members of the subaltern studies collective for my conceptualization of this politics of the governed. See James C. Scott, *Domination and the Arts of Resistance: Hidden Transcripts* (New Haven, CT: Yale University Press, 1990), and Ranajit Guha, ed., *Subaltern Studies, Vol. 1: Writings on South Asian History and Society* (Delhi/New York: Oxford University Press, 1982).

51. The concept of "rightful resistance" coined by O'Brien and Li shows how such gaps are capitalized upon by resisters in China. The Burmese experience, alternatively, highlights situations where the gap cannot be rectified, but rather reminds the polity of the realities of sovereignty. Kevin J. O'Brien and Lianjiang Li, *Rightful Resistance in Rural China* (Cambridge, UK: Cambridge University Press, 2006).

52. For Feminist Legal Theory see Martha Fineman, "Feminist Legal Theory," *Journal of Gender, Social Policy & the Law* 13, no. 1 (2005): 13–23; for Critical Race Theory, see Derrick Bell, *Race, Racism, and American Law,* 3rd edition (Boston: Little, Brown, 1992); for a seminal Marxist critique of law see his "On the Jewish Question" (1843), http://www.marxists.org/archive/marx/works/1844/jewish-question

53. For an overview of the Critical Legal Studies method to which I am indebted in this mode of critique, see inter alia Roberto Unger's book-length article, "The Critical Legal Studies Movement," *Harvard Law Review* 96, no. 3 (January 1983): 561–675.

54. Gustaaf Houtman, "Mental Culture in Burmese Crisis Politics: Aung San Suu Kyi and the National League for Democracy," *Monograph Series* 33 (Tokyo: Tokyo University of Foreign Studies, Institute for the Study of Languages and Cultures of Asia and Africa, 1999): 124–126. I thank an anonymous reviewer for bringing up this additional reason for engaging with forced labor.

55. See Horsey, *Ending Forced Labour in Myanmar,* and Elliott Prasse-Freeman, "Power, Civil Society, and an Inchoate Politics of the Daily in Burma/Myanmar," *Journal of Asian Studies* 71, no. 2 (May 2012): 371–397 for extended discussions of forced labor and justice.

56. Interview conducted by lawyers working for an international legal NGO, 2012.

57. Nick Cheesman, "What Does the Rule of Law Have to Do with Democratization (in Myanmar)?" Paper for the *Myanmar (Burma) Update 2013,* Canberra, Australia, 15–16 March 2013.

58. See Chapter 6 of this volume.

59. First, because fixing formal systems aligns with the normative goals of the respective international lawyers and bilateral patrons who fund the projects, goals that involve replicating their own systems. Second, building rationalized state apparatuses has efficiency appeals: it is much easier to reform one massive bureaucratic system than thousands of informal ones. Third, assuming that for the minimal reason

of increased choice people might want to have the formal system as an option, reforming the formal system can be seen as a collective good; reformers employ a "comparative advantage" argument that they should focus on doing what they do best: working on the formal system. However, for the same reason of increasing choice and options, the informal system deserves proportionate attention.

60. This section is adapted from Elliott Prasse-Freeman, "Animating Reform from Within," *Democratic Voice of Burma*, 24 January 2012.

61. Gyi, *Burmese Political Values*, 147.

62. Brian Z. Tamanaha, *On the Rule of Law History, Politics, Theory* (Cambridge, UK: Cambridge University Press, 2004), 4.

63. For a more thorough review of this literature, see Cheesman, "The Politics of Law and Order," chapter 1. Also see Cheesman, "Thin Rule of Law?"

64. Tamanaha, *On the Rule of Law,* 111.

65. Jürgen Habermas, *The Inclusion of the Other: Studies in Political Theory,* Ciaran Cronin and Pablo De Greiff, eds. (Cambridge, MA: MIT Press, 1998), 225.

66. "Report to the United Nations Human Rights Committee Regarding Racial Disparities in the United States Criminal Justice System," *The Sentencing Project* (August 2013).

67. Whether we can call this a "collective" social commitment or an effective social commitment effected through elite capture is immanent to this discussion.

68. Mattei and Nader, *Plunder,* 15.

69. Ibid.

70. "The [Supreme] Court shuts down challenges to such policies rooted in evidence of their racially disparate impact, requiring instead that plaintiffs show explicit and intentional discrimination on the part of criminal justice personnel. The colorblindness of the Constitution—once a hallmark of the protections of minority rights in the United States—has instead become a mechanism whereby racial minorities are frequently locked out of the courthouse and into prison cells," quoted in *The Sentencing Project* (2013), 17.

71. John Furnivall, *Colonial Policy and Practice: A Comparative Study of Burma and Netherlands India* (Cambridge, UK: Cambridge University Press, 1948), 295.

72. Ibid.

73. David Kennedy, "The 'Rule of Law,' Political Choices, and Development Common Sense," in David M. Trubek and Alvaro Santos, eds., *The New Law and Economic Development: A Critical Appraisal* (Cambridge, UK: Cambridge University Press, 2006), 186.

74. Thomas Carothers, "The Rule-of-Law Revival," in Carothers, ed., *Promoting the Rule of Law Abroad: In Search of Knowledge* (Washington, DC: Carnegie Endowment for Peace, 2006), 4 (article originally published as *Foreign Affairs* 77, no. 2 [March/April 1998]).

75. Ibid., 7. While Carothers's endorsement of Rule of Law here might seem to rhetorically set up an imminent problematization of the concept, none is forthcoming. Rule of Law is consciously announced as technical, and the only critique is of the methods through which it is brought to those not-quite-yet-civilized places struggling with vestiges of premodern charismatic politics. Noteworthy here is how only pages before, Carothers had insisted that instituting the Rule of Law is a fundamentally *political* problem: "The primary obstacles to such reform are not technical or financial, but political and human. Rule-of-law reform will succeed only if it gets at the fundamental problem of leaders who refuse to be ruled by the law (3). Paradoxically, Carothers can only imagine these political problems as solvable through technical fixes.

76. Rachel Kleinfeld, *Advancing the Rule of Law Abroad*, 2012, Carnegie Endowment for International Peace, 21.

77. This theme is drawn out in comparative context by Fionnuala Ni Aolain and Michael Hamilton, "Gender and the Rule of Law in Transitional Societies," *Minnesota Journal of International Law* 18 (2009): 380–402.

78. Jacques Ranciere, *Dissensus: On Politics and Aesthetics*, trans. Steven Corcoran (New York: Continuum, 2010), 36–37.

79. During an October 2013 speech, Aung San Suu Kyi explicitly asked Yale Law School for help designing Burmese law.

80. B. Rajagopal, *International Law from Below; Development, Social Movements, and Third World Resistance* (Cambridge, UK: Cambridge University Press, 2003). See also Julia Eckert, Brian Donahoe, Christian Strümpell, Zerrin Özlem Biner, eds., *Law Against the State: Ethnographic Forays into Law's Transformations*. Cambridge, UK, and New York: Cambridge University Press, 2012.

81. John Comaroff and Jean Comaroff, "Law and Disorder in the Postcolony," *Social Anthropology* 15, no 2 (2007): 133–152.

82. "A Public Address by Daw Aung San Suu Kyi," Harvard Institute of Politics, published 28 September 2012. Available at www.youtube.com/watch?v=-QnBE5Xsx74&noredirect=1.

83. "Aung San Suu Kyi—Remarks to Hawaii Community Leaders," 25 January 2013, published 28 January 2013. Available at www.youtube.com/watch?v=6fvtItKzCBk.

84. Cheesman, "The Politics of Law and Order," 212.

6

Buddhism, Politics, and Political Change

Matthew Walton

Although Buddhist influences seemed subdued during the first year of Myanmar's current political transition, violence between Buddhists and Muslims beginning in June 2012 and a recent resurgence of Buddhist nationalism remind us that religion remains an important factor in Burmese politics. In this chapter, I examine the writings, speeches, sermons, and actions of Buddhists in Myanmar to explore three ways in which Buddhism is playing a role in the transition to democracy. First, Buddhists are gradually taking up the task of not simply defending the compatibility of Buddhism and democracy, but also theorizing the connections between these two institutions in more detail. Second, Buddhism can also engender nationalism and extremism and reinforce gender and status hierarchies in ways that inhibit democratization. Third, the development of democratic thought in non-Western countries like Myanmar not only informs the development of political systems that are relevant and recognizable in local contexts, but also can constructively challenge and revitalize democratic thought in the West.

While Theravada Buddhism is not a totalizing influence on Burmese politics, this chapter argues that it remains the source of the conceptual framework within which most Buddhists in Myanmar think about politics. That is, being embedded in the Theravada moral conception of the universe, Burmese Buddhists understand the political as a sphere of moral action, governed by particular rules of cause and effect. Of course, within this framework, Burmese Buddhists vary as to their interpretation of particular concepts and the degree to which they see Buddhist teachings as relevant to politics; however, this perspective helps to illuminate the ways in which even ostensibly secular discourses are situated within particular cultural and religious worldviews. Beyond this moral conceptual framework, the ways in which Buddhism and national identity have become intertwined in the dominant national narrative also provide an impetus for many Buddhists to prioritize both the preservation of the state and the religion, seeing the two as inseparable and interdependent.

Despite sharing this common moral framework, Burmese Buddhists have developed a wide range of interpretation of the repertoire of "raw materials" that Buddhism provides, particularly its malleable notion of human nature.[1] It should not be surprising that Burmese political thinkers have constructed Buddhist arguments to both legitimate and criticize various forms of political authority and political ideologies or that some of the same monks who participated in prodemocracy protests in 2007 have also encouraged the political exclusion of certain populations just five years later.

Unlike the parliamentary era (1948–1962) or the period following the 1988 protests, in the current transition neither government officials nor opposition figures have talked in detail about the connections between Buddhism and democratic practice. The electoral campaigns of November 2010 and April 2012 featured few references to Buddhism or to candidates' Buddhist practices, which we can likely attribute to sensitivity to the potentially divisive effects of religious rhetoric in the political sphere. However, monks regularly reinforce the moral laws of Buddhism and connect them to political and social situations through their writings and video messages, public sermons, and daily interactions with lay people. In the absence of other political figures explicitly discussing the role of Buddhist beliefs and values in the realm of politics, the actions and sermons of monks take on even more significance.

The current political transition has undoubtedly provided additional political space for the expression of Buddhist perspectives and concerns in the public sphere, some of which support democratic reform and some of which express a more antidemocratic agenda. Additionally, the political, economic, and social changes have created an environment of uncertainty in which both Buddhism and the dominant sense of Burmese national identity as Buddhist have been portrayed as under threat. With a vocal Buddhist majority, the government has been very cautious and restrained in its response to these trends.

It is necessary to highlight two aspects of this analysis. First, the chapter draws mostly on writings, speeches, and sermons of elite political and religious figures. A more popular discourse on religion and politics is only beginning to emerge in the country and it will be important for future research to capture the ways in which public discourse on Buddhism and politics changes.

Second, the examples of Buddhist political thought explored in this chapter are, by default, reflective of the majority Burman tradition. Up to this point it has been very difficult for researchers to study the Buddhist practices and ideas of non-Burman groups in Myanmar, due to linguistic difficulties, lack of sources, and challenges of access. Recognizing the diversity of perspectives on and interpretations of Buddhist thought along ethnic lines (as well as socioeconomic, geographic, and other axes) will be a critically important avenue for future research.

Buddhism as Democratic Legitimator

Since at least the beginning of the twentieth century, some Buddhists in Myanmar have drawn on Buddhist teachings to explain and legitimize democratic governance. This discourse has existed alongside arguments (both Buddhist and otherwise) for centralized, authoritarian control, but Buddhist democratic philosophizing increased after 1988, exemplified most prominently in the writings of Aung San Suu Kyi. The monastic leaders of the 2007 Saffron Revolution also used Buddhist reasoning in their criticism of the former military regime and in their explanations of the compatibility of Buddhism and democracy, and we will likely see more works of Burmese Buddhist democratic thought in the future if political reforms continue to open up space for political discourse.

Aung San Suu Kyi has been the most prominent of the voices calling for democracy in Myanmar. Her status as the daughter of the country's independence hero General Aung San gave her almost instant credibility with much of the Burmese public as soon as she decided to become involved in the demonstrations of 1988. Although the military government consistently attempted to portray her as either under the influence of foreign elements or as a foreigner herself, she proved to be very skilled at situating her ideas about democracy and human rights within a Theravada-influenced Burmese discourse on politics and communicating them to Burmese audiences.[2]

Aung San Suu Kyi usually discusses democracy in a way that is consistent with Western liberal democracy. Human rights, free and fair elections, and a number of other freedoms figure prominently in her speeches. Since the beginning of her political career she has spoken out strongly against what she calls the "twin myths of [Burmese] unfitness for political responsibility and the unsuitability of democracy for their society."[3] In her view, democracy is completely compatible with Buddhism, as the former is an "integrated social and ideological system based on respect for the individual" and the latter "places the greatest value on man."[4]

Aung San Suu Kyi has often explained democracy in Buddhist terms, transposing the traditional "Ten Duties of the King" from a guide for monarchs to a set of expectations for a modern democratic government. In speaking of the second duty, *thila* (morality), she has emphasized the causal links between the conduct of the ruler and the prosperity of the nation, claiming that "the root of a nation's misfortune has to be sought in the moral failings of the government."[5] She insisted that a lack of moral purity in the political authority would set the tone for the conduct of the rest of the people and that living under a political structure characterized by immorality would make the practice of the moral life even more difficult for citizens.[6]

She has not, however, absolved individuals completely from their political responsibilities. In a speech on the topic of solidarity among ethnic groups, she touched on "the real meaning of democracy."[7] She considered why the BSPP (Burmese Socialist Programme Party, the socialist government that ruled from 1962 to 1988) was able to last so long if it was so inept. "I think that the BSPP gained control of the government because the citizens failed to carry out the duties of citizenship," she has said.[8] Democracy requires active participation of its citizens, and Aung San Suu Kyi has conceptualized this participation as a moral duty.

A related understanding of freedom that complicates this liberal rhetoric addresses the question of what individuals are freeing themselves from. One of Aung San Suu Kyi's most well-known English language essays was entitled "Freedom from Fear," and in it she wrote optimistically of a future in which the citizens of Myanmar would no longer be in thrall to fear, either the fear of being subjected to abusive power or the fear among those who exercise that power of losing it. However, closely connected to this democratic change is her call for a "revolution of the spirit," a necessary moral component of the process that will prepare the citizens of Myanmar for democratic practice. Behind those structural elements that would inhibit democratic reform are the qualities that emerge when people ignore their moral practice, namely "desire, ill will, ignorance and fear."[9]

She underscores this understanding of the moral foundation necessary for democratic practice in the following sentences.

> Free men are the oppressed who go on trying and who in the process make themselves fit to bear the responsibilities and to uphold the disciplines which will maintain a free society. . . . A people who would build a nation in which strong, democratic institutions are firmly established as a guarantee against state-induced power must first learn to liberate their own minds from apathy and fear.[10]

First, we should note her usage of the dual sense of freedom/liberation, from political oppression and from moral/mental defilements. Also important, however, is her insistence that each one must purify and liberate his or her mind *before* they can be considered ready for participation in "strong, democratic institutions." Democracy is necessary as the political system that best supports freedom, yet proper democratic participation ideally rests on a foundation of correct moral practice. While she generally presents Buddhist teachings as encouraging broader participation, we can see an interpretation that might actually restrict participation based on an individual's moral conduct.

The preceding quotes, however, are all drawn from Aung San Suu Kyi's speeches and writings of the early and middle 1990s, a period that coincides with deeper Buddhist training and engagement in her personal life. Although her speeches since that time have occasionally included examples and metaphors drawn from the Buddhist tradition, her rhetoric seems to have gradually shifted from its religious emphasis and since her release from house arrest in 2010 has been almost completely free of explicit Buddhist references. This demonstrates how the deployment of Buddhist rhetoric can be situational and strategic and can also change over time, even if by the same person. It will be important to watch for the re-emergence of Buddhist political thought (and not simply Buddhist symbolism) among Burmese political figures. There is, however, a group of Buddhists for whom the use of Buddhist rhetoric and reasoning is an essential part of their political engagement.

Burmese monks have not only been at the forefront of prodemocracy demonstrations in recent years, but have also sought to situate democratic values within a Buddhist context. Nyanissara, also known as Sitagu Sayadaw, is probably the most well known monk in Myanmar today. He oversees a wide network of development projects, including hospitals, clinics, and a Buddhist university based in Sagaing. He also took part in the 1988 protests as a monk, preaching a sermon that criticized the government for not acting in accordance with the "Ten Duties of the King," an interpretation similar to Aung San Suu Kyi's. When the government cracked down on the protests, he left the country, going to study in the United States. Since his return in the mid-1990s, he has successfully navigated the dangerous waters of Burmese politics, maintaining close ties to prominent members of the military while also speaking out against government repression and mismanagement, especially in the period following Cyclone Nargis.

Because of his status in the country and his connections across political divides, at times Sitagu Sayadaw has played a mediating role, particularly between the government and the NLD (National League for Democracy, the largest opposition party). In June 2011, he used the occasion of the opening of the Yangon branch of his Sitagu Buddhist Academy to preach to attendees from both groups about the need for unity in order to have a thriving democracy.[11] In a speech to the UN on 16 May 2011 he shifted his focus from the "Ten Duties of the King" to the ten perfections (*paramis*) as necessary qualities for political leadership.[12] In discussing *thila* (moral discipline), he noted how most interactions between national leaders are devoid of *thila* and instead are based on ego and selfishness (*atta*). Again, we see the Buddhist perspective that perfection in morality is the root of success in any field, including democratic governance.

Another group of monks that has been more explicit about their interest in politics is the small faction that was one of the primary organizing forces behind the 2007 Saffron Revolution. Although responsibility and credit for the coordination of nationwide protests must go beyond any single group, and should include networks of monks, lay supporters, and activists, as well as the often overlooked efforts of the *thila-shin* (nuns), one of the most prominent groups claiming to speak for the monks was the All Burma Monks Alliance (ABMA). According to their own documents, the ABMA was formed on 9 September 2007 by six monks.[13] The founding group included Gambira, a former monk who was jailed in 2007 and released in early 2012, and Ashin Issariya (a.k.a. King Zero), who escaped to Thailand after the protests and has remained a prominent critic of the Burmese government and advocate for democracy. Both before and after the protests, Ashin Issariya led a group of monks and lay people who published and distributed pamphlets and journals that contained poems and articles on topics including human rights, the role of the *sangha* (monkhood) in Burmese society, and democracy. These articles provide another range of perspectives on democracy from a monastic point of view.[14]

In these publications, the contributors advocate for an understanding of *kan* (Pali *kamma*, the Buddhist law of cause and effect) that emphasizes the transformative possibility of change and the role of individual agents in creating change, rather than the common interpretation that stresses the inevitability of experiencing the effects of past actions and the need to simply reconcile oneself with any hardship one experiences. The author of one article declares, "People are creatures who create their own conditions through their own actions, who want to be free, and who have a strong desire to be free. People have a nature and ability that opposes repression and control. That nature is democratic."[15] The author interprets freedom within the context of the Buddhist doctrine of cause and effect, emphasizing people's ability to change their circumstances. From this point of view, democracy is valuable as a political system because it enables and supports human efforts to create their world freely, as they desire it.

The authors of these journals also argue that the Buddha's teachings contain the essence of democracy, a common claim among many Burmese writers. "Democracy is not something that only just appeared. The Buddha had already preached about it twenty-five hundred years ago. In the Buddha's teachings, he thoroughly discussed human rights. . . . The Buddha's doctrine is in accordance with democracy."[16] This writer situates democratic values within the *Kālāma Sutta*, a teaching that many democratic activists in Myanmar revere, and which General Aung San also championed. In this *sutta*, the leaders of the Kālāma people were confronted by many different doctrines and were confused as to which was actually correct. The Buddha advised them not to accept something as truth merely because of tradition or because their parents or teachers told them it was true, or even because the Buddha himself preached it. They should examine it and only when they themselves have determined that it is true, should they accept it as truth. The author concludes that the Buddha never forced his disciples to believe or act a certain way; Buddhism is a religion of free choice. Democracy, as a political system of free choice is thus compatible with Buddhist principles.

The analysis in these articles and speeches is relatively simple and not without its weaknesses (for example, Buddhists in other contexts have found the connection between the Buddha's teachings and rights doctrines to be problematic). However, the important aspect to note is the efforts of both monastic and lay Buddhists to ground versions of democratic politics in Buddhist teachings that will resonate with the majority of the population.

Another Burmese monk who has used his sermons to comment on the connections between Buddhist morality and democracy is Ashin Eindaga, the Twante Sayadaw. In a public sermon delivered in Yangon on 31 January 2011, he stated that, "Democracy is Buddha's doctrine. It is truly Buddha's doctrine." He went on to say, "If you have *taya*, you will have democracy. . . . Democracy means acting in accordance with *taya*, having laws. If society is fully endowed with *thila* (morality), won't it also be fully endowed with democracy?"[17]

This statement represents a particularly Buddhist interpretation of democracy. *Taya* is a requirement for democracy. *Taya* is also a quintessentially moral concept that can refer to fairness, justice, or equality; to moral principles or moral truth; to a natural law or the nature of things; or to the specific law of the Buddha, *dhamma*. By asserting that democracy means acting in accordance with *taya*, Ashin Eindaga reinforced the view that Buddhist moral teachings are not only relevant in the political realm, they are an essential element of a Burmese Buddhist understanding of democracy. On the one hand, democratic political participation ideally allows all citizens to freely create the conditions of their own lives. From this point of view, authoritarianism in any form—whether a monarchy, a colonial administration, or a military dictatorship—would be inconsistent with free human action, the doctrine of the Buddha. This "free" action is, however, constrained by its basis in moral practice. That is, democratic "freedom" also means acting in accordance with the moral truths of Buddhism.

Although direct monastic engagement in politics is still generally frowned upon in Myanmar, there exists a sufficiently gray area between the ideal of complete renunciation of the mundane world and the opposite extreme of monastic political parties as in Sri Lanka for some other monks in Myanmar to carve out a space for political activities. Shwe Nya Wa Sayadaw, a well-known Yangon monk, has a close relationship with the NLD and has frequently given "political" sermons and allowed his monastery to be used for political events. As a result of these activities, he was disciplined by the State Sangha Maya Nayaka Council, the national body that governs monks, in December 2011 and later evicted from his monastery.[18] He has, however, continued to speak out on both politics and issues concerning the protection of Buddhism, a topic examined in the following section.

What we see throughout these Burmese Buddhist perspectives on democracy is an insistence that, as doctrines of human freedom, Buddhism and democracy are unquestionably compatible. In a society that has been ruled by an oppressive military government for most of the past fifty years, this assertion is critical in grounding arguments for basic rights and freedoms as well as increased citizen political participation in the Buddhist worldview that most of the population shares. However, the ambiguity of the concept of "freedom" as well as the understanding that politics is an inherently moral undertaking also potentially challenges or undermines liberal notions of democracy that seek to expand the freedom of the individual as far as possible. Not only that, because Buddhism is the religion of the majority, there is a worrying risk that, as has happened in the past, Burmese Buddhists will seek to implement a system that not only privileges Buddhists but also relies explicitly on Buddhist doctrine, alienating non-Buddhists from meaningful participation in the polity. These concerns, along with the worrying reemergence of a violent and exclusionary Buddhist nationalism are considered in the following section.

Buddhism as Democratic Impediment

While Buddhists in Myanmar have long used the Buddha's teachings to argue in favor of democracy, the current transition has also revealed some potentially antidemocratic tendencies, or interpretations, of Buddhism. One of the most harmful is the recent wave of anti-Muslim violence that has occurred in cities across the country. In this section, I examine the dynamics of the reemergence of an avowedly Buddhist nationalism as well as the "Buddhist" characteristics of the present violence. I also consider several other potential Buddhist impediments to further democratic reform, including the standing of women in Burmese society and the virtually unquestioned position of monks in Burmese society.

In June 2012 riots erupted in western Rakhine (Arakan) State after the rape and murder of a Buddhist girl by three Muslim men and subsequent retaliation by Rakhine Buddhists. There were casualties on both sides, but most observers agree that the Rohingya Muslim minority suffered a disproportionately greater loss of life and property; many people displaced by the conflict are still in temporary camps today. Clashes between Rohingya and Rakhines have continued throughout 2014.

Although the conflict in Rakhine State initially appeared to be the result of local tensions, Buddhist-Muslim violence soon moved across the country, directed at non-Rohingya Muslims. In the central Myanmar town of Meikhtila, riots in March 2013 resulted in dozens of deaths as Buddhists burned Muslim homes, mosques, and schools in response to a jewelry store dispute and the murder of a Buddhist monk by a group of Muslims. Violent incidents occurred in several other cities, including Okkan, Lashio, and Kanbalu. A less prevalent but important counternarrative also began to emerge of effective community policing in some areas, Buddhists sheltering Muslim neighbors from attacks, and religious and community leaders coming together to refute rumors and restrain militant elements of their own communities.

The governmental and legal response to the riots has been somewhat muted and certainly not a representation of the equally administered "rule of law" that

Burmese politicians have been calling for. President Thein Sein pledged that those responsible would be held accountable, but in most cases (despite ample documentation of Buddhists, even monks, attacking Muslims) those arrested and prosecuted have been predominantly Muslim. Prosecutions of those involved on both sides are continuing, but blatantly unequal treatment has led some observers to question the ability of the Burmese legal system to dispense justice equally.

Reports from government-led commissions of inquiry into several of the incidents have studiously avoided using the term "Rohingya," instead referring only to Muslim "Bengalis," increasing the appearance of state bias. The 2014 census also seems to have exacerbated tensions. While insisting that Rohingya was not a recognized ethnic group in Myanmar, the government did initially promise that Rohingya would be able to self-identify in the census under the "Other" ethnic category. However, they reneged on that promise at the start of the census in March 2014, under pressure from Rakhine protesters. At the same time, violence against foreign aid agencies resulted in the withdrawal of almost all aid groups in Rakhine state, leaving displaced populations in an increasingly vulnerable position.

These waves of violence, combined with either persistent anti-Muslim rhetoric or virtual silence on human rights violations from public figures across Myanmar represent an assertive resurgence of Buddhist nationalism that could threaten the reform process as it seeks to silence, vilify, persecute, and even expel particular marginalized groups in Burmese society. Buddhism and nationalism have become almost inseparably intertwined in Theravada Buddhist majority countries like Myanmar; this interconnectedness becomes particularly emphasized at moments in which the majority population feels threatened by a group of "others." Historically, Buddhist kings drew their legitimacy from their institutional support of the monkhood and from a cosmology that presented the well-being of the Buddhist community as an indicator of the strength of the nation. Thus, threats to Buddhism also function as threats to the nation, and calls to defend the "Motherland" (especially when shouted by groups of monks) reiterate the belief that the nation is at its core Buddhist and that non-Buddhists can at best enjoy conditional membership in the national community.[19]

Although there is a generally assumed prohibition against monastic political activity among Burmese Buddhists, monks have regularly engaged in politics, from positions as advisers to kings before colonization to their place at the head of the anticolonial movement at the beginning of the twentieth century. Monks also assumed leading roles in political protests in Myanmar during military rule, including in 1988 and 2007. While for the most part these actions were undertaken in opposition to the oppression of military rule, some Buddhists have directed their efforts at the suppression of minority religions, Islam in particular. Wirathu, one of the leading voices in the current campaign, was imprisoned in 2003 for inciting anti-Muslim riots in Mandalay and the 969 movement of which he is a part initially emerged as one of the primary groups engaging in anti-Muslim rhetoric and actions during the current transitional period.

The movement, which draws its name from the numbers of attributes of the Buddha, the *dhamma* (his teachings), and the *sangha* (the community of monks), imagines 969 as a symbolic counter to the number 786, a numerological shorthand for Islam used among some Muslims in Asian countries. The symbol 786 has a practical purpose, as Muslim businesses (especially restaurants) display a 786 sticker to indicate to customers that they serve halal food, although it also functions as a more general notification that the business is Muslim-owned. The 969 movement has sought to institute a similar self-identification practice by Buddhist-owned businesses through the distribution of 969 stickers and encouragement of Buddhists to only patronize Buddhist-owned establishments.

In this way, 969 has functioned as a sort of "Buy Buddhist" campaign, and its supporters claim that they are merely responding to similarly insular buying practices in Islamic communities. But some 969 literature and monastic sermons have also directly criticized Islam and spread unsubstantiated rumors about Islamic practices in Myanmar. While 969 defenders argue that they are merely encouraging Buddhists to more fervently practice and defend their religion, the movement's literature presents Islam as both a threat to Buddhism and to the Burmese nation and often exhorts Buddhists to "take action" against the threat.

When Wirathu's actions and the 969 boycott movement are framed as "defending Buddhism," it can be very difficult for lay Buddhists to criticize them.[20] As explained in more detail below, the general respect for the *sangha* in Myanmar means that for most Buddhists, even publicly questioning a monk would be almost unthinkable. The framing of the movement as a "defense of Buddhism" campaign rather than an anti-Muslim campaign also influences the way that people view them, with significant social pressure to conform. These dynamics demonstrate the challenges of navigating a changing political landscape in Myanmar where reforms have opened up space for freer speech, but religious norms still prevent public questioning of monks or their interpretations of Buddhist teachings.

Additionally, Wirathu epitomizes more ambivalent and instrumental attitudes toward democracy that are common among many Burmese Buddhists, both monks and laypeople. He has supported seemingly democratic citizen protests (for example, against the controversial Chinese-run Letpadaung copper mine) but has also regularly fronted marches and protests that cast the Rohingya as a threat to the Burmese Motherland and call for their expulsion. He traveled to Meikhtila in the days following the violent conflict there; he was ostensibly there to be a "peacemaker" but in interviews and speeches continued to spread uncorroborated reports of the fighting that put the blame almost solely on Muslim residents.

Other prominent monks have also staked out seemingly contradictory positions, criticizing the former military regime for oppressing its citizens and restricting basic rights, yet supporting proposed bills that would limit and punish interreligious marriage, effectively nullifying the rights of minority religious groups. These laws tap into longstanding fears and rumors in Myanmar that Muslims are attempting to undermine Buddhism by marrying Buddhist women, forcibly converting them, and producing Muslim offspring. Some supporters of the law frame it as designed to protect women's rights (more on this later in the chapter), but women's groups in Myanmar have almost universally condemned the law as patronizing and ineffective. Despite public criticism, some monks have remained vociferous champions of the law, and it has also been taken up as policy by at least one major political party, the ostensibly progressive National Democratic Force.

The State Sangha Maha Nayaka Council (SSMNC), an official group of high-ranking monks, had been noticeably quiet during the unrest until finally issuing a statement at the end of August 2013 that barred groups from using the 969 symbol for political activities.

Their response highlights the challenge of navigating the gray area of monastic involvement in politics. While many Burmese welcome the occasional monastic intervention in times of crisis, many are also conflicted about or even adamantly opposed to regular monastic political engagement. In response to the SSMNC's recent ban on organizations using the 969 symbol for political activism, one monk responded, "We don't take part in political affairs . . . so you cannot say we violate the ethics of a Buddhist monk. We just make our special efforts in order to preserve our race and religion."[21] In fact, since the middle of 2013, Buddhist nationalist efforts have shifted away from the 969 movement and toward groups like the Organization for the Protection of Race, Religion, and Belief that seek political and legal pathways for promoting Buddhism and institutionalizing anti-Muslim policies.[22]

Fortunately, efforts on behalf of interreligious peace and understanding have also been increasing. Prominent monks such as Sitagu Sayadaw, Ashin Seikkeinda, and Ashin Sandadika have issued statements and participated in interfaith gatherings, creating space for lower-ranking monks and lay people to speak out and challenge the hitherto dominant narratives of hate, fear, and exclusion. Lay groups, especially multiethnic and multifaith youth organizations, have also taken the lead in condemning religiously motivated discrimination. In April 2014, civil society groups launched a new movement to guard against hate speech and dangerous speech, promoting "flower speech" (*panzagar*) that combats hate and leads to mutual understanding and respect.[23]

In order for these responses to be effective counters, they need to directly address the logic used by Buddhist nationalists, that Buddhism itself is under threat and that it is appropriate to use any means necessary to defend the religion from the threat of Islam. Of course, an important corollary to these efforts will be debunking the myth of the Islamic threat, while also addressing the social, economic, and political insecurities that make Buddhist communities inclined to accept these fear-based arguments.

It is important to note that there is nothing necessarily doctrinally "Buddhist" about this violence. That is, it has been carried out by Buddhists ostensibly in defense of Buddhism, but those inciting hatred or violence through their sermons have relied on rumors and traditional prejudices rather than the Buddha's teachings in stirring up their audiences. This does not mean that their arguments have not found fertile ground among Buddhists in Myanmar, where suspicion of and discrimination against Muslims is still common. Religious and political leaders have employed "defense of Buddhism" arguments in other contemporary contexts in order to justify bloody, antidemocratic policies, particularly violence against non-Buddhist religious groups perceived as a threat to Buddhism and, as explained earlier, it can be very dangerous for a Buddhist to be seen as refusing to protect the religion.

The role of women in society is another area where Buddhist influences are likely to be found, especially in this transitional period as more women are elected to positions in parliament and as the easing of (some) restrictions on speech and organizing allows more groups representing women's interests to emerge. The common narrative of gender politics in Burmese society has insisted on its egalitarian nature, at least relative to other countries. A 1958 article in the *Atlantic* by the academic and public figure Mya Sein is typical of this type of assessment, noting that the women of Burma have traditionally enjoyed broad rights of inheritance and arguing that what looks like female deference to men simply reflects traditional customs.[24]

However, access to positions of power or influence is by no means equal among the sexes in Myanmar. Mya Sein seemed to think that having six female members of parliament was sufficient in 1958; today there are only "twenty-five women MPs in the 440-seat Lower House . . . [and] four women MPs in the 224-seat Upper House."[25] The first and only female minister was appointed to be health minister in August 2012.[26] Unsurprisingly, women hold few positions of authority either within the *tatmadaw* (Burmese Armed Forces) or the many non-Burman nonstate armed groups currently negotiating cease-fires and political settlements.

In an interpretation of Buddhist teachings that is common in Myanmar and other Theravada countries, women are considered to be spiritually deficient. Mya Sein accepted this view when she explained that, because one can only become a Buddha as a man, men are inherently superior (although women can and do pray for a rebirth as a man, which would allegedly allow them quicker progress on the spiritual path). The quality of *hpoun* (power) and its accompanying political and social legitimacy are restricted to men only, leading many to believe that women cannot be effective in positions of authority. Even today, women are thought to be spiritually "polluting" by many Buddhists, putting further constraints on their opportunities and adding religious approval to misogyny and gender discrimination.

Burmese nuns (*thila-shin*) are one of the most marginalized and least respected groups in the country. Common Theravada tradition holds that, although the Buddha grudgingly agreed to create a female monastic community (*bhikkhuni*), the women of that lineage allowed their moral practice to degrade to such a degree that hundreds of years ago the community completely died out. By this reasoning, the *thila-shin* are not considered to be of the same level of spiritual attainment as (male) monks, despite the fact that they are compelled to follow a far more rigorous code of conduct. Most Burmese Buddhists give donations to monks based on how morally upright and prominent they are believed to be; monks also benefit from an institutionalized system of giving, where their meals and other requisites are virtually assured. *Thila-shin*, on the other hand, are generally not supported, forcing them to beg for donations, which reinforces a vicious cycle in which most people lose further respect for them due to this begging.

There are, of course, examples of respected and successful women in Myanmar's history. Yet gender bias and discrimination will be difficult to oppose when structural constraints and inequities are defended with reference to Buddhist teachings and traditions. One leader of a Buddhist organization defended the proposed interreligious marriage ban by saying that "our Buddhist women are not intelligent enough to protect themselves," an audacious statement that was immediately criticized by women's groups in the country.[27] There are other interpretations of Buddhism that would deny claims of women's "spiritual inferiority" by developing an argument that stems from the Buddha's statements that all physical characteristics are impermanent and ultimately irrelevant when viewed from the standpoint of enlightenment. These more progressive, egalitarian interpretations, however, face a significant impediment in the institutionalized and virtually unquestioned moral authority and social standing of monks.

As men who have ostensibly dedicated their lives to learning, transmitting, and preserving the teachings of the Buddha, members of the *sangha* command significant respect from Buddhists in Myanmar. In most situations when a lay person meets with a monk, he or she must make obeisance and sit lower than the monk during the conversation. The Burmese language even includes a special set of words and honorary titles that govern conversation with monks. Although many monks and lay people have described the organization of the *sangha* as "democratic,"[28] in practice it is an overwhelmingly hierarchical organization, where junior monks are expected to be deferential to those who are more senior and decisions are usually made by senior abbots or their advisers.

While these conventions of monastic authority are crucial in confirming the respect and honor that ought to be given to those who have dedicated their lives to religious practice, they can be an impediment to democratic activity, especially the presumption of equality in participation. In my interviews with political activists in 2011, several Karens (both Buddhists and Christians) expressed frustration that the social conventions that require lay people to be deferential to monks were counterproductive in the context of political organizing because most people found it difficult or impossible to disagree with (let alone criticize) a monk.[29] They also posed challenges in community development workshops that I attended in Chiang Mai in 2011. When discussions in mixed groups (monks, nuns, and lay people) reached a point of disagreement, often a more senior monk would "pull rank" in order to assert his opinion, or the nuns and lay people would simply revert to the deferential positions that they had temporarily abandoned in order to create a more egalitarian working environment.

Buddhism as Democratic Innovator

The theoretical study of politics—and of democracy in particular—has been largely situated within the conceptual boundaries of Western political thought. Increasingly, the relatively new subfield of comparative political theory has encouraged scholars to see non-Western systems of thought as just that: coherent *systems* of thought, with distinctive epistemological and ontological assumptions that sometimes differentiate them from the Western tradition in which most academics operate.[30] We can see this growing subfield as a "corrective" to the cultural specificity of the Western canon in political theory, but an equally important task of this work is to recognize non-Western systems of thought as equal partners in the task of theoretical inquiry.[31]

This section considers several Burmese sources to examine creative ways in which they envision democratic practice as a quintessentially moral activity. This conception of democracy fundamentally challenges dominant Western understandings with regard to both the procedures and purposes of democratic practice. Although these ideas obviously do not reflect the current state of democracy in the country, they do reveal a strand of Burmese political thought that is conscious of the dynamics of institutionalization of democracy and, more importantly, provide a resource for creatively reconfiguring politics to deepen democratic practice around the world.

Within the Burmese Buddhist tradition, one of the most creative innovators was the late nineteenth century royal adviser Hpo Hlaing. Working in the administrations of Mindon and Thibaw, the last two kings of the Konbaung dynasty in precolonial nineteenth century Burma, he attempted to combine insights from his own intellectual tradition with Western knowledge that he encountered. His *Rajadhammasangaha* ("Rules of Kingship"), a manual of advice written for King Thibaw in 1878, is a creative yet pragmatic work that attempts to interpret contemporary political situations using learning drawn from Buddhist texts and provides a starting point for understanding political participation as a moral activity.[32]

In the *Rajadhammasangaha,* Hpo Hlaing frequently situated Western political practices in the context of the Buddha's teachings and of Burmese political traditions, attempting to find a traditional anchor for the new practices he advocated for as well as legitimizing the Burmese tradition by demonstrating that the same principles had been at work there for centuries. He proposed an assembly in which the king would hold discussions with his officials in order to arrive at the best decision for the country, but he also had specific expectations for how this assembly would conduct its business, based on the rule of *sannipata* (unity) and *samagga* (harmony).[33]

Adherence to these rules was also the best way to ensure that a ruler would not fall prey to any of the four *agatis*, variously translated as "biases," "corruptions," or "partialities." The four *agatis* are desire, anger, fear, and ignorance. Hpo Hlaing acknowledged the challenges of living up to these standards, admitting, "for the average person in government service there is no way of avoiding these four wrong ways in his work."[34] However, he claimed that regular meetings would help people to avoid making decisions based on these factors: "In such assemblies what one man does not know another will; when one man has feelings of hate, another will not; when one is angry, another will be calm. When people have agreed in a meeting and preserve their solidarity, there will be no need for fear."[35]

A critical aspect of Hpo Hlaing's political advice is the way he saw mental states (and from a Buddhist perspective, unwholesome states) as influencing political decisions. While, in other parts of the text he prescribed what we might call "religious" methods (such as meditation), here he made it clear that the specific political practice of consulting with advisers could have multiple beneficial effects. It would guard against uninformed, biased, or rash decisions influenced by the four *agatis*, guide the ruler and all who participate away from self-interested action and from the negative mental states that generate ignorance and suffering, and result in consultative decisions that would be better for the country as a whole.

Houtman attributed to Hpo Hlaing "new ideas of law that see the individual as the ultimate self-responsible agent in society," and certainly many Burmese political thinkers have understood the success and development of a political community to depend to some degree on the moral conduct of its leaders and (more recently) its citizens.[36] Since the fall of the monarchy in 1886, they reasoned that political independence brought with it conditions in which each person was not only responsible for the consequences of his or her own actions, but for the effects those actions had on the prosperity of the community as a whole. If individual and collective moral behavior can affect the circumstances of a group, it follows that actions undertaken to strengthen individual moral conduct can also be seen as a type of political engagement, designed to uplift the community as a whole.

The negative qualities that Hpo Hlaing warned against would inevitably lead a nation to destruction. In a 1948 radio broadcast, Ba Lwin, a high school superintendent, turned peoples' criticism of government back on themselves, saying, "I feel that our own personal Government needs checking up first. Are we governed by greed, hatred, pride, suspicion, and ill-will? . . . Spiritual mobilization is the need of the hour."[37] However, attention to individual moral development would build a foundation for political prosperity. The Burmese monk Ashin Thittila has presented individual moral practice not merely as a complement to political participation, but as the only kind of political action that would lead to world peace and harmony. He insisted that, "For all the wheels to revolve in harmony the highest good in each must be developed; this is possible by the performance of daily duties with kindness, courtesy, and truthfulness."[38] Aung San Suu Kyi has also discussed both the challenge and the importance of individual moral practice for political actors. She remarked, "isn't there a saying that 'it is far more difficult to conquer yourself than to conquer the rest of the world?' So, I think the taming of one's own passions, in the Buddhist way of thinking, is the chief way to greatness, no matter what the circumstances may be."[39]

The examples cited above all support the argument that within Burmese Buddhist political thought there is a perspective that holds that the moral standing of an individual involved in politics is critical to the success of a political entity. Unfortunately, this perspective could also lead to disappointing conclusions regarding the feasibility of democracy. This is because of a persistent Buddhist view of human nature, which regards human beings as *pu htu zin*, not evil, yet morally flawed and enslaved to desire and guided by ignorance of the world as it really is. If Burmese Buddhists are skeptical of the ability of the average person to lead his or her own life in a morally upright way, what are the prospects for a democracy in which each person is expected to take part in ruling every other member of the polity?

These same examples contain the seeds of a creative answer to that dilemma. Hpo Hlaing focused on the political benefits of making decisions within an assembly but never considered that the process of engaging in collective discussion with a focus on building consensus could itself have a positive effect on the moral development of participants. Collective decisionmaking, undertaken under ideal institutional structures, can open individuals to alternate or opposing perspectives, eroding their own self-interest and functioning as a moral practice in itself. When, in the assembly, an individual's bias is revealed and he or she can see not only the perspective of another but also the benefit for the entire community of a particular decision, democratic participation can become a morally transformative activity itself.

The phrase "ideal institutional structures" should alert us to the challenge of arranging democratic practice in such a way that it supports these sorts of transformation engagements. Indeed, most activities described as democratic in modern political systems are transactional rather than transformational. Additionally, there is always the danger that communities of moral practice, being led by flawed and worldly human beings, can themselves become arenas of competition and hierarchy as members maneuver to gain status and position in society.[40] It is also possible that, by the same logic, assemblies could be "captured" by powerful individuals in ways that might subvert the expected moral and policy benefits. Yet this line of reasoning represents both a fruitful place for further theoretical exploration and a compelling justification for encouraging, extending, and deepening democratic practice that is rooted in Buddhist reasoning.

There is another important caveat here, in that Buddhism, while the religion of the majority, is only one of many in Myanmar, and Burmese Buddhists themselves exhibit a wide range of interpretations of Buddhist doctrine and traditions. Given the concerns expressed in the previous section about the overlap between Buddhism and Myanmar's national identity, it would be entirely counterproductive for the "moral development" described in this process to be usurped by a solely Buddhist understanding of morality. Yet, while it is true that the idea of completely overcoming the self is unique to Buddhism, the other religious traditions in Myanmar absolutely value the quality of selflessness and attention to the needs of others. Indeed, this could be the basis of an important revisioning of Myanmar citizenship, a conception in which the good citizen is not one who blindly subsumes his or her interests to the interest of the community, but who is an active participant in democratic governance at every level and who values the morally transformative possibilities of democratic political engagement.

These Burmese Buddhist perspectives not only contain resources for strengthening and deepening democratic practice in Myanmar, they are also fruitful sources that can contribute to and revitalize debates on democracy elsewhere. Recognizing democratic participation as a morally productive activity could refocus discussions of democratic institutions and processes, especially those that center on expanding participation. Understanding and incorporating Burmese Buddhist views on politics can complement or challenge the dominance of Western political concepts and practices and contribute to global conversations in which political ideas from all traditions are treated as equal partners in the task of theorizing human political interactions.

Conclusion

Buddhism is an almost infinitely malleable resource in the political realm. It can and has been used in contemporary Myanmar to legitimize democracy, promote political participation and self-government, valorize Buddhism and democracy as practices of "freedom," and claim equality on an ultimate spiritual level. However, it has alternately been used to vilify and restrict the democratic rights of minority communities as alleged "threats" to the religion and state, question the capacity of human beings to effectively govern themselves, argue for limitations on the absolute freedom to commit morally corrupt acts, and denigrate the moral capacity of women. All of these interpretations of Buddhist doctrine and of the role of Buddhism vis-à-vis the polity circulate among Burmese and will affect not only the possibility of continued political reforms but also the character of those reforms and of governance in Myanmar.

Some of these strands of interpretation are not only explicitly undemocratic, they also threaten the institutionalization of democracy by generating communal violence that underscores the long-standing military narrative that Myanmar's citizens require a managed or "disciplined" democracy. Yet the compelling logic of arguments regarding the protection of Buddhism should not be discounted by observers expecting an eventual "secular" transformation in the country. At the same time, Burmese interpretations of the Buddha's teachings contain innovative elements that can not only deepen democratic practice in Myanmar, but also contribute to global discussions of democratic thought. With a huge Buddhist majority, the moral-causal logic of Buddhism, regularly reinforced by the teachings of Buddhist monks, will continue to influence perceptions of politics in Myanmar.

Notes

1. There are also likely important differences *within* Burmese Buddhism, most of which have remained unexplored, for example urban/rural and ethnic distinctions.

2. See Gustaaf Houtman, "Mental Culture in Burmese Crisis Politics: Aung San Suu Kyi and the National League for Democracy," *Monograph Series* 33 (Tokyo: Tokyo University of Foreign Studies, Institute for the Study of Languages and Cultures of Asia and Africa, 1999), and Stephen McCarthy, "The Buddhist Political Rhetoric of Aung San Suu Kyi," *Contemporary Buddhism* 5, no. 2 (2004): 67–81.

3. Aung San Suu Kyi, *Freedom from Fear: And Other Writings* (New York: Penguin Books, 1991), 167.

4. Ibid., 173–174.

5. Ibid., 171.

6. Ibid., 182.

7. Ibid., 229.

8. Ibid., 230.

9. Ibid.

10. Ibid.

11. Zaw Naung Lin and Thant Zin Oo, "At Opening of Buddhist University, Sitagu Sayadaw Exhorts Political, Religious, and Social Organizations to Be United." *The Messenger*, 30 June 2011.

12. Sitagu Sayadaw, "On the Day of the Exalted Buddha's Enlightenment, Buddha's Ten Perfect Messages," *7 Day News*, 30 June 2011.

13. This information is in a self-published pamphlet that includes a narrative of the founding and activities of the group as well as their communications leading up to the protests.

14. According to Ashin Issariya, the articles in these journals were written by him and several other monks. They used a number of different pseudonyms, so none of the names in the following section refer to real individuals.

15. Hti La Aung, "Burma and Democracy," *Ottama Journal,* no. 2 (January 2007): 38. Unless otherwise noted, all translations from Burmese to English are the author's own.

16. Sanda Shin, "Our Desire." *Ottama Journal,* no. 5 (January 2009): 16.

17. Sermon given by Ashin Eindaga at the Thirty-fourth Street *Taya Pwe* on 31 January 2011.

18. "Eviction Order for Burma Monk Shwe Nya War Sayadaw," *BBC News*, 15 December 2011. Available at www.bbc.co.uk/news/world-asia-16198935 (accessed 15 September 2013).

19. Matthew Walton, "Myanmar Needs a New Nationalism," *Asia Times Online,* 20 May 2013. Available at www.atimes.com/atimes/Southeast_Asia/SEA-02-200513.html (accessed 15 October 2013).

20. The following paragraphs are drawn from Matthew Walton, "Buddhism Turns Violent in Myanmar," *Asia Times Online,* 2 April 2013. Available at www.atimes.com /atimes/Southeast_Asia/SEA-01-020413.html (accessed 15 October 2013).

21. May Sitt Paing, "Buddhist Committee's 969 Prohibitions Prompts Meeting of Movement Backers," *Irrawaddy*, 10 September 2013. Available at www.irrawaddy.org /archives/43711 (accessed 15 September 2013).

22. Win Naung Toe and Nay Myo Tun, "Myanmar Leader Backs Buddhist Monks' Calls for Laws to 'Protect' Religion, Race," *Radio Free Asia*, 27 February 2014. Available at www.rfa.org/english/news/myanmar/laws-02272014174350.html (accessed 7 April 2014).

23. Tun Tun Thein, "Nay Phone Latt Leads Campaign Against Hate Speech," *Democratic Voice of Burma,* 6 April 2014. Available at www.dvb.no/news/nay-phone-latt-leads-campaign-against-hate-speech-burma-myanmar/39355 (accessed 7 April 2014).

24. Daw Mya Sein, "The Women of Burma," *Atlantic*, 1 February 1958. Available at www.theatlantic.com/magazine/archive/1958/02/the-women-of-burma /306822 (accessed 15 September 2013).

25. Myat Kyaw Thu, "Burma Has First Woman Cabinet Member in over 60 Years," *Mizzima,* 10 September 2012. Available at www.mizzima.com/news/myanmar/7968-burma-has-first-woman-cabinet-member-in-over-60-years (accessed 15 September 2013).

26. Ibid.

27. "Monks and Religious Leaders Back Interfaith Marriage Ban," *Democratic Voice of Burma,* 26 June 2013. Available at www.dvb.no/news/politics-news/monks-and-religious-leaders-back-interfaith-marriage-ban/28988 (accessed 15 September 2013).

28. See, for example, Gokuldas De, *Democracy in Early Buddhist Samgha* (Calcutta: Calcutta University, 1955).

29. Personal interviews, Yangon, 8 March and 16 July 2011.

30. See, for example, Fred Dallmayr, *Border Crossings: Toward a Comparative Political Theory* (Lanham, MD: Lexington Books, 1999); Roxanne Euben, *Enemy in the Mirror: Islamic Fundamentalism and the Limits of Modern Rationalism* (Princeton, NJ: Princeton University Press, 1999); and Farah Godrej, "Toward a Cosmopolitan

Political Thought: Non-Western Texts and the Methodology of Comparative Political Theory." Ph.D. dissertation (Washington, DC: Georgetown University, 2006).

31. Leigh Jenco, "'What Does Heaven Ever Say?' A Methods-Centered Approach to Cross-Cultural Engagement." *American Political Science Review* 101, no. 4 (2007): 741–755.

32. Hpo Hlaing's text in Burmese is reproduced in Maung Htin, *Yaw Mingyi U Hpo Hlaing's Biography and "Rajadhammasangahagyan"* (Yangon: Unity Publishing House, 2002); however, for consistency in this chapter I use the English translation by L. E. Bagshawe, *Rajadhammasangaha,* Online Burma/Myanmar Library, 2004, which is available from www.ibiblio.org/obl/docs/THE_RAJADHAMMASANGAHA.pdf (accessed 24 June 2012).

33. Bagshawe, *Rajadhammasangaha,* 151.

34. Ibid., 174.

35. Ibid.

36. Houtman, "Mental Culture in Burmese Crisis Politics," 89.

37. Bwa Lin, "Burma," in *Burma Speaks: A Collection of Broadcast Talks from the Burma Broadcasting Station* (Rangoon: Government Printing and Stationery, 1950).

38. Ashin Thittila, *Essential Themes of Buddhist Lectures* (Rangoon, Burma: Department of Religious Affairs, 1987), 55.

39. Aung San Suu Kyi, *Letters from Burma* (London and New York: Penguin Books, 1997), 162.

40. Ingrid Jordt, *Burma's Mass Lay Meditation Movement: Buddhism and the Cultural Construction of Power* (Athens: Ohio University Press, 2007).

7

Ethnic Politics in a Time of Change

Martin Smith

Ethnic conflict and military-backed governments have remained enduring features of state failure and national instability since Myanmar's independence from Great Britain in 1948. In March 2011, another military veteran, ex-general Thein Sein, assumed presidential office, introducing the fourth system of government since the colonial departure.[1] At the time, the Myanmar government was one of the most isolated and condemned in the international community. After decades of unending conflict, Myanmar stood near the bottom of international league tables in everything from health and education to poverty and corruption, and over two million refugees, migrants, and internally displaced persons, mostly ethnic minorities, crowded around the country's borderlands.[2] Economic relations had been improving with Asian neighbors but, located in the international frontline, those neighbors also shared many cautions over what the new political era might bring.

It was thus against most domestic and international expectations that the new system of "disciplined democracy," implemented by President Thein Sein, would do much to change the long-standing patterns of conflict in national politics. Despite a spread of cease-fires with armed ethnic groups during the 1990s, the former State Peace and Development Council (SPDC) regime had done little to address nationality grievances and political reform during more than two decades in power. Moreover, with Aung San Suu Kyi and the National League for Democracy (NLD) also facing repression and restrictions, the 2010 general election that brought Thein Sein and the promilitary Union Solidarity and Development Party (USDP) to office had been widely boycotted by prodemocracy and ethnic groups. In particular, the reservation of 25 percent of all seats for armed forces (*tatmadaw*) representatives in the legislatures was widely regarded as a strategy to ensure military domination in government into the twenty-first century.

Despite this unpromising start, the next three years saw a significant change in the political and ethnic environment, heralding the most important realignment in national politics since General Ne Win and the *tatmadaw* first seized power in 1962. The release of political prisoners, relaxation of some media restrictions, and gradual liberalization in other aspects of daily life were welcomed by Aung San Suu Kyi and the NLD, which won forty-three seats in the legislatures in the 2012 by-elections. Meanwhile the Thein Sein government broadened the ethnic peace offers of the previous SPDC regime, and, from a hesitant beginning, this saw a further spread in cease-fire agreements to include the majority of armed ethnic groups in the country within two years.

The international community was quick to support such change. As the doors to the country opened, international sanctions were reduced, business investors and aid funds poured in, and hopes grew that protagonists on the various political and ethnic sides might finally work together to resolve the country's many serious problems. The need for ethnic peace was a constant refrain. Speaking in July 2013, President Thein Sein promised the international community that by the year's end "the guns will go silent everywhere in Myanmar for the very first time in over 60 years."[3] "We are aiming for nothing less than a transition from half a century of military rule and authoritarianism to democracy," he said.[4]

After three years of the new political system, however, a more cautious sentiment began to set in. Many citizens were yet to see real improvements in the quality of their lives, and parties across the political and ethnic spectrum questioned the reform direction within the country. The perception was widespread that the government's main intention was to entrench the USDP-*tatmadaw* in office. With such negative practices as economic cronyism and political arrests still continuing, constitutional amendments were called for as essential for democratic progress to succeed.[5] "Hopes Were High for Burma But Is the Honeymoon Over?" headlined the *Irrawaddy* magazine in March 2014.[6]

Such opinions resonated among ethnic minority peoples who constitute an estimated one-third of the population and inhabit all the restive borderlands. After decades of warfare, building trust with minority communities was always going to be difficult for the new government. Ethnic leaders and parties also wanted to take part in dialogue and national reform, but they were not strongly represented in the new political system. With armed conflict and repression continuing, ethnic-based parties had generally criticized the 2008 constitution and been marginalized in the 2010 general election.[7] Equally critical, new volatility faced minority peoples in the transition to a new system of government. President Thein Sein's peace outreach to all armed ethnic groups in the country had been welcomed, and this was encouraged by his 2011 decision to suspend construction of the China-backed Myitsone dam in Kachin State. Finally, it was hoped, there was a central government in Myanmar ready to consult with local peoples over political and economic decisions affecting their lives.

Subsequent events, however, raised new concerns, with many ethnic parties questioning whether the government in Naypyitaw really had control over *tatmadaw* officers and business interests in the field. As the ethnic peace intermediary Harn Yawnghwe summarized, "Can President Thein Sein be trusted?"[8]

Since 2011, land-grabbing has increased in the borderlands, major international investments such as the oil and gas pipelines to China have been pushed through, and, despite Thein Sein's promises to halt offensive operations against armed ethnic groups, *tatmadaw* commanders have continued to launch attacks, especially in the Kachin and Shan States where the government has key economic and political interests.[9] Over a thousand combatants and unknown numbers of civilians were reported to have died in these operations, and an estimated 100,000 civilians fled their homes in an area where there had previously been more than seventeen years of ceasefires.[10] The severity of this conflict during 2011–2013 did much to undermine opposition confidence in Thein Sein's peace overtures.

Ethnic tensions were then further raised by Buddhist-Muslim violence that broke out in the Rakhine (Arakan) State in 2012 before spreading to other parts of the country. The communal conflict between the ethnic Rakhine population and the minority Muslims, many of whom self-identify as Rohingya, is undoubtedly one of the most difficult challenges that the country faces. But with the government and security services often appearing to take the side of Buddhist Rakhines, the consequences for Muslim communities have been devastating. Around 140,000 civilians have been displaced (predominantly Muslims) and over 250 persons (also mostly Muslims) were reported to have been killed in a crisis that presently appears no nearer to finding just and inclusive solutions.[11]

After three years of the Thein Sein–USDP government, such continuing outbreaks of violence raised fundamental questions about national reform and the future of multiethnic politics in the country. Ethnic doubts and local conflict renewed in March 2014 when the government decided to go ahead—with international donor backing—with a disputed population and housing census, the first since 1983, to count and quantify the peoples of Myanmar. It was not just Muslim-related groups who raised concerns about the ways in which they were being delineated without effective consultation and input. The name *Rohingya* did not appear on the official census list, while the rest of Myanmar's population was subdivided into an extraordinary "135 national races."[12] This was a list that the Thein Sein–USDP government had uncritically accepted from the former SPDC and which was widely rejected as inaccurate and poorly planned—whether by accident or design.[13]

Thus, as the clock began to wind down toward Myanmar's next general election in 2015, political and ethnic tensions once again began to rise. There was general acceptance that important steps had been started toward dialogue and national reconciliation during the past three years, and there appeared to be no turning back to the isolationist repression of the recent past. For the moment, however, peace and reform were not set in political stone, and a ruling elite from the SPDC era still remained in power. Rather, the national landscape appeared to be one of new "winners and losers" under the post-2011 political system; urgent constitutional change was called for by the NLD and other prodemocracy groups; and ethnic peace and inclusion had yet to be achieved in the troubled borderlands.[14] In short, Myanmar was still at the beginning of a time of change, not at the end, and pressures continued to mount for reform on the many political and socioeconomic tasks still at hand.

The Contemporary Landscape

In July 2013, President Thein Sein acknowledged three key components in Myanmar's process of national transformation: political reform, from a state-centered to a free market economy, and from armed conflict to a "just and sustainable peace."[15] Such words had resonance for citizens from all ethnic backgrounds. Progress in all three areas is regarded essential, if trust in the new political system is to build. The difficulties, however, in delivering such change are immense. There is no shortage of political, economic, and peace ideas on the different sides, but until now, there has not been consensus on national reforms or agreement on the timetable and mechanisms by which inclusive debate and participation can be achieved.

As in all decades since independence, Myanmar's political landscape continues to be fragmented and the number of parties claiming or promoting ethnic representation has increased since the Thein Sein–USDP government came to power. In early 2014, for example, there were over twenty electoral parties that had stood or won seats in the 2010 general election, and another seven still active in the United Nationalities Alliance (UNA) that had won seats in the 1990 election but boycotted the 2010 polls (see Fig. 7.1).

Among armed ethnic groups, there were officially over a dozen with cease-fires with the government, including those that previously had cease-fires from the SPDC era, such as the United Wa State Army (UWSA) and New Mon State Party (NMSP), and those that had only agreed cease-fires with the Thein Sein–USDP government, such as the Karen National Union (KNU) and Karenni National Progressive Party (KNPP). Meanwhile, there were still a number of armed ethnic groups without formal cease-fires, notably the Kachin Independence Organisation (KIO) and Ta-ang (Palaung) National Liberation Army (TNLA) in northeast Myanmar where cease-fires with the SPDC had broken down since Thein Sein assumed office (see Fig. 7.2).

Figure 7.1: Ethnic Political Parties

Elected to the legislatures (2010)
All Mon Regions Democracy Party[a]
Chin National Party[a]
Chin Progressive Party
Ethnic National Development Party[a]
Inn National Development Party[a]
Kayan National Party[a]
Kayin People's Party
Kayin State Democracy and Development Party[b]
Lahu National Development Party[c]
Pa-O National Organisation[a, b]
Phalon-Sawaw [Pwo-Sgaw] Democratic Party[a]
Rakhine Nationalities Development Party[a]
Shan Nationalities Democratic Party[a]
Ta-ang (Palaung) National Party[a, b]
Unity and Democracy Party of Kachin State[d]
Wa Democratic Party[a]

Electoral parties that did not win seats (2010)
All National Races Unity and Development Party (Kayah State)[e]
Asho Chin National Party[f, g]
Danu National Democracy Party[f, g]
Federal Union Party[g]
Kachin Democratic Party[g]
Kachin State Democracy Party[g]
Kachin State Progressive Party[h]
Kaman National Progressive Party
Khami National Development Party
Kokang Democracy and Unity Party[i]
Mro or Khami National Solidarity Organization[i]
Northern Shan State Progressive Party[h]
Rakhine State National Force
Tai-leng (Red Shan) Nationalities Development Party[f, g]
Wa National Unity Party[f, i]

Parties from 1990 election in 2002 United Nationalities Alliance (boycotted 2010 election)
Arakan League for Democracy[j]
Kachin State National Congress for Democracy
Kayin (Karen) National Congress for Democracy
Mon National Democratic Front (now Mon National Party)[j]
Shan Nationalities League for Democracy[j]
Shan State Kokang Democratic Party[j]
Zomi National Congress (now Zomi Congress for Democracy)

Source: Transnational Institute, "Burma's Ethnic Challenge: From Aspirations to Solutions," *Burma Policy Briefing* No. 12 (Amsterdam: TNI-BCN, 2013).

Notes: These are intended as a contemporary snapshot, with parties varying considerably in history, size, and influence. With ongoing changes in the run-up to the 2015 general election, not all details will be exact. The complexity of the ethno-political landscape is only likely to stabilize if inclusive political agreements are reached.

a. Nationalities Brotherhood Federation participant; b. ceasefire group connection; c. party from 1990 election; d. government-backed; e. withdrew due to political pressures; f. Nationalities Brotherhood Federation participant; g. formed 2012–2013; h. registration not accepted due to ceasefire group connection; i. party from 1990 election; j. allied in the 1998 Committee Representing the People's Parliament with the National League for Democracy

Figure 7.2: Armed Ethnic Opposition Groups

Arakan Liberation Party[a, b]
Arakan Army
Chin National Front[a, b, c]
Democratic Karen Benevolent Army[d]
Hongsawatoi Restoration Party
Kachin Independence Organisation[b, c, e]
Karen National Union[a, b, c]
KNU/KNLA Peace Council[d]
Karenni National Progressive Party[a, b, c]
Kayan New Land Party[b, d]
Lahu Democratic Union[b, c]
Myanmar National Democratic Alliance Army (Kokang)[c, f]
National Democratic Alliance Army (eastern Shan State)[d]
National Socialist Council Nagaland (Khaplang faction)[a]
National United Party Arakan/Arakan National Council[c]
New Mon State Party[b, c, d]
Pa-O National Liberation Organisation[a, c]
Rohingya Solidarity Organization
Shan State Army-North[b, c, d]
Shan State Army-South[a]
Ta-ang (Palaung) National Liberation Army[c]
United Wa State Army[d]
Wa National Organisation[c]
All Burma Students Democratic Front[a, g]

Notes: a. Post-2011 ceasefire; b. present or former National Democratic Front member; c. United Nationalities Federal Council member; d. SPDC-era cease-fire, continued post-2011; e. SPDC-era cease-fire, broke down 2011; f. SPDC-era cease-fire, split and breakdown 2009; g. Nonnationality force, based in ethnic territories

Complicating the picture further, there were over twenty ethnic Border Guard Forces (BGFs), some of which were former cease-fire groups, as well as progovernment militia, four of which were headed by elected members of the legislatures (see Fig. 7.3). Equally important, as government restrictions lessened, there has been a rapid expansion in ethnic-based civil society organizations (CSOs). Along with faith-based groups, these are also influential in community life, becoming widespread in many parts of the country today.[16]

Despite such division, many ethnic nationality leaders remained confident that peace and national reconciliation can be achieved, provided that there is progress on two interlinked issues in the future: agreement on political reform and a nationwide cease-fire.[17] "Until and unless we get political rights, we cannot end the civil war," said Tu Ja, a former KIO leader seeking parliamentary election.[18]

Figure 7.3: Border Guard Forces and Militia

Border Guard Forces (established 2009–2010)

BGF Battalion Number	Former Name/Description
1001-3	New Democratic Army–Kachin[a, b]
1004-5	Karenni Nationalities Peoples Liberation Front[a]
1006	Myanmar National Democratic Alliance Army (Kokang)[a, b]
1007	Lahu militia, Mongton, Shan State[c]
1008	Akha militia, Mongyawng, Shan State[c]
1009	Lahu militia, Tachilek-Mongkoe, Shan State[c]
1010	Wa militia, Markmang, Shan State[c]
1011-22	Democratic Karen Buddhist Army[a, b]
1023	Karen Peace Force (ex-KNU 16th battalion)[a, b]

Cease-fire Groups or Breakaway Factions that Have Become Militia (*pyithusit*)

Kachin Defense Army (ex-KIO): now Kaungkha Militia
Lasang Awng Wa Peace Group (ex-KIO)
Mon Peace Defense Group (ex-NMSP)
Mong Tai Army Homein (Homong) Region
Pa-O National Organization[d]
Palaung State Liberation Party[d]
Shan State Army–North (3 and 7 Brigades)

Other Militia Under *Tatmadaw* Regional Commands

There are over fifty local militia, and their titles vary. The strongest are in the Shan State. The best known include:

Common Name	Location
Pansay Militia[e]	Muse Township
Kutkai Militia[e]	Kutkai Township
Tar Moe Nye Militia[e]	Kutkai Township
Mong Paw Militia[e]	Muse Township
Mangpang Militia	Tangyan Township
Monekoe/Phaunghsai Militia	Mongko Township
Monhin/Monha Militia	Mongyai Township
Ahdang Militia	Putao Township, Kachin State

Notes: a. Former cease-fire group; b. Connected party or leaders won seats in 2010 election; c. Former *tatmadaw*-controlled militia; d. Connected party or leaders won seats in 2010 election; e. Leader won seat in 2010 election

The challenge, then, is how this will be achieved. Opposition united fronts have long been a feature of Myanmar's volatile political landscape, and over the years there have also been conflicts between different ethnic groups.[19] But since the Thein Sein–USDP government assumed office, there has been an acceleration in ethnic-based activities and collaboration over common aims that have not been witnessed in many decades. Among armed groups, the twelve-party United Nationalities Federal Council (UNFC) has emerged as the main voice for political representation and negotiations, while among electoral parties a number of unifying activities have been underway. These include the formation of a fifteen-party Nationalities Brotherhood Federation (NBF), which wants to promote a single Federal Union Party (FUP) in the 2015 general election, and there has also been agreement to unite parties from the 2010 and 1990 polls, such as the Rakhine Nationalities Development Party and Arakan League for Democracy.[20] During these discussions, meetings between armed and electoral groups have become commonplace in different parts of the country—a practice that was risky and often forbidden under the SPDC regime.[21]

By early 2014, however, frustration was clearly growing among many ethnic groups over the shape and pace of national reform. While the greater sociopolitical openness in the country was appreciated, many leaders believed that the Thein Sein government, USDP, and *tatmadaw* were playing for time while entrenching their own institutional and economic positions under the new political system. Opposition parties wanted change well before the 2015 general election so that, unlike in 2010, they could prepare for what they wanted to be genuinely democratic and "free and fair" polls. But on neither nationwide peace nor constitutional reform did substantive changes look imminent that would meet many of their most fundamental demands.

Among ethnic groups, three major difficulties stood out in building trust and bringing all sides to the table. First, even while peace talks had been continuing, the *tatmadaw* was still launching attacks—on various pretexts—against the KIO, TNLA, and allied Shan State Army–North (SSA-N) in northeast Myanmar.[22] Such operations and the ongoing suffering of local communities exacerbated doubts as to who was really making government decisions in the country—President Thein Sein or the *tatmadaw* commander-in-chief Senior General Min Aung Hlaing.[23] Notably, too, concerns were also expressed about the ongoing conflict and civilian displacement among the majority Bamar (Burman) population, including by the 88 Generation Students. Charity events were held in Yangon, and in 2013 there were peace marches from Yangon and Mandalay to the KIO "capital" at Laiza—events without parallel in Myanmar's recent history.[24] International worries were also voiced. As Buddhist-Muslim violence spread from the Rakhine State, international agencies estimated that the number of internally displaced persons had grown under the Thein Sein–USDP government to around 650,000, with another 120,000 refugees officially still staying in Thailand—most of them ethnic minorities.[25]

Second and related to this, as opposition groups pointed out, the different Kachin, Shan, and Ta'ang forces in northeast Myanmar had all had cease-fires with the previous SPDC regime. These dated back two decades, during which many efforts had gone into trust and community building.[26] It was, in fact, only under the Thein Sein–USDP government that these treaties had broken down, and this grievance increased the resolve of ethnic parties to ensure guaranteed and durable agreements now. Since independence in 1948, there have been failed peace attempts before.[27] Furthermore, opposition groups were angered in recent years by the *tatmadaw*'s increasing promotion of cease-fire BGFs and local militia as a form of pacification in their areas, some of which were involved in illicit narcotics production and other corrupt activities.[28] As elsewhere in the world, the twin issues of conflict and narcotics have long been interlinked, but in Myanmar's case, illicit opium production has actually escalated during the recent cease-fires, with an estimated 26 percent increase during 2012–2013.[29] Such ambiguities and failures underpinned ethnic mistrust. Speaking on the sixty-fifth anniversary of "Karen Resistance Day," the KNU's veteran chairman General Saw Mutu Sae Poe warned the Karen people and "patriotic leaders" that "due to our experiences as Ethnic Armed Organisations we need to be prudent and cautious."[30]

Finally, and equally contentious, there was growing resentment that, while the Thein Sein–USDP government was gaining all the international plaudits and relief from economic sanctions, the *tatmadaw* and government-favored companies appeared to be using their positions to pursue their own business interests in the ethnic borderlands—whether advantaged by cease-fires in the south of the country or military maneuvers in the northeast. By 2014, Thein Sein's suspension of the controversial Myitsone dam appeared very much a government exception, and, with Chinese lobbying continuing, there were many concerns that this mega project would ultimately be resumed.[31]

Some economic plans were still in their early stages, but a number of major projects were underway. In northern Myanmar, key businesses include the jade mines in Kachin State and the new oil and gas pipelines passing from Rakhine State through the northern Shan State to China.[32] In eastern and southern Myanmar, projects include hydroelectric dams in the Shan, Kayah, and Karen States and the Dawei (Tavoy) development project in the Thanintharyi (Tenasserim) Region.[33] Supported by various Chinese, Thai, and Myanmar investors, there seemed little benefit to the local peoples in many borderland areas, causing ethnic leaders to call for a moratorium on outside investments until real peace has been achieved. "Their existence can lead to land grabbing and forced labour here," claimed Tar Gyoke Jar, the TNLA vice-chairperson. "Moreover, by citing investments, they [the government army] may also wage attacks."[34] Community groups, too, became very vocal in protest. The exploitation of resources in Kayah State, criticized by the Karenni Civil Society Network, was "equivalent to a new economic offensive against the Karenni people," despite the government's 2012 cease-fire with the KNPP.[35]

For such military and economic reasons, leaders of the UNFC and other ethnic parties remained reluctant during 2011–2013 to sign a joint "nationwide cease-fire agreement" between all groups and the government, until there was political dialogue at which such fundamental issues were resolved. All sides recognized the need for such an inclusive agreement, if the whole country were to benefit and progress during a national time of change. It was largely this conviction that kept the peace talk momentum continuing when major crises emerged.

There were, however, some very different views about what such a historic treaty might mean. Ethnic-based parties, for example, wanted firm political commitment in a symbolic accord of the political legitimacy and national resonance of the Panglong Agreement that drew up the ethnic principles for the new Union of Burma back in 1947. In contrast, government officials, while also wanting a high-profile occasion to which they could invite international dignitaries, promoted the signing of a nationwide cease-fire first and only dealing with political and demilitarization issues afterward. Ethnic parties suspected this as a trap to delay real change and marginalize opposition groups further. Thus, although various humanitarian and reconciliation programs in Chin, Karen, Mon, and other cease-fire areas helped to encourage community confidence, these were never going to be enough to achieve a political breakthrough and nationwide peace.[36]

Throughout 2013, this disagreement went back and forth, and toward the year's end the differences between opposition groups and the government grew deeper following a UNFC conference attended by seventeen armed ethnic parties in KIO territory at Laiza. In response to an eleven-point UNFC position statement,[37] a tough twenty-five-point reply was issued by government representatives at the next round of peace talks a few days later in Myitkyina.[38] Reflecting *tatmadaw* input, the new peace draft limited the ability of armed ethnic groups to organize, appearing to blame them for national conflict and calling upon them to disarm.[39] *Tatmadaw* officers were known to be particularly upset that, in the Laiza agreement, ethnic signatories called for a national "federal army" to ensure ethnic inclusion and representation.[40]

Subsequently, peace talks resumed with a new Nationwide Cease-fire Coordination Team (NCCT) set up by sixteen ethnic organizations to negotiate with the government's Union Peacemaking Work Committee (UPWC), headed by Aung Min, a minister in the president's office. They, in turn, set up a joint working group in March 2014 to draft a nationwide cease-fire pact, and it was agreed to bring in parliamentary and *tatmadaw* representatives—a key ethnic demand—during the next stages of discussions. Although government and *tatmadaw* motives were still suspected, the

UPWC team would consist of nine members: three each from the *tatmadaw*, parliament, and government.[41] Previously, *tatmadaw* representatives had often appeared conspicuous by their absence in cease-fire talks. Rather, other actors had appeared to be driving the organization and momentum of peace meetings and activities. These included the government-affiliated Myanmar Peace Centre, Norwegian-backed Myanmar Peace Support Initiative, and Euro-Burma Office-Supported Working Group on Ethnic Coordination.[42] With all sides now apparently on board, a new target deadline of 1 August 2014 was proposed by *tatmadaw* leaders as the date for signing a nationwide cease-fire.[43] It was not achieved.

There were still many challenges. After decades of conflict, it should not be surprising that so many difficulties remained—from politics and the economy to the resettlement of displaced persons and humanitarian affairs. But, as NCCT and UWPC teams continued efforts to draft a nationwide cease-fire (completing a second draft in May), there was still no clear consensus on an inclusive process and political agreement within the country by which so many objectives might be achieved.

Political and Military Challenges

With careful planning and mutual benefit, protagonists on the different sides have long recognized that the actual agreement of cease-fires is not an unassailable task in Myanmar's conflict landscape. Indeed the establishment of cease-fires and the *tatmadaw*'s bolster of local militias had become an increasing feature of borderland life under the SPDC regime. This, however, did not lead to demilitarization nor reduction in the number of government or armed ethnic troops, causing many citizens to ask, "War and peace: what's the difference?"[44] It should be stressed, therefore, that accusations of corruption and human rights violations have not followed government forces alone in the war zones.[45] As in any time of conflict resolution in the world, the transformation to demilitarization and peace will need many different elements, involving different armed groups and stakeholders, to rebuild communities, establish civilian-based government, end human rights violations, and allow democracy and legal justice to grow.

Clearly, then, peace-building in Myanmar will be a complex task. At the same time, cognizance must be paid to the reality that, over the years, ethnic grievance and armed conflict have been sustained by two main issues: political failure and military domination over many aspects of the government and the people's lives.

For this reason, calls have been persistent among ethnic-community and political leaders for many decades that progress is needed in two key areas for a cease-fire process that will truly endure: political reform that restores genuine rights to the peoples and a cease-fire treaty that ensures demilitarization by all sides. It was these two issues that returned to the top of the political agenda in 2014 as attention turned among different parties and stakeholders to what a "nationwide cease-fire agreement" might mean. The gulf between government and opposition groups still appeared very wide.

On political reform, there were still many different opinions. In principle, the 2008 constitution had delineated a greater number of ethnic nationality rights, which included a number of innovations in representation at the three levels of legislature (lower and upper houses of parliament and fourteen state/region assemblies). The seven ethnic states (Chin, Kachin, Karen, Kayah, Mon, Rakhine, and Shan) from the 1974 constitution had been maintained along with seven regions (formerly divisions), where the majority Bamars mostly live. In addition, new "self-administered" territories were demarcated for the Danu, Kokang, Palaung, Pa-O, and Wa in the Shan State and Naga in the Sagaing Region. Equally new, twenty-nine electoral seats were reserved for "national race" populations in the states and regions where they formed smaller minorities. On this basis, another seven nationalities for the first time gained a form of political representation: Akha, Bamar, Intha, Kayan, Lahu, Lisu, and Rawang.[46] This meant that twenty ethnic groups were now demarcated in different ways on Myanmar's political map.

In practice, however, ethnic nationality leaders complained that such political representation had, so far, meant very little. Indeed, as they pointed out, many prodemocracy and ethnic groups had taken no part in drawing up the 2008 constitution. Among many objections, USDP-*tatmadaw* domination existed at all levels of the legislatures; 25 percent of all seats continued to be reserved for *tatmadaw* appointees; the chief ministers of the states and regions were chosen by the president; and the new legislatures had proven quite incapable of representing local peoples in preventing conflict, land-grabbing, and other forms of economic exploitation under the new political system. Moreover, it was not only ethnic-based parties that wanted constitutional change. For example, without reform, the NLD leader Aung San Suu Kyi would be barred from becoming president, even if her party should win the 2015 polls.[47] In response to such criticisms, a parliamentary committee was set up to receive submissions and review the 2008 constitution. As the months pass by, however, doubts are widespread that any major changes will be allowed before the 2015 general election by the *tatmadaw*, which still has effective control over constitutional reform.[48]

To try and break this deadlock, both ethnic and prodemocracy groups continue to put up ideas and proposals for national change. Behind these discussions is the underlying dilemma as to whether the present political system is reformable—and, if so, how? Ethnic representatives, in particular, are very aware that, if they sign a nationwide cease-fire agreement, government and *tatmadaw* leaders want this to signify acceptance of the 2008 constitution—something the ethnic representatives had not, until now, been prepared to do.[49]

Against this backdrop, political brainstorming continued. There were arguments, for example, as to whether the constitution can really be reformed by "amendment," with the UNFC and its ethnic allies instead wanting a complete "rewriting"[50]; there was discussion on proportional representation to secure political and ethnic balance in the legislatures[51]; many nationality parties, including UNFC and UNA members, promoted an ethnic state system for the whole country, adding a new state for the Bamar majority as well[52]; and all opposition groups, including the NLD, wanted an end to reserved seats for military officers in the legislatures. For their part, *tatmadaw* leaders continued to proclaim their special role as protectors of the 2008 constitution during the transition to democracy.[53]

In general, however, the majority of ethnic-based and prodemocracy organizations—whether electoral, armed, or CSO—showed preference for a union or "federal" system of government, as envisaged at independence in 1948, in contrast to the "unitary" system wanted by the SPDC generals and established under the 2008 constitution. Importantly, voicing such a federal demand was allowed in Myanmar's new political environment. After many years of suppression, the *federal* term no longer appeared taboo. During 2013, everyone from the parliament speaker ex-general Shwe Mann and Aung San Suu Kyi to the ethnic-based NBF, UNA, and UNFC spoke of the potential for a federal system in the country.[54] Community-based groups also voiced support, with CSOs calling for a "democratic federal state" on the twenty-fifth-year anniversary of the 8-8-88 protests.[55] And, as interreligious violence rocked the country, faith-based groups also called for profederal change. "This nation belongs to all and a true federalism will bring lasting peace and development," the Catholic Bishops' Conference said in a public statement.[56]

If there were major exceptions to federal demands among ethnic parties, these were groups in the China borderlands, notably the cease-fire UWSA and National Democratic Alliance Army, which had once been close to the Communist Party of Burma and prioritized the establishment of "autonomous states" or "regions" for their peoples. Although invited, these two groups were not taking part in the nationwide cease-fire drafting but said they would be ready to sign if they approved.[57] Leaders of the SSA-S, too, were absent from the drafting, but they also indicated readiness to sign once an acceptable treaty had been achieved.[58]

Important discussions and meetings, therefore, lay ahead. In theory, the challenge appeared not so much the federal goal, but achieving a federal system suitable to Myanmar and which all sides would accept.[59] But whether *tatmadaw* and USDP leaders would allow commitment to federal or any other kind of constitutional reform in a nationwide cease-fire agreement was still widely doubted. During 2012–2014, government leaders had prioritized a nationwide truce, giving very few indications over future intentions or who was actually making the key policy decisions. Indeed it was even unclear whom the *tatmadaw* might support as the next president after 2015, with President (ex-general) Thein Sein, Parliament Speaker (ex-general) Shwe Mann, and the present commander-in-chief Senior General Min Aung Hlaing all thought to be in the frame.

With these concerns in mind, attention began to focus on the second important element in the cease-fire accord: a military agreement that all sides will accept while political reform takes place. In early 2014, the immediate prospects did not look good. Despite various peace and confidence-building measures, ethnic forces remained on military alert.[60] Memories were still raw from the SPDC's 2009 orders for all cease-fire forces to transform into Border Guards Forces under *tatmadaw* control. This was an order most of the larger groups had refused and that witnessed a *tatmadaw* offensive against the Myanmar National Democratic Alliance Army in the Kokang region of Shan State.[61] The operation was led by Min Aung Hlaing, who later succeeded Senior-General Than Shwe as commander-in-chief.

Subsequently, twenty-three BGF battalions were established (see Figure 7.3), further dividing many ethnic minority communities in the field. In consequence, ongoing military attacks during 2011–2014 against Kachin, Shan, and Ta'ang forces in northeast Myanmar strengthened a view that, whatever the peace terms offered by President Thein Sein's negotiation teams, the *tatmadaw* and USDP government were still playing a game of "divide and rule." In particular, the belief remained strong that, whether through cease-fires or military operations, the *tatmadaw* has a long-term strategy of "regional clearance" and "regional control" operations to undermine the resistance of ethnic opposition groups in the new political era.[62]

It was for this reason that UNFC leaders say they put up the headline-grabbing demand for a "federal army" at the Laiza conference in 2013—that is, they wanted to remind all sides that political reform, demilitarization, and national change are not just for ethnic opposition groups but for the Bamar-majority *tatmadaw* as well.[63] After decades of conflict, they argue that a federal-based army, including local ethnic police and military forces, will be essential for national peace and inclusion. But during the first half of 2014, the government still appeared to want ethnic signatories to "disarm and disband" after the agreement of a nationwide cease-fire. This is something that few are likely to agree to. As the NMSP vice-chairperson and NCCT leader Nai Hongsa explained, "From our side, we have our security concerns and also we have a wish to establish a genuine union army. So we still have quite a lot to negotiate to reach a deal on this."[64]

Thus the stage was delicately set. The fact that talks were continuing and cease-fires generally holding demonstrated that there are leaders on all sides who are committed to trying to establish a nationwide peace. But for the moment, even with a national cease-fire accord, there appears to be no inalienable agreement on the key political and military challenges that have long underpinned conflict and state failure in the country. Without sincerity and compromise, a technical exercise in cease-fire procedures will not be sufficient. As political veterans remembered, previous changes in government and national politics have also seen peace talks and cease-fires at different times in the past, notably in 1948–1949, 1963–1964, and after 1988.[65] But none had addressed the root causes of grievance and conflict. The question therefore remained whether, this time, a peace enterprise under a new government will achieve the solutions that have long been desired.

An Outlook to the Future

As the international doors to Myanmar opened during the past three years, it was undoubtedly a time of change. While there may not have been a "fall of the Berlin Wall" moment, new dynamics, space, and energy have emerged in a long-restricted and conflict-torn environment. For the first time in decades, there are hopes of a better future, and there seems no immediate prospect of a regression to the isolationism and totalitarianism of previous military governments. It is accepted that many difficulties lie ahead in democratic and economic transition. But ethnic-based parties and leaders are eager to be central participants in any activities of reform. If the holy grail of just political and cease-fire agreements can be found, then they trust that nationality parties can freely stand in elections for the legislatures; political, cultural, and economic rights will be protected; local autonomy will be respected; internally displaced persons and refugees can return to their homes; and demilitarization will be begun in the ethnic borderlands and conflict zones around the country. All such steps will be needed in the coming years to cement a durable peace.

The problem, however, is that change is still very much at an early stage, often raising more questions than answers. For the moment, unless very dramatic events intercede, the same *tatmadaw* and ruling elite are in power, ensuring that they continue to be the managers of change in the country, as they have in every decade since General Ne Win's "Military Caretaker" administration in 1958. In contrast, both prodemocracy and ethnic-based parties remain uncertain of their places in Myanmar's future.

During the next two years, it is likely that the success or failure of a nationwide cease-fire, constitutional amendments, and the result of the 2015 general election will do much to answer the most immediate questions about the future direction of the country. But at present, it is unclear whether the new Myanmar state will evolve in the multiethnic direction of India, the one-party domination of China or Vietnam, or, as critics fear, the example of Cambodia where, despite an abundance of international aid, the same political and business elite are in power and the majority of the population remains poor and often marginalized.

In Myanmar's present landscape, therefore, it is possible to pick out both negative and positive trends for the future. The legacies of decades of humanitarian suffering and socioeconomic underachievement are still widely visible. During the past three years, important starts have been made on redressing some of these issues, but there is still a long way to go. As the outgoing UN special rapporteur on human rights Tomás Ojea Quintana stated in his final report, although there have been "significant changes" of improvement during the past few years, abuses against minority groups have continued, the *tatmadaw* "retains a prevailing role" in national life and institutions, and democratic transition is still "fragile."[66] "A critical step will be to secure cease-fire and political agreements with ethnic minority groups, so that Myanmar can finally transform itself into a peaceful multi-ethnic and multi-religious society," he said.[67]

On the negative side, as Quintana warned, continuing conflict, political arrests, and economic exploitation have done much to fuel a potential new generation of grievances. Especially concerning, a rise in a militant Buddhist-based nationalism, which the authorities appear to support, has seen a new wave of religious- and ethnic-based violence spread across the country.[68] In consequence, many peoples fear that, rather than being an exceptional case, a dominant Buddhist nationalism will be an increasing feature of Myanmar life in the new political era. As critics noticed, the NLD and other prodemocracy parties also appeared reticent to publicly speak up on the rights of minority peoples during the past two years, knowing that electoral victory in the 2015 polls may depend on taking populist positions among the Buddhist and Bamar majority.[69]

The international community, too, has come in for criticism. For while the influx of Western aid has generally been welcomed, there is a perception that much has been too close to the government, premature, and not always wisely spent.[70]

Various examples can be presented. But in ethnic politics, a particular controversy is the 2014 population and housing census, supported by the UNFPA and Western government donors with a budget of US$74 million. Amid a wide array of criticisms, not only did donors allow the census to go ahead with the confusing "135 national races" list, there also appeared no awareness that under the 2008 constitution the enumeration of ethnic groups could impact the rights of citizenship and representation.[71] Equally unhelpful, as conflict continued in the Kachin, Rakhine, and Shan States, the census went ahead without effective local consultation before a nationwide cease-fire had been completed, war zones could be restored to peace in the ethnic borderlands, and the looming 2015 general election had taken place. All sides have accepted that a national census is needed; the issue is more one of timing and preparation. In Myanmar's future, therefore, it is vital that international aid and development activities are conducted with local participation to support national reconciliation and interethnic understanding, rather than becoming the source of new confusions and protest.[72]

On the positive side, different examples can also be selected to, conversely, show encouraging trends. While political reforms are still in their infancy, there can be no doubt that the increased openness, social liberalization, and media freedoms over the past three years have helped the improving national climate. Progress has been uneven, especially in the ethnic borderlands. But whether in the legislatures, cease-fire talks, or expanding networks of civil society groups, political and ethnic issues are being discussed and dealt with in interactive ways that were previously forbidden or constricted. As yet, there has been no quantum leap of change in state institutions or the functioning of government, but on current trends, there remain hopeful voices that democratic reform will ultimately be sustained. Prodemocracy and ethnic groups, however, stress that they very much want significant constitutional change before the 2015 general election so as to prevent another USDP-*tatmadaw* nexus dominating the next years of government as well. For the moment, such reform change is not guaranteed.

On ethnic peace, the success or failure of a nationwide cease-fire is likely to be the key from which everything follows under the Thein Sein presidency. Whether addressing political, military, or humanitarian challenges, little can be done without an all-embracing cease-fire to which all sides are committed. Experience has long shown that individual agreements between the government and different ethnic groups will not be sufficient to achieve national stability and reform. Over the decades, successive military governments might have become very capable at controlling a conflict-torn environment. But, in the twenty-first century, such a perennial state of strife and unrepresentative system of governance are leaving Myanmar well behind its powerful neighbors.

There are therefore many imperatives why a nationwide cease-fire and political reform are essential. The actual shape and timetable of such measures, however, are yet to be agreed upon. To date, there have been many initiatives, but the phrase "peace process" has been used too early. As critics point out, the real authorities in the government are yet to come to the negotiating table, while presidential appointees and the government-affiliated Myanmar Peace Centre, who are mostly ethnic Bamars and the main intermediary faces, have no mandate to make political decisions.[73] On the conflict frontlines, many of the present cease-fires remain very tenuous.

In summary, as government and ethnic nationality teams continue efforts to achieve a nationwide cease-fire, the stakes are very high. If a nationwide cease-fire is agreed to in the coming months that all sides find politically acceptable and are prepared to commit to, then for the first time since conflict broke out at Myanmar's independence there will be an accord by which an inclusive process toward peace, reconciliation, and reform can be developed. But in the present political era, this cannot simply be a paper document. The warnings from history are very clear. Peace success will very much depend on following through with genuine political, ethnic, and economic reforms in the coming years if the cycles of grievance, conflict, and militarization are to be ended.

Notes

1. The others were parliamentary democracy (1948–1962), General Ne Win's "Burmese Way to Socialism" (1962–1988), and the military State Peace and Development Council (initially State Law and Order Restoration Council [SLORC], 1988–2011).

2. In the United Nations Development Programme's 2011 Human Development Index, Burma was placed 149th out of 187 countries, below all its Asian neighbors except Nepal.

3. "President Thein Sein's Speech at Chatham House (The Royal Institute of International Affairs)," London, 15 July 2013.

4. Ibid.

5. See, for example, Jason Motlagh, "A Promised Political Amnesty in Burma Remains Incomplete," *Washington Post*, 24 February 2014.

6. Thin Lei Win/Thomson Reuters Foundation, "Hopes Were High for Burma But Is the Honeymoon Over?" *Irrawaddy*, 10 March 2014.

7. See, for example, Transnational Institute, "Ethnic Politics in Burma; the Time for Solutions," *Burma Policy Briefing* No. 5 (Amsterdam: TNI-Burma Centrum Netherlands, February 2011).

8. Harn Yawnghwe, "Can President Thein Sein Be Trusted?" *Democratic Voice of Burma,* 16 August 2013.

9. See, for example, John Buchanan, Tom Kramer, and Kevin Woods, "Developing Disparity: Regional Investment in Burma's Borderlands" (Amsterdam: Transnational Institute-Burma Centre Netherlands, February 2013); Karen Human Rights Group, "Losing Ground: Land Conflicts and Collective Action in Eastern Myanmar," Report No. 2013-01 (Thailand: KHRG, March 2013); Earthrights International, "'There Is No Benefit, They Destroyed Our Farmland': Selected Land and Livelihood Impacts Along the Shwe Natural Gas and China-Myanmar Oil Transport Pipeline from Rakhine State to Mandalay Division," April 2013; Bertil Lintner, "A Well-Laid War in Myanmar," *Asia Times,* 2 February 2013; Transnational Institute, "The Kachin Crisis: Peace Must Prevail," *Burma Policy Briefing* No. 10 (Amsterdam: Transnational Institute-Burma Centre Netherlands, March 2013).

10. See, for example, ibid., *Policy Briefing* No. 10; Edward Chung Ho, "Time for Thein Sein to Come Clean About Burmese Losses in Kachin State," *Kachin News Group*, 22 September 2012; Anthony Davis, "Pyrrhic Victory in Myanmar," *Asia Times*, 31 January 2013; UN Office for the Coordination of Humanitarian Affairs, "Myanmar: Countrywide Displacement Snapshot," November 2013; Michel Gabaudan and Melanie Teff, "Myanmar: Act Immediately to Protect Displaced People's Rights," Refugees International Field Report, 17 March 2014.

11. See, for example, ibid, Gabaudan and Teff; IRIN, "Rakhine Sectarian Violence—One Year On," 13 June 2013; International Crisis Group, "The Dark Side of Transition: Violence Against Muslims in Myanmar," *Asia Report* No. 251, 1 October 2013; Fortify Rights, "Policies of Persecution: Ending Abusive State Policies Against Rohingya Muslims in Myanmar," February 2014.

12. See, for example, International Crisis Group, "Myanmar Conflict Alert: A Risky Census," 12 February 2014; International Crisis Group, "Counting the Costs: Myanmar's Problematic Census," Update Briefing, Asia Briefing No. 14, 15 May 2014; "Ethnicity Without Meaning, Data Without Context: The 2014 Census, Identity and Citizenship in Burma/Myanmar," TNI-BCN *Burma Policy Briefing* No. 13, February 2014. Terms for nationality identity in the Burmese language—that is, *lu-myo* ("kinds of people") who are designated as *taingyinthar* (approximately, "indigenous")—can be problematical, relate to groups considered to be inhabitants before the first British annexation in 1824, and do not easily translate into the English word *ethnic*.

13. Ibid.

14. "Suu Kyi Calls on Govt, Military to Help Amend Constitution," *Democratic Voice of Burma*, 6 January 2014.

15. Thein Sein, "President Thein Sein's Speech."

16. For example, 29 Kachin CSOs issued a statement in March 2014 criticizing the national census. "The Statement by Kachin Civil Society Organisations Concerning the 2014 Myanmar Population and Housing Census," 9 March 2014. The same week, 90 Karen Buddhist monks and Christian pastors from religious organizations across Myanmar issued a statement calling for measures to support peace-building: "Karen Monks, Pastors Voice Support for Peace Process," *Democratic Voice of Burma*, 14 March 2014. Elsewhere, the Burma Rivers Network, a 15-group alliance, issued a list of over 33,000 people and 131 CSOs that called for the suspension of all hydro-projects on the Salween River that crosses four ethnic states. Burma Rivers Network, "Press Statement on International Day of Action for Rivers Against Dams," 14 March 2014.

17. See, for example, Lawi Weng and Saw Yan Naing, "KNU Airs Grievances to Thein Sein Ahead of Nationwide Cease-fire Talks," *Irrawaddy*, 6 January 2014.

18. Seamus Martov, "Kachin Rebel Turned Politician Readies for Comeback," *Irrawaddy*, 14 September 2013.

19. See, for example, Martin Smith, *Burma: Insurgency and the Politics of Ethnicity* (London and New York: Zed Books, 1991 and 1999).

20. "Arakan Alliance," *Democratic Voice of Burma*, 9 March 2014. It is intended that the FUP will contest in constituencies countrywide where no local member parties are standing.

21. In 2005, for example, several prominent Shan leaders were arrested and sentenced to jail terms of between 75 and 106 years for high treason following a meeting in Taunggyi. These included Major-General Hso Ten of the cease-fire Shan State Army-North and Hkun Htun Oo of the Shan Nationalities League for Democracy, the second largest-winning party in the 1990 election. They were only released in 2011–2012 under amnesty by the Thein Sein–USDP government.

22. See, for example, Kyaw Kha and Lawi Weng, "Army Increases Attacks in North Burma, Seizes 2 Shan Rebel Camps," *Irrawaddy*, 4 March 2014. The government explanation for military operations has varied, such as to halt illegal logging or for census security. See, for example, Colin Hinshelwood, "18 Kachin Villagers Captured by Burmese Army in Mansi," *Democratic Voice of Burma*, 2 February 2014; International Crisis Group, "Counting the Costs," 14–15.

23. See, for example, "Govt Must Show 'Sincerity' in Peace Dialogue," *Karen News*, 7 February 2014; "After Attacks, Kachin Rebels Must Rethink Peace Process: Gun Maw," *Irrawaddy*, 17 February 2014. See also note 49.

24. See, for example, Transnational Institute, "The Kachin Crisis."

25. See, for example, "Myanmar: Countrywide Displacement Snapshot," UN OCHA, November 2013; "Programme Report: January to June 2013," The Border Consortium, 16–21. The majority are Kachin, Karen, Karenni, Mon, and Shan as well as Muslim populations in the Rakhine State. There are also over two million migrants, many of them illegal, in Thailand, Malaysia, and India.

26. In the Kachin State and northern Shan State, cease-fires with the various Kachin, Palaung, and Shan forces were agreed between 1989 and 1994.

27. Smith, *Burma: Insurgency*.

28. See, for example, *Shan Drug Watch Newsletter*, no. 4 (October 2011); Free Burma Rangers, "Opium, Logging and Gas: the Burma Army's Predatory Rule over the People of Burma," 17 March 2014, www.freeburmarangers.org; Tom Kramer, Ernestien Jensema, Martin Jelsma, and Tom Blickman, "Bouncing Back: Relapse in the Golden Triangle" (Amsterdam: Transnational Institute, June 2014).

29. "Myanmar Opium Fight Failing; Soldiers Shooting Up," Associated Press, 17 March 2014.

30. "Address of KNU Chairman General Saw Mutu Sae Poe on the 65th Anniversary of Karen Resistance Day," 31 January 2014.

31. See, for example, May Sit Paing, "Thein Sein Violated the Official Contract," *Irrawaddy*, 11 March 2014.

32. See, for example, Saw Yan Naing, "From Jade Land to a Wasteland," *Irrawaddy*, 21 February 2014; Shwe Gas Movement, "Drawing the Line: The Case Against China's Shwe Gas Project, for Better Extractive Industries in Burma," September 2013; Earthrights International, "There Is No Benefit"; Buchanan, Kramer and Woods, "Developing Disparity."

33. See, for example, ibid.; Burma Rivers Network, "Press Statement,"; Shan Human Rights Foundation, "Large-Scale Land Confiscation for Salween Dam Infrastructure in Northern Shan State," 13 February 2014; Paul Vrieze and Htet Naing Zaw, "Dawei Awaits Its Destiny," *Irrawaddy*, 22 February 2014; "The Bad Oil—Companies Occupy Relocated Villages' Land," *Karen News,* 19 December 2013.

34. Thida Linn, "TNLA Calls for Postponing Major Investments in Their Region until Cease-fire," *Eleven Myanmar*, 1 March 2014. See also, for example, "KNU Wants Genuine Peace Before Dam Construction Resumes," *Democratic Voice of Burma,* 17 March 2014.

35. Feliz Solomon, "Stop Salween Dams, say 34,000 People in Burma," *Democratic Voice of Burma,* 14 March 2014.

36. See, for example, "Lessons Learned from MPSI's Work Supporting the Peace Process in Myanmar," Myanmar Peace Support Initiative (MPSI), March 2014; and "MPSI Facilitated Projects," available at www.mmpeacemonitor.org /images/pdf/mimu_1024v01_20130613_mpsi_facilitated_projects.pdf.

37. "11-Point Common Position of Ethnic Resistance Organizations on Nationwide Cease-fire," Ethnic Armed Organisations Conference (Laiza, 2 November 2013).

38. Lawi Weng, "Mon Group Rejects 'Unacceptable' Govt Cease-fire Proposal," *Irrawaddy*, 19 November 2013.

39. "The Nationwide Cease-fire Agreement Between the Union of the Republic of Myanmar and the Ethnic Armed Organisations," undated, 2013.

40. "Ethnic Leaders Stress Need for Federal Army in Post-Cease-Fire Myanmar," Radio Free Asia, 26 November 2013.

41. "New Committee Formed to Draft Myanmar Nationwide Cease-Fire Pact," Radio Free Asia, 10 March 2014; "Peace Talks Have Been 'Extremely Positive': Hla Maung Shwe," *Democratic Voice of Burma,* 16 March 2014. It was also planned that there should be nine NCCT and five non-NCCT representatives. But although sometimes present at peace meetings, non-NCCT groups did not take regular part. Opposition suspicions centered on the role of the government's Union Peacemaking Central Committee with which the president and UPWC liaised. Its eleven-man membership was very similar to the powerful National Defence and Security Council. See, for example, "Ethnic Resistance Reps to Meet in Myitkyina," *Shan Herald Agency for News,* 8 May 2014.

42. Since 2011, different international actors have been involved in pro-peace activities, including Japan's Nippon Foundation. For analyses of ethnic and cease-fire events, see, for example, Myanmar Peace Support Initiative, "Lessons Learned from MPSI's Work" 2014; Burma News International, *Deciphering Myanmar's Peace Process: A Reference Guide 2013* (Chiang Mai:Wanida Press, 2013), and updates, including 2014 guide, available at www.mmpeacemonitor.org.

43. "Military Calls for Cease-fire Deal to be Signed by August 1," *Eleven Myanmar*, 11 March 2014.

44. See, for example, Tom Kramer, "Neither War Nor Peace: The Future of the Cease-fire Agreements in Burma" (Amsterdam: Transnational Institute–Burma Centre Netherlands, July 2009).

45. For an analysis of the logging trade in which government, business, and armed ethnic and Chinese groups have been complicit, see, for example, Global Witness, "A Disharmonious Trade: China and the Continued Destruction of Burma's Northern Frontier Forests," October 2009. For recent corruption reports, see, for example, Saw Yan Naing, "From Jade Land to a Wasteland," *Irrawaddy*, 21 February 2014; Saw Yan Naing, "'Peace Permit' Bonanza Puts Ethnic Groups on Defensive," *Irrawaddy*, 20 December 2013. For post-2011 use of child soldiers and landmines by the *tatmadaw* and different ethnic forces, see, for example, Human Rights Watch, "'Untold Miseries': Wartime Abuses and Forced Displacement in Burma's Kachin State," 20 March 2012; "Chance for Change: Ending the Recruitment and Use of Child Soldiers in Myanmar," Child Soldiers International, January 2013; "Landmine Monitor 2013 Myanmar/Burma Country Report," International Campaign to Ban Landmines, November 2013.

46. The complete list: Bamar (5), Karen (5), Chin (3), Shan (3), Pa-O (2), Rakhine (2), Lisu (2), Akha, Intha, Kachin, Kayan, Lahu, Mon, Rawang (1).

47. See, for example, Daniel Pye and Tha Lun Zaung Htet, "Aung San Suu Kyi Says Burma to Amend 'World's Most Difficult' Constitution," *Irrawaddy*, 10 May 2013; Jared Ferrie, Reuters, "Burma's Constitution Likely to Dash Suu Kyi's Presidential Hopes," *Irrawaddy*, 20 June 2013.

48. See, for example, Ei Ei Toe Lwin, "Constitution Body Takes Military Veto off the Table," *Myanmar Times*, 14 March 2014; Sanay Lin, "Army MPs Slam Suu Kyi's Remarks on Charter Reform," *Irrawaddy*, 14 May 2014.

49. See, for example, Nang Seng Nom and Yen Snaing, "'When Political Problems Are Solved, There Will Be No More Battles,'" *Irrawaddy*, 13 March 2014.

50. Sai Wansai, "Amendment or Rewriting: 51 Years on Burma Still Overwhelmed by Constitutional Crisis," *Shan Herald Agency for News,* 13 August 2013.

51. See, for example, "Proportional Representation for Burma?" *Mizzima News*, 31 July 2012; Richard Horsey, "Shifting to a Proportional Representation Electoral System in Myanmar?" paper presented at SSRC Conflict Prevention and Peace Forum, 31 January 2013; Kay Zin Oo, "NLD, Ethnic Parties Unite in Push for Constitutional Reform Before 2015 Election," *Mizzima News*, 20 June 2013.

52. Kay Zin Oo, "New Constitution Will Be Ready in a Month: Ethnic Groups," *Mizzima News*, 5 September 2013.

53. "Tatmadaw's National Politics Is to Safeguard Country," *New Light of Myanmar,* 28 March 2013; "Military Will Continue to Play Political Role, Says Army Chief," *Mizzima News*, 27 March 2013. See also note 48.

54. Nang Mya Nadi, "Shwe Mann Reiterates His Support for Federalism," *Democratic Voice of Burma,* 3 September 2013; "Without Federal System, Myanmar's Peace Agenda Will Be Difficult—House Speaker," *Eleven Myanmar,* 4 September 2013; Nyein Nyein, "Suu Kyi, Ethnic Leaders to Work Toward Federal Union," *Irrawaddy*, 18 June 2013; "UNFC Statement of the Ethnic Nationality Conference," 2 August 2013.

55. "Civil Society Groups Call for Creation of a 'Federal State' During 8888 Anniversary," *Democratic Voice of Burma*, 8 August 2013.

56. "Statement by the Catholic Bishops' Conference of Myanmar: To the Leaders and the People of Myanmar," 24 June 2013.

57. May Kha, "Wa Leaders Ask President for Autonomous State," *Irrawaddy*, 3 March 2014.

58. "Yawdserk Dismissed Media Report on Separate Cease-fire Deal," *Shan Herald Agency for News,* 17 March 2014. One other locally influential group missing from the cease-fire drafting was the National Socialist Council Nagaland, part of which is based upon the Myanmar side of the border with India. The Bamar-majority All Burma Students Democratic Front was also not always involved. But it is not regarded as an "ethnic" party.

59. See, for example, "Speaker Says Myanmar Cannot Copy Federal Systems from Other Countries," *Eleven Myanmar*, 11 August 2013; Bertil Linter, "Finding a Federal Model that Fits," *Irrawaddy*, 8 March 2014.

60. See note 42.

61. See, for example, Tom Kramer, "Burma's Cease-fires at Risk: Consequences of the Kokang Crisis for Peace and Democracy," *Peace & Security Briefing* No. 1, (Amsterdam: Transnational Institute–Burma Centre Netherlands, September 2009).

62. See, for example, "Fresh Tensions with Shan Army Have Implications for Wa," *Shan Herald Agency for News,* 15 February 2013.

63. This view was put to the author by several different ethnic leaders.

64. "Disarm and Disband Proposal Worries Ethnic Armies," *Democratic Voice of Burma,* 14 March 2014; Ei Ei Toe Lwin, "Drop Military Demands or We'll Quit Peace Process, NCCT Warns," *Myanmar Times,* 2 May 2014.

65. See, e.g., Smith, *Burma: Insurgency*.

66. Tomás Ojea Quintana, "Report of the Special Rapporteur on the Situation of Human Rights in Myanmar," Human Rights Council, Twenty-fifth session, Agenda item 4, 12 March 2014.

67. Ibid.

68. The issue remains highly controversial. See, for example, Hannah Beech, "The Face of Buddhist Terror," *Time Magazine,* 1 July 2013; "Time Magazine Misinterpretation Rejected," Republic of the Union of Myanmar President Office, Nay Pyi Taw, 23 June 2013; Htet Naing Zaw and Lawi Weng, "Spiritual, Political

Leaders Question Need for Burma Religious Law," *Irrawaddy*, 19 March 2014. See also note 11.

69. "Suu Kyi Pressed on Rohingya Citizenship," *Irrawaddy*, 16 November 2012; Joseph J. Schatz, "Burma's Aung San Suu Kyi, a Human-Rights Icon, Is Criticized on Anti-Muslim Violence," *The Washington Post*, 23 December 2013; Deborah Snow, "Aung San Suu Kyi: Kachin Ethnic Group Boycotts Visit to Opera House," *Sydney Morning Herald*, 28 November 2013.

70. See, for example, Hanna Hindstrom, "Norway Defends Controversial Peace Initiative," *Democratic Voice of Burma*, 31 May 2012; Bertil Lintner, "Misguided Engagement in Burma," *Development Today,* no. 6/7 (3 July 2012); Carey L. Biron, "Debt Relief Package for Myanmar Unusually Generous," *Inter Press Service*, 28 January 2013; Lex Rieffel and James W. Fox, "Too Much, Too Soon? Foreign Aid and Myanmar," Nathan Associates, March 2013.

71. See note 12. Yen Naing, "Burma Census Data May Be Used Politically: Official," *Irrawaddy*, 22 May 2014.

72. For a few days in March, see, for example, "The Statement by Kachin Civil Society Organisations," 9 March 2014; Nang Mya Nadi, "Shans Plan Their Own Census," *Democratic Voice of Burma,* 13 March 2014; Nang Mya Nadi, "Mons Count Heads to Justify National Race Representatives," *Democratic Voice of Burma,* 15 March 2014; Lawi Weng, "Wirathu Joins Arakanese Protest Against Census," *The Irrawaddy*, 17 March 2014; "International Karen Community Wants Burma's Census Postponed," *Karen News*, 17 March 2014; Ko Htwe, "Burmese Islamic Group Issues Census Directives," *Democratic Voice of Burma,* 19 March 2014.

73. Saw Yan Naing, "Peace Brokers Lack a Mandate: Burma Expert," *Irrawaddy*, 18 March 2014; "Gov't-Sponsored MPC Is Not Trustworthy, Say Ethnic Federations," *Eleven Myanmar*, 13 March 2014.

8

Governance and Political Legitimacy in the Peace Process

Ashley South

The peace process that began in Myanmar in late 2011 probably remains the best opportunity in decades to address political, social, economic, and cultural issues that have driven conflict between the government and ethnic groups since independence.[1] However, the May 2013 agreement that halted fighting between government forces and the Kachin Independence Organization (KIO) remains deeply problematic as of mid-2014, with government forces having recently relaunched military operations against Kachin and allied ethnic armed groups (EAGs) in northern Myanmar. Nevertheless, for the first time in the country's history, most major EAGs are engaged in (albeit protracted and difficult) negotiations to consolidate existing cease-fires and achieve a lasting peace agreement. Despite recent setbacks, this can be considered a significant and historic peacemaking achievement.[2] However, a number of serious issues remain unresolved. The peace process is unlikely to result in a substantial and sustainable process of peace-building, unless these issues are addressed.[3] This will be difficult given the long history of mistrust among key stakeholders and the failures of understanding and action evident among key external actors, including international actors who ostensibly support the peace process.

Despite the agreement of cease-fires between most EAGs and the government, the facts on the ground in many ethnic nationality–populated conflict-affected areas have not changed. For many communities, the Myanmar Army continues to be experienced and perceived as a predatory and violent intruder, although in some cases conflict-affected communities are clearly experiencing the benefits of peace. In order for the peace process to be successful, initial cease-fires between the government and EAGs need to be consolidated (or in the case of Kachin and northern Shan States, respected); a substantial and credible political dialogue needs to commence between the government, the Myanmar Army and other mainstream political actors, and representatives of the country's diverse ethnic communities; solutions need to be found to a number of urgent issues that threaten to undermine trust and confidence in the peace process. It is also necessary that international aid donors, and others (including private sector interests) seeking to support or otherwise engage with the peace process, inform themselves about the complex dynamics of conflict in Myanmar, take care that their interventions are conflict sensitive, and wherever possible do no harm.

There is a risk that, should the peace process fail, the broader reform process underway in Myanmar could be threatened. This is evident in moves by Myanmar politicians in mid-2013 to position themselves vis-à-vis the 2015 elections by criticizing the government's handling of negotiations with EAGs. With Myanmar assuming chairmanship of the Association of Southeast Asian Nations (ASEAN) regional grouping in 2014, in the run-up to elections the following year, political leaders are likely to be increasingly distracted and/or caught up in games of zero-sum electoral politics. Such tensions tend toward a view that in mid-2014 the window of opportunity to make progress on peace in Myanmar is closing. Likewise, the window of opportunity for ethnic political leaders to achieve maximum leverage will begin to recede as the 2015 elections approach. Arguably, for the first time since independence, ethnic issues are at the heart of Burmese politics. Ethnic politicians are therefore keen to maximize the advantage of this historic moment. At the same time, EAGs negotiating cease-fires and a subsequent political dialogue understand that, if they are unable to achieve an agreement that addresses their communities' fundamental concerns and aspirations, such a pact is unlikely to be credible.

The success of the peace process depends on several factors, including the degree to which Myanmar's political leaders feel a sense of ownership. This includes the expectation that whatever government may take power after 2015 will inherit the legacy of many decades of often bitter conflict and also the hopes for a better relationship between the state and the country's diverse ethnic groupings. The key question is the role and positions of the Myanmar Army. Is the *tatmadaw* willing to participate in (or at least allow) negotiations that will address the key concerns and hopes of ethnic communities? Or, are Myanmar Army leaders fundamentally "unreconstructed" and unwilling to envisage the remaking of state-society relations in the country, which will be necessary to achieve a sustainable and equitable peace?

This chapter necessarily has a provisional character, reflecting uncertainties inherent in the peace process itself. Furthermore, there are lacunae, as key events and data are not yet in the public domain. Where not otherwise stated, primary data come from the author's field notes and are current as of May 2014.

This chapter does not address the pressing issue of anti-Muslim violence in Myanmar. Unlike conflict between EAGs and the government and army, which in principle can be solved through political negotiations, the problem of intracommunal violence is perhaps more intractable and difficult to solve. Nevertheless, this is one of the most urgent issues facing the country during this challenging period of transition.

Background[4]

Non-Burman communities make up at least 30 percent of Myanmar's population.[5] During the precolonial period, ethnic identity was diffuse, with ethnolinguistic characteristics being one among several markers of sociopolitical position. The political salience of ethnicity became reinforced during the colonial period, so that by the time of independence in 1948, ethnicity had become a defining category of political orientation. In the lead-up to independence, ethnic nationality elites sought to mobilize communities in order to gain access to political and economic resources, demanding justice and fair treatment for the groups they sought to represent. Burman and minority elites having failed to successfully negotiate a pacted transition to independence, the late 1940s saw widespread outbreaks of violence.[6] By the time the Karen National Union (KNU) went underground in January 1949, the country had embarked on a civil war that was to last more than six decades.[7] The ensuing armed conflict was marked by serious and widespread human rights abuses on the part of both the *tatmadaw* and, less systematically, EAGs.

For more than half a century, ethnic nationality–populated rural areas of Myanmar have been affected by conflicts between ethnic insurgents and a militarized state, widely perceived to have been captured by elements of the ethnic Burman majority.[8] For decades, communist and dozens of ethnic insurgents controlled large parts of the country. Since the 1970s, however, armed opposition groups have lost control of their once extensive "liberated zones," precipitating further humanitarian and political crises in the borderlands. For generations, communities have been disrupted, traumatized, and displaced. In 2011, there were an estimated 500,000 internally displaced people (IDPs) in the southeast alone, plus some 150,000 predominantly Karen refugees living in a series of camps along the Thailand-Burma border.[9] In the nearly two years since the start of cease-fire negotiations in late 2011, the number of displaced people in southeast Myanmar has been considerably reduced, while it has increased dramatically in Kachin and Rakhine (Arakan) States as a result of war and communal violence.

A previous round of cease-fires in the 1990s brought considerable respite to conflict-affected civilian populations. These truces (twenty-five agreements in total) provided the space for civil society networks to (re)emerge within and between ethnic nationality communities. However, the then military government proved unwilling to accept ethnic nationality representatives' political demands for substantial political discussions, resulting in significant autonomy agreements. Therefore, despite some positive developments, the cease-fires of the 1990s did little to dispel distrust between ethnic nationalists and the government. Trust was further eroded in April 2009, when the government proposed that the cease-fire groups transform themselves into Border Guard Forces (BGFs) under the direct control of *tatmadaw* commanders. Several of the less militarily powerful cease-fire groups accepted transformation into BGF formations. However, most of the larger groups resisted, including the United Wa State Army (UWSA), Kokang (MNDAA), KIO, and New Mon State Party (NMSP).[10]

The election of a semicivilian government in November 2010 represented a break with the past, despite the continued role of the military in government and politics. Although opposition groups (including most EAGs) continue to object strongly to elements of the 2008 constitution, the political transition process has nevertheless seen the introduction of limited decentralization to seven predominantly ethnic nationality–populated states. In late 2011 and through 2012, the new government under President (and ex-general) Thein Sein agreed, or reconfirmed, preliminary cease-fires with ten of the eleven most significant EAGs, representing the Wa and Mongla, Chin, Shan, Pa-O, Karen, Karenni, Rakhine, and Mon (for an overview of key stakeholders in the Myanmar peace process, see Fig. 8.1). Despite such positive developments, in June 2011 the Myanmar Army launched a major offensive against the KIO, the main Kachin armed ethnic group in northern Myanmar, breaking a seventeen-year cease-fire. As a result of this resump-

Figure 8.1: Key Stakeholders

- Central Committee for Union Peacemaking and Working Committee for Union Peacemaking; Union-level parliament; provincial (state and regional) parliaments
- Myanmar Government (executive); Myanmar Peace Center (government peace secretariat); local government authorities
- Myanmar Army (and local militias)
- Ethnic armed groups (not homogenous; includes Border Guard Forces and militia); ethnic opposition alliances—UNFC and WGEC
- Conflict-affected communities
- Civil society—CBOs and national NGOs (including exile/border-based organizations)
- Ethnic and other political parties
- Western governments and donors; UN
- Regional actors
- Business interests
- Refugees, diaspora communities, and exiles

tion of armed conflict, at least 80,000 people were displaced along the border with China, with tens of thousands of more IDPs in the conflict zones and government-controlled areas.[11] This resurgence of armed conflict included some of the most significant battles of Myanmar's fifty-plus-year civil war. The reasons behind the resumption of armed conflict in Kachin areas are complex and contested, and largely beyond the scope of this chapter, including sometimes opaque political-economic and geostrategic factors. Furthermore, by attacking the KIA, the Myanmar Army sends a message to other EAGs (particularly the UWSA), regarding the extent to which the military is prepared to envisage a future of autonomous enclaves, controlled by its erstwhile battlefield enemies. In addition, renewed hostilities in Kachin and northern Shan States should be seen in the context of Myanmar Army efforts to move insurgent forces away from key strategic installations, including a gas and oil pipeline from Rakhine State through Myanmar to China's Yunnan province.

Cease-Fires: Peacemaking

Since late 2011, the military-backed government has agreed to preliminary cease-fires with fourteen EAGs (see Fig. 8.2).[12] The agreement of cease-fires between the Myanmar government (and possibly the Army) and all of the main armed ethnic groups in the country is a necessary and important milestone in peacemaking—but is not sufficient alone to achieve significant peace-building and is furthermore threatened by continuing *tatmadaw* offensives in the north. In addition to attacks on the KIO, since the agreement in 2012 of cease-fires with the two main Shan groups (the Shan State Army–South/Restoration Council of Shan State, and the Shan State Army–North/Shan States Progressive Party), scores of clashes have occurred with the Myanmar Army. That cease-fires negotiated with groups based in northern Myanmar (Kachin and Shan States) have been the most unstable is particularly worrying. Presumably, the Myanmar Army prefers to continue fighting with EAGs, which are relatively isolated from the aid and media networks that proliferate along the Thailand border in southeast Myanmar (where Karen, Mon, Karenni, and other armed groups operate). Displaced populations fleeing conflict in the north are less likely to seek refuge across international borders and cause embarrassment for the Myanmar government—unlike in Thailand, where the presence of aid agencies and activist groups would rapidly draw attention to the humanitarian impacts of fighting. It should also be noted that, in some cases at least, clashes have resulted from EAG commanders on the ground patrolling aggressively, seeking taxation from villages, and provoking Myanmar Army interventions.

The continuation of fighting in several areas is clearly of great concern. However, in many areas the cease-fire situation is relatively more stable.

Figure 8.2: Cease-Fire Groups (2013)

United Wa State Army (UWSA), 6 September 2011
National Democratic Alliance Army (NDAA), 7 September 2011
Democratic Karen Buddhist Army (DKBA), 3 November 2011
Restoration Council of Shan State (RCSS/SSA-S), 2 December 2011
Chin National Front (CNF), 6 January 2012
Karen National Union (KNU), 12 January 2012
Shan State Progress Party (SSPP/SSA-N), 28 January 2012
KNU/KNLA Peace Council (KNU/KNLA PC), 7 February 2012
New Mon State Party (NMSP), 25 February 2012
Karenni National Progressive Party (KNPP), 7 March 2012
Arakan Liberation Party (ALP), 5 April 2012
National Socialist Council of Nagaland (NSCN), 9 April 2012
PaO National Liberation Organisation (PNLO), 25 October 2012
All Burma Democratic Front (ABSDF), 5 August 2013

Civilians living in conflict-affected areas where cease-fires are holding benefit in a number of ways: through reduced fear, improved livelihood options, and better opportunities for travel and access to services and assistance—allowing some displaced populations to begin the task of rebuilding their lives.

Research conducted among conflict-affected Karen communities by the Myanmar Peace Support Initiative (MPSI) (see Fig. 8.2) indicates that, before the January 2012 KNU cease-fire, villagers constantly had to flee from fighting and to avoid forced conscription and portering by the Myanmar Army, whereas today people report greatly decreased levels of fear. Many said that for the first time in decades they did not have to worry about fleeing into the jungle to avoid serious human rights abuses. In some cases, displaced people are beginning to return to previous settlements and attempting to rebuild lives long blighted by armed conflict and its impacts. Many villagers mentioned that before the cease-fire they were unable to travel or visit their farms—or could only do so on payment of bribes to Myanmar Army soldiers. Even then, villagers were severely restricted in terms of the amount of food or other supplies they could carry when traveling, as Myanmar Army soldiers often accused them of supporting the KNU. Villagers told stories of terrible abuse at the hands of the Myanmar Army, including multiple beatings and killings.

After the cease-fire, however, villagers can travel much more freely and tend their rice fields. Levels of taxation (paid to the Myanmar Army, and also to EAGs) have decreased significantly over the past two years. In many communities, livelihoods have improved as a result of villagers' better access to their farms and a reduction in predatory taxation. Furthermore, in the past gangs of thieves connected to the local Myanmar Army preyed on the villagers with impunity. These days such criminal activity has decreased.

People who spoke to MPSI greatly appreciate these changes—although they worry whether the cease-fire and emerging peace process can be maintained. One villager said that, "since the cease-fire, I can go to my rice fields and weed regularly, so I got more rice for my family. Now I can also travel freely and, unlike before, sleep out in the rice fields in a little hut without having to fear for my life. Now the Burma army still move around, but we don't have to fear meeting them." Another man told MPSI that "our villagers are like ducklings that have been in a cage for so long, and now they are released. They are so pleased to leave their cage! Our villagers are free to travel day and night, and are more busy and productive than before."

Despite such positive views, civilians in conflict-affected areas are often extremely vulnerable, facing extensive needs in many sectors (e.g., health, education, livelihoods, and food security). Among the dimensions of human security, the primary concern of most conflict-affected communities is physical safety.[13] Many ethnic nationality communities continue to experience high levels of militarization, with Myanmar Army troops often being perceived and experienced as an occupying and predatory force. If the Myanmar Army and EAGs could withdraw from some nonstrategic positions, perceived as threatening by communities, this would provide a boost in confidence to local stakeholders and help people to believe that the peace process can result in sustainable improvements to their situation.

Preliminary cease-fires agreed between the government and EAGs therefore need to be consolidated, with concrete agreements regarding troop positions and the behavior of armed forces—that is, negotiation of a cease-fire "code of conduct." Such details have been discussed between the KNU and the government's peace secretariat, the Myanmar Peace Centre (MPC), but so far have not been clearly endorsed by the Myanmar Army leadership. There is also a need for cease-fire monitoring by local actors (community peace monitoring) and/or by international agencies as specified in a number of cease-fire agreements (e.g., negotiations in 2012 and 2013 between the government and the KNU).

As noted, the continuation of military clashes between the Myanmar Army and cease-fire groups in Kachin and Shan States is deeply worrying. These cease-fire violations raise questions regarding whether the Myanmar

Army is under government control or if military commanders are following their own agendas. The inner workings of the Myanmar government and army are almost entirely opaque to outside observers. Some have suggested that the government and Myanmar Army have adopted a strategy to "divide and rule" EAGs. This approach used the peace process to achieve international rehabilitation (removal of sanctions, etc.) while outmaneuvering ethnic armed groups militarily by picking off recent battlefield enemies one-by-one; in other words, the government and army performed respective "good cop" and "bad cop" roles. In this reading, government strategy in the peace process would be in the first instance to respond positively to EAGs' demands and aspirations. Later, the government would backtrack, leaving the more proactive (propeace) elements on the ethnic side exposed and vulnerable to criticism from hardliners within their own ranks for having been seemingly naive in accepting at face value the government's initial promises to address key ethnic concerns.

Even if this conspiracy theory has some truth to it, political change and peace in Myanmar are dynamic processes, made and remade by doing. Regardless of what dark plans may be playing out, there is a momentum behind the reform and peace processes that needs to be intelligently supported. It is difficult to imagine Myanmar returning to a one-party military dictatorship. However, it is equally difficult to imagine a Western-style bourgeois liberal democracy in Myanmar. Most likely to emerge is a unique Myanmar hybrid regime, reflecting elements from other countries in the region.

Political Negotiations: Toward Peacebuilding?

There is a need to move from the agreement—and credible implementation—of preliminary cease-fires, to discuss long-standing political issues that have structured armed and state-society conflicts in Myanmar since independence and before. At the time of this writing, substantial political talks between the government and key ethnic stakeholders had not yet started, leading to skepticism regarding the government's, and particularly the Myanmar Army's, sincerity in pursuing necessary political talks ahead of elections scheduled for late 2015. Indeed, meetings between the Myanmar government, army, and EAGs in April and May 2014 led to skepticism on the part of ethnic stakeholders regarding the willingness and ability of the government to accede to key demands, or even acknowledge the legitimacy of ethnic grievances and aspirations.

Key stakeholders question whether the government (Aung Min and the MPC, and ultimately the president) have enough political capital to credibly deliver negotiations, especially following recent interventions in the peace process on the part of parliamentary speaker (ex-general and disappointed presidential hopeful) Shwe Mann and democracy icon Aung San Suu Kyi. Shwe Mann, in particular, seeks to bring peace talks more into parliamentary (and thus his own) remit. Skeptics also question whether the government has enough leverage with the Myanmar Army to deliver cease-fires.

As the 2015 elections approach, it may become increasingly difficult to move forward with the peace process, as Myanmar politicians position themselves in relation to the elections. There is a growing reluctance to give the present government credit for achievements in the peace process and increasing skepticism that anything agreed with this government will hold post-2015. In the meantime, the long delay to starting political dialogue has undermined an always-limited confidence in the peace process, especially on the part of ethnic communities, lending credibility to widespread concerns regarding the government's sincerity. Any moves from the government regarding political dialogue must therefore be credible—needing a concrete timetable and real agenda. The window of opportunity here relates also to the motivation of key government leaders (in particular the president and Aung Min) to construct a "peace legacy" before 2015. In this context, individual armed ethnic groups (e.g., the KNU and Restoration Council of the Shan State [RCSS]) have asserted their right to engage directly with the government—and the Myanmar Army—to discuss urgent issues of importance to local communities.

In the second half of 2013, elite-level engagement in the peace process was oriented increasingly around a proposed national cease-fire accord. Originally suggested by the president in early 2013, by the middle of the year this suggestion seemed to have dropped down the political agenda, as it became obvious that EAGs would not be willing to endorse such a symbolic agreement without beginning serious political talks. However, key EAG leaders became alarmed in mid-2013 by moves on the part of Aung San Suu Kyi and Shwe Mann challenging the legitimacy of the peace process. They also feared that, unless a settlement could be reached soon with the government, time would run out for reaching an agreement regarding necessary political dialogue before the 2015 elections. Pragmatic EAG leaders preferred the option of negotiating with the military-backed government, which—despite reservations over whether the president could really deliver a peace process—seemed motivated to engage with EAGs on the peace process. This was preferred over the possibility of negotiating with a post-2015 (presumably NLD-dominated) administration, which would likely have very high levels of domestic and international support, and therefore over which ethnic nationality leaders would have limited leverage.

Therefore, in August and September 2013 key EAG leaders were at the forefront of making proposals to the government regarding the national cease-fire accord, which would be necessary in order to receive significant ethnic support. For the first time in decades, ethnic nationality leaders were setting the agenda at the top table of Myanmar politics. In a meeting of potentially historic importance, leaders of the KNU and RCSS met with the government in Naypyitaw in late August and agreed in principle to a fourteen-point national cease-fire accord, including provision for a framework for political negotiations, cease-fire monitoring arrangements, and an agreement of a code of conduct governing the behavior of armed elements. The framework included other issues as well, such as how best to assist and provide "peace dividends" to conflict-affected communities and the vexed issues of land rights. Participants in such talks would initially include key EAGs, senior government officials (including parliamentary representation through the Central Committee for Union Peacemaking and Working Committee for Union Peacemaking) (see Table 8.1), and the Myanmar Army. Subsequently, it would be necessary to include ethnic political parties and civil society actors in comprehensive discussions.[14]

During 2013, civil society groups and political parties became increasingly worried about their lack of participation in the peace process. Unless these stakeholders feel a sense of ownership and participation, they may become alienated, and even begin to mobilize against the peace process. The exclusion of women from most aspects of the peace process is a particular problem, given the centrality of gender issues in armed and state-society conflicts, and the important contributions women can make toward reconciliation efforts. When political talks begin, there is a need to ensure participation of key stakeholders, including conflict-affected communities, civil society groups and political parties, and women. This will be a logistical challenge, reflected in the complexity of the Framework Agreement (ethnic peace plan) presented to the government by the United Nationalities Federal Council (UNFC, an alliance of some key EAGs) and other ethnic political actors in mid-2013. This proposal specifies roles in political dialogue for the government, political parties and EAGs, and civil society in a multi-stakeholder framework with provisions for discussion of key issues through various working groups.[15]

Alternatively, it may be useful to reframe the talks process, to separate it into two issues. The first focus centers on security issues, which would remain the domain primarily of the government and Myanmar Army and EAGs (with civil society in advisory or watchdog roles). The second centers on a nationwide political dialogue, involving a much wider variety of stakeholders, including representatives of the Burman majority, parliamentarians, and so on. However political talks proceed, it would be useful to map key issues of concern to ethnic and other stakeholders and identify those requiring constitutional change. This is presumably a long-term process involving multi-stakeholder dialogue, and ultimately endorsement by parliament—in which the Myanmar Army has an effective veto. A second set of issues includes those that could be addressed more immediately (e.g., land, language, etc.), in order to provide some peace dividends for conflict-affected communities while the long and complex process of political negotiations plays out. Among the more complex and contentious issues yet to be addressed in relation to political talks (and with serious implications for any constitutional amendment process) is the status of "minorities within minorities"—that is, ethnic communities such as the Pa-O. This concept refers to minorities within areas where the majority or dominant population come from another ethnic nationality, such as in the Shan, Mon, and Karen States.

A number of questions remain unresolved regarding the role of civil society actors in the peace process. While many civil society actors will demand a seat at the peace negotiations table, others may be more effective in a watchdog role, monitoring proceedings and where necessary attempting to pressure key actors to reach agreement. An intermediary role would be for civil society groups to have observer status at peace talks and/or to be consulted on specific issues. Whatever the eventual structure of society participation in peace talks, it will be necessary to ensure systematic and sustained consultation with representatives of Myanmar's diverse social groupings.

A number of cease-fire talks, including those with the Chin National Front, Karenni National Progressive Party, and KNU, have agreed in principle to establish cease-fire monitoring mechanisms. However, at this time (prior to any proposed nationwide cease-fire accord), monitoring has yet to become a reality on the ground. Leaving aside the tricky distinction between monitoring a cease-fire (agreement between EAG and government) and the broader peace process (including more general elements of commitments to human and other internationally designated rights), there remain questions regarding whether monitoring is best undertaken by international or local actors. In principle, there is an important role here for ethnic civil society actors who have access to (and the trust of) conflict-affected communities.

Multiple Stakeholders, Contested Agendas, and Problematic Negotiations

As noted above, EAGs in particular and ethnic stakeholders more generally in Myanmar are a highly diverse group—reflecting the heterogeneity of this country's ethnic and social networks. Among EAGs, a number of different positions are apparent, including both ideological perspectives and some long-standing personal rivalries. Political sensitivities make it unhelpful to anatomize these issues in too much detail.

Internecine, intraethnic concerns were to a certain extent superseded in November 2013 with the creation of a Nationwide Cease-Fire Coordination

Team (NCCT), composed initially of thirteen (at the time of this writing, sixteen) EAGs. The NCCT was established at a historic meeting at Laiza, the KIO's main base and—until the recent Myanmar Army offensives—a bustling town on the China border. The Laiza meeting agreed to an eleven-point strategy to guide EAG negotiations—although questions remained regarding the degree to which key groups, such as the RCSS, and particularly the UWSA, endorsed this approach. In early December, the NCCT met with Aung Min and his MPC secretariat, together with senior Myanmar Army commanders, in the Kachin State capital of Myitkyina. This was a historic occasion, being the first time the government had met officially with an alliance of EAGs rather than negotiating group-by-group. The Myitkyina meeting thus represented government acquiescence in one of the EAGs' key demands: multilateral negotiations to resolve armed conflict in Myanmar.

However, the Myitkyina meeting, and subsequent negotiations between the Myanmar Army, government, and EAGs in Yangon, demonstrated the gulf that existed between the government and ethnic sides. After nearly two years' experience of relatively easygoing talks with Aung Min and the MPC, the Myanmar Army was now at the table (in the first instance, through participation of key figures in the National Defense and Security Council). In terms of process, this was a positive development, as actors and observers had questioned the credibility of a peace process conducted by the executive branch of the government with only limited input (effectively, observer status) on the part of the Myanmar Army—which remained the most important and powerful institution in the country, particularly in armed conflict–affected areas. Negotiations since late 2013 have demonstrated what many EAG and other actors suspected: that the "real" government or Myanmar Army position was considerably more "hard-lined" than that presented by the president's chief mediator and his team. Nevertheless, one positive outcome from these negotiations was the emergence of clarity regarding both sides' positions.

In April 2014, the two sides met again in Yangon and agreed to merge various proposed drafts of a nationwide cease-fire accord into a single document. While this was presented at the time as a breakthrough, there remained large sections of the draft agreement where the two sides disputed not just the wording of individual items but basic issues of policy and politics. Nevertheless, negotiations (including a further, generally more positive meeting in May) continued under the auspices of a Joint Nationwide Cease-Fire Drafting Work Group. This consisted of nine NCCT leaders and nine from the government (three from the executive/cabinet, led by Aung Min; three from parliament, led by ex-general Thein Zaw; three from the Myanmar Army). IF (and the capitalization is significant) a nationwide cease-fire agreement could be agreed upon, there was a commitment to begin substantive political dialogue within six weeks.

The Question of Legitimacy

The stagnation of negotiations toward achieving a nationwide cease-fire agreement revolved around a number of issues, including the Myanmar Army's reluctance to endorse some of the points negotiated during previous bilateral agreements between the government and EAGs, including issues of cease-fire monitoring and agreement of a code of conduct governing the behavior of armed personnel on all sides. The two sides also failed to agree on the language and substance of ethnic demands for a restructuring of state-society relations in Myanmar to achieve a federal settlement. Another sticking point has been the language used to describe EAGs. While the government side—and particularly the Myanmar Army leadership—prefer the designation "armed groups from ethnic areas," the EAGs themselves have insisted on being referred to as "revolutionary ethnic armed organizations." This is more than just semantics.

For many ethnic stakeholders, the current structure of the state of Myanmar is regarded as illegitimate. Although there is widespread support and appreciation for the reform process led by the president, many remain skeptical regarding the extent to which the government—and particularly the Myanmar Army—is really willing to reimagine and renegotiate state-society relations in this troubled country. Ultimately, this is a matter of changing political cultures and attitudes, as much as achieving agreement on paper. Some ethnic leaders take the reportedly rather arrogant and dismissive attitude of senior Myanmar Army commanders in recent negotiations with the NCCT as evidence of the unreconstructed nature of the Myanmar military and state. By claiming the designation of "revolutionaries," EAGs indicate their desire to radically change the nature of the state in Myanmar to better reflect the aspirations and address the concerns of ethnic communities. For the government and army, however, the problem seems rather one of placating restive minorities through the provision of economic development and other benefits in remote areas.

Before the reforms in Myanmar got underway in 2011, the military regime was widely regarded (at least among Western countries) as an illegitimate pariah. However, the reforms of the past three years have altered this assessment, with many international actors understandably keen to support the reform movement by supporting the new government. In this context, donors and diplomats often seem unable to appreciate that the legitimacy of the state, as currently structured, is still fundamentally contested by many ethnic nationality actors. By supporting the extension of state services and governance functions into conflict-affected, previously semi- (or completely) autonomous areas, international donors risk doing considerable harm to the peace process. In order to mitigate against this risk, strengthening of the state should be accompanied by support to EAG governance regimes and service delivery structures, until such time as the conflict over the structure of the state has been resolved through political dialogue.

One of the main demands of ethnic stakeholders in the peace process is for a political dialogue focused on the concerns and aspirations of ethnic communities, and to negotiate changes in the relationship between the state (meaning the central government) and Myanmar's diverse ethnic groupings. It is assumed that ultimately this will require constitutional change. If and when substantial political dialogue starts, it should be more inclusive than the process of negotiating cease-fires and should include representatives of political parties, civil society actors, and women. In this context, there are likely to be increasing challenges to the legitimacy of EAGs. Already, some voices are questioning the degree to which EAGs really represent their claimed constituencies—and to what extent these are essentially "warlord organizations."

It must be acknowledged that most EAGs—and individual field commanders—do have economic agendas. It is hardly surprising, after decades of armed conflict, that political economies in conflict zones sometimes involve economic activities that enrich both EAG and Myanmar Army personnel. Nevertheless, many of the longer-established EAGs do enjoy very extensive—if sometimes contested—support among ethnic communities. Of course, EAGs cannot claim to be the sole political representatives of ethnic communities. As a result of cease-fires, and government tolerance of interactions between EAGs and ethnic political parties, civil society, and communities more broadly, Myanmar's armed groups are in many cases learning to be less "hegemonic." They are being drawn into collaboration with other stakeholders, such as ethnic political parties, in recognition of their legitimacy due to their success in the 2010 (and 1990) elections.

A Different Take on Ethnic Autonomy in Myanmar

An example of political diversity on the part of Myanmar's EAGs is presented by the UWSA. The UWSA split from the Communist Party of Burma when the latter collapsed in early 1989, precipitating the earlier wave of cease-fires in Myanmar.[16] Over the subsequent quarter century, the Wa leadership developed a reputation as Asia's largest narco-trafficking organization, though it subsequently oversaw a total ban on opium cultivation in their area of control. The northern UWSA command was recognized as an autonomous region under the 2008 constitution, although the status and future of the southern command on the Thailand border remains uncertain. In this context, Wa political demands center primarily on territorial autonomy and the desire to see their area of control designated as a state (or state-like territory) of Myanmar, rather than a region of Shan State. While UWSA personnel have participated in various alliance meetings (including those convened by the UNFC and WGEC), the primary Wa objective is decentralization. This concept implies continued authority for the UWSA leadership, with little or no interference from the state, and international involvement limited to the provision of services and relief items to the desperately poor Wa population.[17]

Observers of political and military developments in Myanmar have suggested that recent *tatmadaw* offensives against the KIO and allied Shan and Ta'ang EAGs in northern Myanmar have in part been intended to begin outflanking the UWSA—possibly in preparation for a future offensive against the Wa.[18] Myanmar Army leaders are reportedly unhappy with the degree of entrenched autonomy enjoyed by the UWSA, and would seek to redress this before the transition away from military rule is complete. (Myanmar military leaders no doubt calculate that the international community would be mute in response to offensives against the "Wa drug dealers.")

Outstanding Issues: Incursion of Unregulated Business Activities into Conflict-Affected Areas, Land-Grabbing, and Megaprojects

Business interests could be spoilers in the peace process, or could be engaged to play a more positive role. Most new business activities, including logging and mining, in conflict-affected areas are extractive and are often connected to local or national power holders such as the Myanmar Army or EAGs. Business activities in newly accessible conflict-affected areas are often associated with land-grabbing (e.g., for plantation agriculture).[19] In addition to having negative social and environmental impacts, such activities can undermine communities and other stakeholders' trust and confidence in the peace process. Unless the government, EAGs, and their international partners address these issues, there is a risk that local communities may be alienated from the peace process, as was the case with the previous round of cease-fires in the 1990s. For EAGs, there is a particular risk that their legitimacy and leadership of ethnic communities may be challenged if armed groups are perceived as having strong economic agendas in the peace process.[20] It is therefore in EAG's interests to demonstrate awareness of action on this issue.

Problems of land-grabbing are compounded by the negative impacts of the 2012 Farmland Act and 2012 Vacant, Fallow, and Wasteland Act. These acts do not recognize customary upland land tenure practices but rather seem designed to facilitate the transfer of land from communities to powerful business interests. It may be appropriate to suspend implementation of the 2012 land laws in conflict-affected areas, although the mechanism for doing so will need to be carefully considered.

Ethnic communities are also concerned about major infrastructure projects. Myanmar undoubtedly needs economic and infrastructure development, especially in remote and conflict-affected areas. However, ethnic communities are deeply concerned that the peace process will see the construction of major infrastructure projects, such as hydroelectric dams, that will deprive them of ancestral lands and undermine their human security and livelihoods. Large-scale projects should only be implemented after free, prior, and informed consultation with all stakeholders, and should follow proper impact assessments.[21] For some ethnic stakeholders, there should be no significant outside investment in conflict-affected areas until political dialogue is well established.

Land and Livelihoods

One consequence of the peace process is the growing impact of state penetration, "modernization," and the market economy on traditional cultures and livelihood patterns. The political dimension of this multifaceted issue is addressed below. In relation to local ownership of development (and land), the impacts of socioeconomic and cultural change on traditional communities can be managed through consideration of communal tenure systems—and where appropriate, incorporation of such arrangements in governance aspects of peace agreements.

Other land-related issues with important consequences for conflict and its impact in Myanmar include housing, land, and property rights. As noted above, ethnic nationality–populated, armed conflict–affected areas of Myanmar are "home" to hundreds of thousands of forced migrants. For many of these people, return to their previous villages is a key concern, while other displaced populations have found some kind of (at least semi-) durable solution in their current location and require assistance in order to achieve some degree of human security in situ.[22] Such issues are also important for the 150,000 refugees in camps along the Thai-Myanmar border and the two to three million migrant workers from Myanmar living precarious lives in Thailand. This topic is largely beyond the scope of this chapter but requires the urgent attention of policymakers, and should be a priority item on the agenda of peace talks.[23]

Issues of IDP and refugee return, and restitution of land rights (or failing that, provision of adequate compensation) are complicated by widespread landmine pollution in conflict-affected parts of Myanmar. For many communities, return and resettlement options are constrained—or made very risky—by the prevalence of landmines, laid over many years by all parties to the conflict. The issue is further complicated by the use of landmines by some conflict-affected communities in order to "protect" themselves from military incursion (largely on the part of the Myanmar Army). Landmine mapping and demining operations therefore need to be undertaken with an awareness of the complex political and security context, and in consultation with EAGs and local communities.[24] Furthermore, it will be necessary to guard against land that is identified for landmine clearance increasing in value. This phenomenon provides power-holders with motives to misappropriate community farmland where land rights are not well defined, as is the case under the 2012 land laws.

Economic Agendas

Although largely beyond the scope of this chapter, an appreciation of the peace process should take account of the significant financial and political interests that characterize key conflict actors. Myanmar Army leaders used the incidence of armed conflict to justify the perpetuation of militarization (and military power and prerequisites) in border areas, and to enrich themselves, while some EAG field commanders have made personal fortunes in the course of decades of armed conflict, as have respective (and often interlinked) crony and business networks. This is not to suggest that all conflict actors are motivated only by greed.[25] Ethnic nationality communities in Myanmar have experienced and continue to articulate very significant grievances and aspirations for self-determination and political progress. For many actors, motivations are a complex mix of economic self-interest, strongly held identity constructions, and fierce idealism.

Among the most significant challenges facing both government and ethnic nationality stakeholders (including EAGs, political parties, civil society actors, and, above all, conflict-affected communities) are business and "development" activities in conflict-affected areas. These range from local enterprises, through national-level companies, to the activities of international and multinational corporations.[26] An issue perceived as particularly pressing by many local communities is the growing prevalence of drugs (particularly methamphetamines such as *ya ba*), which seems often to be facilitated post-cease-fire by increased freedom of movement.

After decades of conflict and underdevelopment, there is a great need for economic development and jobs, improved livelihood options, and vocational training. Many minority-populated, conflict-affected areas are sites of significant natural resources. With some resources, such as remaining timber stands and fish stocks, value can be added locally. In others, such as natural gas and oil reserves, income streams for the national exchequer are significant, with possibilities for revenue sharing between the central state and local authorities. Unfortunately, however, much of the industry and investment in remote areas tends to be extractive, with local people receiving little benefit beyond payoffs to political and military elites. Conflict actors' motivations for reaching cease-fires are not limited to war weariness, political vision and entrepreneurship, or humanitarian impulse—but include the desires of military and political elites to benefit from business opportunities, including the exploitation of natural resources. Such extractive industries are often damaging, both socially and environmentally.

Of particular concern in conflict-affected areas are a series of hydropower projects planned for the horseshoe of minority-populated areas in western, northern, and eastern Myanmar, most of which are being planned without adequate social or environmental impact studies. Other concerns focus on mining concessions granted in border areas, unsustainable logging activities (though the extension of road networks into previously inaccessible areas to facilitate such logging also allow remote communities to access markets), and the growing problem of commercial agricultural plantations (particularly palm oil in the south). All of these activities may involve land-grabbing.

The largest infrastructure development project in the country—indeed, in the region—is planned for the Karen (and also Mon, Dawei [Tavoy], and Burman-populated) southern Thanintharyi (Tenasserim) Region. This is the Dawei project, which envisages construction of a deep-sea port on the Andaman coast, a major industrial zone, a road, and other infrastructure links to neighboring Thailand. The first stage of this project alone is estimated to be valued at some US$13 billion. Significant environmental concerns have been raised by the prospect of dirty industries being relocated from Thailand. Other potential problems include the lack of workers' rights and local landowners' vulnerability to forcible appropriation of their farmlands. Previous large-scale infrastructure developments in Myanmar have resulted in "development-induced" displacement and increased vulnerability. As the political-economic relationship between Myanmar and Thailand becomes stronger, this will give the latter a growing stake in stability in the southeast, which may result in greater pressure on the KNU and other EAGs. For Karen and other ethnic nationalities in Burma, much will depend on how community and political leaders position themselves in relation to such economic developments—including "special economic zones"—in the process of being established at a number of locations across the southeast.[27]

The future of the Dawei project, and especially the special economic zone, remains uncertain, given the project's backers inability thus far to raise the huge amounts of financing necessary. On the other side of the country, the largest Chinese investment in Myanmar is the construction of a gas pipeline and related rail and road projects connecting the Rakhine coast on the Indian Ocean to landlocked Yunnan Province. The Shwe Gas project is of huge geostrategic importance, allowing China to tap Myanmar's natural gas resources and providing Chinese access to the Indian Ocean by bypassing the strategically vulnerable Straits of Malacca. However, like other Chinese and state-sponsored infrastructure developments in Myanmar, the Shwe Gas project has been dogged by controversy. Local Rakhine and other communities are concerned about land confiscation, inequitable compensation, environmental damage, and other negative consequences. Furthermore, as noted previously, the oil and gas pipelines connect to China through some of the most conflict-affected parts of Myanmar and have been implicated in repeated Myanmar Army offensives against the KIO and other EAGs in the north.

Given the need for investment, jobs, and sustainable livelihoods in Myanmar, well-regulated companies (particularly, but not exclusively Western corporations) have an important role to play in the country's development and in delivering "peace dividends." Western companies operating in Myanmar are more likely to be on their best behavior, under scrutiny from activist groups, and will therefore exercise relatively high standards of corporate social responsibility (at least compared to Myanmar and regional companies, many of which have well-deserved reputations for putting profits before people and the environment). Western corporate interest in Myanmar cannot be dissociated from geopolitical agendas. The United States and other Western countries have an interest in engaging the government, and encouraging it to reorientate Myanmar away from the Chinese sphere of influence, in order to "balance" against Asia's emerging superpower. Likewise, significant Japanese investment in Myanmar (including many hundreds of millions of dollars in aid money) may be explained by a desire to contain China and to stimulate the economy back home, as well as by Japanese national sentiments regarding its historic closeness to Myanmar.

Local Autonomy and the Politics of Governance

A particularly significant, but largely unremarked, challenge in the peace process lies in conceptualizing and working constructively on the relationship between government structures and those of EAGs. Many armed opposition groups have long-established, though chronically under-resourced, paragovernment structures, including in the fields of education, health, and local administration. Peace talks have yet to address, let alone resolve, how these nonstate local governance structures will relate to formal state structures. These issues have been raised in talks between the government (and more recently, the Myanmar Army) and the NCCT. At this time, the Myanmar Army leadership seems reluctant to acknowledge—or seriously discuss the future of—nonstate governance and service delivery regimes in conflict-affected areas, perhaps considering these as a threat to the integrity and sovereignty of the Union.[28] The issue of "interim arrangements," governing the relationships between state and nonstate regimes in conflict-affected areas, is a particularly pressing question in areas of recent armed conflict. In these areas, communities are subject to multiple authorities, namely the government, the Myanmar Army, and one or more EAGs, plus local militias and other informal power-holders.[29] For many displaced and other communities in the conflict zones, EAG structures and personnel are perceived as more legitimate and effective than those of the state. Civil society actors working on the ground in conflict-affected areas often enjoy very close relations with (and personnel overlap with those of) EAG service provision actors. It is essential that such individuals and networks enjoy a sense of ownership in the peace process if momentum is to be maintained. Deepening of the peace process therefore should include participation of affected communities and other stakeholders, such as civil society and political actors, with special attention to the roles of women and young people.

The government has committed in principle to negotiations regarding decentralization in ethnic nationality–populated areas. Furthermore, the 2008 constitution allows for limited decentralization in some areas of governance. However, on the ground, the cease-fire process has seen the state, and Myanmar Army, pushing to expand its authority into previously contested, conflict-affected areas. This is not necessarily (or entirely) a conspiracy; it is what governments do—apply governance to subjects.

The extension of government services into previously inaccessible, conflict-affected communities can have positive impacts for vulnerable populations (e.g., improved access to health and education services, provision of identification cards), but can also be seen as threatening by local communities, who often continue to regard the state as threatening and the Myanmar Army as violent and predatory. Efforts to expand Myanmar government authority and service-delivery systems should therefore be undertaken in close consultation with relevant EAGs and affected communities, and appropriate civil society groups.

In many conflict-affected areas, local organizations working cross-border and from inside Myanmar have for years been the only agencies providing assistance to conflict-affected communities. It is essential that such individuals and networks enjoy a sense of ownership in the peace process.

There is a risk that international and state agencies entering these areas could undermine and/or overwhelm existing local capacities, damaging confidence in the peace process. Therefore, international actors should only support the expansion of government authority into previously contested areas in consultation with local stakeholders—that is, donors and international agencies should seek to "do no harm" to the peace process.

This call for conflict sensitivity raises important issues regarding the legitimacy and capacity of state and nonstate actors. Aid agencies and donors often understand weak state capacities as the primary obstacle to recovery and postconflict development. However, a recent report by the Asia Foundation points out that the legitimacy of the state may itself be contested—as is the case in Myanmar's ethnic conflicts. Perceived "injustice over governance, political and economic marginalization and threatened identity of the local minority population . . . feed an inter-generational narrative of fear and distrust of the state and security forces and of challenging the state's legitimacy and authority."[30] In this context, unless the state's legitimacy is reimagined and reinvented, building state capacity is likely to have mixed consequences, at best.

Political Cultures

The government's ability to deliver reforms is hampered by deep-rooted conservative-authoritarian institutional cultures and limited technical capacities. This is also the case with Myanmar's diverse EAGs. Furthermore, the government, composed mostly of ex-military personnel, exercises only limited control over the Myanmar Army. One consequence of the Kachin conflict has been to activate and empower hard-line elements within the Myanmar Army, who actively oppose civilian control over the military. Perhaps the greatest challenges facing the government are therefore to ensure that the Myanmar Army implements its policy and to build new civilian institutions. For many actors and observers, such reforms will require significant changes to the 2008 constitution, as well as a reimagining of military identities and roles.

The president having promised so much, Myanmar may experience a "revolution of rising expectation": prospects of change have been talked up and people may become frustrated if the government and its partners are unable to deliver. The reform process in Myanmar may be likened to taking the lid off a pressure cooker. In a society where tensions have been building for more than half a century, ethnic and other grievances can easily spill over, with disturbing consequences. Furthermore, with new freedoms of association and expression, and the removal of a "common enemy" (the militarized government), old political grievances and aspirations are being rearticulated and enacted in Myanmar in ways that were unimaginable just two years ago. One example is the recent violence and ethnic hatred in parts of Rakhine State and central Myanmar. These events remind us that there is not just conflict between the government and Myanmar Army and various armed ethnic groups, but also intracommunal conflict, with the potential to be extremely violent, between some ethnic communities. Outbursts of horrific violence in Rakhine constitute a complex phenomenon, beyond the scope of this chapter, involving deep-seated mistrust of the "other" and the politics of citizenship, immigration, and representation—issues that have been exacerbated and mobilized by local and national-level political entrepreneurs. (The Rakhine nationalist community also experiences many of the same grievances and aspirations common to other ethnic minority groups in the country.) Among other things, these events indicate that there are spoilers on the sidelines, waiting to utilize tensions to provoke violence in order to undermine the reforms.

Despite apparent commitment to the peace process, government and Myanmar Army leaders still seem to regard ethnic communities as "children," whose lives must be developed and improved by the state (with international assistance), rather than seeing ethnic communities (and possibly EAGs) as primary actors in their own stories and legitimacy. Such patrician tendencies are notable among the government's peace envoys, such as the predominantly ethnic Burman staff of the MPC, an initiative established in mid-2012 as a quasi-governmental secretariat to Aung Min. As noted, the peace process is often experienced by conflict-affected communities "on the ground" as the penetration of top-down state services and governance structures into previously inaccessible, conflict-affected areas. Such a process can undermine trust in the peace process.

For many years, citizens of the country were denied access to news and information and suffered severe restrictions on freedom of speech and association. Majority (ethnic Burman) communities have generally not been exposed to the grievances, concerns, and aspirations of ethnic nationalities—although this is beginning to change, with a greater focus in the Myanmar media on armed conflict (e.g., in Kachin State). Should political negotiations result in a settlement (as discussed previously), there is therefore a risk of a backlash among the majority community. Elements of such a community could be mobilized by populist politicians to oppose any deal struck between government and ethnic elites (e.g., in relation to federalism—a concept that is not well understood by the Burmese public). There is therefore a need for public education, exposing the Burman majority community to the realities of their ethnic brethren. Ultimately, what is required is a national conversation on the nature of citizenship and the state in Myanmar. This will have to be a long-term undertaking, involving other minority communities in Myanmar, such as Muslim groups, which have recently been subject to terrible intracommunal violence.

At the international level, there is often a lack of understanding among aid agencies, donors, and diplomats regarding the issues affecting conflict-affected communities in remote, ethnic nationality–populated parts of the country. There is considerable risk that peace and political actors will avoid difficult challenges, preferring self-congratulation and easy options to addressing the many problems still affecting ethnic communities and state-society relations. In this case, opportunities to build a better Myanmar may be lost. In the run-up to elections in 2015, the window of opportunity to act on these issues will likely begin to narrow.

Convergence: Toward "Federalism from Below"?

Political talks between the government and ethnic nationality political elites may be drawn-out, top-down, and blueprint-driven. Negotiations could get trapped in legalistic discussions (e.g., around constitutional reform), with key actors adopting zero-sum approaches—especially in the run-up to the 2015 elections.

It would be helpful if the government could make some symbolic and practical concessions and gestures in order to demonstrate good faith and awareness of ethnic grievances. For example, measures to allow the use of ethnic languages in government schools and state/region-level administrations, and action to address widespread land-grabbing would do much to build confidence in the peace process, on the part of ethnic communities. Thus far, ethnic language provision has been largely absent in formal peace talk negotiations. In the meantime, however, some regional governments have started to introduce ethnic language education into government schools, often at the prompting of above-ground ethnic political parties (e.g., the Karen People's Party in Bago Region and the All Mon Regions Democracy Party in Mon State).

Also, for the peace process to be regarded with confidence in conflict-affected areas, it will be necessary for armed groups on all sides to reposition some troops, especially units perceived as particularly threatening by local communities. Indeed, displaced civilians have repeatedly told this author that the main constraint on IDPs returning to their homes and trusting the peace process to be just and sustainable is the continuing presence of Myanmar Army units in the vicinity of their old settlements.

Given the seeming deadlock in negotiations around a nationwide cease-fire accord, and consequent delay in the commencement of political dialogue, it will be important to ensure that existing bilateral cease-fires between the government and EAGs are successful on the ground in terms of providing peace dividends for conflict-affected communities. This could be achieved through recognition of the legitimacy of "interim arrangements," which safeguard the status of nonstate governance and service delivery systems, in conflict-affected areas—at least during the period of political negotiation before a comprehensive peace agreement is reached. Given the bottlenecks sketched above, this transitional period may be prolonged—probably stretching beyond elections scheduled for late next 2015.

In order to build trust and confidence in the peace process, international and national actors should support local activities that help to address the urgent concerns and needs of ethnic communities—including as identified by credible EAG and other ethnic leaders. Concrete and sustainable attempts to build peace "on the ground" are particularly important, given the likelihood that political negotiations will not produce a deliverable settlement until late 2014 or 2015 (at the earliest). Government and donors should undertake peacebuilding needs assessments in partnership with EAGs, civil society, and conflict-affected communities in order to build common understandings of needs and a joint agenda for addressing them.

It is necessary to promote activities that help to build trust and confidence on the part of key stakeholders, testing the peace process. This would involve seeking out and supporting good practice on the ground (or an "appreciative enquiry" approach) in areas such as education and livelihoods. Donors and policymakers should support convergence between state and nonstate governance regimes and service delivery systems in ways that build on local practice, demonstrating to communities (and EAGs and civil society) that the peace process can create spaces to support local agency. A good start can be made in the field of education, where schools and locally appropriate curricula are provided in many conflict-affected areas by EAGs and associated civil society actors.[31] Less helpful will be large-scale international assistance delivered only through government channels, without the participation of key stakeholders, including EAGs and conflict-affected communities, women, and civil society actors. International programs that bypass local community and civil society actors can also be very damaging. Concrete, locally owned, and sustainable attempts to build peace on the ground are particularly important, given the likelihood that political negotiations will not yield quick results.

Such concerns are particularly evident in relation to sector policy reform. In a number of fields, including education, but also health and general governance reform, donors are eager to engage with the previously pariah Myanmar government. In well-intentioned efforts to support the government and its reform of state structures and institutions, donors and diplomatic actors may be pushing the aid agenda beyond the momentum of the peace process: strengthening state structures and their expansion into previously contested or (semi-) autonomous areas, with deleterious effects on the peace process.

The Aid Industry

The peace process in Burma/Myanmar is indigenous, driven in the first instance by government initiative. In the context of limited international involvement, the process has been quite ad hoc in nature. Furthermore, it is highly complex, with some twenty parallel sets of discussions underway between the government and various EAGs.

Given the essentially indigenous nature of the peace process in Myanmar, the role of the international community is necessarily limited. On the one hand, international stakeholders should continue to remind the government, and EAGs, of their commitments and responsibilities under international human rights and humanitarian law, of the need to resolve outstanding armed conflicts, and of the necessity for an inclusive political dialogue and ultimately a substantial political settlement acceptable to key stakeholders. Beyond that, the international community can support peace-building initiatives that build trust and confidence in the peace process, and at the same time test the sincerity of the Myanmar government and army, and EAGs, to deliver the peace that citizens long for. One way of doing so is to engage constructively with various parties to the process, including civil society actors, encouraging their participation in and principled support for the peace process.

Among the more high-profile interventions has been the MPSI,[32] which aims to build trust and confidence in—and to test—the peace process by supporting agreements between the government and EAGs.[33] The MPSI was initiated in January 2012, when Myanmar asked the Norwegian government to help support the peace process. Since then, a number of other governments and donors have become involved. The MPSI has sought to move quickly in response to political imperatives in a fast-changing context. It is committed to substantial consultations with conflict-affected communities, civil society, and government and nongovernment political and military actors, and to sharing information with a broad range of stakeholders. The MPSI is committed to working in a manner that does not expose vulnerable populations or other partners to increased danger (including due to any future breakdown in the peace process). It is supporting local partners (CBOs and EAGs) to implement projects in Rakhine, Chin, Shan, Karen, and Mon States, and Bago and Thanintharyi Regions.[34] International responses such as the MPSI are premised in part on a desire to avoid the mistakes of the 1990s, when foreign donors failed to support the previous round of cease-fires in Myanmar, missing opportunities to move from peacemaking toward an environment of genuine peace-building.[35]

Unfortunately, international support to the peace process has been mostly characterized by a lack of direction, and strategic drift. Donors seem content largely to provide funding channeled through government structures—an easier approach than seeking out appropriate local partners on the ground, and one which is very tempting in a context where for the first time in decades large aid agencies can have direct relations with the previously pariah state.

This situation is not unique to Myanmar. Other than in contexts where a state's legitimacy is very clearly and persistently challenged (e.g., Myanmar pre-2011), or when regional or global powers' interests are directly involved, donors tend to frame issues in terms of technical problems to be fixed by professional aid regimes, rather than issues as sites of contestation, needing (at least in part) political solutions. As the Asia Foundation report cited above observes, it is not uncommon for peace initiatives to fail to engage with the real issues affecting communities and other stakeholders. This has been largely true of donors to the Myanmar peace process. For example, most Asian governments' support for the peace process is channeled almost exclusively through Myanmar state structures, demonstrating limited consultation with conflict-affected communities and almost none with EAGs. This approach to "peace building" tends to frame armed conflict as a problem to be resolved by the application of foreign aid—rather than (in part at least) an illustration of deep-rooted social and political grievances.

One might reasonably ask what aid donors can do, beyond reverting to the "aid conditionality" of the past two decades, which is unlikely to be helpful in the current context (although possibly necessary in some specific cases). As noted, peace processes in Myanmar are indigenous—with the international community limited to a (hopefully intelligent) supporting role. The primary political responsibility therefore lies with local political actors, especially the government and EAGs. One of the main tasks of international engagement is to support these actors, as well as others when participation in the peace process deepens.

Aid agencies working in conflict-affected areas need to better understand local political cultures and the dynamics of peace and conflict. Often, such actors have limited understandings of how their programs play out in local contexts and are perceived by affected communities.[36]

There are continuing needs for humanitarian assistance and longer-term development aid in ethnic, armed conflict–affected areas. However, large-scale aid in these areas, before the cease-fires are consolidated (which includes troop repositioning and negotiation of a code of conduct) and political dialogue has started, could be dangerously counterproductive. Many ethnic communities are concerned that the government has an "economic development first" agenda, to use aid as an alternative to needed political dialogue.[37] Ethnic communities are concerned that aid interventions represent efforts by the Myanmar government to intensify its presence in and control over ethnic communities. For large-scale aid to be welcomed, it should in most cases be delayed until *after* political dialogue is started. Furthermore, aid needs to be delivered in ways that reflect respect by donors, the government, and implementing partners for the principle of ethnic autonomy.

Turning from policy to ideology, an appreciation of international support to the peace process in Myanmar must take into account critiques of the "liberal peace"[38] and the notion of Western interventions in conflict-affected societies being undertaken in order to promote the triumvirate of liberalism, democracy, and market capitalism.[39] As described by Oliver Richmond, the "liberal peace" has various attributes and articulations but is usually understood as interventions to end armed conflict, paving the way for an extension of Western-style state-building and market-based political economies. Profoundly ideological, such approaches often obscure the political struggles at the heart of armed and state-society conflicts.[40]

Peace, Politics, and the "Anti-politics Machine"

In *The Anti-politics Machine,*[41] James Ferguson argues that "development" can depoliticize contentious issues by framing them as amenable to technical solutions to be implemented by government in partnership with aid professionals, rather than sites of political struggle.[42] Is the same thing happening to ethnic grievances and political agendas as part of the peace process?

The Asia Foundation cautions that postconflict aid projects generally "focus on *development outcomes* such as improving livelihoods, health, and education, and on local economic growth."[43] However, there is little evidence that such development-oriented approaches impact on conflict dynamics—other than in inadvertently negative ways (e.g., by strengthening problematic state structures). This report argues that "transformational strategies and outcomes are fundamentally political in nature," requiring changes in political structures and behavior at national and local levels—and not just local economic or community development. Ultimately, the Asia Foundation report notes that aid can support peace processes (such as those underway in Myanmar), but that local and national leadership is necessary to the success of such transitions.

If state and EAG political leaders can address ethnic concerns through political negotiations, it might be appropriate to transfer some issues from the political agenda onto the aid and development agenda (e.g., in the fields of language use and education, livelihoods). Certainly, conflict-affected areas are in desperate need of economic development, and particularly private investment, which can produce jobs and sustainable livelihoods. However, economic development without widespread consultation—and particularly in the absence of political progress—is unlikely to solve the deep and long-standing problems of armed and state-society conflicts in Myanmar. Peace-building in Myanmar cannot be achieved solely by technical "fixes" and the delivery of aid and economic development.

Tentative Conclusions, Key Questions

As noted at the outset, the dynamic and continuing nature of the peace process in Myanmar makes this analysis provisional in nature, with only tentative conclusions possible. However, a number of key issues can be identified, and questions raised:

- Will the current round of cease-fires see EAGs continue to control autonomous "liberated zones," mostly in the borderlands (like the cease-fires of the 1990s)—in which case, what will be the status of these areas, and how will (or will) such issues be addressed as part of political negotiations? Recent Myanmar Army offensives against the KIO (with the implied threat of future operations directed against the UWSA) would seem to imply that the military is unwilling to see the continuation of autonomous enclaves as a viable long-term solution to Myanmar's ethnic question.

• Will the government and Myanmar Army be willing to engage seriously in discussions on the current status and future of EAG governance and administration regimes, and nonstate service delivery structures, in armed conflict–affected areas—perhaps as part of "interim arrangements" under the nationwide cease-fire accord? These locally owned and implemented structures need to be supported during the likely protracted period of political dialogue before a comprehensive political settlement to Myanmar's protracted ethnic conflicts can be agreed upon. In the middle-to-longer term, how should nonstate governance and service delivery regimes relate to (or integrate with) state structures?

• The peace process has seen EAGs enter a (no doubt long and contested) transformation from insurgent groups toward—what? State and international actors mostly assume that, if a political settlement can be negotiated that is acceptable to key stakeholders, EAGs will disarm. However, while some EAGs may eventually lay down arms, and even become political parties, others will prefer to retain their weapons (conceivably as part of a transformed Myanmar Army?).

• EAGs have been illegal (according to the Myanmar government, which itself has been regarded as illegitimate); also, EAGs are generally not recognized under the international states and legal systems. The president has promised to rescind laws criminalizing contact with EAGs. What are the status and expected roles of EAGs—for the Myanmar government and Army, and international actors (diplomats, donors, aid agencies)?

• It is important to recognize that the main EAGs do enjoy significant—although not exclusive or uncontested—political legitimacy as representatives of ethnic communities. Only by recognizing and responding to this legitimacy can the peace process be sustained. The peace process has brought EAGs into partnerships with government and international actors, and provided some opportunities for armed groups to organize among previously inaccessible communities in government-controlled areas. Where does this leave other ethnic political actors (e.g., political parties that contested the 2010 elections), many of which feel marginalized from the peace process as currently configured? To what extent will the proposed future political dialogue address these concerns, on the part of ethnic political parties and civil society actors?

• Do government—and particularly Myanmar Army—leaders understand ethnic grievances and aspirations? How can Bamar communities, at the elite and popular levels, be helped to gain a better understanding of ethnic realities? Are the Myanmar government and army willing to address ethnic concerns substantively in political negotiations?

• Can donors act with strategic coherence, utilizing assistance and political leverage to support progress in the peace process? Will the government and its international partners be willing to ensure that activities to build peace and bring development to conflict-affected areas are undertaken jointly, in partnership with key ethnic stakeholders? Donors and aid agencies need to demonstrate better conflict sensitivity and act in ways that support political and social transformations in conflict-affected areas (not just building the capacity of state structures). Supporters of the peace process need to recognize that many issues of concern to ethnic communities are inherently political and cannot be resolved through the application of aid or other technical fixes.

• The peace process is an opportunity for EAGs (e.g., the KNU) to break out from their border-based jungle enclaves and reconnect with the Karen community "inside" Myanmar.[44] Many Karen people regard the KNU as legitimate and seek its leadership, but they are expressing serious concerns about the peace process. The peace process represents a chance to mobilize the community and demonstrate to the public that the KNU is aware of and working to address its constituents' concerns.

• If cease-fires are not consolidated, political talks do not start soon, and issues of urgent concern to communities are not addressed, hardliners among ethnic (particularly diaspora and exile) communities are likely to criticize the leaders of armed ethnic groups for "allowing themselves to be put in the pocket" of the government (selling out). Therefore EAG leaders need to communicate better with their publics and demonstrate that they are actively pursuing a political change agenda and engaging the government on issues of concern. More fundamentally, the Myanmar Army needs to stop attacking EAGs and related civilian communities in northern Myanmar.

• Reification of ethnic identity: to what extent is the peace process serving to (re)establish categories of ethnic identity, in politically and economically salient ways, which may not be helpful for the future social and political well-being of Myanmar?

Notes

This chapter began as a presentation made to the "Myanmar in Reform 2013" academic symposium, held at University of Hong Kong, 17–19 June 2013, organized by Ian Holliday. Many thanks for comments on the draft text to Alan Smith, Martin Smith, Stephen Gray, Susanne Kempel, Wolfgang Trost, and Elliott Prasse-Freeman.

1. For a historical overview of ethnic armed conflict in Myanmar, see Martin Smith, *Burma: Insurgency and the Politics of Ethnicity* (London: Zed Books, 1999); see also, Ashley South, *Ethnic Politics in Burma: States of Conflict* (London: Routledge, 2010).

2. *Peacemaking* may be defined as ending violent conflict, through the agreement of a cease-fire or truce.

3. *Peace-building* may be defined as activities designed to transform the underlying dynamics of violence, toward a more peaceful management of conflict. Conrad Brunk reviews the literature and debates around ending violence—specifically the distinction between "negative peace" (ending armed conflict, but not necessarily addressing underlying 'structural violence') and "positive peace" (transforming the political, social, and economic structures of conflict and oppression): "Shaping a Vision—the Nature of Peace Studies," in Larry Fisk and John Schellenberg, eds., *Patterns of Conflict, Paths to Peace* (Toronto: Broadview Press and University of Toronto Press), 11–33; see also Johan Galtung, *A Theory of Peace* (Transcend Press, 2010).

4. This section is drawn from Ashley South, "Prospects for Peace in Myanmar: Opportunities and Threats" (Peace Research Institute Oslo Working Paper, December 2012).

5. Demographic data in Myanmar are notoriously unreliable. See Appendix A for a breakdown of ethnic groups. A census took place in 2014 (prior to the 2015 elections). Although this might give better data, there is also a risk of reinforcing unhelpful essentializations of ethnicity in Myanmar. As discussed further below, ethnicity is a fluid category, subject to reimaginations. While the fixing of ethnic identity may be convenient for administrative and political elites, this does not necessarily reflect lived realities; see Mandy Sadan, *Being and Becoming Kachin: Histories Beyond the State in the Borderworlds of Burma*. Oxford: Oxford University Press, 2013. A key challenge in the census will be to decide who is considered a citizen, in which state or region. How many Chinese immigrants will be registered in Kachin and Shan states? How many Rohingya in Rakhine?

6. On the history and historiography of the 1947 Panglong Conference, see Matthew Walton, "Ethnicity, Conflict, and History in Burma: The Myths of Panglong," *Asian Survey* 48, no. 6 (2008): 889–910.

7. For an analysis of the Karen insurgency, see Ashley South, "Burma's Longest War: Anatomy of the Karen Conflict" (Amsterdam: Transnational Institute/Burma Centre Netherlands, 2011).

8. Gustaaf Houtman, "Mental Culture in Burmese Crisis Politics: Aung San Suu Kyi and the National League for Democracy," *Monograph Series* 33 (Tokyo: Tokyo University of Foreign Studies, Institute for the Study of Languages and Cultures of Asia and Africa, 1999).

9. Thailand Burma Border Consortium, "Program Report 2012: January to June," Bangkok, 2012.

10. Transnational Institute, "Burma at the Crossroads: Maintaining the Momentum for Reform," *Burma Policy Briefing* No. 9 (Amsterdam: Transnational Institute–Burma Centre Netherlands, 2012).

11. Human Rights Watch, "Untold Miseries: Wartime Abuses and Forced Displacement in Burma's Kachin State" (New York: HRW, 2012).

12. "Naypyitaw: Nationwide Cease-fire in October," *Shan Herald Agency for News*, 3 September 2013. For up-to-date coverage of the peace process in Myanmar, see Burma News International's "Myanmar Peace Monitor" at www.mmpeacemonitor.org.

13. Communities have repeatedly stressed to the author, during his numerous visits to conflict-affected areas (including, but not limited to the past two years), that their primary concern is physical safety (protection).

14. For a first-hand account, see "Ethnic Cease-fire Draft Accepted 'in Principle,'" *Shan Herald Agency for News*, 9 September 2013.

15. "Ethnic Working Group Presents Draft Framework for Political Negotiations," *Shan Herald Agency for News*, 20 June 2013.

16. See Smith, *Burma: Insurgency*.

17. On the history of the UWSA, see Tom Kramer, "The United Wa State Party: Narco-army or Ethnic Nationalist Party?" *Policy Studies* 38 (Washington, DC: East-West Center, 2007).

18. Confidential conversations.

19. Karen Human Rights Group, "Losing Ground: Land Conflicts and Collective Action in Eastern Myanmar," Report No. 2013-01 (Thailand: KHRG, March 2013).

20. Political legitimacy may be claimed and/or conferred on the basis of procedural credibility, economic performance, ethnic or religious authenticity, or other factors: Muthiah Alagappa, *Political Legitimacy in Southeast Asia: The Quest for Moral Authority* (Stanford, CA: Stanford University Press, 1995); see also David Steinberg, *Turmoil in Burma: Contested Legitimacies in Myanmar* (Norwalk, CT: EastBridge, 2006).

21. See the *Guiding Principles on Business and Human Rights*, endorsed by the UN Human Rights Council (New York and Geneva: UN Office of the High Commissioner for Human Rights, June 2011).

22. Ashley South, "Burma: The Changing Nature of Displacement Crises," *Working Paper* No. 39 (Oxford: Oxford University Refugee Studies Centre, 2007).

23. See report for Displacement Solutions: Scott Leckie, "Bridging the HLP Gap—The Need to Effectively Address Housing, Land and Property Rights During Peace Negotiations and in the Context of Refugee/IDP Return: Preliminary Recommendations to the Government of Myanmar, Ethnic Actors and the International Community" (Geneva, June 2013).

24. Ashley South, with Malin Perhult and Nils Carstensen, "Conflict and Survival: Self-Protection in South-East Burma," Asia Programme Paper ASP PP 2010/04 (London: Chatham House/Royal Institute of International Affairs, 2010); Local to Global Protection initiative, September 2010.

25. Scholars such as Paul Collier have analyzed the causes of armed conflict primarily in terms of the economic opportunities available to combatants: *Resource Rents, Governance, and Conflict* (Ann Arbor: University of Michigan Press, 2005). David Keen criticizes this approach, pointing out that conflict actors' perceptions of sociopolitical and historic injustices are equally important in understanding their motivation; *Complex Emergencies* (Cambridge, UK: Polity Press, 2008), chapters 2–3. Over time, armed conflicts tend to be transformed, as structural influences move away from original (often "grievance"-based) causes, toward new ("greed"-oriented) factors: Mark Duffield, *Global Governance and the New Wars: The Merging of Development and Security* (London: Zed Books, 2001).

26. For documentation on such concerns, see "Truce or Transition? Trends in Human Rights Abuse and Local Response in Southeast Myanmar Since the 2012 Cease-fire," Karen Human Rights Group, May 2014.

27. South, "Burma's Longest War."

28. Among different sectors of service delivery in conflict-affected areas, probably the greatest advances in "convergence" between state and nonstate provision has been in the field of health, with a number of meetings undertaken between government (primarily Ministry of Health) and EAG health departments, and associated community-based organizations (CBOs), which among other issues have focused on accreditation of nonstate personnel: "The Karen Department of Health and Welfare Continues to Push the Burma Government to Recognize Its Community Health Workers and to Extend Its Health Service," *Karen News*, 3 October 2013.

29. On a number of occasions in early and mid-2013, fighting broke out in Karen State between the KNU/KNLA(Karen National Liberation Army) (particular-

ly Brigade 5), DKBA (Democratic Karen Buddhist Army), and Myanmar Army–influenced Border Guard Force units. Nevertheless, leaders of Karen EAGs, including BGF units, have formed a Karen Reunification Committee, seeking to coordinate military activities and reach accommodations acceptable to local elites, in terms of political and military authority on the ground. This development can be seen as representing a move toward more consociational forms of governance cooperation between Karen elite segments, marking a potentially significant break from previous attempts to reunify disparate and fragmented Karen military and political structures, in the name of "Karen unity," and under a *single* command structure.

30. Thomas Parks, Nat Colletta, and Ben Oppenheim, "The Contested Corners of Asia: Subnational Conflict and International Development Assistance" (Bangkok: The Asia Foundation, 2013).

31. See Marie Lall and Ashley South, "Comparing Models of Non-state Ethnic Education in Myanmar: The Mon and Karen National Education Regimes," *Journal of Contemporary Asia* 2 (2013): 1–24.

32. The author is a senior consultant for the MPSI.

33. The Asia Foundation identifies strategies for peacebuilding in contested states, including confidence-building activities—which "does not mean building confidence in the state; confidence relates to the expectation that the conflict itself (and the political dynamics that influence the conflict) can be overcome and that a credible transition to peace will occur" (Parks, Colletta, and Oppenheim, "Contested Corners of Asia."

34. For regularly updated information on the MPSI, see www.peacedonorsupportgroup.com/myanmar-peace-support-initiative.html.

35. From late 2012, the MPSI increasingly functioned (among other roles) as a secretariat to the Peace Donor Support Group, which includes most Western donors to the peace process.

36. Parks, Colletta, and Oppenheim, "Contested Corners of Asia."

37. The Asia Foundation (in Parks, Colletta, and Oppenheim, "Contested Corners of Asia") challenges the assumptions that economic growth and improved levels of development and service delivery can reduce violent conflict in the absence of political and institutional transformation.

38. Kim Jolliffe, "People's War, People's Peace—How Can International Peacebuilders Facilitate Reconciliation of the KNU Conflict and Address Local Security Concerns?" (London: King's College War Studies Department, 2013).

39. See Oliver Richmond, *The Transformation of Peace* (Basingstoke, UK: Palgrave Macmillan, 2007).

40. See also Duffield, *Global Governance and the New Wars,* and with specific reference to Myanmar, see Mark Duffield, "On the Edge of 'No Man's Land': Chronic Emergency in Myanmar." Working Paper 1, independent report commissioned by the Office of the UN RC/HC, Yangon, and UNOCHA, New York (Bristol, UK: Centre for Governance and International Affairs, University of Bristol, 2008).

41. James Ferguson, *The Anti-Politics Machine: 'Development,' Depoliticization, and Bureaucratic Power in Lesotho* (Minneapolis: University of Minnesota Press, 1994).

42. Compare with Elliott Prasse-Freeman's "abdication of politics" (Chapter 5).

43. Parks, Colletta, and Oppenheim, "Contested Corners of Asia"; italics in original.

44. Ardeth Maung Thawnghmung, *The "Other" Karen in Myanmar: Ethnic Minorities and the Struggle Without Arms* (Lanham, MD: Lexington Books, 2012).

9

Planning for Social and Economic Development

Lex Rieffel

In its first three years, the Thein Sein government has greatly raised expectations, domestically and abroad, that it will rapidly transform the Myanmar economy. Its success in meeting these expectations will depend on many factors, including luck. Other chapters in this book focus on the two most important of those factors: ending internal ethnic and communal conflicts and building a democratic political system consistent with good governance. In this chapter, I focus on the economic planning process: the design and implementation of formal plans that spell out long-term economic and social objectives, as well as the policies and programs adopted to achieve these objectives. Planning is nothing new for Myanmar. One could say that Myanmar/Burma, along with other countries that gained their independence after World War II, was born with a plan in its teeth.

Myanmar's first major economic development plan was the Pyidawtha Plan, adopted in 1953. It was built on a two-year analysis funded by the US government and carried out by a team of economists and engineers led by Robert R. Nathan. Sadly, Myanmar's performance over the next five years fell far short of the objectives of the Pyidawtha Plan. The Ne Win regime was even less successful in achieving the objectives of the plans it sought to implement between 1962 and 1988. Although the plans of the Than Shwe regime (1992–2011) were more realistic and announcements were routinely made that targets had been achieved, the verifiable results were underwhelming.

The Thein Sein government did not long hesitate before initiating a new planning process, partly because it wanted to get a great deal of foreign aid and the donors wanted to see a plan before making long-term aid commitments. The government proceeded on two tracks. It produced a "Framework for Economic and Social Reforms" at the end of 2012 and started work on a twenty-year "National Comprehensive Development Plan."

After elaborating on Myanmar's 1948–2011 planning experience, I will sketch out the current planning process, provide highlights of the framework, and describe the status of the twenty-year plan. Then I will focus on six major planning challenges in the coming years, in light of Myanmar's past experience with development plans. These six challenges are (1) infrastructure, (2) resource extraction, (3) human resource development, (4) the agriculture sector, (5) foreign aid, and (6) macroeconomic management.

The Pyidawtha Plan and Its Successors

Myanmar's track record of planning makes it hard to be optimistic about future planning efforts.[1] It appears that a number of the mistakes in its past are being repeated, and some of the planning challenges that were not met successfully in the past may not be met in the foreseeable future. Moreover, it is conceivable that the tsunami of aid donor interest in Myanmar since 2011 will contribute to producing disappointing planning outcomes.

In seeking to assess the prospects for Myanmar's current national economic development plans, it is important to dwell on both Myanmar's legacy of colonialism and its track record of planning over the sixty-five years since its independence. Tin Maung Maung Than succinctly sums up the former as follows:

> The colonial experience shaped the set of associated concepts concerning the political economy of post-independent Myanmar that became the vision of the emerging political elites. The most persistent vision was that of a socialist economy characterized by anti-capitalist and nationalist themes. Together with the imperative for reconstructing the war-ravaged economy, socialism, economic independence, and planning formed the basis of the dirigiste approach to national economic development.[2]

Work on Myanmar's first national economic development plan was initiated by General Aung San at a "Rehabilitation Conference" convened a month before his assassination in July 1947. It was formally adopted by the government shortly after independence on 4 January 1948.[3]

In 1950, inspired by a newspaper report about an economic assessment of Iran's potential carried out by a private firm, Prime Minister U Nu directed his staff to undertake a similar assessment for Burma. The result was a two-year contract with the US engineering firm of Knappen Tippetts Abbett (KTA) in association with the mining engineering firm Pierce Management and the economic consulting firm Robert R. Nathan Associates.[4]

The U Nu government convened a conference in August 1952 to launch the eight-year Pyidawtha Plan.[5] The analytical core of this plan was a report from the KTA-Nathan team: "Comprehensive Report: Economic and Engineering Development of Burma." It was delivered to the government of Burma in August 1953 in two volumes together containing over 800 pages.[6]

Two features of the historical context for the Pyidawtha Plan are worth mentioning. One is the massive destruction of infrastructure in Burma that occurred during World War II, which explains the leading role of the KTA firm and the emphasis in the plan on infrastructure rehabilitation and development. The other feature is the 1948 constitution, which had many socialist and welfare elements that were aligned with the views of Robert R. Nathan. Nathan had gained prominence as a planner of the wartime mobilization of the US economy, as a liberal thinker, and as an advocate of progressive economic policies.

Around the time the final report was delivered, the government of Burma shut down the US technical assistance program to protest the CIA's support of the remnants of the Kuomintang (KMT) forces that had fled into northern Burma as the People's Liberation Army established control of mainland China. Significantly, Nathan's team of economists continued to work in Burma for the Economic and Social Board, funded directly by the Ministry of National Planning.[7] This arrangement ended shortly after the increasingly dysfunctional U Nu government resigned and ceded temporary authority to the Burmese army in 1958.

Two assumptions underlying the Pyidawtha Plan contributed significantly to its lack of success. First, it explicitly assumed that the insurrections against the government would be resolved by the beginning of 1954, but they continued with little respite. Second, it assumed that the price for Burma's rice exports would remain high. Instead, when the Korean War wound down in the mid-1950s, global demand dropped significantly and prices fell. As a result, the amount of foreign exchange available to fund capital projects was considerably lower than expected.

A third factor may have been equally important in the abandonment of the Pyidawtha Plan after 1958: the *tatmadaw* had been largely neglected in its design and implementation. If General Ne Win had acquired an interest in the plan, some of the economic disasters of his twenty-six years in power might have been avoided.

The goal of the Pyidawtha Plan was to increase national output by 90 percent in eight and a half years, not an overly ambitious goal in the context of postwar reconstruction. Forty-two percent of the capital formation in this period was to be undertaken by the government's programs and projects, with the rest by the private sector.

The Pyidawtha Plan started to veer seriously off track in a political crisis over the 1957/58 budget when U Nu decided to introduce a new four-year plan. Implementation of the Pyidawtha Plan ended in April 1958 when the Anti-Fascist Peoples Freedom League (AFPFL) split, leading to the parliament's decision in September 1958 to relinquish power to a caretaker government led by General Ne Win.

In his analysis of the failure of the Pyidawtha Plan, Louis Walinsky suggested that a strategy of development that placed more reliance on the private sector could have been more successful. One evident shortcoming was that it diverted the attention of Burma's leaders from the crucial task of establishing civil order. Furthermore, it failed to highlight how much effective plan implementation would depend on the active involvement of these leaders.

Implementation of the Pyidawtha Plan was not dependent on foreign aid at the outset, but foreign aid financed more than 50 percent of the public sector's capital expenditures in the second half of the plan period. The main donors, by disbursements in US dollars, were Japan, the United States, India, Russia, and the World Bank. From Walinsky's perspective, the biggest aid problems arose with US assistance. In his view, US aid "was extended slowly, painfully and inflexibly, on a piecemeal basis. Apart from surplus disposals, it was project-tied and oriented. It bore no necessary relation to broad development goals or to the total development program. It was not coordinated in any significant way with aid from any other sources."[8]

In short, Burma's aid programs "seemed, for the most part, to have been centered on the several donors' needs, policies and objectives, rather than on Burma's. . . . Indeed it seemed almost as though [Burma's] experiences were causing her to withdraw, once again, toward her historic isolation."[9]

Walinsky summarized the 1950s development planning experience as follows:

> [The Pyidawtha Plan contributed] a goal, an approach, and a demonstration of the kinds of analysis, organization, procedures and policies necessary to do the job. The effectiveness of this contribution was limited by an incapacity or unreadiness on the part of those whose appreciation was most required to realize its full implications.[10]

An alternative view was set forth in Myanmar economist Thet Tun's 1964 critique of Walinsky's account in which he argued that the "ideology" of the US advisers was at the heart of the plan's failure.[11]

Burma's national planning experiences over the next thirty years, from 1958 to 1988, were even less satisfactory. When General Ne Win came to power in 1962, Burma turned sharply nationalist, isolationist, and socialist. Most modern Burmese enterprises were nationalized; foreign firms were expropriated.

Tin Maung Maung Than divides the Ne Win era into two parts: a period of military rule from 1962 to 1974 and a period of one-party rule from 1974 to 1988. A sixteen-year "Perspective Plan" was issued in 1961 and then a "Military Four-Year Plan" was developed for the period 1966/67 to 1969/70 as a guide for annual plans. However, the first serious planning exercise under Ne Win's regime was the "Twenty-Year Perspective Plan" endorsed by the Burma Socialist Programme Party (BSPP) in 1973 and implemented through a set of four-year plans. This twenty-year plan grew out of the "Long-Term and Short-Term Economic Policies of the BSPP," a document formulated by the party secretariat and approved by the BSPP Central Committee in September 1972. This document "was essentially the economic manifesto of the BSPP."[12]

The four-year plans under the twenty-year plan were implemented but were unable to prevent Myanmar from falling further and further behind its regional neighbors economically. Symptomatic of the policy failures during the Ne Win era were three demonetizations, the first of which took place in 1964. Significantly, the Ne Win regime departed in the 1970s from its initial position of eschewing foreign aid. Even the United States relaunched an aid program that continued at a modest level until the popular uprising in 1988. Nevertheless, the foreign aid provided was not able to stop Myanmar's steady economic decline. In December 1987, the UN added Myanmar to its list of the world's least developed countries.

Tin Maung Maung Than sums up the economic record of the Ne Win era as follows:

> In its 26 years of governance, two generations of Myanmar military leaders had not been able to establish an enduring and strong state structure that would control the commanding heights of the national economy and fulfill their elusive aspirations of transforming Myanmar into an equitable and prosperous industrialized country. Instead, their legacy had been an enervated state that had denied itself of the opportunities offered by markets as well as the human resources and creative endeavors of its citizens.[13]

National economic planning after 1988, under the State Law and Order Restoration Council (SLORC) and the State Peace and Development Council (SPDC), reversed course away from the socialist path back to market-oriented strategies sketched out in a new set of four-year and five-year plans. However, in the wake of the military's suppression of the 1988 uprising, foreign aid from Western donors dried up again. Toward the end of the 1990s, Myanmar experienced severe balance of payments constraints, exacerbated by the financial crises in Thailand, Indonesia, and Korea in 1997 and by the economic sanctions imposed by Western countries. The balance of payments constraints were largely relieved when Myanmar started exporting natural gas to Thailand in 1998, but the economy continued to underperform relative to most other countries in Asia.

The SLORC wasted little time in initiating its own series of plans. Initially, these were a set of annual plans under the regime's Stabilization Program. Then a "Short-Term Four-Year Plan" was formulated for 1992/93 through the 1995/96 fiscal years. It was succeeded by the "Second Short-

Term Plan" for the fiscal period 1996/97 to 2000/01.[14] Next came two five-year plans.

A second attempt to design and implement a comprehensive economic development plan, what might be labeled Pyidawtha 2.0, was launched in 2001 by the government of Japan. For the next two years a resident team in Yangon, supplemented by a large number of Japanese experts, worked with Myanmar counterparts to produce the Myanmar Economic Structural Adjustment Program (MESAP). The MESAP was delivered to the government in 2003, but it was never implemented for two reasons. First, the attack on Aung San Suu Kyi and her entourage at Depayin in May 2003 prompted Japan to suspend most of its aid to Myanmar. Second, the sacking of Prime Minister and Chief of Intelligence Khin Nyunt in October 2004 removed the project's major client from the scene and no other official replaced him to champion the plan.

Cyclone Nargis that devastated much of the delta region of Myanmar in May 2008 had a silver lining in the form of renewed flows of foreign aid. While initially resisted by the SPDC, pressure from its ASEAN partners succeeded in creating a substantial international relief and recovery effort that set the stage for the flood of foreign aid in response to the political and economic reforms initiated in 2011 by the Thein Sein government.

Summing up economic planning in the SLORC/SPDC period, on the positive side it moved the country substantially away from the debilitating socialist economy of the Ne Win era. On the negative side, it failed to utilize the windfall of foreign exchange from natural gas exports to Thailand to end the state of warfare with the armed ethnic groups or to raise the standard of living of the general population.

Planning Under the Thein Sein Government

The economy inherited by the Thein Sein government was underperforming but not in crisis, primarily due to the liquidity provided by natural gas exports to Thailand. Macroeconomic mismanagement was the overriding constraint. Chronic budget deficits were financed by borrowing from the central bank, resulting in high inflation. The official exchange rate was fixed and grossly overvalued, perhaps more than any other in the world. Formal trade was highly restricted, leading to a relatively high level of unrecorded trade and smuggling. Agriculture sector output was depressed by institutional and policy weaknesses. Natural resource extraction was expanding, but the full benefit was not flowing through the budget to the population as a whole. Demonetizations in the 1980s and a banking crisis in 2002 had produced deep distrust of the banking system, so Myanmar's economy was cash-based. Western sanctions remained a significant constraint on private sector investment.

By mid-2013, many of these drags on economic dynamism were gone or sharply reduced as the Thein Sein government launched a series of reforms, although the pace of these reforms was not immediately apparent. In the way that Thein Sein's meeting with Aung San Suu Kyi in August 2011 was the game-changing breakthrough in the political arena, the move to a new managed-float exchange rate system on 1 April 2012 was the game-changer in the economic arena.[15]

At the beginning of 2014, the Thein Sein government was implementing or designing three distinct but overlapping national development plans: a preexisting but revised five-year plan, a new twenty-year plan, and a Framework for Economic and Social Reforms providing a bridge between the other two plans.

Five-Year Plan

When it came to power in 2011, the Thein Sein government decided to implement the Than Shwe regime's five-year plan (fiscal year [FY] 2011/12 to FY 2015/16) rather than abandon it. Annual plans to implement the first two years of this five-year plan were approved by the legislature in the context of passing annual budget laws. In January 2013, however, the Thein Sein government submitted to the legislature a substitute for the final three years of the plan (FY 2013/14 to 2015/16).

Twenty-Year Plan

The twenty-year plan has been labeled the National Comprehensive Development Plan (NCDP). It is being developed using both a top-down and a bottom-up approach; broad goals are set at the top levels of government, while detailed plans, or wish lists, are developed by every township and by every ministry and agency of the government. These goals and plans are being merged into a coherent whole. Implementation will be carried out through a series of four five-year plans beginning with a FY 2011/12 to FY 2015/16 plan.

An important input for the NCDP is the Myanmar Comprehensive Development Vision (MCDV), an exercise being undertaken by the Economic Research Institute for ASEAN and East Asia (ERIA), ASEAN's economic think tank based in Jakarta. The exercise was launched at the Third Mekong-Japan Summit in November 2011 and is funded primarily by the Japan-ASEAN Integration Fund. It has already generated some controversy by proposing a development strategy of "two-polar growth with border development and better connectivity." Some within Myanmar have criticized the strategy as inequitable, suggesting instead a strategy that gives equal attention to each of the fourteen regions and states. As of August 2014, however, the MCDV was still under wraps.[16]

Framework for Economic and Social Reforms

At the request of the Office of the President and in consultation with the Ministry of National Planning and Economic Development (NPED), work on the Framework for Economic and Social Reforms (FESR) began in May 2012 at the Center for Economic and Social Development (CESD) of the Myanmar Development Resource Institute (MDRI). Covering three years, it resembles the "poverty reduction strategy papers" produced by low-income countries in all regions of the world as guides for development assistance from multilateral and bilateral donors. The impetus for producing the FESR was the government's eagerness to convene a conference where donors would pledge funding for specific projects and programs. An important feature is a set of "quick wins" in nine sectors.

Figure 9.1: Framework for Economic and Social Reforms

From the Executive Summary:

- [M]aintaining a stable macroeconomic framework is the first order of reforms . . .
- [T]he [ASEAN Economic Community, AEC] targets will be an important driver of further reforms.
- The government will give highest priority to the drawing up of the necessary procedures as well as environmental and social guidelines for foreign investment in accordance with the new law . . .
- Given a high percentage of agricultural contribution to GDP and employment in the country, agricultural growth is critical for inclusive development.
- In order to ensure that the extraction of natural resources produces real benefits for people, the government is . . . committed to early adoption of the [Extractive Industries Transparency Initiative—EITI] .

From the Text:

Paragraph 42. Four areas of policy priorities:

- Sustained industrial development to catch up with global economies.
- Equitable sharing of resources, both budgetary and foreign aid, among regions and states.
- Effective implementation of people-centered development.
- Reliable and accurate gathering of statistical data.

Paragraph 46. Short and Long-term Goals:

- Full implementation of ASEAN economic integration in accordance with its 2015 schedules.
- Achievement of the Millennium Development Goals by 2015. Graduation from least developed country status by 2020.

Paragraph 47. Targets:

- An average annual GDP growth rate of 7.7%.
- Industry share of GDP rising from 26% to 32%.
- Per capita GDP growth of between 30 and 40% from the base year.

At the monthly donor meeting hosted by the NPED Ministry in December 2012, the government announced that the first Myanmar Development Cooperation Forum would be held on 19–20 January 2013. The draft FESR was approved by the Planning Commission at its 26–27 December meeting, and on 28 December the document was sent to donors in Burmese and English "for your review and comments," but with a couple of missing sections.[17] The draft FESR was highly praised by the donors at the January forum, but as of August 2014 it had not been issued in a complete form. However, the legislature took the FESR into consideration in the course of developing the budget for FY 2013/14. Highlights from the FESR are provided in Figure 9.1.

Next Steps

The ten "quick wins" highlighted in the FESR were the following: (1) fiscal and tax reforms, including replacing the commercial tax with a general sales tax at a single rate; (2) monetary and financial sector reforms, including central bank autonomy and a shift from direct to indirect instruments of monetary policy; (3) liberalization of trade and investment; (4) private sector development (focusing on regulatory reform and tourism); (5) health and education; (6) food security and agricultural growth; (7) governance and transparency, including participation in the Extractive Industries Transparency Initiative (EITI); (8) mobile phones and Internet access (including a target of 80 percent mobile phone penetration by 2015); (9) infrastructure; and (10) effective and efficient government.[18]

Looking beyond the FESR, the success of Myanmar's twenty-year plan will depend partly on its design, partly on its implementation, and partly on external events over which the government has no control.

In the design process, the Ministry of National Planning and Economic Development clearly has the lead responsibility. This is not a new ministry; it has existed in roughly its present form for decades.[19] It is also drawing on expertise in the Center for Economic and Social Development in the Myanmar Development Resource Institute, as noted above. Significantly, while the first NPED minister was a retired general, he was replaced by a technocrat, Kan Zaw, in August 2012.[20] Backed by other technocrats in subministerial positions, the NPED ministry seems to have some influence on a broad range of economic policies. In the first three years of the Thein Sein government, NPED's planning efforts benefited significantly from a small number of expatriate advisers funded by the UN Development Programme and several bilateral aid donors. Responsibility for implementing the twenty-year plan will be widely shared among the government's ministries and agencies, but the NPED ministry is expected to play the central role in monitoring implementation and initiating corrective action where it appears to be lagging.

Another body with a formal role in the planning process is the National Economic and Social Advisory Council (NESAC), consisting of eminent personalities (mostly from the private sector) and reporting directly to President Thein Sein. The NESAC does not make public any of its proceedings, however, and by most accounts its impact on economic policy so far has been marginal.

The success of the twenty-year NCDP will also depend greatly on how the government of Myanmar approaches six major planning challenges: infrastructure, resource extraction, human resource development, the agriculture sector, macroeconomic management, and foreign aid. These are examined in the following sections.

The Infrastructure Challenge

Two facts illustrate the magnitude of Myanmar's infrastructure challenge as of mid-2014:

- Not one single highway or railroad connected Myanmar to any of its five neighboring countries.
- The natural gas exported by Myanmar to Thailand in 2013 generated four times as much electricity as Myanmar consumed from all sources in that year.[21]

Transportation Infrastructure

The SLORC/SPDC regime prided itself on its infrastructure investments. These were substantial—primarily roads and bridges—but they appear to have been selected more for their political and security benefits than their economic benefits. An example is the new highway from Yangon to Naypyitaw. Between the Yangon entrance and the Naypyitaw exit, a distance of roughly 200 miles, there are only three interchanges. As a result, the highway does not provide the farm-to-market benefits or other development benefits normally associated with highway construction.

The Asian Development Bank (ADB) has done a great deal of work on "Asian Connectivity" and has loaned hundreds of millions of dollars for the construction of highways in mainland Southeast Asia. Long-designated and partly constructed corridors that include Myanmar are the East-West Corridor, the Southern Corridor, and the North-South Corridor.[22]

China has built a superhighway to the Myanmar border at Ruili-Muse and has committed to supporting the construction of a high-quality road from Muse to the Indian Ocean port of Kyaukphyu, roughly following the route of the dual oil-gas pipelines. It is not clear when construction will begin and how long it will take to complete.[23]

Thailand has decent roads that go to the Myanmar border in five locations. Segments of connecting roads on the Myanmar side are under construction, but there is no timetable yet for completing any of these links.[24] The Indian government is financing construction of the Kaladan Multimodal Transit Project linking the Indian Ocean port of Sittwe to an inland port up the Kaladan River and then by road to its Manipur State. Reopening the World War II–era Stillwell Road (formerly Ledo Road) between India's Nagaland State and Myanmar's Kachin State is also under discussion. Construction of a bridge across the Mekong River between Myanmar and Laos commenced in early 2013 and is due to finish in 2015, but this is likely to have more political than economic significance in the near term.[25]

In the area of port development, the Thein Sein government has made its priorities clear and these appear sensible. Top priority has been given to the Myanmar International Terminals Thilawa, on the outskirts of Yangon. It will service the Thlilawa special economic zone (SEZ), Myanmar's top priority SEZ (see below).

Second priority has been given to a deep seaport at Kyaukphyu on the Arakan coast where the dual gas and oil pipelines to China begin. Funding has been earmarked for building out the port and a connected SEZ (see below). China may feature prominently in developing this area.

The Than Shwe government awarded a concession in late 2010 to one of Thailand's biggest construction companies to develop a deep seaport and heavy industrial zone at Dawei [Tavoy] in Thanintharyi [Tenasserim] Region, with road, railroad, pipeline, and electrical power links to the Thai border 99 miles (160 kilometers) from the port.[26] The Thein Sein government effectively terminated this concession before any part of it had been completed.[27] In 2013, the Thai government decided to put its weight behind the project. The result is a major redesign, a new private sector partner on the Myanmar side, and an extended timetable.

With regard to airports, improvements have been and continue to be made at the international airports serving Naypyitaw and Mandalay to handle the heavier traffic for the Southeast Asian Games (hosted by Myanmar in December 2013) and for the ASEAN and East Asian Summit meetings in 2014, as well as growing tourist arrivals. In August 2013, South Korea's Incheon International Airport Corporation won a tender to build a new international airport for Yangon, but it was unable to conclude a contract with the government, and in February 2014 the government began negotiations with a consortium led by Singapore's Changi Airport Authority. The government also plans to issue in the last quarter of 2014 a tender for upgrading thirty-nine smaller airports.[28]

Electric Power Infrastructure

One of the most dismal statistics about Myanmar is electricity consumption per capita.[29] Assuming a population of fifty million, per capita consumption in 2011 was 100 kilowatt-hours, the lowest in the ten-nation ASEAN community. In part this reflects a relatively low level of investment in electricity generation over the past fifty years, but even more it reflects the decision of the Than Shwe regime to export natural gas and electricity to Thailand and China. In 2011, more than 85 percent of Myanmar's natural gas production was exported to Thailand, and 25 percent of the electric power generated by seventeen hydropower plants in Myanmar was exported to China.

The Thein Sein government has fast-tracked a number of new power generation projects to help meet the escalating demand for electricity in the country's urban centers. It is also negotiating to increase the shares of electricity and gas retained for domestic consumption. For example, a news report in February 2014 noted that one-third of the gas produced in Phase One of the Zawtika project would be retained for domestic consumption.[30]

The most daunting challenges in this area relate to dam projects initiated under the previous government with Chinese, Thai, and Indian companies but not yet completed. Among these is the Myitsone dam project on the upper reaches of the Irrawaddy River in Kachin State, conceived as one of a series of seven dams in the same general area designed primarily to export electricity to China. Arguably the biggest of the early economic reform actions by the Thein Sein government was suspending construction of the Myitsone dam in September 2011 for the remainder of his term (until 2015). The suspension delivered a major shock to China-Myanmar relations, and how the affair will play out is far from certain. (See Chapter 12.)

Myanmar's hydropower potential is enormous, estimated at more than 100 times the current installed capacity. Twenty-two hydropower dams have been completed, fourteen are under construction, and another fifty have been approved by the government. Ninety percent of the total are financed by Chinese sources.[31] Myanmar has one coal-fired power plant and three more are to be built in the near term.

There are serious environmental and population displacement issues related to all of these projects, in addition to ownership and financing issues. It will not be easy for the government to reorganize the Myanmar Electric Power Enterprise into a set of more efficient production, transmission, and distribution companies, some of which could be privatized. Negotiating respectable contracts with new private-sector operators will be necessary to mobilize the private capital required for a rapid increase in energy production. Adjusting the balance to favor domestic energy consumption over energy exports will take time and the renegotiation of legacy contracts.[32] Transparency sufficient to meet popular expectations in a democratic system will be difficult in all areas of electricity sector development. Resisting political pressure to subsidize electricity tariffs will be a challenge. What is certain is that demand for electricity will soar in the coming years as long as Myanmar's three transitions remain on track.

Industrial Zones and Special Economic Zones

The Than Shwe regime encouraged the establishment of industrial zones at the district level in the mid-1990s.[33] By 2012, eighteen such zones had been established and seven more were under construction. Few of the existing industrial zones are fully developed, and most of them suffer from serious infrastructure weakness, notably unreliable electricity supply.

Shortly before ceding power to the Thein Sein government, the Than Shwe regime promulgated a general SEZ law and a parallel law specifically for an SEZ at Dawei in Thanintharyi Region. Recognizing serious deficiencies in these laws, the Thein Sein government drafted a new national SEZ law with a view to giving the SEZs a major role in Myanmar's development strategy. It was passed by the legislature in January 2014.[34]

Three major SEZs are now on the drawing boards. The most advanced is at Thilawa, on the outskirts of Yangon, linked to an existing port (see above) and undertaken with strong support from the government of Japan. A public company was funded in April 2014 to manage the Thilawa SEZ.[35] Great efforts are being made to provide fair compensation for land being acquired and to meet a high standard on other social and environmental issues.

The second most advanced is an SEZ at the Kyaukphyu port in Rakhine (Arakan) State, the terminus of the dual gas and oil pipelines to China. In March 2014, a Singapore-led consortium won the tender to design the development of this SEZ.[36] The third SEZ, at Dawei, is in the process of being restructured in a major way as noted in the section above about port development.[37]

There are difficult issues associated with SEZ development. One issue is whether the SEZs will be open to domestic investors or only to foreign investors and joint ventures. Another issue is financing. Current policy emphasizes the contribution of private capital to develop the SEZs, but there is always pressure on the government in these projects to provide too much funding (or "tax expenditures") or to seek too much funding from bilateral aid agencies in the form of loans either directly to the government or guaranteed by the government. The alternative to SEZ development is to focus on removing obstacles to job-creating domestic and foreign investment across the country. However, a small group of SEZs can serve to kick-start investment at the beginning of an economic transition, as it has in China, by concentrating essential infrastructure and service support (electricity, port access, customs clearance) in one place.

Information and Communications Technology

Myanmar ranks among the most underserved countries in the world for mobile phone penetration and Internet access. Happily, these are areas where the Thein Sein government has advanced rapidly and relatively skillfully. The process for awarding mobile phone licenses in mid-2013 to two foreign companies, Telenor of Norway and Ooredoo of Qatar, came close to matching international best practice. The government's coverage target of 80 percent of the population by 2015 is ambitious, and internal conflicts, both ethnic and communal, may prove to be insurmountable obstacles to achieving them. Fortunately, the financing risks associated with this part of Myanmar's infrastructure development seem to be close to zero. The risks overwhelmingly lie in the direction of not meeting coverage and access targets.[38] A Singapore firm using French technology launched a mobile money service in January 2014. Services of this kind have had a remarkably large and positive economic impact in other parts of the world (notably Africa) and have the potential of being transformational in Myanmar.

Urban Development

Urban development is a financial bottomless pit, with insatiable demand for government-funded residential, commercial, industrial, and infrastructure projects. This is illustrated in the construction of the new capital of Naypyitaw, an enormous sunk cost. The challenge in Yangon is to modernize and build up the city without destroying so much of the heritage architecture that the city loses its character and becomes a clone of Bangkok or Manila. Properly done, much of the financing for urban development will come from private sources, both direct investment and lending, but the pressure for government funding is likely to be intense, especially as Myanmar's democratic institutions advance.

Financing Infrastructure

At the heart of the infrastructure challenge is finding appropriate forms of financing for the many projects Myanmar wants to undertake in the near term. The risks probably lie in the direction of too much financing rather than too little.

An abundance of infrastructure financing will be available from private sources, but on commercial terms that can lead to debt-servicing problems down the road. Public-private partnerships (PPPs) are promoted so vigorously nowadays that they sound like a panacea, but they are devilishly difficult to structure in ways that produce high-quality service without saddling governments with risks they cannot afford to bear. Funding from multilateral development banks also burdens low-income borrowing countries with significant risks because of their treatment as preferred creditors; unlike bilateral aid agencies, the multilateral banks do not restructure or write down repayment obligations when problems arise. Competition among foreign infrastructure suppliers is expected to be fierce with much of the competition coming in the form of financing terms that are difficult to assess and compare. Myanmar will be hard pressed to avoid PPP failures or debt-servicing problems in the medium term associated with infrastructure projects.

The Resource Extraction Challenge

Most economists would agree that Myanmar is among the countries in the world where an abundance of natural resources has proven to be more of a curse than a blessing. In Myanmar's case, the curse has come partly in the form of rent-seeking behavior that enables members of the social elite to capture the lion's share of the value of the resources being extracted.[39] Another issue is the conflicts ongoing since independence between the resource-poor ethnically Bamar heartland and the resource-rich borderlands inhabited by ethnic minorities.

A large portion of Myanmar's forest resources has been depleted, but the Thein Sein government has taken steps to reduce timber extraction toward a sustainable rate, notably by banning the export of logs after 1 April 2014. It will be difficult, however, to stop illegal log exports from the mountain regions on Myanmar's borders, many of which are controlled by ethnic armed groups and others by regional commands of the *tatmadaw*.

The immediate challenge in the period ahead is the pace of extraction of oil, gas, and minerals. Natural gas exports to Thailand have been the single biggest foreign exchange earner for Myanmar for the past ten years. Myanmar's earnings from gas exports are now increasing by leaps and bounds because of a new field supplying more gas to Thailand and because the gas pipeline to China became operational in mid-2013.[40] If these were Myanmar's only sources of foreign exchange, there would be little reason to worry. However, foreign exchange earned from exporting jade, copper, tin, and rubies is increasing. In addition, direct investment is beginning to flow into nonresource sectors and foreign aid is ramping up. Furthermore, the Ministry of Energy announced in October 2013 the award of tenders for the exploration of oil and gas in thirteen onshore blocks and in March 2014 in twenty offshore blocks.[41]

A recent study out of Harvard University's Kennedy School of Government argues that Myanmar has sufficient resource wealth to avoid dependence on foreign aid, explaining that "if reasonable taxes were imposed on natural resources, there would be adequate funds to finance enhanced efficient infrastructure investment and spending on health and education."[42] The study focuses on jade, hydroelectric power, and the controversial Letpadaung copper mine, estimating that billions of dollars of revenue would flow to the government if these resources were taxed to the degree that they are in other neighboring countries.

The Thein Sein government is to be commended for its announced goal of participating in the EITI, which will help to ensure that the revenue the government obtains from resource extraction is fully disclosed and fully on budget.[43] EITI, however, does not address the rate of extraction, which arguably is too high. Indeed a case can be made for announcing a moratorium—for five years, perhaps—on new mining licenses and land concessions, as Laos did in June 2012. A "time out" of this kind would make it easier for the government to build the institutional capacity to address the environmental and social impacts of proposed projects and manage larger flows of foreign exchange.

The Human Resource Challenge

Myanmar may have depleted its human resources at a faster rate over the past sixty years than its natural resources. Of course this is not true on a simple numerical basis because Myanmar's population at independence was 18 to 19 million and stood at 51 million in the 2014 census. The depletion thus is not in population size, but in the dearth of professional-level expertise in areas ranging from government administration to medicine to business. Consider the fact that U Nu was one of the leaders of the Non-Aligned Movement in the 1950s and U Thant became the third secretary general of the United Nations in 1961. Apart from Aung San Suu Kyi, Myanmar personalities with this kind of global stature do not exist. Myanmar at independence had one of the finest medical schools in Asia and today by most measures it must rank at or close to the bottom. Under Myanmar's military rulers from 1962 to 2011, government investment in people was focused primarily on military personnel, while the educational standards in state-supported civilian schools and universities steadily declined.

A vignette of higher education illustrates how far behind other Asian countries Myanmar has fallen. In 2013, ambitious students at the Yangon Institute of Economics could take "tuition classes" for a month that guaranteed high marks on the final examination for particular courses. Tutors were often a recent graduate who worked with a copy of the textbook assigned for the course in which the professor had highlighted answers to all of the exam questions. The students paid the tutor around MMK7000 (roughly US$7) per tutorial, of which MMK2000 went to the professor.[44]

It is hard to imagine Myanmar achieving the objectives of its twenty-year plan without some early breakthroughs in the education sector. Some of the most crucial breakthroughs will not be obvious because of rapidly evolving learning technology. The scope given for private education is an especially key policy issue that will have a great impact on outcomes, and one where a social consensus may be elusive. Substantial foreign aid resources are targeting the education sector, and fortunately the risks of doing harm with aid projects may be lower here than in any other sector.

The Agriculture Sector Challenge

An argument can be made that the most important sector for Myanmar's future development is the agriculture sector. According to the 2014 census, 70 percent of Myanmar's population is rural and dependent on agriculture. Furthermore, in all of the other Asian countries that have achieved middle-income status, raising the incomes of rural households has been a vital first step; the outstanding example is China.

Like the education sector but unlike the information-communications sector, there is no "cookbook" for developing agriculture. Every country is different, and within a country as large and diverse as Myanmar, there is no single development strategy that will work across the country. Sadly, it looks as though the Thein Sein government has wasted more than three years trying to raise agriculture production through top-down measures, such as decreeing that rice farmers plant a particular kind of hybrid rice.

One especially complex issue here is land-grabbing: taking land away from people who have farmed it for years, even generations, for commercial farming or real estate development or infrastructure projects like dams. The sitting Myanmar legislature has passed three separate laws since its members were sworn in at the beginning of 2011, but all have serious potential flaws that seem likely to contribute to land alienation and rural unemployment and underemployment.[45]

The Thein Sein government has raised the amount of seasonal crop credit that the parastatal Agricultural Development Bank can offer, but the scope of government-supported crop credit is too limited to have a significant macroeconomic impact. The measures taken so far seem piecemeal and reactive instead of being strategic and comprehensive. Myanmar has one outstanding advantage in the agriculture sector: its soils have not been damaged by excessive use of agricultural chemicals as they have been in other Asian countries. This is one reason why the benefits to agriculture sector development could be as high as the benefits to manufacturing sector development in the long run. To benefit from this comparative advantage, however, the government will have to act quickly to reduce farm-to-market costs and discourage harmful cultivation practices.

The Challenge of Foreign Aid

The best that can be said about foreign aid is that it is a mixed blessing.[46] It has the potential, however, of being a curse in the case of Myanmar. To start with the extreme case, it is possible that Myanmar will be "smothered in love" from the foreign aid community: UN agencies, multilateral development banks, bilateral aid agencies, international nongovernmental organizations, and so on. It is hard to find a respectable foreign aid organization in the world that does not have an active program in Myanmar or is not in the process of establishing one.

One problem with all this attention is simply the time being devoted by senior officials in the Myanmar government to meeting with representatives from all these organizations. If they had only these representatives to receive, it might be manageable. But these officials are also drowning in meetings with foreign investors, foreign politicians, global personalities (entertainers, athletes, philanthropists, former presidents, etc.), the media, and more. It is not uncommon for senior officials to spend entire working days receiving visitors and then focus on their work after hours when they are tired. As a result, crucial policy decisions are delayed or given less thought than they deserve. This problem is especially acute in Myanmar's cultural context where there is little delegation of authority and the effectiveness of the bureaucracy is low.

A related problem is the conflicting advice being given to senior officials. With little experience on which to base choices, it is easy to imagine that a lot of suboptimal choices are being made.

Problems with foreign aid in other countries have been well documented, including aid dependency.[47] It is possible that Myanmar is sufficiently different and it is possible that aid donor behavior in Myanmar will be much better because of the horror stories elsewhere. There is some encouraging evidence here. To begin with, a small group of leading donor agencies began working in early 2012 on a set of principles to guide their activities in Myanmar.[48] This work led to the "Naypyitaw Accord on Aid Effectiveness" proposed by the Thein Sein government and approved by acclamation by all the donors participating in the first Myanmar Development Cooperation Forum in January 2013.

In short, the rhetoric is encouraging. It is hard to believe, nevertheless, that these steps will have a measurable and positive impact on day-to-day activities. The pressure from political capitals and agency headquarters to disburse rapidly and show results will be intense. Competition among donors for the best projects is unlikely to give way to cooperation. Promises not to hire government officials and other key people to staff their aid missions will be broken. The bewildering differences in programming and project management among donor agencies will remain.[49] It is possible that well-meaning efforts to strengthen democratic institutions in Myanmar, including the legislature and the judiciary, will have the tragic result of undermining good governance. It is even possible that the best intentioned efforts by foreigners to assist the peace process to resolve the decades-old internal conflicts will backfire, actually making it harder to achieve the peace that the country so desperately needs to reach its development objectives.

The role to be played by foreign aid is an important part of the design of Myanmar's twenty-year plan. If Myanmar is lucky, the role will be sensibly laid out and the donor agencies will fall into line. Sadly, experience in the rest of the world suggests that the odds are stacked in favor of a planning process where results often fall short of the targets, providing more ammunition to the critics of foreign aid globally. It would be especially tragic if the twenty-year plan fails for some of the same reasons that the Pyidawtha Plan failed sixty years ago.

The Challenge of Macroeconomic Management

The staff report on the International Monetary Fund's (IMF's) 2013 Article IV consultations with Myanmar summarizes the near-term outlook as follows:

> Growth is accelerating, driven by gas production, construction and services, while inflation climbed to 4.7 percent [year over year] in March 2013. External balances remain stable even as the current account deficit has widened due to large inflows of foreign direct investment. The short-term economic outlook remains favorable, with growth expected to accelerate slightly in 2013/14, and inflation to remain contained. International reserves are projected to continue to rise. Fiscal policy is striking an appropriate balance between providing for much-needed investment and social spending, and supporting macroeconomic stability. Risks to the outlook are tilted slightly to the downside.[50]

The staff report is more bullish on Myanmar's longer-term prospects. Assessments of Myanmar's macroeconomic performance by the World Bank, the Asian Development Bank, and other respected organizations present much the same story. It would be wise, however, to take all of these prognostications with a grain of salt. The most honest statement that one can say about Myanmar's macroeconomic performance in mid-2014 is that it seems okay and that no terrible problems cry out for attention.

One reason for the uncertainty is that Myanmar's economic statistics are not reliable. The World Bank website includes the following statement: "Comparable country data for Myanmar can't be provided at this time. The World Bank and other agencies are re-engaging with the Myanmar government and will support Myanmar in its effort to address the scarcity of reliable data for the country."[51]

Another reason is that the economy is changing rapidly in many ways, one of the most positive being the modernization of the banking sector that is beginning to move Myanmar away from having a cash-based economy. A third reason is that insufficient time has passed to develop a good sense of the links between policies and performance.

In reflecting on macroeconomic management in Myanmar going forward, one finds contradictory factors. On the positive side, the Asian countries as a group have achieved above-average results compared with developing countries in other regions of the world. One reason for this success seems to be a cultural predisposition to save more and consume less. On the negative side, one major concern is the weakness of the government institutions responsible for macroeconomic management, specifically the finance ministry and the central bank.

Another concern is Myanmar's quasi-democratic political system. As a historical fact, the Asian countries that experienced rapid economic growth in the past sixty years began their "takeoffs" under authoritarian regimes. Almost all of them began their transitions to democratic systems after reaching middle-income status. The contrasting experience of democratic versus authoritarian regimes is illustrated by the cases of China and India. Most explanations of why India's growth has been slower give great weight to its political system, which makes policy consensus harder to achieve and policy implementation less effective.[52]

Unless the social chemistry of Myanmar turns out to be very different, the Asian experience suggests that macroeconomic management will be one of the biggest challenges for the government that takes office after the 2015 election and for subsequent governments during the period of the twenty-year plan. Myanmar's social chemistry may be revealed in 2014 and 2015 under the strains of chairing ASEAN and conducting national elections. These strains would most likely be visible in the form of increased budget spending and delays in implementing essential reforms having an adverse impact on vested interests.

Wise management of Myanmar's hard-currency earnings, primarily from resource extraction, represent an especially daunting challenge in a country with so little experience in hands-on macroeconomic management and with a central bank that has insufficient tools for insulating the domestic economy from forces driving the exchange rate to appreciate. Some modest depreciation of the exchange rate will probably be necessary to encourage rapid growth in nonresource exports and job creation in the manufacturing sector. One way to ease exchange rate pressure is to create a "sovereign wealth fund" for excess hard currency earnings, but currently the government budget is highly dependent on these earnings.[53] Consequently, the efforts being made by the Thein Sein government to increase revenue from other sources, such as effective income tax collection and introducing a general sales tax, will be a major determinant of the success or failure of Myanmar's economic transition.

For a country with so little recent experience in macroeconomic management, it is difficult to appreciate the sweeping, all-encompassing nature of its impact. One of the risks for the economic transition, therefore, is that it will not get the attention it deserves. In fact, for each of the planning challenges discussed above, sound macroeconomic management has the ability to greatly improve the odds that these challenges will be met successfully.

Conclusion

Readers would be mistaken to conclude from this overview that Myanmar's future economic prospects are poor. There are positive developments, many of which have been noted in other chapters of this volume. The Thein Sein government has pleasantly surprised experts at regular intervals: the president's inaugural speech in March 2011, his dialogue with Aung San Suu Kyi that began in August 2011, the move to a managed float exchange rate system in April 2012, the well-conceived Framework for Economic and Social Reforms in December 2012, and the well-orchestrated Myanmar Development Cooperation Forum a month later. More pleasant surprises are possible. President Thein Sein's midterm speech on 9 August 2013 is also remarkable for the mandate he gave to his ministers for urgently accelerating implementation of the government's policies across the board in the remaining thirty months of his term. The "delivery units" he directed to be established by the Union ministries and by the region and state authorities may succeed in "changing their mindset," as Thein Sein requested and as necessary to be more effective in the period ahead. Another source of optimism is the general orientation of the government's development strategy, which is distinctly more private sector–oriented than the strategy adopted in the 1950s.

As of mid-2014, it is hard to be optimistic about the planning process per se. Muddling through seems the most likely result of the twenty-year Myanmar Comprehensive Development Plan (MCDP).[54] Gross domestic product (GDP) growth averaging above 6 percent per year over the next twenty years, the kind of growth seen in the other Asian countries that took off beginning in the 1970s, seems out of reach. But then GDP growth may not be the best measure of success in Myanmar. Achieving a peaceful and just society may be more important in the medium term than achieving a prosperous society.

Notes

1. Much of this section is drawn from Louis Walinsky, *Economic Development in Burma, 1951–1960* (New York: Twentieth Century Fund, 1962).

2. Tin Maung Maung Than, *State Dominance in Myanmar: The Political Economy of Industrialization* (Singapore: Institute of Southeast Asian Studies, 2007), 19.

3. Myanmar's first national economic plan, the "New Order Plan," emerged under the government of Ba Maw in 1943 during the Japanese occupation. A "Two

Year Plan for Economic Development of Burma" was promulgated in April 1948 but not implemented. These and eighteen more four-year, five-year, seven-year, sixteen-year, and twenty-year plans, some overlapping, are listed in Than, *State Dominance in Myanmar,* 38–39.

4. The dollar costs of the undertaking were funded by a US$10 million grant from the US government. Local-currency costs were met by the Burmese government. The grant was made by the Economic Cooperation Administration (ECA), later renamed the Technical Cooperation Administration (TCA).

5. *Pyidawtha* has been translated commonly as "happy land," but "prosperous land" may be closer to current usage.

6. Nathan Associates, the current name of the firm founded by Robert R. Nathan, has digitized the Pyidawtha Plan and posted it on their website at www.nathaninc.com/myanmar.

7. The Ministry of National Planning had broad responsibility for drawing up and monitoring the five-year plans and the annual plans. The Economic and Social Board, chaired by the prime minister, provided cabinet-level oversight for the planning system.

8. Walinsky, *Economic Development in Burma,* 606–607.

9. Ibid., 545.

10. Ibid., 149.

11. Thet Tun, "A Critique of Louis J. Walinsky's Economic Development in Burma, 1951–1969," *Journal of the Burma Research Society* 47, no. 1 (1964): 179. It is worth noting that the Pyidawtha Plan took a Keynesian approach that was quite different from the development strategy advocated at the time by the eminent Burmese economist Hla Myint. As a professor at the University of Rangoon (after earning a Ph.D. from the London School of Economics) and an advisor to the National Planning Department, Hla Myint argued in the 1950s for an approach that was more private sector–oriented and that emphasized agricultural development over industrialization. He was skeptical of planning and favored a more organic approach to development. In two areas, however, the Robert R. Nathan approach and the Hla Myint approach were similar: investing in infrastructure and improving the administrative capacity of the government.

12. Than, *State Dominance in Myanmar,* 119.

13. Ibid., 226. Later, he writes: "it is this curious interplay between personality, agency, and structure informed by particularistic interpretations of historical experiences that led to Myanmar's path towards bankruptcy through the failure of its state-led industrialization effort" (324).

14. Than, *State Dominance in Myanmar,* 363.

15. For an excellent overview of the strengths and weaknesses of the Thein Sein government's policies in 2013, see Sean Turnell, "The Glass Has Water: A Stock-Take of Myanmar's Economic Reforms: Exchange Rate, Financial System, Investment, and Sectoral Policies" in N. Cheesman, N. Farrelly, and T. Wilson, eds., *Debating Democratization in Myanmar* (Singapore: Institute of Southeast Asian Studies, 2014).

16. The MCDV exercise was split into two phases because of funding delays. The first phase covering selected sectors of the economy had been submitted to the president's office but approval for publication was still pending. The sectors are: agriculture development, industrial development, SME development, rural development and poverty reduction, infrastructure and energy, and financial sector development. The second phase was due to begin in May 2014. Personal correspondence, 14 May 2014.

17. The Planning Commission was established in 2012. It provides policy guidance and oversight of the NPED Ministry and is chaired by President Thein Sein. Other members include the two vice presidents, the union ministers, the attorney general, the auditor general, the Civil Services Board chairman, the chief ministers of the regions/states, deputy ministers, chairpersons of self-administered regions, and department heads. The Planning Commission reviewed the FESR before it was formally presented to the donors in January 2013.

18. A status report on the FESR was presented at the Second Myanmar Development Cooperation Forum. See Zaw Oo, "Implementing the Framework for Economic and Social Reforms," PowerPoint presentation, 27 January 2014.

19. In the postindependence governments led by U Nu, there was a Ministry of Planning and Finance. In the Ne Win era, a separate Finance Ministry emerged and the Ministry of Planning established regional offices at the township level.

20. Kan Zaw was the rector of the Yangon Institute of Economics before being appointed minister. Two more technocrats were appointed as deputy ministers. Set Aung was subsequently appointed as deputy governor of the Central Bank of Myanmar. Khin San Yi was subsequently appointed as minister of education in February 2014.

21. The Asian Development Bank–Accenture report *New Energy Architecture: Myanmar* (June 2013) puts Myanmar's natural gas exports to Thailand at 303 billion cubic feet. The Asian Development Bank report *Myanmar: Energy Sector Initial Assessment* (October 2012) puts Myanmar's total electricity consumption in 2011 at 6,312 gigawatt-hours. At a typical gas energy content (1,000 cubic feet = 1 million BTU [British thermal units]) and gas turbine conversion rate (11,000 BTU produces 1 kilowatt-hour), the gas exported to Thailand in 2011 would have produced 25,600 gigawatt-hours of electricity.

22. Respectively, the alignments of these corridors are as follows: from Danang (Vietnam) to Mawlamayine [Moulmein] via Laos and Thailand; Ho Chi Minh City (Vietnam) to Dawei via Phnom Penh and Bangkok; Kunming (China) to Bangkok via Tachilek and Chiang Mai (Thailand). The Mekong-India Economic Corridor extends the Southern Corridor to Myanmar's border with India.

23. In February 2014, the *Eleven* website published a story that China had offered a US$2 billion loan to finance the construction of this road. A few days later it reported that the Myanmar government had declined the loan because the annual interest rate of 4.5 percent was above the World Bank and ADB interest rates.

24. From north to south, Thai side first, these links are as follows: Mae Sai-Tachilek, Mae Hong Son-Loikaw, Mae Sot-Myawaddy, Songlaburi-Mawlamyine (via Three Pagodas Pass), and Kanchanaburi-Dawei. *Irrawaddy* on 8 April 2014 reported that an upgrading of the eastern half of the road from Mawlamyine to Myawaddy is due to be completed by the end of 2014. See www.irrawaddy.org/burma/asean-highway-link-set-2014-completion-karen-state-official.html (accessed 31 May 2014).

25. "Laos, Myanmar Begin Bridge," *The Bangkok Post*, 18 February 2013, accessed 5 October 2013, www.bangkokpost.com/breakingnews/336551/laos-myanmar-begin-bridge-construction.

26. The Thai border is roughly 80 km east of Dawei, but the road alignment to the border is twice as long because of the mountainous terrain.

27. The government also ruled out building a coal-fired power plant there, part of the original vision involving more than US$50 billion of investment when fully built. "Big Shift to Dawei Predicted" Welcome to Dawei Sea Port website,

www.daweiport.com/cms/index.php?option=com_content&view=category&layout=blog&id=2&Itemid=2 (accessed 5 October 2013).

28. "Govt Tender for Upgrade of Domestic Airports Expected in October," *Irrawaddy,* www.irrawaddy.org/business/govt-tender-upgrade-domestic-airports-expected-october.html (accessed 31 May 2014).

29. This section draws heavily on Asian Development Bank, *Myanmar: Energy Sector Initial Assessment*, October 2012.

30. Thailand's PTTEP is the operator of the Zawtika field. "Thailand's PTTEP Plans $3.3B Investment in Burma as Gas Project Nears Production," *Irrawaddy,* www.irrawaddy.org/business/thailands-pttep-plans-3-3b-investment-burma-gas-project-nears-production.html (accessed 31 May 2014).

31. *Daily Eleven* on 10 February 2014 via the Euro-Burma daily news summary.

32. It will not be easy to make the right trade-off between exploiting energy resources to meet domestic energy demand or exporting energy to earn foreign exchange to pay for essential imports (and reduce dependence on foreign borrowing).

33. This section draws on Aung Min and Toshihiro Kudo, "New Government's Initiatives for Industrial Development in Myanmar," in Hank Lim and Yasuhiro Yamada, eds., *Economic Reforms in Myanmar: Pathways and Prospects*, Report No. 10 (Chiba, Japan: Bangkok Research Center, 2013).

34. There were $21 million of shares sold. Nine Myanmar companies hold 41 percent of the shares and the government of Myanmar holds 10 percent. The rest is held by Japanese investors. The Union of Myanmar Federation of Chambers of Commerce and Industry is playing a major role in the project. www.pwplegal.com/documents/documents/044d8-Myanmar-Times-Special-Economic-Zones-Law-1.pdf (accessed 31 May 2014).

35. http://consult-myanmar.com/2014/04/29/thilawa-sez-shares-sold-out-following-strong-demand/ (accessed 31 May 2014).

36. http://www.irrawaddy.org/business/singapore-led-consortium-wins-kyaukphyu-sez-consulting-tender.html (accessed 31 May 2014).

37. On 29 April 2014, *Irrawaddy* reported that a Chinese-Myanmar joint venture is planning to build a refinery complex in Thanintharyi Region, 20 kilometers south of the Dawei SEZ project.

38. http://www.mobilepaymentstoday.com/news/oberthur-platform-fuels-myanmar-mobile-money-launch/ (accessed 31 May 2014).

39. This process is neatly captured in Elliott Prasse-Freeman, "Power, Civil Society, and an Inchoate Politics of the Daily in Burma/Myanmar," *The Journal of Asian Studies* 71, no. 2 (May 2012): 371–397.

40. Surprisingly, oil is not yet flowing through the completed pipeline to Yunnan Province because of objections raised by residents in Kunming to the site chosen for construction of a refinery to process oil from the pipeline. www.irrawaddy.org/business/china-cutbacks-put-burma-oil-terminal-pipeline-doubt.html (accessed 31 May 2014).

41. www.irrawaddy.org/business/burma-awards-offshore-oil-gas-deals-foreign-firms.html (accessed 31 May 2014).

42. David Dapice, *Creating a Future: Using Natural Resources for New Federalism and Unity* (Boston: Ash Center for Democratic Governance and Innovation, Harvard Kennedy School, July 2013), 5.

43. Myanmar was accepted as an EITI "candidate" country in July 2014. "Myanmar Granted Candidate Status with EITI." http://www.mizzima.com

/mizzima-news/myanmar/item/11649-myanmar-granted-candidate-status-with-eiti/11649-myanmar-granted-candidate-status-with-eiti. (accessed 8 September 2014). www.elevenmyanmar.com/index.php?option=com_content&view=article&id=5830:myanmar-to-submit-for-eiti-membership&catid=44:national&Itemid=384 (accessed 31 May 2014).

44. Interview, Yangon, 9 August 2013.

45. See Chapter 11 in this volume. The lower chamber of India's legislature passed a new land acquisition bill at the end of August that could be a good starting point for a smarter policy in Myanmar.

46. Much of this section is drawn from Lex Rieffel and James W. Fox, *Too Much Too Soon? The Dilemma of Foreign Aid to Myanmar* (Arlington, VA: Nathan Associates, March 2013).

47. See Raghuram Rajan and Arvind Subramanian, "Aid, Dutch Disease and Manufacturing Growth," *Journal of Development Economics* 94, no. 1 (January 2011): 106–118.

48. These principles are largely inspired by the Paris Declaration on Aid Effectiveness agreed in 2005.

49. A potentially explosive issue emerged in May 2014 when a local news service reported that UNICEF was paying rent of $87,000 per month to the family of a former military general for its headquarters in one of Yangon's most upscale neighborhoods. www.irrawaddy.org/burma/unicef-confirms-87000-month-rent-rangoon-office.html).

50. International Monetary Fund, "Myanmar: 2013 Article IV Consultation and First Review Under Staff Monitored Program." *IMF Country Report* 13/250, August 2013, 1. The IMF's 2014 Article IV consultation report was published too late to be reflected in this chapter.

51. Myanmar's first population census in 30 years was launched in March 2014. It had controversial features, however, that are discussed in other chapters.

52. A recent assessment of India's prospects is Teresita C. Schaffer, "India's Sagging Economy: Strategic Consequences" (Washington, DC: Brookings Institution, 23 September 2013), www.brookings.edu/research/opinions/2013/09/23-india-economy-schaffer (accessed 11 October 2013). A comparable assessment of China's prospects is George Friedman, "The End of the Chinese Economic Miracle," *Forbes* (23 July 2013), www.forbes.com/sites/stratfor/2013/07/23/the-end-of-the-chinese-economic-miracle/ (accessed 11 October 2013). A comparison of the two is Murtaza Syed and James P. Walsh, "The Tiger and the Dragon," *Finance and Development* 49, no. 3 (September 2012), www.imf.org/external/pubs/ft/fandd/2012/09/syed.htm (accessed 12 October 2013).

53. A "sovereign wealth fund" invests "excess" hard-currency earnings in foreign assets that can generate budget revenue long into the future after the resources have been depleted.

54. According to a presentation at the Second Myanmar Development Cooperation Forum in January 2014, the MCDP was "in advanced stages of preparation." It had not emerged by May 2014, making it more than six months behind the initially scheduled launch date.

10

Economic Reforms: Expectations and Realities

Moe Thuzar and Tin Maung Maung Than

In this chapter we assesses—at the broadest visible level—the impact and implications of the economic reforms in Myanmar, focusing on the gaps and challenges in their implementation.

Myanmar's opening up had a quiet start amid skepticism. The Union Solidarity and Development Party's (USDP's) sweep of the November 2010 elections was expected as a foregone result of a process that many in the international community decried as a sham. From this low base, the rapidity and range of reforms initiated by President Thein Sein since taking office in March 2011 were all the more remarkable in the eyes of the world. After Aung San Suu Kyi's release from house arrest on 13 November 2010, Thein Sein's inaugural speech on 30 March 2011 highlighted a commitment to economic renewal and poverty alleviation (an unprecedented official recognition in decades that poverty existed in the country), correcting the human rights record, ensuring good governance, and resolving the decades-long ethnic conflict, and it set the tone of the political, economic, and social reforms that are now in the "third stage" as determined by the government.[1]

The heady atmosphere caused by the reforms that the Thein Sein administration initiated was largely due to the reform measures being centered on the people. It seemed to get off to a good start with an inclusive policy-level workshop on economic development held in August 2011, which highlighted rural development and poverty alleviation and also brought Aung San Suu Kyi to the discussion table alongside representatives from Myanmar's policy and business communities. Issues and priorities discussed at that workshop later found their way into a Framework on Economic and Social Reforms (FESR) launched in 2013. The FESR identified priorities under the various national plans and policies in the economic and social sectors, aligning them with the government's twenty-year national development plan. It was a consultative exercise between the executive and legislature, with the aim of liberalizing the country's economy "to grow on a par with the dynamic Asian economies" and identifying policy priorities for the period 2012–2015.

Freer speech has come to Myanmar together with measures to liberalize the economy. A decades-long multiple exchange rate was finally unified in April 2012, readying the ground for a revamp in the Myanmar Investment Commission setup and a new foreign direct investment (FDI) law in November 2012. Restrictions on the media were progressively lifted, culminating in the dissolution of the infamous Press Scrutiny Board and in allowing private dailies to operate. The opening of the economy was also accompanied by the passing of a law allowing workers to organize and strike. Several amnesties since May 2011 led to a commitment to free all prisoners of conscience by the end of 2013 (which is still lagging in fulfillment), and the National League for Democracy (NLD) rejoined the political process after a watershed by-election in April 2012 that saw democracy icon Aung San Suu Kyi make the transition to a legislator in Myanmar's *hluttaw,* or parliament.[2]

This did not go unrewarded. Countries such as the United States, UK, Australia, and those in the European Union sought closer engagement with the Thein Sein administration, resulting in the easing of sanctions and a landmark visit by President Barack Obama on 19 November 2012, the first for a sitting US president. This was all in the name of supporting and encouraging further reforms. The Association of Southeast Asian Nations (ASEAN) also placed its faith in Myanmar's reforms and agreed to that country's bid for ASEAN chairmanship in 2014.

An oft-asked question on Myanmar's reforms revolves around the motivation for the reforms at this specific juncture, and the implications of rapid changes. Myanmar obviously wishes to catch up with the rest of ASEAN and make up for the lost decades, particularly in economic development. Through this prism, the political reforms become a necessity to facilitate the opening up of the economy. With the reforms now focused on "people-centered" policies and a comprehensive national development strategy that ties in with regional priorities, the Thein Sein administration is showing its awareness of linking its national commitments to regional priorities. As Myanmar's reforms are taking place in the midst of regional change, ASEAN's economic integration processes can reinforce and provide additional impetus to Myanmar's economic reforms. Even so, as ASEAN moves closer to the launching date of the ASEAN Community (including the ASEAN Economic Community [AEC]) by 31 December 2015, ASEAN members are grappling with the geopolitical implications of tensions in the South China Sea and the association's own challenges in meeting AEC commitments.[3]

The Quest for Foreign Direct Investment

Myanmar put an end to the confusing and nonproductive dual exchange rate on 1 April 2012 with an announcement to unify the multiple exchange rates and to phase out the Foreign Exchange Certificate (FEC) scheme. This is an important first step toward reforming the financial sector and ensuring macroeconomic stability for greater foreign investment. The exchange rate unification via a managed float system may be one of the most important economic reform measures to improve the economic climate in Myanmar in view of its past history of different "official" rates, the huge gap between the official and black market rates, and the loopholes created for informal remittances (known as *hundi*) bypassing the rigid bank requirements.[4]

Since the exchange rate unification in April 2012, the Central Bank of Myanmar (CBM) now holds an auction each morning among seventeen of Myanmar's banks to determine a reference rate for the Myanmar kyat (MMK) against the US dollar (US$), the euro, and the Singapore dollar. Once set, other banks and money changers can then exchange the kyat within a band of ±0.8 percent above or below the reference rate. Consistent with the rationale of a managed float, the CBM maintains that it will not intervene in the foreign exchange market in order to achieve any particular rate, but only when it perceives the market for the kyat has become disorderly or divorced from (unspecified) fundamentals.[5]

The new exchange rate mechanism appears to be working well, with the kyat recently trading at around MMK997 to US$1.[6] The current official rate indicates that the CBM's auction system is providing a technical solution of sorts in response to murmurs from the business community that the initial managed float (about MMK800 to US$1) was not representative of the actual supply and demand in the market. Thus far, the divergences in exchange rates are not great. This has encouraged the government to consider moving to the next step of a free float. However, this warrants monitoring, particularly because Myanmar still lacks an effective financial system. This gap is keenly felt in present circumstances, and the CBM has initiated several measures to remedy the situation. Policymakers are aware that the longer Myanmar's financial sector reforms lag, the more inhibitions will be displayed in Myanmar's economic growth and the competitiveness of Myanmar's business sector, ultimately affecting foreign direct investment (FDI) inflows.

Sean Turnell has analyzed the gains and gaps of the financial sector reforms undertaken by the Thein Sein government, most of which were initiated in 2012.[7] It should be noted that the most significant impact of reforms was actually of an external origin—the easing of financial sanctions, which had effectively caused Myanmar's isolation from most of the international financial system. The sanctions had not only limited the provision of international financial services to Myanmar, but also the flow of new ideas, methods, and technology that have become international standards. The hope is that going forward Myanmar will leapfrog in adopting the more advanced technologies and know-how from around the world. However, the following summary of Turnell's analysis shows that in reality, the whole banking and resource mobilization infrastructure, including financial and capital markets is being built from scratch. This daunting task is expected to be achieved by 2015, as a performance indicator of the reformist government's commitment.

• Increasing the deposit base by lowering the long-standing capital-to-deposits ratio requirement on banks from 1:10 to 1:25.[8] This measure, which facilitates deposits mobilization, seems to have worked from the data on increased deposits.

• Expanding allowable collateral to include (beyond urban land) gold, as well as three agricultural commodities—rice, beans, and sesame. This measure, which was aimed at assisting farmers and traders, has not, however, increased the availability and accessibility of loans, as the loans have to be repaid in full before the collateral is sold. There has been little take-up, as small-holders have limited funds and would thus have to wait for the best market conditions before selling their crop.

• A series of cuts, over 2011–2012, to the interest rates that banks are allowed to charge (on loans) and pay (on deposits), ultimately to 13 percent and 8 percent, respectively. But as the CBM still sets the maximum and minimum interest rates, they are not yet market-determined.

• Banks were authorized in late 2011 to offer hire-purchase products on durable consumer goods. The take-up has been low, however, with only one private bank (Kanbawza Bank) offering the product. This is because apart from the goods themselves serving as collateral, borrowers must also have their loans guaranteed by another person.

• Allowing the banks to provide automatic teller machines (ATMs) and to issue debit cards. But there are still restrictions on the number of withdrawals that can be made each day from standard accounts, and a separate (noninterest-bearing) account is required for each ATM card, which cannot be used for any other purpose. The ATMs are expensive to operate, as the frequent power failures that are a part of everyday life in Myanmar require that each machine have its own (diesel) generator.[9] The use of debit cards beyond ATMs is still in the trial stage, with a limited range of retailers for point-of-sale transactions. A number of the private banks are also seeking to introduce credit cards, but these are, as yet, not permitted by the CBM.[10] Still, with these developments, global card-issuing firms such as Visa and MasterCard have partnered with private banks to provide familiar card services to the growing numbers of foreign tourists and visitors to Myanmar.[11] It is interesting to note that this initiative was led by the private banks, especially Kanbawza Bank, which is also partnering with Japan's Sumitomo Mitsui Banking Corporation to upgrade its internal systems.[12]

• One of the biggest obstacles to the proper functioning of ATM networks is the lack of any interbank settlement system that would allow consumers to use debit cards other than in machines at their own bank, or to use in widespread electronic payment systems such as Electronic Funds Transfer at Point of Sale (EFTPOS).[13] In 2012, the CBM selected Japan's Daiwa Corporation to design and construct an interbank settlement system, based around the CBM's hubs in Naypyitaw, Yangon, and Mandalay, and using cloud computing as a way of sidestepping the frequent power shortages.[14] There is a large capacity gap to be bridged in the implementation of the system, which will eventually form the technical backbone of what is envisaged as the "Myanmar Payments Union."[15]

• The issuing of permits to banks (to all but Yoma Bank) to open money change counters to deal in foreign exchange. By September 2012 some 62 foreign currency exchange booths had been set up inside bank branches and as stand-alone shop fronts. This has been by far the most visible of the changes to Myanmar's banking sector under the new government. For the banks, the money-changing business has proved to be one in which it is difficult to make profits.[16] This can be attributed as a direct result of the managed float.

• In August 2012, most of the private banks that had foreign exchange dealing licenses were given permission to issue and accept letters of credit for international trade transactions. Hitherto these could only be traded by the state-owned Myanmar Foreign Trade Bank and Myanmar Investment Corporation Bank. The letters of credit are, however, fairly expensive (US$30 for exports, US$50–$150 for imports), suggesting they will be used primarily for larger transactions.

• In March 2012, four of Myanmar's private banks (Kanbawza Bank, Co-operative Bank, Asia Green Development Bank, and Ayeyarwady Bank) were given permission to set up offices overseas (in Malaysia, Indonesia, Thailand, and Singapore) to facilitate the remittances made by the large community of overseas Myanmar workers and professionals. Ayeyarwady Bank linked up with Maybank of Malaysia and Kanbawza Bank with Thailand's Siam Commercial Bank.[17]

• In September 2012, Myanmar Oriental Bank (MOB) signed an agreement with the world's largest international money transfer firm, Western Union, to offer inward remittance services into Myanmar. As part of the arrangement, MOB staff have been receiving training from Western Union Vietnam.[18]

In tandem with the measures for financial sector liberalization, the 1988 foreign investment law was also updated to attract much-needed investments. The new Foreign Direct Investment Law enacted on 2 November 2012 is another visible measure (in addition to the exchange rate unification) that the Thein Sein government has undertaken as a key component of the economic reforms. It took much back-and-forth deliberation between the *hluttaw* and the executive branch to agree on the regulatory framework of the new law, and necessary assurances to allay investor concerns. While responses by Myanmar's business community to the new FDI law has been mostly positive, the prevailing sentiment in the country is that more should be done to support domestic firms in competing with foreign investors.[19] This stems from earlier concerns that Myanmar's business community is not ready to compete effectively in the single market and production base envisaged by 2015 under the AEC.

The experience of the Asian tiger economies in the 1990s shows that growth policies helped to reduce poverty. This was actually a result of collaboration with multinational corporations (MNCs) investing in the countries. Myanmar obviously views its FDI trajectory as following the same path. The most prominent deal inked after the new FDI law came into effect was the agreement signed with Japan in December 2012 to develop a special economic zone for the Thilawa Port and its surrounding areas in Yangon Division, followed by agreements with three of Japan's largest corporations—Mitsubishi, Marubeni, and Sumitomo—in October 2013.[20] The other high-profile event was the opening up of the telecommunications sector to foreign operators. A competitive bidding process involving international and local companies saw Norway's Telenor and Qatar's Ooredoo emerge as the winners in June 2013. These companies have started operations in Myanmar, again starting from a "greenfield" situation in terms of infrastructure and capacity, especially in the more remote areas of the country. The investment projects may change the Internet and mobile phone penetration rate in the near future. Current subscriptions are at 10 per 1,000 population and cellular phone density is at 26 per 1,000 population.

There are differing views on the extent of the new law's timeliness in encouraging new investments, with analysts providing a cautiously optimistic view that it is a step in the right direction (in the context of political transition). Myanmar reported US$625.12 million in FDI for the last quarter of fiscal year (FY) 2012/13, and a total of approximately 18,000 jobs created during that period.[21] Starting from a low base, these numbers do seem an incredible achievement. There is acknowledgment of the "dire state of physical and institutional infrastructure in Myanmar and financial and political risks involved in doing business in the country."[22]

Myanmar's new FDI law still needs to be tested with regard to intellectual property rights policies and dependable dispute settlement mechanisms for economic agreements and undertakings. A general improvement in the rule of law (and the perception of investors that there is improvement) would facilitate investor attraction and confidence in the country and also support Myanmar's participation in regional economic integration. One of the concerns voiced over the provisions of the law focused on the perceived extraordinary powers of the Myanmar Investment Commission (MIC). This is an exaggeration in the government's view, which maintains that the MIC's new "powers" are just to cut away swathes of red tape. Certainly the approval process has been streamlined, and the MIC is responsible for the whole process. Still, it takes one to two months for an investment proposal to be approved (after all due diligence requirements have been carried out). Registering a company or a branch office is a much faster and less complex process, taking only a few days.

Additionally, despite being the designated regulatory authority on foreign investments, the MIC can issue orders, directives, and notifications and amendments to existing rules and regulations only with the government's approval. Major economic decisions such as the setting up of special economic zones, for example, require additional approval from the regional or state governments and the local communities concerned. Additionally, mega projects have to be presented to the parliament for review. This last requirement has not yet been tested; it is not clear whether the parliament's recommendations and suggestions could lead to further changes or amendments to the initial investment proposal. Given that the FDI law itself was extensively discussed and debated in the legislature and behind the scenes, it is possible that the mega investment proposals will meet the same scrutiny.

A judicious management of the reforms should contribute to establishing a welcoming climate for FDI in Myanmar. It is also time for the business community in Myanmar to support this development by improving their domestic competitiveness. A general improvement in the rule of law and the perception of the investors of this improvement would greatly facilitate this. Other ongoing concerns to ensure macroeconomic stability and attract more investors are

- improving legal and regulatory enforcement of new laws and regulations;
- fostering better communication and coordination among local businesses and their foreign counterparts, including helping the private sector interact on an equal basis with foreign counterparts;
- improving and expanding the existing human resource base, which is currently very limited in terms of organizational, managerial, and marketing skills;
- upgrading infrastructure and improving communications systems, including more reliable and cheaper access to the Internet and the possibility of introducing mobile banking; and removing barriers to international trade and investment, including the current state of public utilities provision (electricity, water, etc.).

These concerns highlight the reality that Myanmar remains one of the riskiest countries in which to do business. In its 2014 survey of 197 countries on their legal and regulatory environment, UK-based risk analyst Maplecroft lauded Myanmar's efforts to improve its business environment but cautioned that the country still remains a challenging place to do business due to poor governance.[23]

Equally important is the lifting of sanctions and embargoes to ease the constraints on Myanmar's economic opening. Steps toward the latter were taken by the United States and the European Union (EU). The EU suspended sanctions in April 2012 and lifted all sanctions except the arms embargo the following year. The United States started the targeted easing of bans on exports of US financial services and investment,[24] followed by the US Treasury Department's Office of Foreign Assets Control (OFAC) authorization of "certain" US financial services and new US investments in Myanmar in July 2012, provided that they do not partner with military-owned businesses.[25] During the high-profile visits by both Thein Sein and Aung San Suu Kyi to the United States in October 2012, sanctions banning the import of goods from Myanmar were eased. On 16 November 2012, the United States authorized the importation of Burmese-origin goods, except jadeite and rubies. On 22 February 2013, the authorization came through for US persons to conduct financial transactions, which include the opening and maintaining of accounts, with four banks: Asia Green Development Bank, Ayeyarwady Bank, Myanma Economic Bank, and Myanma Investment and Commercial Bank.[26] In May 2013, the visa ban in place since 1996 prohibiting entry of former members of the military junta, their business partners, and immediate family members was lifted in time for Thein Sein's official visit to Washington, DC.[27]

While lifting or easing sanctions is necessary to help accelerate the reforms, the dismantling of sanctions applied reflexively, especially those enacted into law, will not be as reflexive, nor will the process be as immediate, as ASEAN countries have called for. Former US Secretary of State Hillary Clinton justified the easing of financial sanctions to support the legitimate economic actors in Myanmar, but it is difficult to define legitimacy beyond the obvious examples of those known to be involved in money-laundering activities of the previous junta. It is also difficult to differentiate which business entities are linked to the military, as former military personnel—now retired and "civilianized"—have benefited from the sale of state-owned assets that include former government offices in Yangon, port facilities, and shares in the national airline.[28] While the hope may have been to create some form of competition and at the same time generate some revenue for the USDP's political platform, this move also runs the risk of entrenching more oligarchic forms of society where wealth is concentrated in the hands of a select political and economic elite, even as Myanmar strives to build a capitalist democracy.

Still, it is significant that the countries that led the imposition of the sanctions regime on Myanmar for the past half century are now also at the forefront of easing the sanctions and readily admitting that sanctions alone did not work in inducing change in Myanmar.

Myanmar also lifted some blacklists of its own. More than 2000 names on a blacklist of both Myanmar nationals and foreigners hitherto barred from (re)entering the country were removed in August 2012 in a public announcement.[29] This measure was made to complement Thein Sein's "invitation" in May 2012 to the Burmese diaspora around the world to return to the country to contribute to and participate in the transition.[30] It was the closest the government would get to a public admission of the brain drain from the years of military rule. However, even with assurances that the government would facilitate conditions (especially for investors and businessmen), and similar requests made by Aung San Suu Kyi in her meetings with the diaspora during her travels, the take-up rate has been slow. One factor could be the financial costs of resettlement, including expectations of equivalent remuneration for professional jobs. A survey of salary trends in Myanmar's private sector shows that whether earnings are in MMK or US$, the wage levels are still relatively low despite significant increases over the past decade (see Tables 10.1 and 10.2).[31]

A corollary to this scenario can be found in the rising incidence of labor disputes.[32] This is a direct result of the new labor laws, which have created a space for workers to voice their dissatisfaction over low wages. The labor disputes have been mainly over low wages and will likely continue in the wake of the new minimum wage law enacted in March 2013, which requires employers to pay at least the prevailing minimum wage set by a government committee. This committee, formed by the president's office, will set the minimum wage per sector, based on research of prevailing minimum wages in industries across the country, and taking into account "the needs of the employees and their families, the current living standards, the cost of living, the state of the country's economy, the well-being of the employee vis-a-vis his profession, and other considerations presented by the relevant ministry."[33] Prior to the new law's enactment, the Ministry of Labor set a temporary factory minimum wage (MMK56,700) in 2012, but many workers have complained that factory owners neglected to follow this wage. On 1 May 2014, workers called for a minimum daily wage of MMK5600, but conflation of the US$2 per day poverty line with minimum wage in a statement made later in May by Vice President Nyan Tun has compounded negative perceptions.[34] The noncompliance penalties in the 2013 minimum wage law—which also has requirements for equal wage—will affect how employers continue (or start) their business operations.

This places Myanmar in an interesting nexus in the debate on labor relations and human rights, even as the Myanmar Investment Commission

Table 10.1: Median Monthly Salaries Paid in MMK, All Companies

	General Manager	Manager	Supervisor	Factory Worker	Accountant	Secretary	Office Staff	Driver
2003	60,000	40,000	30,000	16,000	40,000	25,000	18,000	18,000
2004	85,000	60,000	35,000	20,000	50,000	35,000	25,000	25,000
2005	100,000	70,000	38,000	25,000	60,000	45,000	30,000	30,000
2006	150,000	100,000	60,000	30,000	65,000	48,000	40,000	42,000
2007	250,000	120,000	70,000	35,000	80,000	60,000	45,000	50,000
2008	300,000	160,000	80,000	40,000	100,000	70,000	55,000	50,000
2009	300,000	160,000	80,000	45,000	100,000	70,000	55,000	55,000
2010	350,000	200,000	100,000	45,000	120,000	100,000	70,000	80,000
2011	400,000	250,000	120,000	50,000	120,000	120,000	80,000	90,000
2012	400,000	300,000	150,000	60,000	150,000	150,000	85,000	100,000
2013	500,000	350,000	250,000	90,000	250,000	150,000	120,000	150,000

Source: Crossroads 1, no. 1 (June 2013).

Table 10.2: Median Monthly Salaries Paid in US$, All Companies

	General Manager	Manager	Supervisor	Accountant	Secretary	Office Staff	Driver
2003	400	250	150	150	100	80	75
2004	500	350	180	300	180	120	100
2005	500	350	200	280	150	120	100
2006	600	450	250	320	180	150	100
2007	650	450	300	320	150	120	120
2008	800	500	300	320	150	120	120
2009	700	450	250	300	150	110	100
2010	800	500	350	325	250	160	125
2011	800	600	400	400	250	171	150
2012	1,000	700	400	400	300	195	175
2013	1,200	800	450	460	380	220	200

Source: Crossroads 1, no. 1 (June 2013).

stresses mandatory corporate social responsibility contributions from companies investing in the country and the International Labour Organization starts engaging with multiple stakeholders in government and the nascent trade unions to promote its decent work agenda. The 2011 Labour Organizations Law (which entered into effect in March 2012) provides the legal framework for the establishment and operation of trade unions. Under this framework, more than 400 basic-level unions were registered in 2012 alone, but at the time of writing, the dispute resolution procedures do not yet seem to have taken effective hold. The role of government as mediator in labor disputes is not yet clear, nor yet the emergence of a framework for industrial relations to negotiate labor disputes beyond wage issues. And, as the special economic zone (SEZ) projects move forward with implementation, they hold both promise and problems for industrial relations. For example, in the Thilawa SEZ, which is described in the Myanmar Thilawa SEZ Holdings brochure as a "monumental project strongly supported by both Myanmar and Japan government," US manufacturer Ball and Japanese auto parts maker Koyo Radiator have signed agreements to open factories, while more than forty companies from eight countries have expressed interest.[35] Yet, the project's first-phase implementation is dogged by poor infrastructure woes and compensation issues raised by the families asked to relocate from the area.

As workers, employers, and government continue to grapple with the new labor realities in Myanmar, an additional concern looms as a potential threat to the current pace of reforms. With freer speech, the right to organize, and greater access to information, economic nationalism is finding popularity among the people of Myanmar today.

Economic Nationalism

It is mainly due to the Thein Sein administration's reform agenda that Myanmar has attracted the current overwhelming interest by many countries around the world. Much of this interest is related to Myanmar's yet unrealized economic potential. The extractive resource sector has seen the most significant FDI (see Fig. 10.1), especially in natural gas, timber, mining, and power generation. These sectors continue to attract the greatest interest today and will most likely do so in the foreseeable future. Yet, Myanmar's comparative advantage also lies in the potential of its labor-intensive manufacturing sector, which may see a revival with the lifting of sanctions. Other areas with potential to grow are in the tourism, financial, and other business services related to liberalization of the economy. Yet, as mentioned above, much more needs to be done in terms of providing the supporting infrastructure, communications, and regulatory environment.

Figure 10.1: Myanmar's FDI by Sector (as of October 2013)

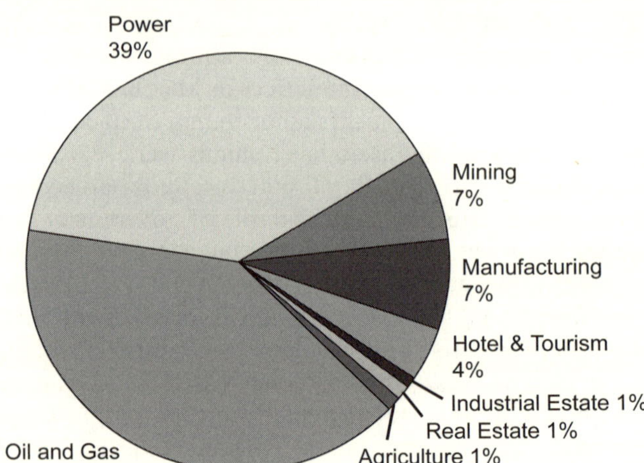

Source: Ministry of National Planning and Economic Development, 2013.

Figure 10.2: Foreign Investment of Existing Enterprises (selected countries in US$ millions, as of October 2013)

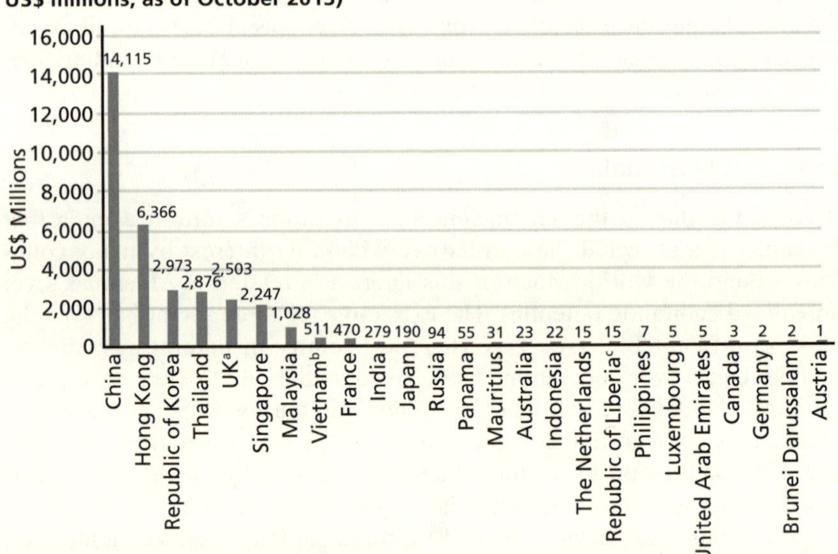

Source: Ministry of National Planning and Economic Development, 2013.

Notes: a. British Overseas Territories; b. Includes loan of US$12 million from Anh So Viet Pharma Co. Ltd; c. Name, promoter, and principal organization changed from Singapore.

Since 1988, Myanmar's economic relations have mainly been with countries in the Southeast and East Asia regions (see Fig. 10.2). China is Myanmar's largest investor and second largest foreign creditor. The recent thawing of relations with Japan, which led to Japan forgiving US$3.7 billion of Myanmar debt,[36] indicates the former's rising role in Myanmar's economic development.

This intense foreign interest in Myanmar's natural resources is a double-edged sword. If foreign and local investors (1) renege on promises or offers to invest in Myanmar, (2) increasingly adopt a wait-and-see attitude to the reforms until after the 2015 elections, or (3) get scared away by the government's commitments to undertake environmental impact or social impact assessments for extractive projects, Myanmar's decisionmakers will face problems in seeking financers for the massive infrastructure needs for missing links in transport and communications to connect with the rest of Southeast Asia. As far as current investments go, those from China are bearing the brunt of popular protests, which compelled the government to suspend the US$3.6 billion Myitsone hydroelectric dam project in Kachin State and renegotiate the Letpadaung copper mine project.

The conflation of resentment against past actions of military junta and the Chinese investments, which are widely perceived as keeping the military in power, continue to simmer. With the heightened global emphasis on good governance, transparency, and accountability, these issues will need careful handling by both the Chinese and Myanmar authorities. The crackdown on local communities protesting land acquisition and compensation issues of the Letpadaung project—a joint venture between the military-owned Union of Myanmar Economic Holdings and a Chinese mining company, Wanbao—resulted in temporary suspension of operations in November 2012 and the formation of an investigation committee led by Aung San Suu Kyi to assess the project's viability. However, a new contract has since been negotiated and work will resume, raising fresh concerns.

About 70 percent of Myanmar's labor force is employed in the agricultural sector, which accounts for just over 40 percent of the country's GDP. Concerns of the small-hold farmers, whose family farms have produced rice and practically all of Myanmar's important foodstuffs over the past five decades, should not be neglected. Aspirations for large-scale plantation-type farming should bear in mind possible fallouts from enactment of the Farmland Law and the Vacant, Fallow, and Virgin Lands Management Law, which were passed by parliament in March 2012. These laws have been criticized as having "mistakes, weaknesses and were incomplete and calls for their review were made since 2012."[37] A revised farmers' protection law was approved in October 2013 with more provisions protecting the rights of farmers.[38] Still, concerns over land grabbing for development continue, highlighting current weaknesses of Myanmar's judiciary and providing further grounds for protests and dissent against the government's drive for economic development. This has found a ready outlet in the religious animosities sparked by the June 2012 acts of violence between Rakhine and Rohingya communities.

The tensions from the June 2012 communal violence in Rakhine state have shown the dark side of transition. Notwithstanding many efforts (albeit with an urban bias) made to promote interfaith dialogue and understanding, religious animosities continue to be incited by nationalist sentiments that seem to find favor with those who feel they are losing out from the changes taking place in the country.[39]

The government's poverty reduction efforts also seem to have stalled. In several public statements, including his monthly radio messages, the president has reiterated the importance of economic development in the border areas to assist poverty alleviation. Yet, there are few concrete projects, although there is a significant push by Japan to ramp up assistance to Myanmar through several channels, including rural poverty reduction and improving human immunodeficiency virus infection/acquired immunodeficiency syndrome (HIV/AIDS) care. The Asian Development Bank (ADB) recently announced that its Japan Fund for Poverty Reduction would fund a US$12 million program for rural poverty reduction in the Ayeyarwady (Irrawaddy) Delta, Thanintharyi (Tenasserim) Division, and Shan State where poverty rates are double that of urban poverty rates, while another US$10 million will go to financing programs for better access and quality to health and HIV/AIDS services.[40]

One progressive measure that has been implemented without much fanfare, though, is the establishment of a poverty reduction fund as part of the decentralization process undertaken under the rubric of the FESR. An assessment of state and region governments in Myanmar, carried out by the Myanmar Development Resource Institute (MDRI)'s Center for Economic and Social Development (CESD) in partnership with the Asia Foundation hailed this development as a major innovation in the subnational fiscal system. Introduced in 2011 as a lump sum development grant called the Poverty Reduction Fund, the initiative stands out as "the only fully devolved resource transfer from the union to state and region level," allocating (in FY 2012/13) about MMK1 billion (roughly US$1 million) to each state or region, with Chin State—due to its extreme remoteness and lack of facilities—receiving triple.[41]

Myanmar's emergence from its former cocoon has catapulted every event taking place in the country—be it economic challenge or ongoing reform moves—into the thick of international and regional attention. The domestic concerns may distract Myanmar from its regional responsibilities as ASEAN chair in 2014. A broader concern is whether Myanmar—long the laggard in ASEAN economic integration—can lead regional preparation for the announcement of the AEC by the stated deadline of 2015.

Myanmar and the AEC

In January 2013, the government launched its Framework for Economic and Social Reforms (FESR) to development partners and donors. The document, which sets out a medium-term strategy to achieve longer-term development goals toward "a modern, developed and democratic nation by 2030," identifies policy priorities for 2012–2015. The FESR lists specific plans for reforms in government, finance and taxations, monetary and financial sector policies, trade and investment liberalization programs, education, governance and transparency, improvements in telecommunications, development of infrastructure, and improved government efficiency. What is interesting, however, is that the FESR acknowledges that Myanmar's economic development needs to link to regional (i.e., ASEAN) processes; the FESR language shows that Myanmar is seeking assistance under bilateral and ASEAN cooperation frameworks to accomplish identified priority tasks.

With the assumption of ASEAN chair responsibilities for 2014, Myanmar has also taken on chairmanship of key meetings under ASEAN economic cooperation. This entails not only key sectoral meetings under the AEC but also the ASEAN Business and Investment Summit and related meetings, which are usually held in conjunction with the ASEAN Summit, providing the opportunity for the captains of industry in ASEAN countries to meet with the ASEAN heads of state/government to discuss AEC implementation relevant to business. The Republic of the Union of Myanmar Federation of Chambers and Commerce and Industry (RUMFCCI) took over chairmanship of the 2014 ASEAN Business and Investment Summit at a meeting of the ASEAN Business Advisory Council (ASEAN-BAC) in Yangon on 29 November 2013. The RUMFCCI will organize meetings of the ASEAN-BAC and the ASEAN leaders in May 2014, and in November 2014, when the ASEAN Business and Investment Summit and the East Asian Business and Investment Summit are scheduled to be held in conjunction with the 25th ASEAN Summit. With the theme "Myanmar: The Gateway to ASEAN," Myanmar is leveraging its unique location in Southeast Asia for strategic accessibility by businesses from the wider East Asia region and beyond.

One of the main topics for discussion at these meetings will be on support for the small and medium enterprises (SMEs) in ASEAN as a whole. This resonates with Myanmar's economic opening up, as SMEs make up the bulk of the country's economy. The topic is also opportune, as Myanmar's parliament is currently debating a draft SME law that will provide a better regulatory and supporting framework for SMEs in Myanmar to build up their domestic competitiveness in preparation for the AEC. As regards preparedness for the AEC, the RUMFCCI president U Win Aung has frankly admitted that the private sector in Myanmar is not yet ready for the "onslaught" of trade, services, and capital flows that AEC realization in

2015 would bring.[42] This concern is widely shared by the business sector in Myanmar, which is clamoring for wide-ranging capacity development—for individual entrepreneurs and businesses as well as the human capital needed for these businesses to operate competitively. An additional concern is about establishing responsible business practices in Myanmar as a priority to be undertaken in tandem with Myanmar's economic opening up. RUMFCCI sees its role as a bridge between the government and the private sector, voicing the private sector's concerns to the policymakers' attention. However, differences of opinions between the RUMFCCI members, and the "government-linked" operations of some of the RUMFCCI-listed businesses, indicate that this role is viewed with some skepticism.

The current process in Myanmar to review and reform laws and procedures is encouraging for Myanmar's ASEAN integration efforts. Effective participation in ASEAN processes, especially the AEC, requires policy reforms and consistency in policy and in its application. Important changes will also need to be made to the country's education and labor policies, so that the workforce will be creative, competent, and competitive. To this end, the effectiveness of Myanmar's AEC implementation efforts should be monitored in the efforts for ensuring adequate infrastructure (e.g., electricity), technically skilled workers, adequate pay, and transparent rules and regulations. All this redounds to the need to attract investors to Myanmar; boosting investor confidence requires a multisector, multistakeholder effort, as Myanmar is still struggling to emerge from the dark legacy of decades of mismanagement. The main imperative is to level the playing field for domestic firms, in order to ensure their competitiveness. Measures to this end would include (1) fair access for all to the country's natural resources, (2) fairness in granting licenses and permits to take up business opportunities, (3) equal treatment in applying rules and procedures, (4) getting rid of arbitrary and ever-changing rules and regulations, (5) reducing official corruption, (6) ending payment of arbitrary dues or donations, and (7) transparency and accountability in applying rules and procedures.[43]

For its part, the government seems to be aware of the many practical implementation issues, despite entertaining a more optimistic view of Myanmar's AEC readiness. This optimism is fueled by Myanmar being largely on track with the other ASEAN member states in meeting AEC commitments for facilitating free flow of goods and services, and freer flow of capital, in the region. Still, ASEAN as a whole faces challenges in fully implementing customs harmonization through the ASEAN Single Window (ASW); countries like Myanmar, Cambodia, and Laos need to complete their National Single Window processes to join the ASW. With regard to the priorities for equitable economic development and the external economic relations of ASEAN, Myanmar needs to take on a more active (and proactive role) during its chairmanship year.

Challenges to liberalizing the economy also have implications for Myanmar's AEC participation. The private sector has made it clear that the current infrastructure is not satisfactory enough to attract overseas investment. There is also an important need for skilled manpower, especially in the AEC's priority integration sectors. Some of these sectors are important for Myanmar's economic development, including agriculture and agro-based industries and fisheries. Currently, silo mentalities across sectors give rise to difficulties in coordination and communication. This is a critical issue, especially in ensuring the successful implementation of the ASEAN Single Window and in facilitating freer flow of services. Services sector liberalization is still far from full integration in ASEAN, not to mention in a newly opened economy such as Myanmar.

Myanmar's implementation of ASEAN agreements on trade in goods and services, while largely on track, shows some mixed results. There are uneven levels of awareness, understanding, and commitment to AEC and its goals and requirements among the private business and government departments. While on track in tariff reduction, Myanmar's score on trade facilitation, compared to other ASEAN member states, is still low. Table 10.3 shows Myanmar's implementation of tariff reduction under the ASEAN Common Effective Preferential Tariff scheme. Myanmar also has some way to go in achieving the commitments under the ASEAN Trade in Goods Agreement (ATIGA), which entered into force on 17 May 2010.[44] Under the ATIGA, ASEAN member states are to eliminate import duties

Table 10.3: Myanmar's Common Effective Preferential Tariff (CEPT) Schedule

Category	1998 HS 96	2004 AHTN2002	2005 AHTN2002	2006 AHTN2002	2007 AHTN2002	2008 AHTN2002	2010 AHTN2007
Inclusion List (IL)	2,356 43.06%	8,936 83.60%	10,461 97.87%	10,521 98.43%	10,611 99.27%	10,615 99.31%	8,240 99.28%
Temporary Exclusion List (TEL)	2,987 54.59%	1,646 15.40%	135 1.26%	77 0.72%	0	0	0
Sensitive List (SL)	21 0.38%	36 0.34%	34 0.32%	32 0.30%	27 0.25%	23 0.22%	11 0.13%
General Exemption List (GEL)	108 1.97%	71 0.66%	59 0.55%	59 0.55%	51 0.48%	51 0.48%	49 0.59%
Total	5,472	10,689	10,689	10,689	10,689	10,689	8,300

Source: Ministry of National Planning and Economc Development (2011 and 2013).

Notes: HS = Harmonised commodity description and coding system or HS Code; AHTN = ASEAN Harmonised Tariff Nomenclature.

on all products traded between the member states by 2010 for the ASEAN-6 countries, and by 2015—with flexibility to 2018—for Cambodia, Laos, Myanmar, and Vietnam (the CLMV countries). Free flow of goods entails effective logistics capacity. Currently, Myanmar ranks the lowest in logistics performance. Table 10.4 shows the World Bank's comparison of ASEAN member states' logistics performance against the regional average for East Asia and Pacific.

The AEC Scorecard, which tracks the performance of ASEAN members' implementation of the AEC commitments, shows that Myanmar also scores low in trade facilitation.[45] It lags behind the other member states in customs modernization (Myanmar ranks lowest) and implementation of the National Single Window (second lowest after Laos). Myanmar is second last (after Cambodia) in implementing the ASEAN agreements on trade facilitation.[46] The situation is similar for Myanmar's performance in lowering technical barriers in standards and conformity assessments, and in technical regulations. These challenges are also true for facilitating implementation and coordination of services liberalization in Myanmar.

Table 10.4: Myanmar's Logistics Performance

Country	LPI	Customs	Infra-Structure	International Shipments	Logistics Competence	Tracking & Tracing	Timeliness
Cambodia	2.37	2.28	2.12	2.19	2.29	2.50	2.84
East Asia & Pacific (regional ave.)	2.73	2.41	2.46	2.79	2.58	2.74	3.33
Indonesia	2.76	2.43	2.54	2.82	2.47	2.77	3.46
Lao PDR	2.46	2.17	1.95	2.70	2.14	2.45	3.23
Malaysia	3.44	3.11	3.50	3.50	3.34	3.32	3.86
Myanmar	**2.33**	**1.94**	**1.92**	**2.37**	**2.01**	**2.36**	**3.29**
Philippines	3.14	2.67	2.57	3.40	2.95	3.29	3.83
Singapore	4.09	4.02	4.22	3.86	4.12	4.15	4.23
Thailand	3.29	3.02	3.16	3.27	3.16	3.41	3.73
Vietnam	2.96	2.68	2.56	3.04	2.89	3.10	3.44

Source: World Bank Logistics Performance Index 2010.

Note: LPI = Logistic Performance Index rank.

Raising the level of the ASEAN region's economic competitiveness thus relies heavily on infrastructure and institutional capabilities. These are key components under the Master Plan on ASEAN Connectivity, adopted by the ASEAN leaders in 2010. Myanmar was one of the earliest ASEAN members to welcome the Master Plan's adoption. Myanmar's strategic location in Southeast Asia, connecting India and China, and serving as a crucial link in the Asian/ASEAN Highway Networks, Singapore-Kunming Rail Link, and Trans-Asia Railway Network, highlights the importance of Myanmar as a key node in connecting global trade. As such, implementation of the Master Plan on ASEAN Connectivity will continue to be a priority for Myanmar to monitor nationally and regionally. However, challenges exist. Myanmar is currently one of the least connected countries in ASEAN. Presenting Myanmar as the gateway to ASEAN cannot ignore the imperatives of regional connectivity with the rest of ASEAN. The Dawei (Tavoy) Deep Sea Port project in southern Myanmar (with investment from Thailand and Japan) and the Thilawa Port project in Yangon (with Japan as the main investor) present considerable potential for the connectivity choices of the Mekong riparian states with ASEAN.

Governance and Corruption

Myanmar's political reforms inform, and are informed by, economic reforms. Chief Presidential Economic Adviser U Myint has recalled General Aung San's observation on politics and economics being closely linked, highlighting that the instability of one affects the other.[47] In pursuing the quest to catch up with the rest of the region, it is becoming increasingly evident that Myanmar needs to undertake substantial improvements to the overall legal framework, including the application of the various laws and regulations, as well as ensuring an environment that is conducive to attracting visitors and investors to come en masse to Myanmar. Table 10.5, which compares governance indicators identified by the World Bank in its world governance indicators project, shows the extent of the effort required for Myanmar to catch up with its ASEAN neighbors.

Corruption certainly poses a hurdle for potential investments, without which the much needed economic growth will not progress far. While it can be said that the president's pronouncements on clean government and good governance, coupled with the commitment to the Extractive Industries Transparency Initiative, are all signals that Myanmar means to clean up its act. The reality of doing business in Myanmar today produces a litany of wrinkles that need ironing out. Legal uncertainty still prevails, especially in ensuring local enforcement of investment deals. Lack of legal capacity—especially in the civil service bodies and related agencies that are responsible for expediting the implementation of investment projects—is a handicap

Table 10.5: Governance Indicators (Percentile Rankings as of 2012)

Country	Voice and Accountability	Political Stability	Government Effectiveness	Regulatory Quality	Rule of Law	Control of Corruption
Brunei	33	77	75	85	73	72
Cambodia	19	41	22	39	17	14
Indonesia	51	27	44	43	34	29
Lao PDR	5	47	21	22	23	15
Malaysia	38	45	80	70	66	66
Myanmar	**4**	**18**	**4**	**2**	**6**	**11**
Philippines	48	15	58	52	36	33
Singapore	54	97	100	100	96	97
Thailand	37	13	61	58	50	47
Vietnam	9	56	44	27	38	35

Source: World Bank, "Worldwide Governance Indicators," 2013, http://data.worldbank.org/data-catalog/worldwide-governance-indicators.

Note: LPI = Logistic Performance Index rank.

that will take several years to address. This uncertainty on the ground is in some ways amplified by the uncertainty over who are the legitimate economic actors in Myanmar today. Being off (or not on) the sanctions blacklist does not automatically translate into being a good business partner, as the uncertainty over sanctions and the state of flux engendered by the reforms have created large gray areas where supernormal profits can be made if one does not dig too deep into due diligence.

Since taking office, Thein Sein has frequently spoken on the need to "eliminate" corruption. In December 2012, in a meeting with cabinet ministers, regional leaders, and senior officials televised live, the president explicitly stated that "bribery and corruption must be effectively prevented in order to implement good governance." He emphasized that the third wave of reforms would include cleaning up and overhauling bureaucracy, which he observed as still lacking transparency and failing to listen to the voices of the people.[48]

In late July 2013, Myanmar's legislature approved an anticorruption bill that had been debated for almost a year since being tabled in 2012. The bill was passed into law in August 2013. The new anticorruption legislation provides for the establishment of an anticorruption commission. In February 2014, Thein Sein followed up by proposing to the Pyidaungsu Hluttaw (Union Legislature) the formation of an anticorruption commission with fifteen members.[49]

The president established an anticorruption commission in January 2013, but the road toward a better ranking in the governance and corruption index will still be an uphill task in view of the deeply entrenched nature of corruption in Myanmar's political and business systems.

Aung San Suu Kyi, in her capacity as chair of the Pyithu Hluttaw Committee for Rule of Law, Peace, and Tranquility, is also promoting civil society efforts to complement implementation of the anticorruption law. In November 2013, she called for the formation of an antibribery society.

Concluding Thoughts

Myanmar's economic reforms have reached an important juncture. While expectations continue to be high at home and abroad on getting the economic policy right so as to produce favorable outcomes that will in turn prove Thein Sein's reforms as "good politics," there are equally high frustrations on the administration's inclination toward being consultative and inclusive in programs and areas whose implementation requires a stronger hand on the part of the government.[50] As things stand, the consensus on the need for macroeconomic stability is being conflated with the populist sentiments arising from more nebulous arenas opened up by reduced government intervention. Thein Sein and his cabinet are also up against "opposing" forces to reform identified by Merilee Grindle and John Thomas, all extant in today's Myanmar: the economic and political "elites" who enjoyed, and benefited from, past systems of patronage and networks; the entrenched mindsets of the bureaucracy; and the military's economic organizations, which enjoyed little or no scrutiny in the past.[51]

Charts and figures aside, and expectations and frustrations notwithstanding, the impact of the economic reforms in Myanmar as felt by ordinary Myanmar citizens can be summed up in three main points. This is the reality, which matches the expectations of some but falls far short for many citizens in the country impatient to see and feel the results of the currents of change that have caught the attention of the rest of the world.

1. Broader access to a wider range of consumer goods and services, as well as information and technology, empowers the people, but the lack of physical and institutional infrastructure results in higher transaction costs. This may improve over time as Myanmar becomes more connected.

2. Affordability, however, remains an issue, given prevailing low income levels in the country. Fiscal and monetary policy reforms, while necessary, could lead to higher inflation and loss of purchasing power in the interim. Expertise and exposure are still very thin among those with the task to undertake these reforms, especially among the lower levels.
3. Myanmar's economic opening has brought more competition for local entrepreneurs and less job security for workers. The adventurous will continue to seek better opportunities at home and abroad.

Despite the obvious challenges, the message is clear from the incumbent reformist government: Myanmar is ready for some serious business.

Notes

1. It also paid tribute to the "sound foundations" laid by the State Peace and Development Council (SPDC), referring to the role of the *tatmadaw* "saving the country" from "deteriorating conditions" at several points in the country's history.

2. Radio Free Asia reported on 10 June 2014 that according to the Assistance Association for Political Prisoners (AAPP), as of the end of May, at least 59 people were serving prison sentences on political charges. See www.rfa.org/english/news/myanmar/political-prisoners-06102014165749.html.

3. The AEC Blueprints identifies four components or pillars, each listing priority measures to be completed by stated deadlines. The pillars are: (1) single market and production base, (2) economic competitiveness, (3) equitable economic development, and (4) integration into the global economy.

4. The *hundi* system is an informal network of money carriers, which stretches primarily over West and Southeast Asia as well as the Middle East and parts of Africa. It is mostly used by migrant workers. Many Myanmar nationals use it as a convenient form of funds transfer. Its popularity in Myanmar is also due to the country's lack of banking connections up to now. For more details on the *hundi* system, see Box 2.1 in the Organisation for Economic Cooperation and Development's *Multi-dimensional Review of Myanmar, Volume 1, Initial Assessment* (Paris: OECD, 2013).

5. Sean Turnell's paper presented to the conference "Myanmar: Setting the Stage for Economic Transition" held in Naypyitaw on 25–26 October 2012.

6. CBM rate as of October 2014, at www.cbm.gov.mm.

7. Turnell paper, "Myanmar," 2012.

8. The capital to deposits ratio was implemented in the wake of the 2003 financial crisis in Myanmar to limit the amount of leverage that banks took on. The measure created a situation where some banks were turning depositors away.

9. Nevertheless, the most savvy of the private banks with respect to ATMs (Kanbawza Bank and CB Bank, especially) seem committed to their continued rollout. Increasingly, however, the actual machines used will be secondhand ones purchased abroad.

10. Apart from the Kanbawza and CB Banks, Myanmar Apex Bank, Myanmar Oriental Bank, and the Asia Green Development Bank are also actively seeking to distribute both debit and credit cards. See Myat May Zin, "Five Private Banks to

Offer Point of Sale Cards," *The Myanmar Times* 32, no. 639 (13–19 August 2012).

11. Amidst the many reports detailing the visits of envoys of the global debit and credit card issuers, see Victoria Bruce, "Visa, MasterCard on the Way," *The Myanmar Times* 32, no. 639 (13–19 August 2012). An immediate motivation for setting up the infrastructure to allow debit cards, first for foreign tourists and then for locals, was the tourist influx for the 2013 Southeast Asian Games, which were hosted by Myanmar in 2013. May Lay, "Visa, MasterCard for 2013 SEA Games," *Irrawaddy,* 21 July 2012, www.irrawaddy.org/archives/9681 (accessed 6 September 2012).

12. "SMBC to Give Technical Help to Myanmar Bank," *Daily Yomiuri Online,* 23 May 2012, www.yomiuri.co.jp/dy/business/T120522004229.htm (accessed 12 September 2012).

13. EFTPOS is, internationally, the most significant vehicle for noncash payment services.

14. Antoni Slodkowski, "Daiwa Looks to Lead $380 Million Investments in Myanmar," *Reuters,* 23 July 2012, www.reuters.com/article/2012/07/23/us-Myanmar-japan-investment-idUSBRE86M07B20120723.

15. Elsewhere around the world, wholesale interbank markets are the areas via which central banks inject or extract liquidity in order to impact upon interest rates that banks levy, and the funds they have available to lend. As noted below, in Myanmar such indirect methods of monetary policy management are replaced by direct controls in the form of interest rate caps, ceilings, and other nonmarket instruments.

16. The exchange rates that the banks are forced to offer are, in fact, considerably better than those offered by the hitherto ubiquitous informal money changers, who are also greatly suffering under the new arrangements.

17. Notwithstanding these new products and arrangements, the informal *hundi* remittance system remains preferred by many Burmese nationals abroad. This is partly because *hundi* continues to be cheaper for smaller remittance payments, but partly too because it remains greatly trusted. See Soe Sander Oo, "Ayeyarwady Bank Begins Remittance Service," *Myanmar Times,* 27 February–4 March 2012. See also Myat May Zin, "KBZ Bank Starts Thai Remittance Service," *Myanmar Times* 32, no. 635 (16–22 July 2012).

18. May Lay, "Western Union to Open in Burma," *The Irrawaddy,* 14 September 2012.

19. Aye Thidar Kyaw, "Myanmar's Business Community Ponders the Future as Foreign Investment Law Enacted," *Myanmar Times*, 12 November 2012.

20. "Burma Inks Thilawa Deal with Japanese Investors," *The Irrawaddy,* 30 October 2013, www.irrawaddy.org/latest-news/burma-inks-thilawa-deal-japanese-investors.html.

21. Write-up on the Foreign Investment Law 2012 in the *Crossroads* magazine inaugural issue, June 2013. *Crossroads* is a collaboration between the Ministry of National Planning and Economic Development and Information Matrix Co. (which also operates *7Days News Journal*) to provide analyses and information on different aspects of the economic reforms.

22. Ibid.

23. In Maplecroft's fifth annual survey, Myanmar is listed as the country that had made the most improvements to its business environment. Myanmar rose from the bottom of the ranking in 2012 to third from the bottom in 2013 and fifth from the bottom in 2014. Nevertheless, Myanmar is still in the lowest percentile of the survey rankings, where countries are under the "Extreme" category. See "Business

Environment Improving in Myanmar, Mozambique and Senegal—Legal and Regulatory Risk Atlas," http://maplecroft.com/portfolio/new-analysis/2014/01/08/business-environment-improving-myanmar-mozambique-and-senegal-legal-and-regulatory-risk-atlas/.

24. US Department of State, "Recognizing and Supporting Burma's Reforms," Statement by US Secretary of State Hillary Clinton, 4 April 2012.

25. Fried Frank Harris Shriver and Jacobson LLP, Mario Mancuso, J. R. Kraemer, and Robert P. Mollen, "US Eases Economic Sanctions Against Burma, Opens Door to US Financial Services and Investment," 13 July 2012.

26. Condensed by Network Myanmar from the US Department of Treasury's FAQ on US Burma Sanctions, www.networkmyanmar.org/index.php/sanctions (accessed 23 April 2013).

27. www.reuters.com/article/2013/05/02/us-myanmar-usa-sanctions-idUSBRE9411AR20130502.

28. www.deccanherald.com/content/57579/content/197821/F#.

29. Including (bizarrely) former US Secretary of State Madeleine Albright and former Philippine president, the late Corazon Aquino.

30. AFP, "Myanmar Urges Millions of Exiles to Return," 11 May 2012, citing the *New Light of Myanmar* as source for the president's invitation.

30. The survey was carried out by Myanmar Survey Research and highlighted in the inaugural issue of *Crossroads* magazine in June 2013.

32. "Labour Disputes on the Rise in Myanmar," *Eleven Media*, 21 May 2013, reported by Asia News Network.

33. http://www.vdb-loi.com/vdb/wp-content/uploads/2013/04/Myanmar-New-Law-on-Minimum-Wages_VDB-Loi-Analysis_30Apr13.pdf.

34. Vice President Nyan Tun spoke of US$2 per day being "enough to survive" daily. See Kyaw Phyo Tha and May Sitt Paing, "Burmese Vice President Draws Ire With Cost of Living Comment," *Irrawaddy,* 22 May 2014, www.irrawaddy.org/burma/burmese-vice-president-draws-ire-cost-living-comment-2.html.

35. Simon Roughneen, "Myanmar, Japan See Promise, Problems in Economic Zone," *Nikkei Asian Review*, 13 June 2014.

36. "Japan to Forgive Myanmar Debt to Support Reforms," *New York Times*, 21 April 2012.

37. Sandar Lwin, "Farmland Law Should Be Amended: Committee," *Myanmar Times* 32, no. 632 (25 June–1 July 2012).

38. Analysis, *Myanmar Times,* no. 702 (4–10 November 2013).

39. See also Moe Thuzar, "Myanmar in Transition," in *CSCAP Regional Security Outlook 2014,* 38–43 (Council for Security Cooperation in the Asia Pacific, 2013).

40. "$22 Mln in ADB Programs to Reduce Poverty, Improve HIV/AIDS Care," *The Irrawaddy*, 14 February 2014.

41. "State and Region Governments in Myanmar," September 2013.

42. Win Aung shared his views at a public talk show event on Myanmar's ASEAN Year on 23 November 2013 in Yangon.

43. These challenges were highlighted by U Myint, the chief presidential economic advisor and chief of the Myanmar Development Resource Institute (MDRI), in his keynote address to the above-mentioned workshop.

44. It was adopted by the 14th ASEAN Summit on 26 February 2009.

45. AEC Scorecard Phase II Report.

46. The agreements for trade facilitation are the ASEAN Framework Agreement on Facilitation of Goods in Transit (AFAFGIT), the ASEAN Framework

Agreement on Facilitation of Inter-State Transport (AFAFIST), and the ASEAN Framework Agreement on Multimodal Transport (AFAMT).

47. U Myint's theme paper presented to a seminar at the National Defense College, where he highlighted the importance of getting the macroeconomic fundamentals right in order to reintegrate Myanmar into the regional and world economy.

48. "Myanmar Leader Voices Concern About Corruption," *Associated Press*, 25 December 2012.

49. The proposed set-up of the anti-corruption commission comprises retired senior military officials and civil servants.

50. Rodrik talks about the dilemma faced by economists between the conflicting perspectives of good economic policy proving good politics, and the need for an element of authoritarianism in ensuring economic reforms. See Dani Rodrik, "Understanding Economic Policy Reform," *Journal of Economic Literature* 32, no. 1 (March 1996): 9–41.

51. Merilee Grindle and John Thomas, *Public Choice and Policy Reform: The Political Economy of Reform in Developing Countries*. Baltimore: Johns Hopkins University Press, 1991.

11

Re-envisioning Land Rights and Land Tenure

Christina Fink

As in many other countries in Southeast Asia, land rights and land use in Myanmar have become hotly contested, with multiple stakeholders vying for access to and control over land. This has created substantial challenges for Thein Sein's government. As Chapters 9 and 10 illustrated, Thein Sein's administration has been eager to forge ahead with large-scale infrastructure projects, resource extraction, and industrial ventures that could fuel economic growth. Yet President Thein Sein has also asserted that his government is committed to people-centered development. Given that most people in Myanmar live in rural areas and are engaged in agriculture, and that rural agriculturalists have fared poorly for many years, the government has recognized the need to address smallholder and landless farmers' demands for land tenure security and support. Citizen anger about past and ongoing land-grabbing have also compelled the government to reevaluate its policies. At the same time, land policy has been a key issue of contention between ethnic nationalist organizations seeking greater autonomy and the central government, with disagreements over which level of government should control land use and receive revenues from resource exploitation.

This chapter considers how land rights and land use have been determined in Myanmar and highlights potential options for the future, particularly for smallholder and landless farmers. Ultimately, the decisions made about land-related policies will have a significant impact on how the economy is reshaped, if the well-being of the poor majority is improved, and whether peace can hold in the ethnic states.

Land and Agricultural Policies from 1948 to 2011

A mix of socialist, authoritarian, and capitalist approaches informed the development of land and agricultural policies under Myanmar's governments from independence in 1948 until Thein Sein's transitional government came to power in 2011. However, all three constitutions (1947, 1974, and 2008) written during that period granted the state ultimate ownership of the land. Successive governments used this power to redistribute land and regulate its use in order to achieve national self-sufficiency in food production and control over the agricultural sector, with variable impacts on the lives of the country's citizens.

From 1948 until late 1988, the government's land policy was largely based on socialist principles, although these were not fully realized in practice. Underpinning policy in the early years was a desire to reclaim the vast tracts of land that had ended up in the hands of foreigners and to provide landless Burmese agriculturalists with secure access to farmland. Such thinking was reflected in one of General Aung San's speeches during the 1947 constitution drafting process when he asserted that land ownership should be limited to a prescribed acreage so that a new class of landlords would not be able to arise.[1] The 1947 constitution restricted landholdings to 50 acres and gave the state the right to nationalize land for collective or cooperative farming. A more detailed land nationalization law was passed by the parliament in 1953 to enable the reclamation of over 6 million acres of land. One-third of the acreage was in the possession of *chettyar* moneylenders who had arrived during British rule and acquired land that had been put up as collateral, particularly during the difficult years of the Great Depression.[2] By 1959, the government had nationalized 3.35 million acres and redistributed 1.45 million acres to 190,000 farmers.[3]

The ruling Anti-Fascist People's Freedom League was committed to improving the lot of landless citizens and increasing rice production, a staple in the Burmese diet and an important export crop. At the same time, the government used the land redistribution program as a means to win over rural citizens who were attracted to the Communist Party, which was waging an insurgency.[4] However, farmland was not collectivized. Farmers leased plots from the government, and they could pass the leases on to their heirs. The land could not be taken away because of debt, and it could only be sold to others who would farm it. Lease fees and taxes on crops were low, and the government sought to provide reasonably priced credit, although it could not provide sufficient amounts. Nevertheless, in order to achieve national production targets, farmers were not legally allowed to let the land lie fallow without reasonable cause.

Land nationalization was resisted by some ethnic state leaders, because of tensions between the ethnic state governments and the union government. The 1947 constitution gave control over land and agriculture in the ethnic states to the respective state governments, but the 1953 law contravened this by stating that land nationalization would apply to the entire Union of Burma. In Shan State, the largest land-holdings were in the hands of Shan princes who viewed land nationalization as a means to undermine their power and extend central government control.

After General Ne Win came to power in 1962, the government sought to develop the country in isolation. Large businesses were nationalized and turned into state enterprises, foreign investment was no longer allowed, and only state-run banks were permitted. Agricultural policies were centered on making the country fully self-sufficient in the production of food, particularly rice, and partially self-sufficient in the production of raw materials needed for domestic industries. Farmers' food security and well-being were often disregarded. Central planners determined the crops farmers had to grow, regardless of whether that resulted in the most productive use of a particular plot of land. Because the authorities controlled the distribution of agricultural inputs and credit but were unable to provide sufficient assistance, farmers found it difficult to make improvements to their land or to achieve higher yields.

Quotas for paddy rice were imposed, and farmers had to sell the prescribed amount of rice to the government at a set price well below the market rate. To meet government quotas, farmers who suffered poor harvests sometimes had to resort to buying additional rice in the market, absorbing the difference in price themselves.[5] Those who could not meet their quotas were often jailed. In addition, local authorities could confiscate farmers' fields if they did not use them in the prescribed manner. The state's compulsory procurement policies and monopoly over rice distribution enabled the government to sell rice to civil servants and urban residents at subsidized prices. This helped avert urban organizing against authoritarian rule. At the same time, the government exported some of the crop, which brought in much-needed foreign exchange.

Notably, the state did not have control over land and agricultural practices in many upland areas in the ethnic states. The majority of these areas were under the sway of ethnic nationalist armies, while others were simply too difficult to access due to a lack of roads and scattered populations. In such areas, as in other Southeast Asian uplands, farmers typically practiced rotational agriculture under a community-organized system of usufruct, or use rights.

Following the 1988 prodemocracy demonstrations, the military regime cautiously introduced some market-oriented economic policies and encouraged domestic and foreign investment in agriculture and industry in order to stimulate the economy. Agricultural policies continued to be based on the objective of increasing production and agricultural exports; however, the means changed due to the failure of past methods to significantly boost output. The government began selectively encouraging the development of large-scale commercial farms and plantations. This policy privileged well-connected businesspeople over smallholder farmers and relied primarily on private investment.

In 1991, the military government issued instructions regarding the management of "Culturable Land, Fallow Land, and Waste Land," which allowed the state to transfer land use rights to state-owned enterprises, domestic businesses, joint-ventures, and private individuals. Five-thousand-acre blocs of land could be leased for the cultivation of perennial crops, such as rubber and oil palm, as well as for livestock grazing and aquaculture. Companies that developed at least 75 percent of their land would be eligible for additional 5,000 acre plots, up to a total of 50,000 acres. Slightly smaller tracts could be leased for orchard crops, and in both cases, the land could be held for thirty years. Unlike smallholder farmers, businessmen were able to access loans, import machinery and other inputs tax-free, and export half of their crop. Some were able to develop successful enterprises, but others struggled to turn a profit because of their lack of experience in agriculture, the large investments required, and the country's poor infrastructure.

Meanwhile, most of the previous policies geared toward smallholder farmers remained in force. As Ardeth Thawnghmung contends, the military's desire for control over the rural population was an important reason for this.[6] Farmers remained beholden to the government for access to land and were compelled to do the government's bidding, although farmers also sought to evade government regulations and quotas to the extent that they could. After 1988, the government made greater efforts to extend roads, railroads, and irrigation works, but poor rural families bore much of the cost, because they were routinely forced to provide their unpaid labor for the projects.[7] The agricultural ministry also pushed land reclamation and required the planting of second crops of paddy, with mixed results for farming families. Paddy farmers whose fields received sufficient water saw their incomes increase while those who could not channel enough water into their fields suffered. As in the past, the state agricultural bank was allocated insufficient funds to meet farmers' needs, and although the government allowed a limited number of private banks to open, smallholder farmers could not obtain loans from them.

In 2003, the government lifted restrictions on what farmers could plant on nonirrigated agricultural land, leading to increased profits for some farmers. However in the irrigated areas, the government's system of directed production ensured that more than half of the cultivated area was planted in paddy rice, cotton, and sugarcane, even though farmers in some areas would have earned more by growing other crops.[8] Acreage classified as paddy land had to be used for growing rice, and changing the classification to the broader category of agricultural land was difficult and often could only be approved as an unofficial agreement, with the payment of a bribe.[9] Yet, restrictive government policies were not the only challenge for farmers. They also frequently had to contend with corrupt local authorities who sought to augment their insufficient salaries through extortion and the sale of subsidized fertilizers on the private market.[10] At the same time, as Thawngmung has stressed, some sympathetic local authorities did try to minimize the burden of inappropriate central policies on farmers in their jurisdictions.

Government policy was often unpredictable, as demonstrated by the Ministry of Agriculture and Irrigation's 2005 nationwide program to have citizens plant over 7 million acres in *jatropha curcas*, a biofuel plant. This program was implemented despite the fact that the government did not have the technology to process the plant into fuel and did not have a market for it abroad.[11] Farmers were required to buy the seeds and dedicate part of their land to the crop, while agricultural and grazing land was confiscated in numerous parts of the country for jatropha plantations.[12] The project was later quietly discontinued as its failure became increasingly obvious.

In the wake of the massive damage caused by Cyclone Nargis in 2008, the regime compelled certain wealthy businessmen to provide financial and technical assistance during the recovery and rehabilitation process. They were then compensated by being given paddy land, which they were supposed to develop into commercial farms with the help of soft loans. However, given the challenges of establishing viable agribusinesses in Myanmar at that time, not all businesspeople were pleased with the arrangement.

As Kevin Woods has described, some business owners handled this by taking on tenant farmers or making contract arrangements with local farmers.[13] In the case of tenant arrangements, landless farmers, who may have formerly occupied the land, had to pay a rental fee, generally a portion of their crop, to farm the land. In the "2+3" contract farming model, an arrangement common in other low-income countries, the land and labor is supplied by the local farmer while the company provides capital, technical assistance, and market access. Some local farmers benefited from contract farming, because they could obtain credit from the contracting company at a lower rate than they could from informal moneylenders and the company bought the produce at the market rate or higher.

In general, though, smallholder farmers did not fare well under military rule. Farmers with small plots, poorer quality land, and insufficient water were particularly vulnerable. Farmers sought to cope by borrowing money at high interest rates from unofficial moneylenders. If they could not manage the debt, they sold their land-use rights through informal transactions. The number of landless agriculturalists increased steadily after 1988, with some becoming wage laborers locally while others sought work in other parts of the country or in neighboring countries. Well over two million people crossed into Thailand alone for work, with most coming from farming families who could not make ends meet.

Land Confiscation Between 1962 and 2011: Causes and Consequences

Land confiscation took place throughout the period of military rule from 1962 to 2011, but because of previous governments' control over the media and the lack of official reporting on the subject, the scale was unknown. Since the partial liberalization of the media beginning in 2012, the domestic press has reported widely on previous and ongoing cases of land confiscation, and it has become clear that large numbers of people in many parts of the country have been affected.

Land confiscation was justified on the basis of the 1894 Land Acquisition Act, a colonial-era law that allows the government to take land for public purposes as well as for transfer to businesses.[14] In addition, agricultural land could be confiscated if it was deemed to be unoccupied, fallow, or not being used according to government regulations. However, in many cases, the land that was taken was not vacant or fallow. It was being cultivated by smallholder farmers who did not have official land-use documents. According to the law, farmers must first register the land they are using and then apply for a land-use certificate. However, under military rule, farmers were reluctant to initiate the process, because they distrusted the authorities and because land registration was expensive due to the need to pay bribes.[15] In practice, the authorities did not require land-use registration but only the payment of an annual rental fee, for which farmers were issued receipts. Thus, many plots of land were marked vacant on the state land records department's cadastral maps even though they had been tilled for years. Farmers whose land was taken for state use or commercial ventures had little recourse in such situations. Challenging government authorities or influential people could lead to arrest, and taking the case to court would be futile, because higher authorities could insure that judges ruled in favor of the government or company. Some farmers received minimal compensation, but most received nothing and ended up landless.

Upland cultivators who practiced rotational systems of agriculture were also in a legal bind. The military regime, like many other governments in mainland Southeast Asia, did not recognize this form of customary agriculture as a legitimate use of the land. Rotational farming can enable productive use of hilly land when population densities are low. Each household in a community has use rights for several plots, and each plot is cultivated for one or two seasons and then left to regenerate for several years. However, upland cultivators could not obtain official documentation for such agricultural practices. Thus, their land, which was officially classified as reserved forest land, could be legally expropriated for other purposes.

Before 1988, land in periurban, rural, and upland areas was taken by various ministries for state-owned enterprises, demonstration farms, and livestock projects, and by the *tatmadaw* for bases and other military facilities. However, after 1988, when the military government began encouraging private enterprise in order to stimulate the economy, land seizures for private development became increasingly common. By 2011, nearly 2 million acres had been leased to the private sector for agribusiness; aquaculture; mining for minerals, metals, and precious stones; and other commercial ventures. Choice pieces of coastal land were handed over to businessmen to develop hotels and other tourist-related enterprises, again with little or no compensation provided to those who were dispossessed.

Businesspeople who acquired agricultural land did not always put it to use, because of the high cost of investment or the marginal location of the land. Farmers who lost their land to such investors were particularly upset to see their land left vacant, rented out to other landless farmers, or sold. In contravention of the 1991 land rules, such investors were not ordered to return the land to the state, or to the original farmers, although in some cases they rented the land back to the original farmers on an annual basis. In cases where land was handed over to mining companies, this led not only to landlessness, but also, in some instances, to damaging health and environmental consequences for those living in the vicinity of such projects.

In the northern and eastern ethnic states, as Mary Callahan has described, the political and economic picture was complicated because of mixed or shared sovereignty patterns.[16] Ethnic armed groups, militias, the *tatmadaw*, and government administrators exercised authority over patches of territory, while in some cases, two or more groups had overlapping influence. As the *tatmadaw* extended its reach into regions previously under the control of ethnic nationalist armed groups, *tatmadaw* commanders confiscated large tracts of land for a number of purposes. Some land was confiscated for military bases and camps while other land was taken for battalion-run economic ventures. From 1997 on, military units were ordered to provision themselves, meaning they had to produce or procure their own food. Besides requisitioning food from villagers, the battalions in some areas began growing food on land confiscated from villagers, sometimes with the villagers' forced labor.[17] Local *tatmadaw* commanders also took land for plantations and other enterprises, with the profits being used for the battalion's upkeep or for personal enrichment. Land seized for the construction of military bases was often in excess of what the military needed, and extra land was in some cases sold for a profit.[18]

Fear of being conscripted as a porter, raped, tortured, or killed by the *tatmadaw* or other nonstate armed groups led hundreds of thousands of villagers in conflict areas to flee into the forest or cross the border into neighboring countries as refugees. Vacated land was taken over by the *tatmadaw*, other armed groups, or in-migrants, while in other cases, *tatmadaw* troops laid landmines around former village sites to prevent villagers from returning. Both state and nonstate armed groups also planted landmines along footpaths and around strategic sites to protect themselves, making many sites in the conflict or former conflict areas unsafe for habitation or cultivation.

With the country's opening to foreign investment in the 1990s, neighboring countries began looking to Myanmar for opportunities to address their energy and transport needs. The Myanmar government and state-owned enterprises established a range of joint ventures with foreign-owned companies to build gas and oil pipelines, deep seaports, hydropower dams, highways, and railroads. Many of these projects were located in or transversed ethnic conflict areas. Thus, between 1996 and 2006, the *tatmadaw* forcibly evicted the residents of more than 3,000 villages in eastern Myanmar for both counterinsurgency purposes and to facilitate the development of infrastructure projects.[19] Those who had to move or lost part of their farmland received little or no compensation, and only some of the investing companies dedicated any money to local development.

Ethnic armed groups in northern and eastern Myanmar also appropriated land for commercial plantations, mining, and other ventures.[20] As with confiscations by the *tatmadaw* and central government authorities, villagers were not consulted about the planned projects, and they received little or no compensation for the loss of their land. In areas near the Chinese border primarily under the control or influence of ethnic armed organizations and local militias, commercial plantations were developed by local businesspeople with links to businesspeople in China. China's national opium crop substitution program provides financing to companies engaged in developing perennial crops, such as rubber, which not only replace opium but are also needed for China's industrial economy.[21]

With increasing business opportunities in the ethnic states, the composition of the population has been changing. For example, in 2006, with the facilitation of the then northern commander, Burmese businessman Htay Myint's Yuzana Corporation was permitted to take possession of 200,000 acres in Kachin State's Hukawng Valley for the development of sugarcane and cassava plantations and a facility that could process the crops into biofuel. Over 600 households lost their land as a result, and although they filed a lawsuit, only a small portion of the land was returned.[22] Some of the landless became workers on the plantations, but many more came from lower Myanmar. With former conflict areas being pacified and developed, migrants from other parts of the country—and from China—have moved in. This has potential political consequences. As the populations become more mixed, ethnic nationalists may have less justification in asserting the need for ethnic rights based on ethnic territoriality.

The security of land tenure in urban areas was generally greater than in rural areas, but at various times, urban residents were compelled to move as well. For instance, between 1958 and 1960, General Ne Win's caretaker government removed 300,000 squatters from Yangon and relocated them to satellite towns. In addition, after the 1988 prodemocracy demonstrations, the military government forcibly evicted as many as 1.5 million people from Yangon, Mandalay, and other towns and resettled them in satellite towns or rural areas.[23] Communities that had been active in the demonstrations were particularly targeted, but their removal also allowed for the commercial development of prime real estate.

All in all, as a result of the land confiscation and the post-1988 governments' land, agriculture, and national security policies, Myanmar has been reverting to the preindependence pattern of highly unequal land ownership with large numbers of impoverished people. Among the poor, food insecurity is common, and this is reflected in high rates of malnutrition. In 2009, UNICEF found that 41 percent of children were stunted, 30 percent underweight, and 11 percent wasted.[24] Although the numbers vary in different parts of the country, in 2013, the percentage of landless people overall was estimated at 30 to 50 percent of the population.[25] Without sufficient alternative employment opportunities or social protection services, landless agriculturalists in particular have struggled to provide for their families.

Land Laws and Policies Under the Thein Sein Government

President Thein Sein has emphasized in domestic and foreign speeches that he wants to help low-income farmers. At a conference in London in 2013, he declared, "As part of our drive to foster growth for all the people of Myanmar, we will develop clear, fair and open land policies."[26] In addition, during his first year in office, he bowed to widespread public pressure and suspended the Chinese-funded Myitsone dam project, which was expected to flood 766 square kilometers of land in Kachin State and send almost all the electricity generated to China. However, he and his administration have also sought to facilitate the development of other large-scale infrastructure projects and the expansion of agroindustry in order to modernize the economy. The difficulties of catering to the interests of both rural agriculturalists and corporations are reflected in the two land-related laws drafted by the executive branch, namely, the Farmland Law and the Vacant, Fallow, and Virgin Land Law.

Like President Thein Sein, many members of Myanmar's first parliament in fifty years also want to deliver concrete improvements for ordinary people. Thus, in 2012, they rushed to pass the land laws, despite not being able to fully assess the merits and potential weaknesses of the proposed legislation. As Chapter 4 describes, the parliamentarians had no prior experience with the legislative process and were provided with no staff or other legal resources, so it was not easy for them to critique or suggest improvements to the bills. Nevertheless, there was some lobbying by prominent businesspeople in and out of parliament as well as by civil society organizations speaking on behalf of smallholder farmers. The final versions of the laws included some provisions that pleased smallholder farmers, but they largely favored agribusinesses, while also upholding broad powers for the state.

The Farmland Law grants citizens the right to sell, exchange, inherit, lease, and pawn farmland. This is a significant change from the past, which should enable farmers to borrow from sources other than the Myanmar Agricultural Development Bank and informal money lenders. International development assistance programs were already providing microfinance to farmers in various parts of the country, but this opened up possibilities for farmers to obtain private bank loans and to establish cooperatives from which they could borrow.

Property holders are to be issued official land-use certificates, which in theory should make land tenure more secure than in the past. However, the Farmland Law reaffirms Article 37(a) of the 2008 constitution, which states that "the Union is the ultimate owner of all lands and all natural resources above and below the ground, above and beneath the water and in the atmosphere in the Union." Thus, the government can still rescind citizens' property rights in order to construct special economic zones, hydropower dams, mines, or any other type of project the ministries think will be beneficial, although the law also states that the government must pay compensation in such cases.[27] The government can reclaim the land with no payment if the farmer is using the land for purposes not mandated by existing regulations.

In addition, farmers who have land disputes must resolve them through local committees established under the auspices of the Agriculture and Irrigation Ministry. This system may work well for inheritance and intravillage disputes, because the process is not complicated, costly, or time consuming. However, it is less appropriate for cases in which land has been claimed by government departments, the military, or companies. Government-appointed committee members would be reluctant to challenge such entities. Technically, villagers cannot take land disputes to the courts although some lawyers representing farmers have used criminal charges such as trespassing in order to do so.

The Farmland Law and the August 2012 Farmland Rules enshrine the importance of national food sufficiency, as previous laws did, through the continuation of rigid land classification categories and supervision over land use.[28] Farmers must go through a formal application process if they want to shift from planting seasonal to perennial crops. It is theoretically possible to change the classification of paddy land to the broader category of agricultural land, but only after the government determines that this will not affect national rice sufficiency. As before, farmers must apply for permission to build a shed to store a tractor or a silo to store grain. Failure to do so can result in the state reclaiming the land.

The Vacant, Fallow, and Virgin Land Law was based on the 1991 instructions and specifies the requirements for turning tracts of land into plantations, orchards, and aquaculture enterprises. In the future, the government intends for many more large tracts of land to be leased in this fashion. The passage of the Foreign Investment Law in 2012 enables this by allowing foreign companies to apply for special approval to invest in the agribusiness sector without a joint partner. Moreover, foreign companies can hold leases for seventy years or longer in underdeveloped areas of the country. In effect, the laws grant business enterprises much more leeway over how they can utilize the land than smallholder farmers.

Nevertheless, in a nod to smallholder farmers, the laws note that lands recorded as vacant, fallow, and virgin or as reserved forest land are in many cases being cultivated by farmers. Nonrotational upland farming (*taungya*) is recognized as legitimate, but the government's Farmland Rules call for the elimination of rotational agriculture and the substitution of terraced fields. Still, the rules do not contain a mechanism for the conversion of reserved forestland into farmland.

Notably, the Farmland Law allows farmers to establish farmers' organizations. In addition, according to the 2011 Law on Peaceful Assembly and Peaceful Procession, farmers and other citizens can demonstrate legally if they apply for and are granted permission in advance. In theory this should allow farmers to have a greater voice in land and agricultural policymaking. In practice, however, farmers have found it nearly impossible to get permission for demonstrations against land confiscation, and farmers have been arrested and charged for going ahead with unapproved demonstrations.

Farmers' groups felt that the 2012 laws did not provide sufficient protections for smallholder farmers, and within months called for their amendment. Some of the points that were agreed on at an August 2013 conference in Yangon that drew hundreds of farmers were

> an end to the arrest and charging of farmers [involved in land disputes] and the people who are helping them, fair investigations of farmers' claims, and for authorities to stop using the term "compassionate grant" instead of "compensation" for grabbed land [and] . . . that authorities compensate them directly for lost land, discuss plans with them first before proceeding with project implementation, and identify undeveloped land for them to farm in the event that their property is to be used for a project.[29]

Moreover, the 2012 land laws did not explicitly nullify the various preexisting acts and rules. It is difficult for small-scale farmers to know all the laws and regulations, and as Tin Htut Oo, the former director-general for the

Department of Agricultural Planning, has pointed out, this creates opportunities for exploitation and corruption by officials at various levels.[30]

In October 2013, the parliament responded to smallholder farmers' concerns by passing the Protecting Rights and Enhancing Economic Welfare of Farmers Law. This law was drafted by the Lower House's Agriculture, Livestock, and Fisheries Committee, with the support of both Shwe Mann, the speaker of the Lower House, and Aung San Suu Kyi. After much debate and some revisions, the final provisions include protection against unlawful land confiscation, the right of farmers to cultivate crops of their choosing, and guarantees of access to necessary inputs, agricultural credit, and insurance on appropriate terms. The law also states that farmers should receive appropriate and fair prices for their crops, although it was ultimately decided not to specify how this would be ensured. That will be the task of the leading committee overseeing the implementation of the law, which, significantly, must include not only government representatives but also representatives from farmers' associations. While some smallholder advocates were disappointed that the law's definition of a farmer was made broad enough to include middlemen and businesspeople, landless farmers were pleased that the definition incorporated them.

The executive branch has taken other actions as well to facilitate more rationalized land policy development and to support rural agriculturalists. In 2012, the government formed the Land Allocation and Utilisation Supervisory Committee to prepare a land use policy in collaboration with local and international experts. The committee was also tasked with examining existing laws, rules, and regulations; drafting revisions; and conducting a review of the land revenue system. Meanwhile, the state agricultural bank began providing larger loans to farmers, and international organizations have been able to expand the provision of small loans to farmers as well. In 2013, the president's office ordered the Settlement and Land Records Department to begin issuing new land-use certificates. In his meetings with state, regional, and local government officials during that year, the Coordinating Minister for Economic Development, Soe Thane, emphasized the urgency of completing the land titling process.[31] There has been a significant increase in the issuance of land titles, but the cost of off-the-books payments for issuing the titles continues to be an obstacle in some localities. Soe Thane also stated that the government would begin providing landless farmers with opportunities to obtain vacant land in 2014.

In addition, under Soe Thane's leadership, the government initiated procedures to become a member of the Extractive Industries Transparency Initiative (EITI). The purpose of the initiative is to increase transparency over payments and revenues in the extractive sector in order to ensure that the proceeds are used for sustainable development that benefits the public. EITI signatories are also expected to allow independent civil society organizations to participate actively in EITI implementation. Before 2011, the military government recorded gas earnings in published accounts at the official exchange rate of 6 Myanmar kyat (MMK) to the US dollar (US$), while the unofficial exchange rate hovered around MMK1000 to the US dollar.[32] In this way, less than 1 percent of the country's annual natural gas revenue of around US$3 billion per year at that time was actually put into the state budget. If the initiative is fully implemented, then there should be far more money available for public sector investment, enabling the government to build the infrastructure necessary for the development of a more advanced economy while also supporting rural development.

Similar to the parliamentary period in the 1950s, the central government and ethnic nationalist groups have different positions regarding whether union or the (ethnic) state governments should exercise control over land rights and which level of government should receive revenue from extractive industry projects. The 2008 constitution provides only limited powers to the states and regions, including with regard to land. The union-level government has responsibility for land administration including town and village land; the reclamation of vacant, fallow, and virgin land; settlement and land records; and land surveys. State- and regional-level governments are only assigned responsibility for collecting land revenue, municipal taxes on land, and the sale or lease of state or region-owned land.

The executive and legislative branches have been considering decentralizing more powers to the states and regions as a means to secure peace in the ethnic states. However, as of 2014, major decisions regarding land policy and land rights remained under the control of the union-level government. This meant that the approval of large development projects and mining, agribusiness, and other concessions, continued to be handled by the Union administration with no formal processes for consultation with state and regional governments or with affected local citizens. In addition, there was no revenue sharing mechanism in place, so all revenues from such projects went exclusively to the Union government.

Government Responses to Land Confiscation

The most challenging land-related issue for Thein Sein's government has been how to handle widespread anger and protests over past and ongoing land confiscation. With less repression, rural and urban dwellers have become increasingly determined to get their land back or receive adequate compensation. However, with rising land prices and a desire to establish many more large-scale projects, the government has found it difficult to handle citizens' demands.

Parliamentarians from all parties have been urged by their constituents to address land confiscation, and they have raised the matter repeatedly.

Even Myat Kyi, a former agricultural officer in Naypyitaw who became a USDP parliamentarian, declared, "It is disgusting that the peasants who have cultivated land there for years were evicted through lawsuits—in which they were branded as squatters—when [so-called] forest land and virgin land in Nay Pyi Taw were given by the state to entrepreneurs in parcels of 50 acres to 300."[33]

In 2012, the parliament formed a land seizure inquiry commission, which, in less than a year, received 565 complaints detailing the military's seizure of 247,000 acres of land.[34] In 2013, the commission recommended that the military return any undeveloped land to the previous owners or hand it over to the state. If the land had been developed, the commission asked the military to provide affected farmers with adequate compensation. Defense Minister Lieutenant-General Wai Lwin told the parliament in July 2013 that the military would give back 18,364 acres of unused farmland, but other lands close to areas used by the military could not be returned for security reasons.[35] He did not offer any compensation. The *tatmadaw,* meanwhile, continued to press ahead with land confiscations in conflict and post-conflict areas, particularly where hydropower dams and other development projects were planned.

As of mid-2014, the land inquiry commission had not released figures on land seized by other state bodies or private companies, but there has been public pressure for all who have seized land to return it or make amends. The parliament continued to push the executive branch to take action, setting a deadline of June 2014 for paddy land and September 2014 for other types of agricultural land to be given back. Some well-connected businesspeople have returned parcels of land or paid compensation to some former owners, but they have preferred to use the value at the time the land was taken rather than the current price, which would be far higher. Approximately 70 percent of the land that had been given to Myanmar companies under the previous government remained fallow in 2011 and, according to government regulations, should have been returned to the state.[36] Nevertheless, government authorities have been reluctant to take action against influential businesspeople and may still hope that such land will be developed into profitable enterprises.

Even when companies do return land to the state to hand back to farmers, there can be difficulties. In 2013, Aye Shwe Wah Company, which reportedly holds 40,000 acres in Irrawaddy Division, gave up control of 2,000 acres. However, the division government faced a dilemma. Both the original owners and the tenant farmers whom the company had brought in since 1991 were claiming rights to the land.[37]

Aung San Suu Kyi and the National League for Democracy, whose symbol is the *kamauk*, or farmer's hat, have also been caught up in land issues. In 2012, Aung San Suu Kyi chose to run for election in Kawhmu

Township, an impoverished agricultural area outside Yangon, but she has been less clearly pro–poor farmer than many expected. Given her presidential ambitions, she has had to think about how to balance the interests of many different stakeholders.

In late 2012, she agreed to chair a parliamentary investigation commission into the police's handling of the Letpadaung copper mine protests against land confiscation and negative environmental impacts. In 2010, 7,800 acres of land had been confiscated for the mine, and twenty-six villages were affected. During the 2012 protest, the police responded with force, using incendiary devices that injured 100 people, including several Buddhist monks who were badly burned. Domestic human rights and environmental groups supported the protesters, because they felt that this project, like so many other large-scale projects approved by the former government, benefited the military elite and its affiliates at the expense of local people. The parliamentary commission concluded that the copper mine should continue operations, but that the companies involved should compensate the villagers fairly, invest in their communities, and put in place environmental protections. The commission said nothing about holding officials accountable for the brutal crackdown.

Although Aung San Suu Kyi visited the Letpadaung area to urge the villagers to accept the commission's recommendations, the villagers reacted angrily. Their rallying cry of "End the Crony System!" indicated that they felt that their interests were still being marginalized.[38] In the months that followed, the companies offered higher compensation and built new houses for the villagers, but they did not build a school or hospital as promised. Many villagers refused the compensation, saying that it was insufficient and they would rather have their land back.

While the government has been sympathetic to the plight of those who have lost their land to a certain extent, the administration has been unable or unwilling to fully meet the demands of land confiscation victims. With the rapid expansion of civil society organizations in the country and concerns that the window of opportunity for obtaining land or compensation might not last, it is possible that a broader anti-land-grabbing movement could emerge.

Turning to upland areas, as in other parts of mainland Southeast Asia, the privatization of forested commons has severely affected nearby villagers' livelihoods, as they can no longer hunt, search for edible forest products, graze animals, or collect firewood in these areas. Some upland communities in northern Myanmar have tried to protect their access to forests by using the 1995 Community Forestry Instructions, which were drafted based on the 1992 Forest Law and 1995 Forest Policy. The instructions allow rural communities to comanage forests with Forestry Department oversight in order to collect firewood and meet other basic livelihoods needs.[39] This is a rare example of local communities being able to use the law to their advantage.

Again like other countries in the region, land conflicts are at the heart of development challenges in Myanmar's urban and periurban areas, with the problem being particularly acute in and around Yangon. Land speculation has driven up the prices of land so much that in 2013, square footage in parts of the city was more expensive than in New York City. This has become a critical barrier for both domestic and foreign businesspeople who wish to establish offices, commercial ventures, and factories in the city and its outskirts. Foreign companies have also questioned whether it is worth investing in Myanmar, given the high price of land, in combination with poor infrastructure, a weak regulatory framework, and an insufficiently developed banking system.

Thein Sein's government has recognized the seriousness of the problem but has struggled to find a workable solution. In 2014, the government introduced a progressive tax rate on land sales with significantly higher rates on expensive properties in Yangon and lower rates on less costly properties. Nevertheless, land prices are also rising rapidly in other towns, along roads where people expect that commercial development will be allowed in the future, and in rural areas where development projects are planned or rumored to be under consideration.

The government-backed Thilawa Industrial Zone south of Yangon has also faced difficulties because of rapidly escalating real estate prices. In 2013, the government asserted that villagers whose land was confiscated for the project would be compensated according to World Bank and Japanese standards.[40] The nearly 6,000-acre zone is being developed by the Japanese government, a consortium of Japanese companies, and the Union of Myanmar's Federation of Chambers of Commerce and Industry. With plans to include a deep sea port, factories, a power plant, and housing complexes, it could potentially generate up to 200,000 jobs.[41] However, skyrocketing land prices complicated negotiations over the compensation rate, and in the short term, no jobs were available for those who lost their land and livelihoods.

The dramatic increase in apartment and room rental prices has also made it more difficult for low-income workers to afford proper housing, and this has led to the expansion of squatter communities around factories on the outskirts of Yangon. Unhappy with the illegal settlements, the Yangon Division government evicted thousands of squatters from government and privately owned land in late 2013 and early 2014, although President Thein Sein promised in a radio address in early 2014 that the government was developing plans to accommodate squatters and provide jobs to landless people.[42] The government has little experience managing competing demands in an economy where many factors seem to be beyond its control.

With insufficient funds to meet all the pressing needs and a tendency by some officials to resort to the types of authoritarian methods used in the past, the government has not yet been able to fulfill its promise of people-centered development.

At the same time, large-scale displacement has continued in some parts of the country because of communal violence and civil war. Since 2012, communal violence has led to the dislocation of Muslims in Sittwe (Akyab) and other parts of Rakhine (Arakan) State, in Meiktila, and in other scattered communities in central Myanmar. As of April 2014, there were 146,000 internally displaced people in Rakhine State, the vast majority of whom were Muslims who had been driven from their homes in and around Sittwe.[43] The local Rakhine population has insisted that they will not accept the return of the Muslim population, and neither the Thein Sein administration nor the parliament was willing to stand up for the Muslim property owners' rights.

Although the government had successfully negotiated cease-fires with most of the ethnic armed groups by mid-2012, in Kachin State, a seventeen-year-old cease-fire broke down in 2011. Between 2011 and 2014, over 100,000 Kachin residents fled their homes because of the resumption of armed conflict and the occupation of villages by *tatmadaw* troops. Given the *tatmadaw*'s interest in securing control over land around energy projects and areas with rich timber and mineral resources, it may be the case that even after the conflict ends, not all of the displaced will be able to reclaim their property.

Looking Forward

Despite the many challenges, perhaps the most remarkable change since President Thein Sein came to power was his frank acknowledgment of the mistakes that were made in the past and his stated commitment to developing more inclusive policies. With input from previously silenced sectors of society, opportunities emerged to improve policymaking on land rights and rural development for the well-being of the general population. The government and other stakeholders have also been interested in drawing on suggestions from a range of organizations with expertise in land policy and in learning from the experiences of countries in the region.[44] This could be extremely useful, as China, Vietnam, Cambodia, and Laos have also gone through transitions from socialist economies to more liberalized economic systems.

The development of a comprehensive land policy is key to creating the conditions for secure land tenure, transparency, and economic development. One lesson from other countries is that major land-related policy changes should be made early on in reform processes, because it only becomes more difficult as time passes. In crafting policies, much consideration should be given to balancing the interests of rural agriculturalists, urban residents, businesspeople, and future generations. Agribusinesses, resource extraction projects, and special economic zones can generate jobs and revenue. They can contribute to citizens' well-being if proper environmental safeguards and worker protections are in place. At the same time, creating the conditions that enable smallholder farms and small and medium enterprises to succeed is equally important, both for overall economic growth and for equitable development. As a 2003 World Bank analysis of land policies in over seventy countries demonstrated, countries with more equitable initial land distribution achieved growth rates that were significantly higher than countries where land distribution was less equitable.[45] Indeed, smallholder farms can be highly productive, and they can do more to reduce poverty than agribusinesses.[46]

Arguments can be made for state ownership of land as well as for the privatization of land rights. State ownership can ensure that the poor have access to land, if the government is committed to keeping sufficient land available for small-scale farming and guarantees security of tenure. This system has been discredited in Myanmar, because previous authoritarian governments arbitrarily confiscated land and treated rural agriculturalists more like feudal tenants than citizens with rights. In China as well, millions of citizens have been dispossessed, often without compensation, as the government has pursued rapid urbanization, energy projects, and resource extraction. However, in Vietnam, the government maintained state ownership but generally ensured security of tenure, resulting in the steady growth of agricultural incomes. If a new social contract between the government and citizens is established in Myanmar, it is possible that state ownership could serve the broader public's interests.

Full private ownership gives citizens a greater sense of control, and in theory, it would be more difficult for land confiscation to take place, because the government would be under greater pressure to justify why the confiscation was necessary. Companies would have to buy land from freeholders at the market rate, assuming the owner agreed. Private ownership also has the potential to incentivize greater investment and more conscientious stewardship of the land. However, in a context of intense land speculation and widespread indebtedness, these benefits could be lost as poor farmers feel pressured to sell their fields to pay off debt and end up landless.

The government's current model of state ownership with land-use certificates can work if the government puts other supportive measures in place. Banking regulations need to be changed to enable farmers to borrow from private banks and cooperatives. The government could also use various forms of taxation to rein in speculation and support small-scale farmers. For instance, high land-transfer taxes on agricultural land, payable by the buyer, could dampen speculation. There could also be a high tax imposed on fallow land. Taxes could also be increased for large land-holdings and reduced for small land-holdings.

The formalization of community ownership over land, with access to land understood as a social right, is another approach that has been adopted in some countries. Community members automatically have a right to community-owned land according to criteria determined by the community. The use of community titling can be used to formalize existing customary use arrangements and can also provide a degree of sovereignty and security to ethnic minority communities. This policy has been introduced in upland Lao communities. At the same time, community titling and other forms of cooperative arrangements can allow for communities to benefit from new opportunities. For instance, groups of farmers can negotiate with domestic and foreign companies who want to lease part of the land or enter into contractual farming arrangements with members of the community.

The government may want to consider recognizing different types of ownership systems in different parts of the country. As the World Bank has argued, it is generally more productive to formalize the various types of arrangements that currently exist in a country than to impose a new, uniform system.[47] Community titling could be introduced in upland areas, while in certain forested areas, there could be provisions for community forestry. In urban, periurban, and rural areas where there has been greater population mobility and commercial farming, private ownership or transferable land-use certificates make more sense.

More generally, the government should consider land rights and land use within the context of decentralization of power to ethnic states and regions and even local governments. Much of the support for the ethnic nationalist struggles has been derived from local populations' desire to safeguard their land rights and live undisturbed. Previous governments' decisions to carry out large-scale infrastructure and resource extraction projects in the ethnic states sparked even greater outrage, as large numbers of people were displaced without any consultation or compensation. Some degree of decentralization of the management over land rights, land use, and resource extraction in the ethnic states, and perhaps the regions as well, could help establish greater land security and citizen input into decisions that affect their communities. Revenue sharing between the states and the central government could also help secure peace. These provisions would require the acquiescence of the *tatmadaw* and the various nonstate armed groups as well as significant demilitarization.

Land rights must also be considered with regard to citizenship. Many people who should have citizenship or should be granted citizenship do not currently have official documentation. This includes villagers in remote areas and the hundreds of thousands of internally displaced people and refugees who want to reclaim the land they previously occupied, receive compensation, or obtain new land. The 1982 Citizenship Law may need to be revised to permit refugees and their children to establish their citizenship and to enable Muslims in northern Rakhine State, many of whose families have lived in Myanmar for generations, to achieve citizenship. Moreover, Chinese purchases of land in northern Myanmar, in and around Mandalay, and along major transportation arteries have bred resentment that could lead to communal tensions. Some of the buyers come from families long resident in Myanmar, while others have moved to Myanmar in recent years and obtained Burmese citizenship through the payment of bribes. Still others live in China and have used proxies to purchase the land. The government will face mounting pressure to resolve citizenship rights with regard to land as refugees begin to return, foreign ownership of land increases, and land prices continue to rise.

National land policy in Myanmar has been gender-blind in the past. Women can be property owners or land-use certificate holders, although customary practices in some parts of the country restrict land inheritance for females. Allowing joint titling, which has been implemented in Cambodia and many other countries, would be a more progressive policy, with space on land titles for two names to appear: that of both a husband and a wife, for instance. Joint titling would provide much greater security for women, who could use the titles to obtain credit and invest in the land and in home-based businesses. If a husband were to die or migrate, the wife would still have clear title to the land. Joint titling could also help women overcome discriminatory customary practices in some communities.

Rigid land classification categories and other restrictions and requirements should be reevaluated as they may be preventing farmers from being able to achieve food security and improve their incomes. For instance, if there were more flexibility, smallholder farmers might choose to grow a mix of rice, beans, and vegetables; plant fruit trees; and have a fish pond. If farmers could choose to grow whatever cash crops best fit with their land and could respond to market shifts by changing what they grew, they would likely be more prosperous. A review of Myanmar's agricultural policies shows that after 1988, the production of crops under government control showed little improvement, while those not under government control did much better.[48] If the 2013 Protecting Farmers Law is implemented as written, greater autonomy for farmers could potentially result in higher yields and increased revenues from exports.

If needed, the government could use incentives rather than coercion to encourage the production of certain crops. With regard to rice, options such as lower tax rates could be considered. The government should also consider eliminating burdensome requirements for permits to erect buildings, including storage sheds, on agricultural land. Farmers and commercial businesses of all sizes also require the extension of rural infrastructure for transport and communications. This would increase access to information and markets and reduce transportation costs. Agriculturalists also require sufficient water for their fields; without adequate water supplies, many farmers will not be able to increase their productivity. Social protection measures such as providing low-cost crop insurance and reducing taxes when natural disasters have caused crop losses would also help farmers remain solvent.

If the government is committed to building an equitable society, the needs of the landless must be addressed. Ideally, those with no land or less than 5 acres would be granted land, which would provide them with the means to support themselves and serve as an asset which they could use to obtain credit. At the same time, the government should consider how best to facilitate the development of rural nonfarm livelihoods and urban job opportunities, provide vocational skills training, and enable more rural families to send their children to school for longer, so that they have more employment opportunities.

A standard policy on handling past and continuing land confiscations would help build trust in the government and provide justice to citizens. With regard to past confiscations, decisions must be made about how far to go back in time and what options can be offered to those who lost their land. Options could include returning the land to the original occupants, providing land of equal value, or providing monetary compensation. With regard to the future, the government should narrow the parameters for when land can be taken from occupants and provide suitable compensation. Compensation rates need to be standardized, although variations can be built in. India's 2013 fair compensation for land acquisition law is worth looking at. Compensation is set at four times the market value for rural land and two times the value for urban land, plus livelihood support for a certain number of years. India's policy recognizes that those who are dislocated have also lost their homes and require time to establish themselves in a new location or prepare for a new vocation. India's law also requires compensation for those who lose access to livelihoods on land that has been confiscated. This includes tenant farmers, fishermen and -women, and people who grazed their livestock on the land.

Myanmar's future economic development will require that land be expropriated for various purposes. Many of the projects will presumably benefit the public, such as road expansion, electricity generation for domestic use, and the development of airports and seaports. Still, the government will be under much greater pressure than in the past to obtain the informed consent of those who will be dispossessed, to ensure that they will be fairly compensated, and to appropriately mitigate any negative social and environmental impacts.

Accurately updating department records on land registration and use and making this information easily accessible will help reduce conflicts and enable better decisionmaking. Open Development Cambodia is a good example. It is a public data platform with interactive maps that allow users to view land concessions, large-scale development projects, forest reserves, and community forests, as well as land- and development-related laws and relevant reports and news.

Judicial reform and strengthening, and broadening the scope for land-related cases to be heard in courts, could enable greater economic stability by reassuring investors and smallholder farmers that such cases can be fairly resolved.

Finally, the government must consider how the needs of poor migrant workers and long-term urban residents can be met. Options include the expansion of economic opportunities in smaller towns and rural areas so that fewer poor rural citizens feel compelled to come to large urban centers to find employment, as well as the construction of low-cost housing in urban areas, and the regularization of informal settlements through the provision of land titles and public services.

Despite the many challenges, Myanmar has the opportunity to create a society that begins to live up to the sense of promise so many people felt at the time of the country's independence in 1948. Thoughtful, inclusive policies, which focus on equity and well-being, could enable the people of Myanmar to finally put the decades of economic hardship and insecurity behind them.

Notes

I would like to thank George Washington University's Sigur Center for Asian Studies for a research grant in 2013, and Win Min and Keila Franks for their invaluable research assistance.

1. Aung San, *Burma's Challenge* (Rangoon: self-published, 1946), cited in Maung Maung, *Burma's Constitution* (The Hague: Martinus Nijhoff, 1959), 107.

2. Maung, *Burma's Constitution,* 108.

3. Frank N. Trager, *Burma: From Kingdom to Republic* (New York: Fredrick A. Praeger, 1966), 152.

4. Hugh Tinker, *The Union of Burma: A Study of the First Years of Independence.* (London: Oxford University Press, 1961), 238.

5. Nancy Hudson-Rodd, Myo Nyunt, Saw Thamain Tun, and Sein Htay, *The Impact of the Confiscation of Land, Labor, Capital Assets and Forced Relocation in Burma by the Military Regime*, NCUB/FTUB Discussion Paper, 2003, 6.

6. Ardeth Maung Thawnghmung, *Behind the Teak Curtain: Authoritarianism, Agricultural Policies and Political Legitimacy in Rural Burma/Myanmar* (London: Kegan Paul, 2004), 79.

7. Reports by the International Labour Organization, Human Rights Watch, Earthrights International, the Karen Human Rights Group, and others document the widespread use of forced labor for infrastructure projects from 1988 to 2011.

8. United Nations Development Program, *Myanmar Agricultural Sector Review and Investment Strategy*, Volume 1, Sector Review, 2004, 158.

9. Personal communication, September 2013.

10. Thawnghmung, *Behind the Teak Curtain*, 148–149.

11. Many Myanmar citizens believed the military regime promoted the planting of jatropha as a magical means to counteract the power of Aung San Suu Kyi. The pronunciation of the word *jet su*, jatropha in Burmese, is almost a mirror reversal of Suu Kyi.

12. See Ethnic Community Development Forum, *Biofuel by Decree: Unmasking Burma's Bio-energy Fiasco* (Yangon: 2008).

13. Kevin Woods, *Agribusiness Investments in Myanmar: Opportunities and Challenges for Poverty Reduction* (Kunming: Yunnan University Press, 2013), 74–75.

14. Scott Leckie and Ezekiel Simperingham, *Housing, Land and Property Rights in Burma: The Current Legal Framework* (Geneva: Displacement Solutions and the HLP Institute, 2009), 194–196.

15. Personal communication, October 2013.

16. Mary P. Callahan, *Political Authority in Burma's Ethnic Minority States: Devolution, Occupation, and Coexistence* (Washington, DC: East-West Center, 2007).

17. Karen Human Rights Group, *Development by Decree: The Politics of Poverty and Control in Karen State* (Thailand: KHRG, 2007), 60.

18. Lawi Weng, "Army MP Halts Talks on Military Land Grabs in Burma's Parliament," *Irrawaddy*, 16 August 2013.

19. Thailand Burma Border Consortium (TBBC), *Internal Displacement in Eastern Burma: 2006 Survey* (Bangkok: TBBC, 2006), 27.

20. See, for instance, Karen Human Rights Group, "Losing Ground: Land Conflicts and Collective Action in Eastern Myanmar," Report No. 2013-01,March 2013, and Transnational Institute, *Access Denied: Land Rights and Ethnic Conflict in Burma* (Amsterdam: Transnational Institute–Burma Centre Netherlands, May 2013).

21. Tom Kramer and Kevin Woods, *Financing Dispossession: China's Opium Substitution Program in Northern Burma*, Amsterdam: Transnational Institute, February 2012.

22. Seamus Martov, "World's Largest Tiger Reserve 'Bereft of Cats,'" *Irrawaddy*, 16 November 2012.

23. UN Habitat, *Human Settlements Sector Review, Union of Myanmar* (Nairobi: United Nations, 1991), 10.

24. UNICEF, *State of the World's Children*, 2009.

25. *USAID Country Profile: Property Rights and Resource Governance–Burma* (Washington, DC: USAID, 2013) 8.

26. "Myanmar's Complex Transformation: Prospects and Challenges," Transcript of President Thein Sein's speech, London, 15 July 2013.

27. Robert B. Oberndorf, *Legal Review of Recently Enacted Farmland Law and Vacant, Fallow and Virgin Lands Management Law* (Yangon: Food Security Working Group's Land Core Group, November 2012), 19–20.

28. For a full discussion of the 2012 land laws and earlier laws, see ibid.

29. "Myanmar Farmers Call for Amendments to Land Law," *Radio Free Asia*, 20 August 2013.

30. Tin Htut Oo, "New Agricultural Strategy to Enhance Myanmar's Rural Economy," in Nick Cheesman, Monique Skidmore, and Trevor Wilson, eds.,

Myanmar's Transition: Openings, Obstacles, and Opportunities (Singapore: Institute of Southeast Asian Studies, 2012), 172–173.

31. Personal communication, September 2013.

32. Sean Turnell, "Finding Dollars and Sense: Burma's Economy in 2010," in Susan L. Levenstein, ed., *Finding Dollars, Sense, and Legitimacy in Burma*, Washington, DC, Woodrow Wilson Center for Scholars, November 2010, 30–31.

33. Win Ko Ko Latt, "Rep Tells of Land Grabs in Nay Pyi Taw," *Myanmar Times*, 20 August 2012.

34. Htet Naing Zaw and Aye Kyawt Khaing, "Military Involved in Massive Land Grabs: Parliamentary Report," *The Irrawaddy*, 15 March 2013.

35. Zarni Mann, "Only Fraction of Land Seized by Military Will be Returned: Minister," *Irrawaddy*, 18 July 2013.

36. Thomas Kean, "Pro-poor Land Program Unveiled," *Myanmar Times*, 2–8 July 2012.

37. Shwe Aung, "Land Seized by Crony Companies to Be Returned to Locals," *Democratic Voice of Burma*, 25 June 2013.

38. Lawi Weng, "Stop Protests Against Copper Mine, Suu Kyi Tells Communities," *Irrawaddy*, 13 March 2013.

39. Kevin Woods and Kerstin Canby, *Baseline Study 4, Myanmar: Overview of Forest Law Enforcement, Governance, and Trade*. (Washington, DC: Forest Trends, 2011), 18.

40. Ibid.

41. Sanay Lin, "Govt to Compensate 90 Farmers Affected by Thilawa SEZ," *Irrawaddy*, 11 June 2013.

42. "Yangon Parliament Urged to Deal with Squatters," *Eleven Media*, 25 February 2014.

43. UN Office for the Coordination of Humanitarian Affairs, *Humanitarian Bulletin Myanmar* no. 4 (1–30 April 2014).

44. USAID, Displacement Solutions, the Land Core Group of the Food Security Working Group, the Transnational Institute, and Earthrights International have all put forward recommendations on land policy.

45. Klaus Deininger, *Land Policies for Growth and Poverty Reduction*, World Bank Policy Research Report (The World Bank and Oxford University Press, June 2003).

46. USAID Burma, Michigan State University, and the Myanmar Development Resource Institute's Center for Social and Economic Development, "Strategic Choices for the Future of Agriculture in Myanmar: A Summary Paper," July 2013, 5–6.

47. Deininger, *Land Policies*.

48. Koichi Fujita and Ikuko Okamoto, "Agricultural Policies and Development of Myanmar," *Discussion Paper* 63 (Chiba, Japan: Institute of Developing Economies, 2006), 23.

12

China and Myanmar: Moving Beyond Mutual Dependence

Yun Sun

China's relationship with Myanmar has been a heated topic in the process of Myanmar's reform. Though China enjoyed overwhelming influence in Myanmar during the military government, it now faces serious challenges to its political, economic, and strategic interests in Myanmar. In the recent decades, Myanmar has been one of the few rare cases where China's policy has encountered major setbacks in its periphery diplomacy. Chinese investment projects have come under rising criticism and opposition by locals. China's previous blueprint to utilize Myanmar's strategic utilities is also put on hold, at least temporarily, until bilateral relations improve.

Within the broader history of Sino-Myanmar relations, Myanmar's overdependence on China during its military government era is a deviation from the country's traditional foreign policy principles. For the majority of the six decades of Sino-Myanmar relations, Myanmar pursued a neutralist, nonalignment foreign strategy and maintained a relatively balanced but calculated policy toward China. However, from 1990 to 2011, Myanmar grew increasingly dependent on China due to the pressures of international isolation and sanctions as a result of its repressive domestic politics. During this period, China was a primary source of political and economic support for Myanmar. China's advantageous position in the unbalanced bilateral relationship, combined with the country's rising demand for foreign natural resources and business opportunities, translated into a conscious policy intended to exploit the economic benefits Myanmar offered. To this end, China launched massive investment campaigns in Myanmar in the late 2000s. The confidence about Myanmar's presumed "loyalty," made possible by the country's continued isolation, further emboldened Beijing's ambitions to pursue strategic goals such as energy transportation routes through Myanmar. During this stage, China and Myanmar formed a largely asymmetric, mutually dependent relationship, but for vastly different goals.

However, contrary to Beijing's initial assessment of Myanmar politics after the 2010 elections, the Thein Sein government quickly undertook genuine democratic reform in 2011. The reform freed Myanmar from previous domestic and foreign constraints, removing the precondition of its involuntary dependence on China but not China's growing reliance on Myanmar. Myanmar's changed domestic politics and external relations deprived China of its primary strategic leverage against Myanmar and fundamentally altered the power balance between the two, leaving China in an uncomfortable position.

China still enjoys certain influence in Myanmar. The rapidly declining Chinese investment greatly affects the economic outlook of the country. China's strong ties with border ethnic groups continue to impact the future of Myanmar's national reconciliation, a key task for the Myanmar government in the foreseeable future. How to wield these influences to China's advantage without further damaging Sino-Myanmar relations is a key question for Beijing in the years to come. Meanwhile, Myanmar also faces important challenges in managing its shifting relations with China. Most importantly, Myanmar needs to consider how to manage economic cooperation with China to maximize the benefits for its own country, determine the correct alignment (or nonalignment) of foreign policy to navigate great power competition, and exploit the collective regional architecture to advance its interests vis-à-vis China.

The Asymmetric Dependence Between China and Myanmar

The asymmetric dependence between China and Myanmar was a relatively recent phenomenon made possible by a unique historical context. As a deviation from the relatively balanced ties throughout the history of the bilateral relations, it was temporary and short-lived. Myanmar's dependence on China was the direct result of Myanmar's international isolation after the 1990 general election and the lack of alignment choices. On the other hand, China's dependence on Myanmar stemmed from Beijing's confidence in Myanmar's continued "loyalty" and therefore growing aspiration to exploit Myanmar's economic and strategic utilities. Although the dependence was mutual, it was not equal or symmetric: Myanmar depended on China for critical issues such as national security and regime legitimacy, while China only utilized Myanmar to advance certain interests. Moreover, while China had different partner options to achieve these goals, Myanmar's options were extremely limited.

The Historical Context of Sino-Myanmar Relations

For the majority of the six decades of Sino-Myanmar bilateral relations since the founding of the Union of Burma in 1948 and the founding of the People's Republic of China in 1949, China and Myanmar have enjoyed a relatively stable and friendly relationship compared to the turbulent relationships between Beijing and many of its neighbors. Sino-Myanmar relations were blessed with a positive beginning. After the founding of the People's Republic of China, Burma was the first noncommunist country to extend diplomatic recognition and one of the first countries to establish diplomatic relations with Beijing.[1] In its early years, Beijing attempted to build friendly relations with the newly independent states in Asia, to consolidate the international legitimacy of the communist regime, and to prevent neighboring countries from joining the so-called "imperialist" camp.[2] Meanwhile, Burma, sandwiched between two regional powers—China and India—gradually adopted a neutralist and nonalignment foreign policy in order to balance the two without antagonizing either.[3]

The convergence of goodwill between Beijing and Rangoon sparked warming personal ties between the top leaders of the two countries. Between 1954 and 1965, Chinese Premier Zhou Enlai paid nine visits to Burma, a unique case in Chinese foreign relations.[4] Burmese leaders U Nu and Ne Win reciprocated by visiting China six and twelve times, respectively.[5] The two countries achieved several important landmark successes during this period. They reached consensus to jointly advocate the "Five Principles of Peaceful Coexistence," a boost of the new China and its foreign strategy. To this day, China still takes great pride in the Five Principles as the political and historical foundation of Sino-Myanmar relations and as the central theme of China's foreign policy.[6] China and Burma settled the demarcation of the Sino-Burma border, removing the largest obstacle to the bilateral relations. Despite the abundant complaints within China about Beijing's "unilateral territorial concession" to Burma for a better bilateral relationship, Chinese authorities nevertheless view the case as a "brilliant model" of boundary settlement.[7]

The Chinese Cultural Revolution significantly disrupted this warm trend in the mid-1960s. During this period, China launched a radical revolutionary foreign policy characterized by countering imperialism, revisionism, and all reactionaries of various countries, as well as supporting and aiding the revolutionary movements in Asia, Africa, and Latin America.[8] In the case of Burma, China's ideology-driven foreign policy transpired as an "export of revolution" through material support, training of the Burmese Communist Party (BCP) against the central government to implement Mao Zedong's ideology of world revolution.[9] Although the efforts faded soon after the anti-China riots in June 1967, China's support to the BCP continued well into the 1980s, contributing to the lingering ethnic group issues hindering Myanmar's national reconciliation even today.[10] The disruption damaged Sino-Myanmar relations, which reached its nadir at that time.

As the result of its ideology-driven revolutionary foreign policy, China's external environment deteriorated severely from fighting against both superpowers—the "imperialist" United States and the revisionist Soviet Union—and the "export of revolution" took a toll on China's relationships with the governments of third world countries.[11] To mitigate international isolation, Beijing toned down its revolutionary policy in Burma, reacting only mildly toward the local anti-China riots. This moderate stance helped redirect Sino-Burma relations back to its previous stable course through the following two decades.

From Burma's end, Burma pursued a neutralist, nonalignment foreign strategy and a balancing diplomacy toward China during the first four decades of their relations. Burma has always been suspicious, fearful, and anxious about China's intentions toward Burma. Besides the vast difference of their size and national power, historical memories of invasions from the north during the Yuan and Qing dynasties as well as the more recent example of Beijing's support of the Burmese Communist Party against the Burmese government were reminders of the potential threats from China.[12] The uncertainty regarding China reinforced the country's momentum to diversify its foreign relations. As explained by U Nu in the 1950s, "Burma shall not ally herself with any bloc of countries, shall develop friendly relations with all countries and eliminate estrangement between the two blocks in order to promote world peace."[13] It was believed that a neutralist and nonalignment foreign policy would give Burma maximum maneuverability not only between its immediate neighbors, but also between the two superpowers during the Cold War.[14]

Sino-Myanmar Asymmetric Mutual Dependence (1990–2011)

The Convergence of Two Isolated Countries

The democratic movement in Burma in 1988 and the general elections in 1990 were watershed events for the nation. They also fundamentally changed the country's external environment. After the military coup suppressed the 8-8-88 uprising, the Burmese military (*tatmadaw*) came into power through the State Law and Order Restoration Council (SLORC).[15] In the 1990 general elections held by SLORC, the National League for Democracy led by Aung San Suu Kyi won a prevailing victory (80 percent of the seats in the People's Assembly).[16] Ill-prepared for the failure of the National Unity Party, the military's favored party, the SLORC refused to hand power over to the elected government.

The military's repression of the 8-8-88 uprising and refusal to honor the 1990 elections vitally damaged its external environment and foreign relations in the following two decades. Burma soon found itself faced with accumulating international sanctions. With immediate suspension of all aid to Burma, the United States adopted a series of sanction legislations and executive orders targeting Burma's export industry, financial transactions, foreign investments, and political leaders. (These include the Free Burma

Act of 1995, section 570 of the Omnibus Consolidated Appropriations Act of 1997, Presidential Proclamation 6925, the Burmese Freedom and Democracy Act of 2003, the Thomas Lantos Burmese JADE [Junta's Anti-Democratic Efforts] Act of 2008, etc.) Similarly, European countries echoed US sanctions with an arms embargo, cessation of trade preferences, and suspension of almost all aid.[17]

Among Burma's neighbors, India critically condemned the junta's suppression of the democratic movements and closed its border with Burma in 1988 (although it changed its policy in 1993).[18] Although Myanmar became a member of the Association of Southeast Asian Nations (ASEAN) in 1997, its poor human rights record greatly affected its status within the regional organization. Myanmar had to relinquish its turn to hold the rotating ASEAN presidency in 2006 due to other members' concerns.[19]

Besides the deterioration of external relations, the military government also had to deal with mounting challenges at home. Due to its inexcusable rejection of the 1990 election's results, SLORC's legitimacy became widely questioned. The democratic oppositions, although suppressed, remained a major threat to the military's rule. The unsettled status of the armed ethnic groups and the lack of cease-fire agreements challenged national security and unity. The military officers did not possess the professional knowledge or skills to manage the country's economy, sending the nation back to a chronic stagnation.[20] When the Western sanctions sank trade, foreign investment, and economic cooperation, the Burma government faced the daunting task of generating economic growth.

At the same time, China ran into a similar international quagmire after its crackdown on the students' movement in June 1989. After the Tiananmen Square massacre, Beijing's relationship with the West rapidly deteriorated. The United States and European countries imposed a series of diplomatic and economic sanctions against Beijing, including suspension of high-level official visits and official aid, as well as an arms embargo.[21] Under pressure, the World Bank and the Asian Development Bank also agreed to halt lending to China.[22]

The "abandonment" by the international community faced by both the Burmese and Chinese governments created a unique external context for affinity and alignment between the two. Based on mutual sympathy and shared antagonism, a closer Sino-Myanmar tie was made possible and necessary by their limited options at hand.[23] Beijing needed close ties with foreign governments that would validate its legitimacy and thus help it to "break free from the western isolation and sanctions."[24] So did Rangoon.

Myanmar's Growing Dependence on China

The different attitudes of the world toward China and Burma in the following years, however, put the two countries on very different tracks. Despite the sanctions, China was able to re-engage the world and normalize relations with the West. Burma never had such luxury. While the George H. W. Bush administration conducted several senior-level visits to Beijing and eased some sanctions as early as December of 1989,[25] the West remained critical of Burmese repressive politics—the United States introduced new punitive sanctions throughout the 1990s and 2000s targeting the Burmese government's human rights violations. Such measures peaked in 2007, when the West pushed for a UN Security Council Resolution to condemn and criticize Burma's human rights record and spotlight the repressive rule of the military government.[26]

It was during this period that Burma's dependence on China grew exponentially and disproportionately, deviating from the country's traditional neutralist nonalignment course. Most significantly, the military government largely came to rely on China to protect its national security, reinforce its domestic legitimacy, and mitigate international and regional pressure. At that time, the military regime saw its survival as under serious threat from the United States, whose policy was aimed at eventual regime change.[27] From this perspective, China's tacit security guarantee against a potential US invasion, accompanied by arms sales, military training, as well as equipment and technology transfer, were of high importance for the survival and security of the Myanmar state.[28] China was the only country that provided military assistance to Myanmar during this period and pursued broad military cooperation with it, including a US$1.2 billion arms sales package and training of military officers and engineers to maintain and operate Chinese weapon systems.[29] In addition, the Chinese People's Liberation Army Navy (PLAN) dispatched seventy military officers and engineers to naval and radar bases in Myanmar to train their Myanmar counterparts in operating related equipment.[30]

Beijing also provided diplomatic and political support to Myanmar within the international community. On the bilateral level, Beijing's willingness to maintain a normal relationship with Myanmar, pursue economic cooperation, and host its senior leaders was a public demonstration of support from a major power. China, together with Russia, vetoed the 2007 draft UN Security Council Resolution on Myanmar's political system and ethnic violence, citing the "internal" nature of the affairs and the lack of threat to "international security."[31] China's support was greatly appreciated by the Myanmar government. The official Myanmar television station made a rare interruption of its normal news program to broadcast China's veto and convey Myanmar's gratitude for China's protection.[32]

From 1990 to 2011, China was an important contributor to Myanmar's national economy and its economic development through trade promotion and direct investment. In sharp contrast to the West's financial sanctions and trade embargoes, China's trade with Myanmar increased significantly—at an annual average growth rate of 25 percent from 1988 to 1995 and 35.8 percent from 2000 to 2008.[33]

China also lobbied the Myanmar government about the need and desirability of economic reform. According to a senior Chinese analyst, China wished for the Myanmar military government to understand that "an authoritarian government does not have to democratize to be legitimate. The ability to generate economic growth could also be a source of legitimacy."[34] Economic reform, in China's hope, would also stabilize the domestic politics of Myanmar and diffuse the international pressure China had to carry for the political and economic failure of the military government.

China's Growing Economic Interests in Myanmar

In the 2000s, China's close relationship with Myanmar and protection of the military government was seen primarily as a political liability for Beijing in the international arena. As the political relationship created pressure, China grew increasingly interested in the economic opportunities in Myanmar. The broader context of this evolving priority was China's economic reform and opening up, which determined the directions and tasks of Chinese foreign policy. From the beginning of the reform and opening up in 1979 to the mid-1990s, the focus of China's foreign policy shifted from the revolutionary ideology of the Cultural Revolution to supporting domestic economic development through creating a favorable, conducive international environment.[35] In the mid-1990s, the theme was specifically pointed toward "utilizing both domestic and international markets and resources."[36] This led to booming international economic cooperation and the initiation of the "Going Out" strategy in 1996 by then-president Jiang Zemin, to encourage Chinese companies to go abroad to utilize international natural resources and market opportunities.[37] The strategy was then endorsed by the Politburo in 2000 as a national strategy.[38]

Myanmar fit China's "Going Out" strategy perfectly for several reasons. First, Myanmar is rich in natural resources that China desires to fuel its domestic growth—such as hydropower, minerals, timber, and hydrocarbon resources. Second, Myanmar's proximity makes the transportation and communications easy for Chinese companies. Its location at the junction between South Asia and Southeast Asia, as well as on the Indian Ocean, also qualifies the country as a potential transportation corridor between China and these three regions. Internally, business opportunities in Myanmar and its transportation potential create great incentives for China's landlocked and less-developed Yunnan Province to enhance economic ties with Myanmar to boost trade.

Last but perhaps most importantly, in the Sino-Myanmar power equilibrium, Myanmar was believed to be at a disadvantaged position vis-à-vis China, to the extent that many Chinese scholars jokingly referred to the country as "another province of China." Myanmar had few foreign partner options given the international isolation, forcing it to depend on China for critical resources, including political protection and economic aid. This overdependence was perceived as ensuring that Myanmar would not adopt any unfriendly moves against China.

Reassured by Myanmar's reliance, China soon indulged itself in massive economic activities in Myanmar in the late 2000s. Historically, China had never been a top investor in Myanmar, lagging behind ASEAN nations such as Thailand and Singapore. From 2008 to 2011, however, China's cumulative investment in Myanmar jumped from less than US$1 billion to nearly US$13 billion.[39] The boost came primarily in the year of 2010, through the finalization of the investment agreements on the Myitsone dam, the Letpadaung copper mine, and the China National Petroleum Corporation oil and gas pipeline. By the end of 2012, China had made a cumulative investment of US$14.1 billion in Myanmar, more than one-third of the country's total foreign direct investment.[40]

Beijing viewed Myanmar's dependence as a positive trend for China because China could exploit its advantaged position to influence the terms of the bilateral relationship. The growing confidence gradually rendered a sense of entitlement that Myanmar's dependence on China was a matter of determined fact and a predetermined assumption about the bilateral relations. Under these assumptions, Beijing comfortably made heavy economic and strategic investment in Myanmar despite the potential uncertainties associated with the 2010 elections. The three largest Chinese investment projects were all finalized under Beijing's push before the November elections in 2010. In addition, Beijing began to pursue additional strategic agendas in Myanmar. These included (1) diversification of China's energy transportation routes through the Sino-Myanmar oil and gas pipelines; (2) heavy investment in Myanmar's hydropower sector to increase power export to China, hence improving China's energy security; (3) investment in Myanmar's copper industry to boost China's own strategic copper reserve; and (4) a bridgehead strategy that would turn Myanmar into China's outpost for Southeast Asia, South Asia, and the Indian Ocean.[41]

These strategic aspirations subtly changed the power balance between China and Myanmar by conferring Myanmar with more potential leverage in the bilateral relations. Simply by virtue of possessing a number of key strategic and economic resources that China desired and had heavily invested in, Myanmar enhanced its own position and bargaining power vis-à-vis China. This bargaining leverage would not be viable or meaningful had Myanmar continued to rely on China for more vital resources, such as its national security and international support. But when such constraints were removed, the equilibrium tilted toward the other side, in Myanmar's favor. What Beijing failed to foresee was that the deepening imbalance between China and Myanmar would promote the disadvantaged Myanmar to pursue internal and external changes to rebalance its foreign strategy. And the price Beijing later had to pay for its misjudgment turned out to be high and serious.

China and Myanmar: Moving Beyond Mutual Dependence

How to handle relations with big powers is an eternal problem that weak states have to address in their foreign relations. There are generally several approaches with which weak states seek to improve their position vis-à-vis big powers: internally, weak states strengthen national power and reduce dependence on big powers; externally, weak states seek to balance big powers against each other and/or to form an alliance among weak powers to increase collective strength. In the case of Myanmar's relations with China, all three patterns can be easily identified. The political reform by the Thein Sein government in 2011 paved the way for changing the power equilibrium between Myanmar and China. The Myanmar government gained recognition from both its domestic population and the international community for its democratization efforts, which removed the most acute internal and external existential threats. Its reform efforts convinced the West to lift most of its financial sanctions, removing the foundation of Myanmar's previous overdependence on China. Externally, Myanmar improved relations with the West and introduced new foreign partners to compete with the existing Chinese influence on the ground.

Myanmar's Internal Efforts to Mitigate Dependence on China

Myanmar's political reform reconciled the government's relationship with the democratic oppositions and ethnic groups, increasing the nation's cohesion and internal capacity. A more internally cohesive Myanmar is more capable of protecting its security, economic, and political interests, reducing dependence on Chinese assistance and enhancing its bargaining position.

The reforms pursued by the Thein Sein government established the foundation for its political legitimacy and facilitated nation-building among different political parties. The inclusion of democratic oppositions in the political process helped to forge a new sense of national identity based on a democratic system. Reconciliation between the democratic oppositions and the former military was signified by the improvement of relations between Aung San Suu Kyi and the top leaders of the government, especially President Thein Sein and Speaker of the Lower House Shwe Mann. With the normalization of their relations as leaders of the democratic oppositions, government and parliament forged a new political reconciliation that has gradually become the foundation of Myanmar's democracy.[42] The reconciliation strengthened Myanmar's internal power, largely by freeing up resources formerly dedicated to suppressing democratic forces and shoring up internal cohesion of the nation. It also reduced the sense of vulnerability and insecurity of the government, the root of its dependence on China.

The Myanmar government also sought to improve relations with ethnic groups. As a multiethnic nation with more than 135 so-called ethnic groups, the difficult relationship between Burmans and the ethnic minorities has in the past undermined the nation's identity and internal resilience. Since 2011, the government has launched new efforts on nation-building through engaging ethnic minorities for peace negotiations and political solutions to their decades-long hostility. Although the lengthy, strenuous negotiations since have proved difficult in resolving economic and political differences, the reform nevertheless has improved the prospects for peace and genuine reconciliation compared to the age of the military government.

Problems still exist. The government's lack of capacity, the conflicts among different interest groups, the ambiguous position and role of the military, and the uncertainty associated with a permanent solution to the ethnic conflicts raise questions about the future and success of the reform. However, through its reform efforts, the Myanmar government has managed to reestablish the bases for its domestic legitimacy and boost the nation's internal strength, freeing itself from dependence on China for such resources.

Myanmar's External Efforts to Mitigate Dependence on China

The most direct foreign policy impact of Myanmar's political reform is the country's improvement of relations with the West, especially the United States, which began to recognize and reward Myanmar's reform effort. Three months after President Thein Sein's historical meeting with Aung San Suu Kyi, US Secretary of State Hillary Clinton visited Myanmar in November 2011, followed by the appointment of the first US ambassador to the country in decades and a visit by President Barack Obama in late 2012. Myanmar leaders toured the world, applauded everywhere for their historical achievements. The warming political ties soon led to the lifting of most sanctions: the European Union lifted all sanctions on Myanmar except the arms embargo; the United States lifted the investment ban as well as other financial sanctions.[43] Foreign aid began to pour into the country, including planned infrastructure projects from Japan and from multilateral development organizations such as the World Bank and Asian Development Bank.[44]

The improvement and normalization of relations with the West has generated significant economic benefits. Other than the forgiven foreign debts and foreign aid, the largely untapped natural and labor resources in Myanmar and its considerable market potential turned the country into the most coveted destination for foreign investment.[45] Although there are still uncertainties associated with the investment environment, government policies, and internal conflicts, the enthusiasm of foreign investors remains high. The Myanmar government has taken serious measures to attract foreign investors, including the introduction of the new Foreign Investment Law, preferential policies for foreign investment, special economic zones, and investment promotion procedures.[46]

The improvement of the external environment and diversification of foreign economic partners after the West's removal of trade and investment restrictions helped Myanmar to expand export markets and foreign investments, mitigating its reliance on China for economic cooperation. In fact, many Chinese and Burmese pointed out that "Myanmar now pursues a pro-West policy in economic cooperation to offset China's overwhelming existence and influence in Myanmar." The more diversified Myanmar's external economic ties are, the better-positioned Myanmar becomes to cope with its powerful northern neighbor. China is reduced from Myanmar's most important foreign partner to "one of the partners."

China's Awkward Position

The changes in Myanmar's domestic politics and foreign relations put China in an awkward position. While Myanmar enjoys new options and partners, China had forged and pursued a series of economic and strategic initiatives in Myanmar even before the beginning of the reform. Important Chinese national interests therefore had become deeply associated with and dependent upon Myanmar's continued cooperation and consistent support. However, once Myanmar no longer perceived such cooperation as a necessity, China had to deal with a changed Myanmar with drastically less policy leverage.

China's dependence on Myanmar's cooperation is first reflected in its need for the smooth implementation of large mining and energy projects in Myanmar. While Beijing inked the agreements on the oil and gas pipelines, the Myitsone dam, and the Letpadaung copper mine before the 2010 elections to avoid policy uncertainties and potential Western competition, the majority of the construction took place after the inauguration of the new Myanmar government in 2011.

The shifting balance between Myanmar and China brought unexpected downturn to these projects, most of which ran into local opposition. For example, the US$3.6 billion Myitsone dam invested by the China Power International was suspended in September 2011 by President Thein Sein as his response to "people's will." Then in November 2012, the Letpadaung copper mine invested by Chinese Wanbao Mining was forced to temporarily shut down due to local oppositions and protests. Due to the capital-intensive nature of these projects and their fixed geographical locations, Chinese companies could not easily withdraw their investment without complete or major losses. Yet while Beijing expressed strong dissatisfaction about the suspension of the projects, it has little power or leverage to force the Myanmar government to change its decision.

Second, China has to rely on Myanmar for the smooth operation of Sino-Myanmar oil and gas pipelines, China's fourth-largest energy transportation route after the Central Asia pipelines, Sino-Russia pipelines, and the sea lanes of transportation.[47] Diversification of energy transportation routes has always been a key concern of China's energy security. Most of China's crude oil imports from the Middle East and North Africa is shipped through the Malacca Strait, a region perceived to be under the United States's overwhelming military dominance. Therefore, the initial strategic design of the Sino-Myanmar oil and gas pipelines was to "free" China from its Malacca dilemma, or at least reduce such dependence.[48] The strategic purpose of the pipelines is the primary reason for its categorization as a "national strategic project."[49] Internally, the strategic design of the pipelines is intended to promote the energy development of China's southwest region. Refineries dependent on the pipelines have been constructed in Yunnan, Sichuan, and Guangxi Provinces.[50] In a sense, the Sino-Myanmar oil and gas pipelines have become one main pillar of the energy supply of southwest China.[51]

However, as Sino-Myanmar relations soured, China's Malacca dilemma quickly translated into a "Myanmar dilemma" because of its increased dependence on Myanmar for the smooth operation of the pipelines. The new political reality of Myanmar has cast dark shadows over China's original blueprint. Because Myanmar owns a critical share in the stakes, management, and protection of the pipelines, there are strong criticisms inside China that China made a strategic mistake in handing over the energy security of its southwest region to an unreliable Myanmar.[52] Such a risk had been acceptable when China held critical leverage against Myanmar. However, as such leverage has been lost, the future of the pipelines is now uncertain.

Last but not least, before 2011, China had developed strategic blueprints for Myanmar to play a larger role in China's foreign policy toward South Asia, Southeast Asia, and the Indian Ocean. Basic considerations included for Myanmar to provide support of China's positions at regional organizations such as ASEAN, to be the corridor for China to expand its presence and influence into South Asia and Southeast Asia, and to even become China's outpost in the Indian Ocean.[53] However, after the downturn of bilateral relations, it became widely acknowledged in China that China needed to tone down its strategic expectations for Myanmar regarding these endeavors.[54]

Myanmar's Strategic Options in Its Relations with China

Although Myanmar has improved its position vis-à-vis China within the bilateral relations, there are numerous potential uncertainties. As a small and weak state, Myanmar bears no illusion that it could outpower China.

The power balance has shifted in Myanmar's favor, but the imbalance between the two countries' national power persists. China may rely on Myanmar to advance economic or strategic interests, but the inability to do so by no means threatens China's fundamental national security. However, on the other hand, regardless of how much more bargaining power Myanmar has gained since 2011, China remains capable of inflicting vital damage to Myanmar in the short and long term. China continues to enjoy major influence over the border ethnic groups and hence Myanmar's national reconciliation process. Chinese economic strength remains a vital force that could play a major role in Myanmar's national development.

How to handle the relationship with China in a new era is a delicate yet critical question for Myanmar. Antagonizing China is unwise, yet China already feels antagonized. This is particularly because of its previous dominant influence in Myanmar, which aggravated both the material damage and psychological sense of loss. How to pacify China's dissatisfaction, promote and manage economic cooperation with China, and deftly rally external resources to counterbalance China's influence to maximize its own policy options should be a top priority for Myanmar in the years to come.

Economic Pragmatism

Economic pragmatism is a policy wherein a state seeks to maximize economic gains from its direct trade and investment links with a big power, regardless of any political problems that might exist between them. It signifies a neutral position in that the act of profit-maximizing itself does not carry any value of power acceptance or rejection. In Myanmar, economic growth is essential for success of the political reform. Continued economic engagement and cooperation with China will be conducive to Myanmar's economic development as long as the government provides proper management. Due to uncertainties of the investment environment, internal ethnic and religious conflicts, and the poor government capacity, Western investment into Myanmar has yet to make up for the steep drop in investment from China as of mid-2014. According to official Myanmar government data, the annual approved foreign investment for fiscal year 2013 (ended 31 March 2014) still significantly lags behind the peak year of 2010, although the overall trend of inbound foreign investment is upward since 2011. Indeed, according to Myanmar government statistics, China's investment in Myanmar dropped by more than 90 percent in the fiscal year (FY) 2012/13, from US$8.27 billion to US$407 million. This caused the total foreign investment in Myanmar to fall to US$1.42 billion, down from US$4.64 billion in FY 2011/12 and $US20 billion in FY 2010/11.[55] The decreasing foreign investment is certainly not positive news for the country's economic development.

Properly managed, economic cooperation with China will not only benefit Myanmar, but also help to maintain its advantageous position within Sino-Myanmar relations. Currently, China's large economic and strategic investment projects in Myanmar are a key reason that Beijing pursues a conciliatory rather than coercive approach to address the problems in the bilateral relations. If Myanmar abandons these projects, China will face fewer concerns and constraints in its behaviors.

As the Myanmar government mobilizes all available internal and external resources to boost domestic economic growth, the potential and utilities of Chinese investment should not be neglected, especially in infrastructure development. One major obstacle to the industrialization of Myanmar has been its underdeveloped and inadequate infrastructure, such as electricity shortages and an inadequate electric transmission system, along with a poor national transportation network. These are areas where Chinese investors could make a key contribution.

Chinese investments and projects should be closely managed and supervised by the Myanmar government and local communities given their past poor records in environmental protection, sustainable development, corporate social responsibilities, and so on. These are critical tasks for Myanmar policymakers. However, instead of rejecting "bad" Chinese investment, Myanmar might consider how to transform them into "good," responsible investments for the future of its people and nation.

Alignment/Nonalignment Choice

Changing alignment choices has been both the catalyst for and the result of Myanmar's domestic reform. While the two decades from 1990 to 2011 were characterized by close alignment with China, since the beginning of the reform, Myanmar has been moving in a new direction. Western partners have been introduced to mitigate China's dominance. The new environment raises a key question about Myanmar's strategic orientation with two broad alignment choices ahead: Should Myanmar now seek a new "ally"—most likely the United States—or should it return to its previous "neutralist" nonalignment strategy?

The temptation to align with the United States is strong. After all, strategically speaking, sandwiched between two regional powers (China and India) and subject to China's overwhelming influence for the past twenty years, it is highly tempting for Myanmar to invite a comparable force as an offshore balancer. A closer alignment with the United States will arguably bring Myanmar significant political, economic, and reputational benefits and protect the country against potential pushback from China. Internally, Myanmar's admiration for the US democratic system and practice could lay a solid political and public opinion foundation for close alignment between the two countries.

However, the strategy also has evident drawbacks. Although Washington appreciates a pro-US Myanmar, it may not be willing to antagonize Beijing and jeopardize US-China relations over Myanmar's strategic utility. Senior US officials repeatedly emphasize that US-China relations is the most important bilateral relationship, and US engagement in Myanmar is not targeted at China. If US-Myanmar alignment transpires, it would directly feed into the Chinese argument and solicit China's reaction in other areas. In other words, Washington's willingness to align with Myanmar depends on the tradeoff between the strategic benefits Myanmar could render and the potential damage China would inflict. The calculus may not turn in Myanmar's favor.

Alignment with the United States would inevitably further alienate China, which could retaliate on other fronts. Given China's ties with border ethnic groups and its existing economic influence, China could adopt more radical measures against Myanmar if it believed a US-Myanmar alliance would threaten China's national security and strategic interests. Chinese officials and analysts have never been shy of reminding Myanmar that "countries cannot choose their neighbors." The implied message is that since China is right on Myanmar's border and the United States is geographically afar, Myanmar should be wise about its alignment/nonalignment decisions.

In comparison, a neutralist, nonalignment policy appears to be much less detrimental for Myanmar. Alignment with any big power will create problems of power disparity within the alliance. Without an effective countervailing force to balance the powerful ally, the risk is high for Myanmar to become overaccommodating. Meanwhile, a healthy competition among the big powers will broaden Myanmar's policy options and improve its position. Neither the United States nor China wishes to see Myanmar become a client state of the other. Their willingness to make concessions to curry favors with Myanmar would be highest if they perceive that Myanmar's support is attainable.

A nonalignment strategy would require Myanmar to make strategic and conscious efforts to balance its paths between the two powers. Myanmar would need hedging strategies to balance against and bandwagon with China and the United States at different time to offset risks and ensure an optimal position. To balance against China, Myanmar might need to develop strategic, even security, cooperation with other powers (especially the United States) to mitigate the risks of Chinese coercion and diversify foreign investment and development assistance to counterbalance the existing Chinese capital. Essentially, Myanmar needs to keep China engaged but with measures to counter its dominance. Myanmar's foreign policy since 2011 indicates such a direction.

Multilateral Engagement

There is a general consensus on the lack of effectiveness of weak state alliances, especially if such alliances are directed against a great power. The limited utilities, the varying national interests of each member state, and the difficulty in coordinating political and military activities given the high stakes, all contribute to the secondary status of small state alliances in international security. In this sense, ASEAN is not necessarily a strong alliance of ten small Southeast Asian nations and cannot provide military security to its member states. However, in terms of international negotiations and collective binding capabilities, ASEAN has played an irreplaceable role in enhancing the ability of its members to deal with great powers, especially China. Historically, ASEAN has successfully adopted a collective engagement and binding strategy to hold China to regional norms, enmeshing China in the regional framework and tying it down to abide by such regional norms.[56] Examples would include the ASEAN–China Free Trade Agreement in 2002 and China's accession to the ASEAN Treaty of Amity and Cooperation in 2003, as well as the Declaration of the Code of Conduct of Parties in the South China Sea in 2002.

Myanmar joined ASEAN in 1997 together with Vietnam and Laos (Cambodia joined later). However, its role and influence in the regional institution has been to a certain extent suppressed due to its domestic politics, including the forced relinquishment of its presidency in 2006. Given ASEAN's success in engaging China collectively on regional issues, it would be a useful and effective mechanism for Myanmar to advocate for its positions and deal with China through collective bargaining and regional norms. Since Myanmar regained recognition of the international community, it has yet to demonstrate a keen enthusiasm in participating in ASEAN to advance the region's collective cause and its own national interests. However, as it assumes the presidency of the regional organization in 2014, it is hoped that Myanmar will develop a distinct policy agenda for ASEAN to foster the development of the organization, while benefiting from it.

China's Strategic Options in Its Relations with Myanmar

The changes in Myanmar and the Sino-Myanmar power balance present a great policy dilemma for China. As Myanmar rallies internal and external support, China's importance and policy leverage have declined in contrast with a large amount of vested interests and stakes on the ground. China still possesses major policy influence in Myanmar, through its traditional relationship with some political forces such as the military, its ties with border ethnic groups, and through its existing and potential economic influence. However, much of this leverage is a double-edged sword. Exercising them, such as supporting the conservative political forces against the reformists, manipulating the border ethnic groups to hinder Myanmar's national reconciliation process, or cutting investment in Myanmar, would only further alienate the Myanmar government and the Myanmar people, thereby undermining China's future position in the country.

Play the Ethnic Card?

In the near term, China possesses two key leverages that could have a critical impact over the future politics and economy of Myanmar. The first is the border ethnic groups, especially the Wa and the Kachin. The armed forces of these two ethnic groups, the United Wa State Army (UWSA) and the Kachin Independence Army (KIA), have maintained a de facto semi-independent autonomy from the central government along the border, largely thanks to their trade with and assistance from China. Although it would be an overstatement to attribute their semi-independent status to their ties with China, the Wa and the Kachin would not have been able to maintain such a status without such ties. Business transactions with various Chinese actors have been a key source of revenue for both the UWSA and the KIA, and rumors have been rampant that China has been supplying the UWSA with weapons to enhance its security.[57]

Chinese strategic thinkers are well aware of China's influence over the border ethnic groups and the importance of national reconciliation for the Myanmar government. Many argue that since Myanmar has disregarded China's national interests by suspending Chinese projects and warming ties with the West, China should naturally enhance its policy leverage against Myanmar by hindering the eventual solution of the ethnic group issue or at least delaying the process. For them, "to play the ethnic card well" reflects a fundamental calculation that by keeping the ethnic issues simmering, China will be able to keep the ethnic groups both as a geographical buffer and a bargaining chip against the Myanmar government. This would inevitably require China to provide certain support to the ethnic groups.

For China to adopt such an approach is essentially an implicit act of coercion and an interference in Myanmar's internal affairs. The counterargument from the proponents of this strategy is that although the ethnic issues are the internal affairs of Myanmar, how the issues are resolved directly impact China's border stability and national security, which gives China a legitimate role in the resolution. However, opponents point out the hypocrisy of such an argument in that China fiercely opposes a similar logic/position of US policy toward Taiwan.

Play the Investment Card?

China also sees future Chinese investment as a key leverage in Myanmar. This is particularly true given the slow inflow of Western investments since 2011. China hopes that Myanmar will soon realize that the so-called "reward" promised by the West for Myanmar's reform is nothing but lip service. Chinese analysts observe that foreign investments might flow in eventually, but their volume is yet to compete with the pre-2012 level of Chinese investments for the foreseeable future.

Therefore, to "play the investment card" and reduce Chinese investment in Myanmar would arguably benefit Beijing. It would stop fueling the anti-China sentiment among the local population about Chinese economic "takeover" of Myanmar. It would demonstrate to the Myanmar government the importance of good relations with China and preach caution on further so-called "China-unfriendly" moves. It might even encourage Myanmar to reconsider its alignment/nonalignment choices.

However, the difficult question for China is how and how much to use its ethnic and economic leverages. Any form of negative incentive is a double-edged sword. Playing the ethnic card by supporting the ethnic groups might command fear and respect, but it will inevitably worsen bilateral relations. Furthermore, it will fuel Myanmar's traditional suspicion about China's true intentions and create more hostility. Similarly, withholding investment in Myanmar might convey China's displeasure to the Myanmar government in the short term. However, in the long run, to withdraw from Myanmar as revenge is to voluntarily give up the market to other countries. Furthermore, to play these leverages would potentially backfire and further damage China's existing economic and strategic endeavors, including but not limited to the smooth operation of the Sino-Myanmar oil and gas pipelines.

Understanding the pros and cons of these strategies, Beijing's most likely policy course would be one that combines implicit coercion and explicit inducement. China will try to maintain its leverage in terms of the border ethnic groups so as to keep its deterrence and retain a role in Myanmar's internal affairs. Although China will not go as far as to provide financial and military assistance to the UWSA and KIA, Beijing is unlikely to block their lifelines either. In public, Beijing will accede to and applaud Myanmar's progress for national reconciliation, but in private, it is unlikely to push the ethnic groups to make major compromises. (In Beijing's view, such compromises could become a trigger for future conflicts anyway.) Meanwhile, Beijing will most likely continue to participate publicly in the negotiations between the border ethnic groups and the Myanmar government to monitor and mediate the pace of the talks.

China will almost definitely use its investment to induce China-friendly policies. Such inducements will possibly be offered when Myanmar needs major financing for key large infrastructure projects but fails to obtain it from Western or multilateral financial institutions. Chinese investors have to a certain extent stopped attempts to secure projects through outbidding others, to prevent further encouraging Myanmar's sense of empowerment vis-à-vis China. This was attested by China Mobile's withdrawal from the bidding for the telecom service license in 2013. Meanwhile, both the Chinese government and Chinese companies will try to improve the damaged image of Chinese projects on the ground through public relations campaigns and more corporate social-responsibility programs.

Conclusion

Myanmar's foreign policy course between 1990 and 2011 represents a deviation from the country's traditional neutralist nonalignment foreign policy principle. Due to internal constraints and external isolation, Myanmar developed an overwhelming dependence on China for political and economic support vital to its national security. The confidence in its advantageous position in the bilateral power equilibrium prompted China to enhance its dependence on Myanmar through a series of economic and strategic initiatives. During this period, the two countries therefore formed an unbalanced, asymmetric mutual dependence.

Since 2011, the Thein Sein government's political reform consolidated domestic support, enhanced its internal strength, and improved its external environment. These largely freed Myanmar from its previous overdependence on China. However, this resulted in an awkward position for China, with its important economic and strategic investments at the mercy of the new Myanmar government.

The future of the China-Myanmar relations will likely be characterized by Myanmar's return to its traditional neutralist, nonalignment policy. Meanwhile, Myanmar should resort to economic pragmatism in the bilateral relations while seeking multilateral engagements to balance China's strong influence. On the other hand, China will most likely try to navigate a delicate balance between implicit coercion and explicit inducement to repair the damaged ties and improve its positions.

Notes

1. Yin Chengde, "In Celebration of the 60th Anniversary of the Five Principles of Peaceful Co-existence Proposed by Premier Zhou Enlai," *Guo Ji Wang*, 6 May 2014.

2. Shu Jianguo, "The Essence of Mao Zedong's 'Anti-Imperialism, Anti-Revisionism' Foreign Policy Strategy and Its Implementation," *Global View,* May 2008.

3. Fan Hongwei, "China-Burma Geopolitical Relations in the Cold War," *Journal of Current Southeast Asian Affairs* 31, no. 1 (2012): 7–27.

4. "Premier Zhou Enlai's Nine Visits of Myanmar," Chinese Embassy in Myanmar.

5. Cheng Ruisheng, "The Strong Virility of the Five Principle of Peaceful Coexistence Shown in the Sino-Myanmar Friendship," *People's Daily Website,* 19 September 2009.

6. Ibid.

7. In his conversation with U Nu in 1956, Zhou Enlai clearly stated, "We are willing to settle the border issue and set a good example." "The Handling of Sino-Burma Border Issue," *Zhou Enlai Studies Association*, 25 November 2011.

8. David Steinberg and Hongwei Fan, *Modern China-Myanmar Relations: The Dilemma of Mutual Dependence* (Copenhagen: NIAS Press, 2013), 91.

9. Song Yongyi, "The Cultural Revolution and the War Against Fascism: Why The Past Matters," *China Rights Forum* No. 4, 2005, 23.

10. Xu Yan, "The Rise and Fall of the Burmese Communist Party," *WenShiCanKao*, 13 September 2010.

11. Cheng Yinghong, "Exporting Revolutions to the World: Exploring the Impact of Cultural Revolution in Asia, Africa and Latin America," Hua Xia Wen Zhai, *China News Digest*, 7 November 2007.

12. As put by Burma's vice prime minister U Ba Swe in 1957, "Our fear is very natural because in history big countries always were buckoes. Burma lies between big powers." Quoted in Fan Hongwei, "China-Burma Geopolitical Relations in the Cold War," *Journal of Current Southeast Asian Affairs* (January 2012): 10. Prime Minister U Nu further elaborated the lack of bargaining power of Burma in front of the giant China: "Our tiny nation cannot have the effrontery to quarrel with any power, and least among these, could Burma afford to quarrel with the new China?" Aung Zaw, "The Great Game over Burma," *Irrawaddy*, 11 April 2013, www.irrawaddy.org/archives/31998.

13. Fan, "China-Burma Geopolitical Relations," 9.

14. Interview with a Chinese Myanmar expert, Kunming, December 2012.

15. "88 People's Uprising–SLORC Coup in Burma," *Global Security*.

16. Michael Martin, "U.S. Sanctions on Burma," Congressional Research Service Report R41336, 19 October 2012.

17. Celeste Montera, "EU Restoration of Myanmar Preferential Trade Regime: Neglect of Human Rights Concerns?" *EU-Asia at a Glance* (Brussels: European Institute for Asian Studies, August 2013).

18. Thin Thin Aung and Soe Myint, "India-Burma Relations" (International Institute for Democracy and Electoral Assistance [IDEA], 2001), 7.

19. "Myanmar Gives Up 2006 ASEAN Chairmanship," *The New York Times*, 26 July 2005.

20. Priscilla Clapp, "Burma's Long Road to Democracy," *Special Report* 193 (United States Institute of Peace, November 2007), 6.

21. "Tiananmen Sanctions: 20 Years & Counting," Duihua Foundation, 29 January 2010.

22. Harry Harding, "The Impact of Tiananmen on China's Foreign Policy," National Bureau of Asian Research, December 1990.

23. Interview with former Chinese ambassador to Myanmar, Beijing, October 2009.

24. Liu Wu, "Evolution of Myanmar's Foreign Policy Since Independence and Development of Sino-Myanmar Relations" [miandian duli waijiao zhengce de yanbian yu zhongmian guanxi de fazhan], *Journal of Contemporary Asia-Pacific Studies* 1 (2010): 116.

25. Ren Donglai, "Bush and Sino-US Relations," *Lanxun*, www.lanxun.com/bmx/bmx036/nm03602.htm.

26. "Security Council Fails to Adopt Draft Resolution on Myanmar Owing to Negative Votes by China, Russia Federation," UN Department of Public Information, 12 January 2007.

27. Alvin Powell, "U.S. Pushes for Regime Change in Burma," Harvard News Office, 23 February 2006.

28. Interview with former Chinese ambassador to Myanmar, Beijing, October 2009.

29. Liu Wu, "Evolution of Myanmar's Foreign Policy Since Independence and Development of Sino-Myanmar Relations" [myandian duli houwai zhengci de yanbian yu zhongmian guanxi de fazhan], *Journal of Contemporary Asia-Pacific Studies* [*dang dau yatai*] 1 (2010): 116.

30. Ibid.

31. "China and Russia Veto US/UK-backed Security Council Draft Resolution on Myanmar," *UN News,* 12 January 2007.

32. Li Chenyang and Lye Liang Fook, "China's Policies Toward Myanmar: A Successful Model for Dealing with the Myanmar Issue?" *China: An International Journal* 7, no. 2 (September 2009).

33. David Steinberg and Fan Hongwei, "Modern China-Myanmar Relations: The Dilemma of Mutual Dependence" (Copenhagen: NIAS Press, 2013), 208 and 210.

34. Interview with a Chinese analyst, Beijing, June 2009.

35. Xia Daosheng, "Chinese Foreign Policy Since the Beginning of Reform and Opening Up," speech by former Chinese ambassador to Belgium at the seminar on the 55th Anninversary of the Foreign Policy of the New China, Office of the Commisioner of the Ministry of Foreign Affairs of the People's Republic of China in the Hong Kong Special Administrative Region, 27 September 2004.

36. In 1993, the 3rd Plenary Meeting of the 14th Party's Congress defined China's foreign economic agenda as follows: "fully utilize the two markets—international and domestic and the resources of them." *Decision of the CPC Central Committee on Some Issues Concerning the Establishment of a Socialist Market Economic Structure*, Central Committee of the Communist Party of China, 22 November 1993.

37. Chen Yangyong, "The Creation of Jiang Zemin's 'Going Out' Strategy and Its Importance," *Ren Min Wang*, 10 November 2008.

38. Ibid.

39. "China Now No.1 Investor in Burma," *Mizzima News*, 18 January 2012.

40. "Chinese Chamber of Commerce Hosted New Year's Reception in Mandalay," Ministry of Commerce, 3 January 2013.

41. Yun Sun, "China's Strategic Misjudgment on Myanmar," *Journal of Current Southeast Asian Affairs* 31, no. 1 (January 2012): 73–96.

42. Interviews with Burmese political observers, Yangon, July 2013.

43. Shibani Mahtani, "Sanctions Lifted Against Myanmar," *Wall Street Journal*, 22 April 2013.

44. Danial Ten Kate and Kyaw Thu, "Myanmar Clears ADB, World Bank Overdue Debt with Japan Help," *Bloomberg News*, 27 January 2013.

45. Aung Hla Tun and Jared Ferrie, "Foreign Investment in Myanmar Surges, Office Rents Sizzle," *Reuters*, 20 September 2013.

46. "Myanmar: Tax Incentives for Foreign Investors," *Global Trade Alert*, 15 May 2013.

47. "Sino-Myanmar Gas Pipeline Begins Operation," China Energy Web (China5e.com) is a Chinese energy consulting company based in Beijing. July 2013.

48. Jasnea Sarma and Matthew Reinert, "The Malacca Dilemma" IIT Madras China Studies Centre, 13 August 2013.

49. Cao Guoxing, "Sino-Myanmar Oil and Gas Pipelines: 'Strategic' Interests Outweigh Commercial Interests, Costs Exceed Original Plan Without Guaranteed Volume," *Radio France*, 24 June 2013.

50. "Experts Say the Negative Results of the Sino-Myanmar Oil and Gas Pipeline Have Transpired: A Strategic Misjudgment on the Changing Politics of Myanmar," *Caijing*, 17 June 2013.

51. "The Full Operation of the Sino-Myanmar Gas Pipeline Signifies the Formal Establishment of the Southwest Energy Transportation Corridor," *Shi Dai Zhou Bao*, 24 October 2013.

52. "Experts Say the Negative Results."

53. Sun, "China's Strategic Misjudgment on Myanmar."

54. Interviews with Chinese analysts, Beijing and Kunming, July 2013.

55. "Chinese Investment in Myanmar Falls Sharply," *Wall Street Journal*, 3 June 2013.

56. Jeong Seok Lee, "Hedging Against Uncertain Future: The Response of East Asian Secondary Powers to Rising China," Paper prepared for the International Political Science Association XXII World Congress of Political Science, 8–12 July 2012.

57. "China Provides Fighter Copters to Burma Armed Group: Report," *Radio Free Asia*, 30 April 2013.

13

US–Myanmar Relations: Developments, Challenges, and Implications

Jürgen Haacke

Although Myanmar's recent political transition has been characterized by Secretary of State John Kerry as "incomplete," there is a strong consensus in Washington that the country which the US government officially still calls Burma has embraced significant reforms since Thein Sein assumed the presidency in March 2011.[1] Along with domestic political changes in Myanmar have come major improvements in US-Myanmar relations as epitomized by the landmark visit undertaken by President Barack Obama to Yangon in November 2012, the first ever visit to that country by a sitting US president.

Considering that the United States treated Myanmar as an international pariah until quite recently, the rapid development of US-Myanmar ties presents several questions: How was it possible for the bilateral relationship to evolve in the way it has? What is the present nature of bilateral ties? To what extent do difficult or unresolved issues remain that prevent the relationship from reaching a still higher level? What prospects are there for tighter relations, both short-term and in the medium- to long-term? In this regard, what impact, if any, has the change in bilateral relations had on Myanmar's foreign policy outlook? Based on these questions, this chapter has three objectives: first, to offer an account of contemporary US-Myanmar relations; second, to identify issues on which Washington's stated preferences and Naypyitaw's policy practice are not in sync; and third, to examine both how US Burma policy remains constrained at home and in what ways Myanmar's domestic program is coupled to any significant restructuring of its foreign relations. Accordingly, the chapter is structured into three main parts. The first explores factors that led the United States and Myanmar to mutually adjust their bilateral ties and provides an overview of key developments that have reshaped the relationship. The second discusses the issues in relation to which the United States is looking for further breakthroughs. And the final part looks briefly at the extent of congressional pressure on the Obama administration over Myanmar as well as at the impact of changing Myanmar-US relations on Naypyitaw's basic foreign policy orientation and alignment posture.

Beyond Sanctions and Ostracization

After 1988, US Burma policy was for two decades focused on ostracism and an increasing number of sanctions. Seeking regime change, successive administrations and Congress called for the restoration of democracy on the basis of the 1990 elections, which the National League of Democracy (NLD) had won with an overwhelming majority. Over the years, US Burma policy was decisively shaped by outrage over the various restrictive measures imposed against Aung San Suu Kyi, the daughter of Burma's independence hero Aung San, who was also the 1991 Nobel Peace Prize recipient and the NLD's secretary general. This led US Burma policy, as set by Congress and the executive, to be primarily reactive rather than proactive, and outspoken criticism of Myanmar's military junta—the State Peace and Development Council (SPDC), formerly called the State Law and Order Restoration Council (SLORC)—was the norm for US administrations, Democrat and Republican. In the second half of the 1990s, Secretary of State Madeleine Albright insisted unequivocally that Myanmar's military leaders needed to change course if they wanted to avoid ruining both themselves and their country.[2] Her successor, Colin Powell, upon learning of the violence at Depayin that targeted Aung San Suu Kyi and an NLD convoy in May 2003, referred to Myanmar's military rulers as "thugs."[3] His replacement, Condoleezza Rice, in turn identified Myanmar as one of several "outposts of tyranny" at the beginning of George W. Bush's second term.[4] Such language, which reflected but also amplified the sentiments by many a US senator and congressperson, made very clear that Washington sympathized with the suffering and democratic aspirations of the Myanmar people and was strongly opposed to the military regime in power.

By contrast, the SPDC leadership did not approach relations with the United States with equal loathing. To be sure, US government support for prodemocracy groups and related rhetoric engendered suspicion, frustration, and even anxiety. Some accounts suggest that Myanmar's military leaders on more than one occasion took seriously the possibility of US intervention.[5] However, the evidence also suggests that the SPDC would have preferred a better relationship with the George W. Bush administration. From the junta's perspective, this was just not possible though, given the unbridgeable divide between Washington's persistent demands and the leadership's perceived political-security imperative, which led the military to vilify and crush its internal political opposition while positioning itself as the only institution that could defend the country against threats to sovereignty and/or national unity.[6] Even during the latter stages of the Bush presidency, Beijing-facilitated talks between the two sides in June 2007 came to nothing because Naypyitaw was not prepared to put forward the kind of political concessions that the US participants considered essential to move bilateral relations forward.

Toward Dialogue

Former president George W. Bush was himself strongly antagonistic toward Myanmar's military junta, and then First Lady Laura Bush also publicly positioned herself as a keen supporter of human rights and democracy in the country. Both personally met with antiregime activists, and these meetings seem to have strengthened their moral resolve to stand up against the perceived tyrannical rule of Myanmar's military junta. One might thus hold that timewise the origins of US-Myanmar rapprochement lie squarely in the period following the announcement of the Obama administration's Burma policy review until September 2009, the month the review was formally concluded. Elsewhere, I have argued, however, that it would be more persuasive to partially locate the origins of this rapprochement in earlier years, when foreign policy entrepreneurs proposed new ways to deal with Myanmar.[7] Although Congress then remained overwhelmingly supportive of exerting continued pressure on the SPDC, the appreciation that sanctions alone would not force political change in Myanmar slowly took hold. Testifying to this realization, the Tom Lantos Block Burmese JADE (Junta's Anti-Democratic Efforts) Act of 2008 already specified the creation of a new post of special representative and policy coordinator for Burma who was to promote "direct dialogue with the SPDC," among other responsibilities.[8] In August 2008, President Bush announced his intention to nominate Michael Green for this position, but when he did some months later, the Senate did not confirm the appointment given the timing and the focus on the US financial crisis.

The US Burma Policy Review

Secretary of State Hillary Clinton in February 2009 announced a Burma policy review when on her inaugural visit to Japan and Indonesia. Though the announcement of the review was accompanied by the acknowledgment that Washington's previous sanctions-heavy approach had failed to bring about political change in Myanmar, she also suggested that ASEAN's "constructive engagement" approach toward Myanmar was equally a failure in this regard. The key idea that emerged from the policy review, which involved interagency exchanges and discussion with different stakeholders on Capitol Hill and civil society, was that the administration should introduce a second key pillar to influence developments in Myanmar in addition to the continued reliance on sanctions, namely the pursuit of a political dialogue at a senior level. As such, the decision to embark on direct dialogue did not imply an abandonment of the main goals underlying US Burma policy: to foster real political change ("credible democratic reform"), to improve human rights ("immediate, unconditional release of political prisoners"), and to promote national reconciliation ("serious dialogue with the opposition and minority ethnic groups").[9] That said, the administration was very keen on moving beyond the instrument of sanctions. How keen becomes clear when considering that the policy review was not abandoned even when the SPDC leadership decided in May 2009 to charge and then, in August, to sentence Aung San Suu Kyi for harboring US national John Yettaw after the latter unexpectedly gained access to her property in an apparent attempt to warn her about dangers to her life.

The resolve to opt for so-called "pragmatic engagement" is arguably best understood if one analyzes the shift in approach vis-à-vis Burma in the context of Washington's wider regional interests and policy. The US relationship with ASEAN seems particularly relevant in this regard. First, the Obama administration was intent on improving ties with ASEAN as it recognized that Washington's hitherto inflexible line on Burma had affected its relations with the grouping. Relations between Myanmar and fellow ASEAN members had also not been free from problems, but Southeast Asian governments were opposed to Western countries holding their relations with the association hostage to the preparedness of the SPDC to embrace the West's prescription for political change.[10] Also, ASEAN, whose members have opted to create a political-security, economic, and social-cultural community by 2015, has also been at the center of a number of institutional platforms, which provide a locus for discussions regarding the future of East Asia regional cooperation and regional order.[11] The consensus in Washington has been that the United States should play its part in these discussions, especially at the East Asia Summit. Notably, Washington has also been wary about China developing in the future a two-ocean navy, a development that would be facilitated in the event of any regular People's Liberation Army (Navy) access to Myanmar's ports. Given this regional and geopolitical context, it is not surprising that the new administration did not favor still regarding US Burma policy as separate from Washington's broader East Asia policy.

From Naypyitaw's perspective, the US policy review outcome seems to have been a logical conclusion. Following the analysis of Myanmar officials, Washington's efforts to strengthen relations with ASEAN in the broader context of geopolitical currents in East Asia required a rethink of the very antagonistic position pursued toward Myanmar for years.[12] Significantly, Myanmar's leadership was itself keen to send signals that would encourage greater pragmatism in US Burma policy. Having already in late March 2009 received a US emissary, the military government in August offered a warm welcome to Senator Jim Webb, a long-time proponent of adjustments to US strategy toward the Asia-Pacific and a more pragmatic approach toward Burma. While the sentencing of Aung San Suu Kyi demonstrated that the implementation of Naypyitaw's roadmap to a "disciplined democracy," as outlined in the 2008 constitution, would proceed without major concessions to the regime's critics, the junta also signaled its preference for more constructive bilateral relations as Senior General Than Shwe commuted Aung San Suu Kyi's sentence into house arrest and allowed Senator Webb to take John Yettaw back home to the United States.

Progress in Bilateral Relations

Since then, progress in US-Myanmar relations has by some yardsticks been quite spectacular. Normal diplomatic relations have been reestablished, economic sanctions imposed against the SPDC have been eased significantly, military-to-military ties are being cautiously revived, and reciprocal state visits have already taken place. To what may this positive trend in bilateral relations be attributed? Arguably, four main factors have underpinned the level of progress achieved so far.

The prerequisites of improved bilateral ties. When under SPDC rule, a debate raged about whether engagement or combined international pressure, moral castigation, and isolation would bring about political reforms and improvements to the human rights situation in Myanmar. One astute long-term observer of the country predicted, however, that it would be political reforms undertaken by the Myanmar leadership that would lead to improved relations between Washington and Naypyitaw.[13] This assessment has proven accurate. After all, the government of President Thein Sein took several bold decisions without which the US government would not have normalized diplomatic relations or eased sanctions, relating to the release of political prisoners, the passing of new legislation more broadly compatible with Western understandings of political freedoms, and moves enabling Aung San Suu Kyi and the NLD to participate as a constitutionally legitimate opposition in parliament. Inevitably, some discussion has focused on what prompted the reforms in the first place, with some analysts suggesting that sanctions did work after all, while others see the reforms as being of the government's own making, not least because of their timing. Testifying before Congress, the aforementioned observer of Burmese politics said unequivocally: "These are Burmese reforms and they must be seen that way."[14]

Irrespective of what particular goals have been pursued by Myanmar in the context of its reforms, what matters here is that the reforms largely met the initial expectations for change articulated by US diplomats and decisionmakers. The political process and compromise that subsequently allowed Aung San Suu Kyi to participate in the 2012 by-elections answered Washington's long-lasting call for a genuine political dialogue, even if it meant the NLD was obliged to at least temporarily accept a constitutional framework put in place by the SPDC. Also, progress in Myanmar-US relations has relied on Naypyitaw taking a number of further crucial steps that US decisionmakers have for long wanted the Myanmar side to take (i.e., release of political prisoners, working toward an end to armed conflict with ethnic nationalities).

Secondly, progress in bilateral relations has occurred because US decisionmakers have appreciated the importance of properly acknowledging the reforms. Indeed, the reforms enacted by the Thein Sein government were perceived by the Obama administration as the first and possibly only opportunity for years to come to help bring about the kind of political changes that Washington had long advocated. Importantly, the officials concerned also clearly understood by the autumn of 2011 that for bilateral relations to progress and normalize, it would be necessary for Washington to respond constructively to Naypyitaw's calls to reciprocate its reform steps. Secretary Clinton's chosen approach focusing on "action-for-action" speaks clearly to this.

Third, improved bilateral ties have moreover depended on the evolving attitudes and positions of those members of Congress who for years had been influential critics of Myanmar's government and shapers of US Burma policy. Very early on, the Obama administration sought to win and then maintain support from these key congressional stakeholders for a new direction in Burma policy by establishing a close consultation process. Crucially, even Senator Mitch McConnell, Senate Republican leader since 2007, supported the administration in its attempt to proceed with a more pragmatic approach toward Myanmar. For many years, the senator had been one of the most vocal if not leading critics of the SPDC and supporters of the political opposition based around Aung San Suu Kyi. Within a few months of the Thein Sein government committing to what President Obama called "flickers of progress," several members of Congress paid a visit to Myanmar and were encouraged by the reforms.[15] Some held subsequent meetings with Myanmar decisionmakers when they visited Washington (e.g., Foreign Minister Wunna Maung Lwin), and this helped to maintain the momentum in their dialogue with the Thein Sein government. That said, Congress has passed key legislation in support of Burma's reforms only once—in September 2012 in the context of a visit to the United States by Aung San Suu Kyi and Thein Sein. This legislation waived the requirement that US representatives to international financial institutions vote against loans to Myanmar.

Progress has, fourth, also depended on support for bilateral reengagement from Aung San Suu Kyi. After all, as David Steinberg argued, "Her role, both explicitly when she has been able publicly to articulate her views, and implicitly in the interpretation of her attitudes and positions by her acolytes, has been more than simply influential in determining U.S. policy toward Burma/Myanmar."[16]

Upon her release from house arrest in November 2010, US policymakers regularly looked to Aung San Suu Kyi for signals, and it seems—at times at least—de facto instruction. Particularly in the period from mid-2011 to 2012 the administration was very careful not to take any major steps without consulting her beforehand. Her views have also continued to guide members of Congress in their respective conclusions about whether the administration's Burma policy was on the right track and, subsequently, whether to endorse substantive policy shifts, such as the easing of sanctions. In that case, Aung San Suu Kyi agreed with the Thein Sein government and the Obama administration that the time for a continued reliance on sanctions had passed.

From engagement to partnership? When the Obama administration embraced "pragmatic engagement" in September 2009 to attempt to influence Naypyitaw on such issues as political prisoners and national reconciliation, its expectations about immediate results were limited. Consequently, its inability to persuade the then military regime to allow for inclusive elections in 2010 left the administration disappointed but not surprised.[17] The reform commitment articulated by incoming president Thein Sein in his inaugural speech was noted in Washington, but skepticism prevailed and was expressed even in June 2011.[18] However, over the summer and autumn that year, Myanmar's new president and government took a number of steps that led President Obama to ask Secretary Clinton "to explore whether the United States can empower a positive transition in Burma."[19] Key was President Thein Sein's offer and Aung San Suu Kyi's acceptance that the two would work together for the benefit of their country. During her celebrated stay in Myanmar, Secretary Clinton made clear that the United States would accompany Myanmar's leaders on the path to reform if they chose to keep moving in that direction.[20]

The administration adopted an approach to engagement where the United States would "meet action with action."[21] This approach was in keeping with the notion that while Myanmar's reforms were "real and significant," the reform process was also "fragile and reversible."[22] Within weeks of Secretary Clinton's visit, this approach was plainly put into practice as, following a substantial release of political prisoners (totaling around 650) including high-profile political activists, Washington announced its intention of moving toward exchanging ambassadors. This decision also took account of the positive response by the Myanmar government to a range of previous US recommendations: allowing the International Committee of the Red Cross access to conflict areas, announcing early the date for the 2012 by-elections, and the substantial and positive interaction between the government and ethnic groups (not least the cease-fire with the Karen National Union [KNU] in January 2012).

The 1 April 2012 by-election proved another milestone in bilateral ties. In response, Secretary Clinton outlined several action steps, which would involve sending an accredited ambassador, re-establishing an in-country US Agency for International Development (USAID) mission (to strengthen democracy, human rights, and the rule of law; to advance peace and reconciliation; and to meet humanitarian needs), creating the framework for private organizations based in the United States to commit to nonprofit activity designed to assist the population at large, and facilitating travel to the United States for select government officials and parliamentarians. Clinton also suggested Washington would begin easing financial and investment sanctions, although sanctions and prohibitions would continue to apply in cases where institutions or individuals remained on the "wrong side of [Burma's] historic reforms."[23]

On the occasion of the visit by Myanmar foreign minister Wunna Maung Lwin to Washington in May 2012, the Obama administration not only announced the nomination of Derek Mitchell as the first US ambassador to Burma since 1990, but also outlined its decision to permit US investment activity as well as the export of US financial services to Myanmar.[24] Presented by the administration as a strong signal of US support for reform, the announcement followed considerable controversy, as various US-based advocacy and rights groups found the move premature and said so clearly. Secretary Clinton nevertheless waived the 1997 ban on new investment in Burma (congressional authorization for which was set out in the Foreign Operations, Export Financing, and Related Programs Appropriations Act of 1997), while the license authorizing new investment became subject to some limitations and requirements. The latter were designed to prevent new investment in Myanmar that involves agreements entered into with the Ministry of Defence, state or nonstate armed groups or entities owned by the above, or a person blocked under the current sanctions program.[25] Moreover, reporting requirements apply in connection with cases where new investment by US companies exceeds US$500,000, in part to encourage responsible investment by US companies. To promote transparency, as well as to reduce corruption and to strengthen accountability, the Obama administration communicated its expectation that Myanmar should join the Extractive Industries Transparency Initiative (EITI). The Thein Sein government agreed.

Meeting President Thein Sein for the third time, in September 2012 on the sidelines of the UN General Assembly meetings in New York, Secretary Clinton announced that the United States would begin easing restrictions on imports of Burmese goods. Following consultations with Congress, a relevant waiver by the State Department and a general license by the US Treasury were issued in mid-November. One key rationale for the waiver was that the easing of import restrictions, which was badly sought by Naypyitaw, would help Myanmar to begin establishing a viable manufacturing sector. It also meant to reward Naypyitaw's continued reform efforts, including the removal of prepublication censorship, the passing of a new labor law and a new Foreign Investment Law, Myanmar's efforts to join the EITI, as well as its moves to promote ethnic reconciliation. Notably, the importation of jadeite and rubies as well as articles of jewelry containing them would continue to be subject to sanctions in accordance with the 2008 JADE Act. As with the other steps taken before, the administration highlighted that Aung San Suu Kyi was in favor of this easing of trade restrictions.

November 2012 marked another milestone in Myanmar-US relations as President Obama visited Yangon while en route to the ASEAN Leaders Meeting in Phnom Penh. The visit had the aim of locking in the government's various reform measures, but it was also designed to boost the legitimacy of Myanmar's reformers given the perceived possibility of political backsliding. President Obama suggested that if the Myanmar leadership followed the United States in promoting core freedoms judged fundamental to democracy, Naypyitaw would have "in the United States of America a partner on that long journey."[26] Indeed, by some accounts these objectives for Myanmar squarely reflect the shift of the Obama administration from a relatively cautious approach toward Naypyitaw focusing on "action-for-action" to a position where Washington aims to play a major part in helping to deliver Myanmar's political, economic, and social reforms.[27] While the United States announced US$171 million in development assistance during the Obama visit, the Thein Sein government also made several further commitments.[28] For instance, it reaffirmed Naypyitaw's commitment to UN Security Council Resolution 1874, signed the International Atomic Energy Agency (IAEA) additional protocol, started a process on so-called "prisoners of concern," signed a joint antitrafficking plan, embraced an International Labour Organization (ILO) action plan on forced labor, and vowed to pursue a durable cease-fire in Kachin State as well as prevent communal violence in Rakhine (Arakan) State.

Continuity in Obama II. Although Senator John Kerry replaced Hillary Clinton as secretary of state in President Obama's second term in office, US Burma policy has continued very much as before. Bilateral cooperation has been agreed in a number of key areas. For instance, USAID has begun collaborating in relation to democracy, human rights, and the rule of law; transparent government; peace and reconciliation; and prosperity. Significant emphasis, for example, has been put on political education and support measures designed to ensure free, fair, and credible elections in 2015 (including political party development and general voter education). To this end, USAID in March 2013 announced a three-year multimillion-dollar program.[29]

In line with its reform objectives, strengthening Myanmar's civil society is thus key. As Daniel Baer, deputy assistant secretary of state for democracy, human rights, and labor, explained in general terms:

> We are well aware of the need for political change in many places, and we are also well aware that durable change is most likely to come from within. That means we can be effective by standing up for civil society, throwing civil society actors a lifeline of support when they need it, and helping to preserve the space for them to make the case for change in their own societies.[30]

In this context, US diplomats have also pushed Naypyitaw to engage civil society directly and to explore and establish ways to work together with civil society in partnership. Among other outcomes, this led to the formation of a committee charged with establishing the number of remaining political prisoners in Myanmar.

In May 2013, President Thein Sein traveled to the United States. He committed himself to continue to build a new democratic state, while seeking the improvement of bilateral economic ties. The two governments signed a Trade and Investment Framework Agreement during the visit, reflecting Naypyitaw's interest in exporting more products to the United States.[31] Important from Myanmar's perspective was also the recognition gains associated with Thein Sein's visit, the first by a Myanmar head of state since Ne Win's trip in 1966.

Evolving military-to-military ties. At the time of writing, the administration was legally prevented from offering to Naypyitaw any of the usual security assistance programs: International Military Education Training (IMET), Foreign Military Financing (basically grants for the acquisition of US military equipment, services, and training), and Section 1206 of the National Defense Authorization Act, which involves the use of Department of Defense funds to build military capacity of another state in order for that country to participate in or support military or stability operations in which US Armed Forces are a participant.[32] Notably, Ambassador Derek Mitchell has emphasized that the United States is "not even close" to arms sales or operational training.[33] Nonetheless, contacts with the Myanmar military are being sought and gradually expanded. In June 2012, then defense secretary Leon Panetta suggested that Washington would strengthen military ties if political and human rights reform continued.[34] Following this up, US Pacific Command commander Lieutenant General Francis Wiercinski and Deputy Assistant Secretary of Defense for South and Southeast Asia Vikram Singh traveled to Myanmar in November 2012 as part of a larger delegation to discuss Myanmar's human rights situation. During the event, the two sides agreed on dialogue and some training, particularly in the areas of humanitarian issues, human rights, and greater professionalization provided by the Defense Institute for International Legal Studies (DIILS). By September 2013, two DIILS scoping delegations had visited Myanmar with backing from both Senator McConnell as well as Aung San Suu Kyi. Myanmar participants have also been invited to attend courses at the Asia-Pacific Center for Security Studies, which is run by the Department of Defense in Honolulu.

Washington has also welcomed and supported the idea of integrating Myanmar into multilateral regional defense frameworks. Given the legal strictures under which the administration has been operating, the Obama administration "agreed" to Thailand's request to allow a small contingent of *tatmadaw* officers to observe certain parts (e.g., humanitarian assistance/disaster response) of the 2013 and 2014 multilateral Cobra Gold exercises, the largest Asia-based military exercise in which the United States participates. The two sides have also used other multilateral venues to meet. For instance, Defense Secretary Chuck Hagel met with his counterpart Lieutenant General Wai Lwin on the sidelines of the ASEAN Defence Ministers Plus 1 meeting in Brunei in August 2013, seemingly in part to voice US support for Myanmar's efforts relating to defense events organized while Naypyitaw holds the ASEAN chairmanship in 2014. Moreover, Myanmar has been represented at ADMM exercises (which tend to focus on rescue, recovery, and disaster relief). The Myanmar defense minister also joined other ASEAN counterparts in traveling to Hawaii in 2014 for an informal (inaugural) US-ASEAN defense ministers' meeting. Moreover, the administration has been contemplating the benefits that could be derived from restoring the IMET program, especially in the context of the UK defense secretary extending an invitation for thirty *tatmadaw* officers to participate in a flagship course in January 2014.[35] Eventually, officials from both the Department of State and Department of Defense in congressional testimony offered in late 2013 opted to merely suggest the adoption of an expanded-IMET, or E-IMET. For financial year 2015, the State Department has requested IMET funds for Burma at the same level as for Papua New Guinea (US$250,000). There is considerable support in parts of the wider policy community for engaging the *tatmadaw* to greater extent.[36] The same is true for security sector reform generally, including capacity-building measures to better confront Burma's resurging opium poppy cultivation and narcotics trafficking challenge.

In short, within about two years US-Myanmar relations have substantially improved. Even a dialogue involving defense officials has been slowly developing. In the words of the administration, the "United States is supporting an historic political and economic transition in Burma and is taking an active role in the country."[37] While Washington-Naypyitaw ties thus have transformed, it is noteworthy that in some ways the success of their budding partnership would seem to depend on the willingness of Myanmar's leadership to further embrace US and wider international expectations concerning domestic reform measures and a new politics of inclusion. However, as the next section will show, on several issues of concern to Washington, the Thein Sein government has so far resisted US advice and admonition.

Difficult Issues in Bilateral Relations

The Obama administration has repeatedly praised the courage and reform commitment demonstrated by President Thein Sein and his administration. At the same time, the administration has made clear that there are a number of issues on which it expects Naypyitaw to make further progress. In this chapter, four such issues are identified: constitutional issues, ethnic conflict, communal violence, and military and trade relations with North Korea. Because most of these issues are dealt with in some detail elsewhere in this volume, this chapter merely outlines Washington's take on them and explains why Myanmar's current government is more likely to continue to resist rather than to adopt Washington's recommendations and prescriptions, thus making for challenges in bilateral relations.

Constitutional Changes

The Obama administration may have strongly supported the idea that for Aung San Suu Kyi and the NLD to be able play a meaningful and constructive political role in the country's domestic politics following the 2010 elections, seeking election to parliament would be the appropriate step to take even if that meant working within the political and constitutional parameters set by the SPDC. That said, the 2008 constitution—much criticized by US policymakers already during the drafting stage, let alone after its passing by a flawed referendum in May 2008—remains deeply problematic from Washington's perspective.

In part, this has to do with the role that the constitution has reserved for the military, which is incompatible with unambiguous civilian rule. But the Obama administration also finds other constitutional provisions problematic, not least Article 59f. This provision does not allow the legitimate children of presidential contenders to owe allegiance to a foreign power. It is this provision that, likely by design, prevents Aung San Suu Kyi from becoming president or vice president at the time of this writing. For the administration, the 2008 constitution also fails to resolve the longstanding ethnic conflict given the limited degree of autonomy it offers to the country's ethnic nationalities.

The administration's position parallels and perhaps reflects wider concerns in Washington. Senator Mitch McConnell, long the key voice on Burma in Congress, has been quite blunt about the need for constitutional amendments: "Simply put, if Burma is to take the next big step toward economic and political reform and toward fully normalizing its relations with the United States, it needs to revise its Constitution."[38] The constitutional changes he considers essential include bringing the *tatmadaw* under civilian control by ending their special role in Myanmar's politics and allowing Aung San Suu Kyi to be eligible for the office of president. Like others, he has also focused on the importance of judicial independence and constitutional assurances for ethnic minorities. According to Senator McConnell, "These provisions, if left unamended, would cast a pall over the upcoming 2015 elections. . . . If the 2015 elections are viewed as illegitimate, it will lead many to conclude that reform efforts have stalled in Burma and the country's stated commitment to democracy is hollow."[39]

How much constitutional change is in the offing? The 2008 constitution remains also for many in Myanmar an obstacle to serious political change. Indeed, Aung San Suu Kyi and the NLD campaigned for constitutional change in the 2012 by-election because the constitution did "not conform with democratic norms and standards." More recently, in October 2013, the NLD leader argued—not least when on international travel—that a failure to amend the constitution would mean that the 2015 elections might perhaps be free but not fair. In this context, she has also made plain her desire to see amended the very constitutional provision (Section 436) that would make it so difficult to actually change the constitution in key areas because amendments have to pass not only the parliamentary threshold of 75 percent plus, but also depend on the majority of eligible voters supporting the constitutional change in a nationwide referendum.

How much constitutional change is forthcoming in the near future remains unclear at this time. Views on what constitutional amendments are necessary have varied widely, not least within parliament. With Aung San Suu Kyi having declared her interest in becoming president, the NLD is of course hoping for an amendment that would allow their leader to assume the highest office in the event of her party sweeping the 2015 elections. The USDP seems supportive of some amendments, but has not specified its preferred changes.[40] Meanwhile, ethnic groups primarily want to see constitutional amendments that would create a more federalist system to allow for greater autonomy.

To identify possible changes to the constitution, the Union Parliament formed in 2013 the Constitutional Review Joint Committee.[41] Notably, the joint committee's specification was that precedence was to be given to provisions "that are conducive to the nation."[42] Potential constitutional amendments were also to be enacted in line with current constitutional provisions. Eventually, the joint committee collected many thousands of submissions for constitutional change but failed to reach any conclusions. In its stead was then created, in February 2014, the Parliamentary Constitutional Amendment Implementation Committee. This committee has yet to complete its deliberations and to formally submit any proposals, but it seems that the committee may recommend reducing the threshold for constitutional change to a two-thirds majority.

However, the prospects for wide-ranging amendments to the constitution that would downgrade the military's future role in Myanmar's national politics seem limited. When asked about constitutional reforms, President Thein Sein has been cautious, pointing to the role of parliament and the Myanmar people. Yet the president has signaled opposition to amendments that would reduce the constitutionally sanctioned role and autonomy of the military.[43] As concerns the commander-in-chief, Senior General Min Aung Hlaing has similarly taken the position that it is for the *tatmadaw* to protect the 2008 constitution.[44] To be sure, even the senior general apparently believes that the participation of the *tatmadaw* in Myanmar's politics will be reduced over time.[45] However, it is unclear to what extent he already considers the country's political players and civilian institutions sufficiently "mature" for the military to possibly step back early. What seems clearer is that the representatives from the military in the legislature will surely be guided by his views.

Moreover, even by May 2014, the constitutional amendment necessary for Aung San Suu Kyi to become at least the next vice president cannot be taken for granted. The president indicated that it was up to parliament rather than the executive to ensure that Aung San Suu Kyi would not remain debarred. He has also repeatedly clarified that he does not oppose her candidacy. However, the foreign citizenship of a family member has once before prevented a contender from assuming the post of vice president, and there are questions about whether the provision as it stands is not in fact in Myanmar's national interest. Also, trust between Aung San Suu Kyi and the NLD and what in effect is a "hybrid government" is still lacking, which may reduce the likelihood of the military supporting constitutional change in this specific area.[46] Meanwhile, representatives of the ethnic parties apparently tend not to regard the eligibility issue as being of primary significance. At the very least, therefore, for an amendment that would in principle allow Aung San Suu Kyi to become eligible for the highest office to pass through parliament, significant political horse-trading might become necessary.[47] To subject not least the military leadership to greater pressure, Aung San Suu Kyi—together with the 88 Generation Peace and Open Society organization—has launched a people's movement style campaign to influence the outcome on constitutional change. There are already signs of possible blowback, however, which raises renewed questions about the willingness of the ruling elite to allow for constitutional change.

Ethnic Conflict

Since 2011, the Myanmar government has spent considerable energy on moving toward a nationwide cease-fire and eventual peace agreements with the country's armed ethnic groups.[48] While Naypyitaw has been successful in reaching new cease-fire accords with several nonstate armed groups, the cease-fire arrangement with the Kachin Independence Organisation (KIO) and its military wing, the Kachin Independence Army (KIA), broke down in June 2011. With the two sides unable to forge a new formal cease-fire, Kachin State has since seen significant fighting and displacement.[49]

Washington has consistently supported national reconciliation between the government and ethnic nationalities but eschewed assuming a prominent role as facilitator or mediator. Indeed, the US Embassy in Yangon has stated that, "we support dialogue as the best and only way to address the root causes of longstanding conflict."[50] Similar to other countries, Washington's diplomatic staff has maintained regular contact with ethnic groups, but also even participated as international observers in some peace talks, as between the government and the Karenni National Progressive Party as well as the KNU in 2012.[51] Washington was invited to join the Peace Donor Support Group the year after.

That said, the United States has registered deep concern about the fighting in Kachin State. With the deterioration of the humanitarian situation in Kachin State, Washington turned openly critical of the military approach taken by Naypyitaw in order to deal with what the United States regards as a political problem. Washington's concern was demonstrated by the visit that US Ambassador Derek Mitchell undertook to Kachin State in December 2012. Soon thereafter the *tatmadaw* escalated military operations against the Kachin by bombarding positions near the KIO's headquarter in Laiza, involving the unprecedented use of fighter planes and helicopters. Washington called this use of airpower "extremely troubling." As Ambassador Mitchell moreover declared, "both sides have to recognize that there is no military solution to this question, and that an eye for an eye will leave everyone blind."[52] Mitchell also warned Naypyitaw that its approach risked Myanmar's improving international reputation and would set back the government in relation to its stated goals of peace, reconciliation, and development. Following the apparent violation of a cease-fire due to take effect on 19 January 2013, the United States publicly chastised Myanmar's authorities in part by expressing deep concerns about the safety of civilians and calling on Naypyitaw for both unhindered access to those requiring assistance and greater efforts to bring about dialogue.[53]

For their part, both the Myanmar Foreign Ministry and the Ministry of Defence have at times reacted irately to US criticism. With the government having already condemned the "terrorist" KIA for ambushing military ration supply convoys and persistently destroying important infrastructure as well as invoking the right to act in self-defense, both ministries in early 2013 rejected the perceived partisan representation in relation to fighting in Kachin State. Having clearly overstepped what to Naypyitaw and especially the military represents welcome or acceptable involvement, US diplomacy thereafter returned to a cautious, less publicly vocal mode in responding to the conflict and its management. This has been a challenge because international coverage of the conflict, not least the humanitarian crisis still faced by the internally displaced people, which involves both Kachin, many of whom are Christians, and Shan, continues unabated, and the administration has been criticized by human rights organizations and Kachin diaspora groups for not doing enough to help stem the conflict if not for relaxing sanctions against Myanmar too early. The situation in Kachin State has also attracted considerable interest on Capitol Hill, where, for instance, Senator McConnell has highlighted the historical connection between the Kachin and the United States and warned that the full normalization of bilateral relations between Naypyidaw and Washington will in part depend on building peace in Kachin State. Given the failure by the Myanmar government and the KIO/KIA to conclude a new full cease-fire accord, Ambassador Mitchell thus urged both sides to engage in mutual restraint to create trust and conditions for lasting peace in what is seen as a "critical juncture in the peace process."[54] This has continued to prove difficult, however.

Under the circumstances, in April 2014, the administration openly welcomed General Gun Maw, formally the KIA's deputy chief of staff, who outlined to a wide range of administration officials his concerns about Naypyitaw's demands and negotiation strategy in order to buttress his request for US involvement in the process. The general extracted from newly appointed assistant secretary of state for democracy, human rights, and labor Tom Malinowksi a commitment to "firm U.S. support for the post-cease-fire peace process." The symbolic significance of the Obama administration receiving a military leader of an armed ethnic grouping should not be underestimated; but the administration has still continued to make any formal direct involvement in support of ongoing dialogue dependent on a request from both the ethnic groups and the government.[55] For its part, the Myanmar government seems not yet to have asked; indeed, presidential spokesperson Ye Htut has characterized the government's conflict with nonstate armed ethnic groups as a domestic issue. Meanwhile, the *tatmadaw* continues to respond to the KIA in declared self-defense, while capturing important KIA bases.[56]

Communal Violence

Another sensitive and difficult issue in bilateral ties concerns the ongoing communal conflict and violence in Myanmar, particularly as regards relations between Rakhine Buddhists and the Muslim community that refers to itself as Rohingya. (The government does not recognize the Rohingya as one of the country's ethnic nationalities and instead routinely refers to its members as "Bengalis.")[57] However, communal violence even in Rakhine State has targeted and affected different Muslim communities, as is clear already from the October 2012 attacks. Since, communal violence has erupted in several other locations across Myanmar, including Meikhtila, Lashio, and Thandwe (Sandaway), and thus represents a much wider challenge.[58] Some observers have suggested that the state itself has been complicit.[59]

Although perhaps taken by surprise by the ferocity and ugliness of the aggression and the destruction perpetrated in northern Rakhine State and around Sittwe (Akyab) in June 2012, it is notable that Secretary Clinton preferred to depict the events as communal violence rather than as a religious issue, as did Naypyitaw. US officials in September 2012 availed themselves of the opportunity to visit affected areas and to discuss the situation in Rakhine State with Myanmar government representatives. This was at the time seen by one senior official to "[speak] volumes about the changed relationship between the United States and Burma, that they would have enough trust in us to allow us to visit."[60]

With regards to the Rohingya, the US position is that this community has experienced severe legal, economic, and social discrimination. As the then special representative and policy coordinator for Burma Patrick Murphy put it in early 2013, "There is no excuse for violence, however, or persecution of the stateless Rohingya."[61] General goals formulated by US officials for Rakhine State include achieving lasting peace and stability, rebuilding trust between the communities, allowing access for humanitarian assistance, and offering the Rohingya greater freedom of movement. The United States also seeks a longer-term solution that will include addressing citizenship issues.[62] As regards anti-Muslim attacks more generally, Washington has deplored and condemned these outbreaks of communal violence and called on government and local authorities to do more to stem the sources of ongoing tensions. The warning is that if religious and civil society leaders do not actively oppose the violence targeting Muslim communities, the country's broader reform process could be threatened.

Wary of unwelcome international interference, including possible external support for local insurgency, Naypyitaw has recognized the importance of responding appropriately to what gripped Rakhine State in 2012. The Thein Sein government thus formed an investigation commission tasked to offer both analysis of the events and recommendations for the future. Notably, among the steps taken since, the Union government has established a committee responsible for overseeing peace, stability, and development in Rakhine State, and for addressing "root causes" of intercommunal conflict. It also disbanded the NaSaKa border security force, which has been associated with human rights violations in Rakhine State, a move promptly welcomed by the US ambassador.[63] President Thein Sein has also spelled out a "zero-tolerance" policy as far as sectarian violence is concerned.

That said, the intolerance and discrimination against the Rohingya community and anti-Muslim sentiments generally make for a difficult agenda. Buddhist Rakhine nationalists feel hard done by history and resent their community's perceived marginalization in the face of the Rohingya's identity claims and political goals.[64] For many Bamar, the depiction of Rohingya as "illegal immigrants" does have a historical base in that the country was subjected to periods of significant and often unrestricted immigration not only during colonial times but also in Myanmar's postindependence period, immigration that in turn led to a variety of legislative, administrative, and security countermeasures by the state. The aforementioned Inquiry Commission report highlights the contested nature of Rohingya identity claims. Its authors, in line with prevalent understandings in Myanmar, conclude that *Rohingya* is not the name of a distinct race or people.[65] The report also argues that there is no connection between people who entered the country under the British during the colonial period and those earlier people who originally invoked the term *Rohingya*. Significantly, the commission's conclusion (p. 56) is that "should the Bengalis continue to insist they should be called Rohingya, the majority in the country will not accept this and there could be further unrest. . . . Bengalis now pushing the term Rohingya are surely fanning the flames of sectarian violence."

The likelihood of the Union government accepting the Rohingya as equal citizens of Myanmar thus remains remote. There is, for instance, still little or no parliamentary support for amending the 1982 citizenship law. Indeed, legislators will have noted that Rakhine Buddhists were incensed when in 2010 Myanmar's main political party touched on the issue of citizenship to Rohingya in their political campaigning, but ended up boosting the vote for the Rakhine Nationalities Development Party.[66] Even Aung San Suu Kyi, after prolonged silence on the issue, has only asked for a review of the 1982 citizenship law so that it meets "international standards." Also, the strength of anti-Muslim sentiments running throughout the country cannot be underestimated, and these are shared if not reinforced by Buddhist monks. Analysts have captured this phenomenon in terms of rising "Buddhist nationalism" or even—as regards the Rohingya—"genocidal Buddhist racism."[67] How constraining these sentiments are has again been exemplified by the cautious approach Aung San Suu Kyi has taken on the issue.[68] Wider mass public opinion will therefore surely be taken into account by legislators and party operatives as the country prepares for the 2015 elections.

Meanwhile, for the Obama administration, communal tension and violence remain problematic as the president alluded to when in Yangon in November 2012. It is certainly not an issue on which the Obama administration can stay silent, especially given widespread international condemnation of the situation and sustained if not increasing pressure from advocacy and solidarity groups that aim to influence the administration and Congress. The 2014 US human rights report, prepared by the State Department, describes the humanitarian and human rights crisis in Rakhine State "as the most troubling exception and threat to the country's progress."[69] Notably, the difficult situation in Rakhine State has continued, punctuated by allegations in January 2014 of a massacre at Ducheeratan middle village, which have been strenuously denied as unconfirmed and unverified by the authorities; threats and mob violence directed against employees of the UN and international non-governmental organizations; and the government's decision not to allow for self-identification of Rohingya in the March 2014 census. The mob violence in Sittwe, which also affected US aid workers, led to the US embassy again expressing deep concern over the region's lack of adequate security forces and the lack of the rule of law. But the concern was also transmitted once more at a much higher level. Notably, the deteriorating human rights situation in Rakhine State featured strongly during the visit to Myanmar by Assistant Secretary of State Daniel Russel in April 2014. And the keen US advice that Myanmar adopt a more active role to arrive at a durable solution to address the underlying causes of conflict there was powerfully reinforced by Samantha Power after the UN Security Council was informally briefed on developments in Rakhine State days later. Even President Obama himself, speaking in Malaysia, warned that if the rights of Myanmar's Muslim population were not protected, the country would not succeed. Nonetheless, movement on core issues remains absent.

Military Relations with North Korea

Concerns about the military relationship between Pyongyang and Naypyitaw go back many years; already in the early 2000s concerns emerged that Myanmar was pursuing in secret a nuclear weapons program. However, serious analysis on the subject found that the supposed evidence was weak or at least inconclusive.[70] Myanmar's then military leadership refuted the allegations. In November 2011, Lower House Speaker Shwe Mann, who had led a secret visit to North Korea in 2008, also denied that Myanmar was intent on pursuing a nuclear weapons program.[71] When President Obama visited Myanmar in November 2012, the Thein Sein government sought to dispel remaining concerns by vowing to sign and ratify the IAEA Additional Protocol, as well as by updating its Small Quantities Protocol and strengthening cooperation with the IAEA.

Question marks have, however, remained over the extent of cooperation between Myanmar and the Democratic People's Republic of Korea (DPRK) in relation to military and especially missile technology. Though in mid-2009 Naypyitaw did not permit the North Korean vessel *Kang Nam* to dock in Myanmar, a vessel suspected of illicitly carrying missile components, the Obama administration has reported that since then North Korean companies arranged for Myanmar to receive military equipment and supported Naypyitaw's efforts to build and operate military-related production facilities.[72] The Directorate of Defense Industries (DDI) has been said to carry out missile research and development at its facilities, which are linked to a memorandum of understanding on DPRK assistance to Burma to build medium range, liquid-fueled ballistic missiles.[73]

The Obama administration has routinely stressed to Myanmar the importance of completely cutting military ties with North Korea. The issue apparently featured prominently during Secretary Clinton's first visit. According to one official, Myanmar's military trade with North Korea has constituted a "top national security priority."[74] Speaking at his confirmation hearing, US Ambassador Derek Mitchell asserted that US-Myanmar bilateral relations "can never be fully normalized until we are satisfied that any illicit ties to North Korea have ended once and for all."[75] In July 2012, President Obama signed a new executive order that allows Washington to impose sanctions against relevant entities or individuals. A year later, the US Treasury "designated" Lieutenant-General Thein Htay, the head of DDI, for his apparent role in arms purchases from North Korea.

For the Thein Sein government, remaining military ties with North Korea constitute a tricky issue. Essentially, it was the previous military government that entered into relevant agreements, and as these concern defense matters they would be for the *tatmadaw* to manage. The Obama administration clearly understands this. Some observers therefore believe that the administration has tried to play down the issue of military ties between Naypyitaw and the DPRK in US-Myanmar relations.[76] Whether accurate or not, Naypyitaw's military relationship with Pyongyang, past and present, will likely remain a major talking point in US-Myanmar ties, especially given that these ties have been for years a particularly prominent issue on Capitol Hill. To the extent that more evidence for continuing military technology and weapons transfers becomes available despite repeated US demands, DPRK-Myanmar military contacts are bound to remain one of the more problematic aspects in US-Myanmar relations.

Prospects for Bilateral Ties

Naypyitaw's reforms have already allowed the Myanmar and US governments to move toward fully normalizing their relationship. When assessing

Myanmar's prospects, both the Obama administration and interested members of Congress remain cautiously optimistic for the most part despite the challenges Myanmar is facing. In the longer term, some administration officials indeed hope the US relationship with Myanmar will be even stronger than the strategic partnership Washington aims to forge with Vietnam. The problem for the administration is that more and more members of Congress, following a period of relative restraint on Burma-related issues, have become very insistent that Myanmar's power-holders do more to break with the era of military rule. For instance, Senator Marco Rubio (Republican from Florida), the ranking member of the Senate Subcommittee on East Asian and Pacific Affairs, already in 2013 noted "significant backsliding" and insisted that Washington should not "continue to reward Burma for pledges it has not implemented."[77] In other words, while the administration may be interested in pushing for the further deepening of bilateral relations with Myanmar, various well-positioned Congresspeople aim to ensure that lawmakers do not surrender control over the next chapter in US-Myanmar ties. Key positions expressed in Congress are of course shared by the administration anyway, but in many ways certain members of Congress are less pragmatic in dealing with the developing situation in Myanmar.

As the 2015 elections draw closer, the question of what constitutional amendments Myanmar's parliament might agree on is assuming ever greater importance for US officials and policymakers, particularly as regards the reform of Article 59f. The reason is twofold: first, as suggested, there is a strong sense across much of Washington that Aung San Suu Kyi deserves and ought to be Myanmar's next president. Since she has herself unequivocally declared her interest in becoming president, there is significant support for her position, especially in Congress. While, according to the 2008 constitution, it would be for Myanmar's parliament and, after that, its people to decide on constitutional change, it should probably be assumed that the administration has already indicated to Naypyitaw that Washington would very likely strongly object if Aung San Suu Kyi's eligibility was not sanctioned in time by Myanmar's legislators. Perhaps administration officials have also pointed in this regard to the limited legitimacy enjoyed by the country's present parliament in international eyes given that the 2010 elections were considered neither free nor fair, and 25 percent of parliamentarians are military appointees. This would broadly chime with the position and expectations adopted by congressional heavyweights such as Senator McConnell. While, strictly speaking, the Myanmar government does not control decisions on future constitutional amendments, bilateral relations may suffer regardless if certain key US expectations are not met.

Congress does continue to constrain the administration, too, however, which will also impact bilateral ties. Since late 2013, against the backdrop of emerging calls in favor of US-Myanmar military-to-military cooperation, congressional resistance to the administration's perceived lax approach to human rights violations in Myanmar has visibly increased, in part because for many a congressperson and human rights advocate, bilateral military-to-military cooperation represents the last remaining keystone of US leverage vis-à-vis Naypyitaw. Toward the very end of 2013, Senator Robert Menendez, chairman of the Foreign Relations Committee, thus introduced legislation to prevent Department of Defense funds for security assistance to Burma without Naypyitaw first meeting core demands, such as civilian oversight of the armed forces, constitutional amendments, and greater *tatmadaw* restraint as well as improvements in behavior.[78] The legislation explicitly only allows for basic training on human rights and disaster relief. An identical bill was introduced soon thereafter in the House by Representatives by Joseph Crowley, a long-time critical voice on Burma, and Steve Chabot, chairman of the House Subcommittee on Asia and the Pacific; and a revised version clarifying precisely the extent of the security assistance to be denied was subsequently referred to the House Committee on Foreign Affairs in an apparent attempt to maintain a tight leash on the administration regarding the development of military-to-military relations.[79] Congress has also explicitly focused on the situation in Rakhine State. In May 2014, the House agreed to a simple resolution that calls on the Myanmar government to end all forms of persecution and discrimination of the Rohingya people, to recognize the Rohingya as an ethnic group indigenous to Burma, and to work with the Rohingya to resolve their citizenship status.[80] Senator Menendez followed this up by a publicly released letter sent to President Thein Sein. At the very least, the renewed greater congressional activism and pressure has also forced the administration to insist vis-à-vis Naypyitaw that progress be attained in relevant areas and to accept, at least for now, congressional limits to further developing the bilateral relationship with Myanmar.

Yet the likelihood of winning further key concessions from Naypyidaw is not straightforward. While Myanmar's present government seems intent on further improving relations with Washington, both nationalism and suspicions of foreigners continue to shape Naypyitaw's foreign policy outlook. Moreover, even Ambassador Mitchell has readily admitted that legacies of the pre-2011 mindset regarding US-Myanmar ties remain, a mindset that was built on fear and alienation.[81] Importantly, the current state of US-Myanmar relations arguably already serves Naypyitaw's interests quite well. Above all, the substantial easing of US sanctions has paved the way for new US investments and a resumption of exports to the US market. The fact that the underlying authorities for sanctions generally remain would not appear to be too much of an issue, not least because the Myanmar leadership sees US policy toward Naypyitaw as being increasingly shaped by regional as well as geopolitical considerations rather than simply by moral or ideological drivers. Another major benefit of the United States's engagement policy is that it has also helped Naypyitaw turn a corner in many of its other diplomatic ties—the benefits derived from much improved relations with Japan are particularly notable—and that international financial institutions have returned to work with the government.[82] Taking these factors into account, it seems that while Myanmar has a big stake in the continued development of relations with Washington, the latter may not find it as easy as before to bring Naypyitaw to make more challenging political compromises, even with appeals that would make reference to Myanmar's international status. This applies in particular to issues on which the Thein Sein government feels it cannot compromise.

Myanmar Foreign Policy

If things go well, however, how close could bilateral ties get? In foreign policy terms, Washington's engagement policy vis-à-vis Myanmar—though it preceded the rhetoric of the "pivot to Asia" and US "rebalancing"—fits well with the Obama administration's broader ambition to strengthen the US presence in East Asia.[83] Engagement has certainly made for a more coherent approach toward Southeast Asia, which tends to be regarded as the key addressee of the US rebalance toward the Asia-Pacific. The more interesting question is, however, whether the significant improvements in bilateral relations between Washington and Naypyitaw signal a major departure from Myanmar's traditional foreign policy posture.

From independence, Burma/Myanmar's declared foreign policy has been one of neutralism or nonalignment.[84] Even during the SPDC era, when US intervention was considered possible, the military government described its foreign policy as independent, active, and nonaligned, though in practice it pursued a rather passive position vis-à-vis the major powers that arguably entailed a form of limited alignment with China.[85] That said, China has historically been viewed with considerable suspicion and especially the increasing reliance on China in the economic sphere in the 2000s has been understood as an important factor for the Thein Sein government to embrace reforms and to open up vis-à-vis Washington.

Significantly, from Naypyitaw's perspective, better ties with Washington seem primarily designed to achieve greater balance in the country's foreign relations in line with the ideas of independence and nonalignment. Indeed, improved relations with Washington have been for Naypyitaw the catalyst to strengthen simultaneously various external relationships, not least with Japan, European powers, and Australia. The Thein Sein government is also keen to upgrade its role within ASEAN, not least because it assumed the organization's chair in 2014. Such balance in its foreign relations is meant to avoid future exploitation and to build national resilience.

Though Naypyitaw has sought to escape China's growing stranglehold over the Myanmar economy and the political dangers of serious economic dependency, Myanmar's government retains an interest in cooperative and stable relations with Beijing. Indeed, notwithstanding real problems in the bilateral relationship with China both past and present, the Thein Sein government is not about to seriously entertain the idea of pushing for the kind of strategic cooperation with Washington that some other Southeast Asian countries have sought. From Naypyitaw's perspective, much improved political ties with the United States are already sufficient to change the calculations of other powers about Myanmar, including China. This is likely to lead Naypyitaw to develop military-to-military relations with all major powers, including China.

Whether any serious foreign policy restructuring might be pursued by Myanmar in the future will remain to be seen. Should Aung San Suu Kyi succeed in becoming the next president, which cannot be taken for granted, she might, as is imagined by some, in practice want to "lean" more toward the West given her many and close personal ties with members of the political elites in the UK and the United States. Indeed, at least for now, her relations with the ASEAN countries and China are weak and her interest and efforts in seriously developing these have been almost negligible to date. That said, Aung San Suu Kyi should probably not be expected to be able to comprehensively prevail over the views and advice of the bureaucracy and military in foreign policy and security matters, and both are not likely to favor a major departure from traditional tenets of foreign policy.

Conclusion

Following a successful rapprochement during the first term of the Obama administration, US-Myanmar relations have improved quickly and beyond initial expectations. Now, however, bilateral ties are more clearly defined as much by progress as by differences in perspective, values, and interests. They will therefore require careful management. The Obama administration seems prepared for this. At the same time, the administration has no interest in seeing Myanmar's reform policies remain "incomplete" because it sees these as serving as a model. Indeed, in advance of the 2012 Obama visit to Myanmar, the administration suggested there were important lessons to be learned for other authoritarian countries from Myanmar's preparedness to embrace comprehensive change. As then national security adviser Thomas Donilon indicated, if North Korea embraced denuclearization it would also find the United States a partner in reform.[86] Current assistant secretary Daniel Russel has reiterated the point that "Burma remains important to U.S. interests as a demonstration of the benefits that can accrue to a nation that pursues a progressive path to change."[87] Beyond just pointing to Myanmar as a model for other authoritarian states, the president has more recently also suggested that the role the United States played in initiating Myanmar's political transition highlights the kind of US leadership he thinks can be very successful. As the president said: "We're now supporting reform and badly needed national reconciliation through assistance and investment, through coaxing and, at times, public criticism. And progress there could be reversed, but if Burma succeeds we will have gained a new partner without having fired a shot. *American leadership*."[88]

As such, political stasis or even regression in Myanmar toward and beyond the 2015 elections would stand to expose the Obama foreign policy doctrine as ineffective, likely followed by a deterioration of bilateral ties. Such a turn of events would also be politically damaging to one of the main authors of recent US Burma policy, former secretary Clinton, should the latter decide to run for the White House in 2016. While the Obama administration should thus be expected to want to reinforce both Myanmar's internal reforms and strengthen bilateral relations with Naypyitaw, it is likely they will find for the time being in Naypyitaw a government and a military leadership that seem hesitant if not unwilling to cede as much political ground as they are asked to relinquish and which aim to actualize the country's declared independent and nonaligned foreign policy. Indeed, at least until 2015 the Myanmar government will aim to limit any great power competition over Myanmar by continuing to work for balanced relations with all.

Notes

1. For a contextualizing scholarly perspective, see, for instance, Michael Aung-Thwin and Maitrii Aung-Thwin, *A History of Myanmar Since Ancient Times: Traditions and Transformations* (London: Reaktion Books, 2012); also see Robert H. Taylor, *The State in Myanmar* (London: Hurst, 2009).

2. Madeleine Albright, *Madam Secretary: A Memoir* (New York: Pan Books, 2003), 201.

3. Colin L. Powell, "It's Time to Turn the Tables on Burma's Thugs," *Wall Street Journal*, 12 June 2003.

4. "Rice Names 'Outposts of Tyranny,'" *BBC News*, 19 January 2005.

5. Andrew Selth, "Even Paranoids Have Enemies: Cyclone Nargis and Burma's Fears of Invasion," *Contemporary Southeast Asia* 30, no.1 (December 2008): 379–402.

6. On Myanmar's security policy, see Tin Maung Maung Than, "Myanmar: Preoccupation with Regime Survival, National Unity, and Stability," in Muthiah Alagappa, ed. *Asian Security Practice: Material and Ideational Influences,* 390–416 (Stanford, CA: Stanford University Press, 1998); Andrew Selth, *Burma's Armed Forces: Power Without Glory* (Norwalk, CT: EastBridge, 2002); Morten B. Pedersen, *Promoting Human Rights in Burma: A Critique of Western Sanctions Policy* (Lanham, MD: Rowman & Littlefield, 2008), chapter 2. Also see Jürgen Haacke, *Myanmar's Foreign Policy: Domestic Influences and International Implications* (Abingdon: Routledge for IISS, 2006), and Renaud Egreteau, *Histoire de la Birmanie Contemporaine: Le pays des prétoriens* (Paris: Fayard, 2010).

7. Jürgen Haacke, "Explaining Change in U.S. Burma Policy: The Role of Foreign Policy Entrepreneurs," paper presented at London School of Economics, 19 February 2014; Priscilla Clapp, "Prospects for Rapprochement Between the United States and Myanmar," *Contemporary Southeast Asia* 32, no. 3 (December 2010): 409–426. Also see, for example, Michael Green and Derek Mitchell, "Asia's Forgotten Crisis: A New Approach to Burma," *Foreign Affairs* 86, no. 6 (November/December 2007): 147–158. Also David I. Steinberg, "The United States and Its Allies: The Problem of Burma/Myanmar Policy," *Contemporary Southeast Asia* 29, no. 2 (August 2007): 219–237.

8. See Section 7 of the Tom Lantos Block Burmese JADE Act of 2008, www.govtrack.us/congress/bills/110/hr3890/text.

9. See US Department of State, "Hillary Rodham Clinton Remarks at United Nations After P-5+1 Meeting," (New York, 23 September 2009).

10. On ASEAN and Myanmar, see, for instance, Stephen McCarthy, "Burma and ASEAN: Estranged Bedfellows," *Asian Survey* 48, no. 6 (2008): 911–935; Jürgen Haacke, "The Myanmar Imbroglio and ASEAN: Heading Towards the 2010 Elections," *International Affairs* 86, no. 1 (January 2010): 153–174; and Christopher Roberts, *ASEAN's Myanmar Crisis: Challenges to the Pursuit of a Security Community* (Singapore: ISEAS, 2010).

11. See Michael J. Green and Bates Gill, eds., *Asia's New Multilateralism: Cooperation, Competition, and the Search for Community* (New York: Columbia University Press, 2009); and Evelyn Goh, *The Struggle for Order: Hegemony, Hierarchy, and Transition in Post-Cold War East Asia* (Oxford: Oxford University Press, 2013).

12. Interview with Myanmar official, March 2012.

13. See David I. Steinberg, "The United States and Its Allies: The Problem of Burma/Myanmar Policy," *Contemporary Southeast Asia* 29, no. 2 (August 2007): 227.

14. David I. Steinberg, Testimony before Senate Foreign Relations Committee, Subcommittee on Asian and Pacific Affairs, 26 April 2012.

15. Among those who traveled were Senators John McCain, Mitch McConnell, and Joseph Lieberman as well as Representative Joe Crowley. See, for instance, Ron Corben, "US Senators Signal Conditional Support for Lifting Burma Sanctions," *Voice of America*, 20 January 2012.

16. David I. Steinberg, "Aung San Suu Kyi and U.S. Policy Toward Burma/Myanmar," *Journal of Current Southeast Asian Affairs,* no. 3 (2010): 36–37.

17. See, for instance, "Statement by President Obama on Burma's November 7 Elections," 7 November 2010. As the president put it, "Ultimately, elections cannot be credible when the regime rejects dialogue with opponents and represses the most basic freedoms of expression, speech, and assembly."

18. See Joseph Yun, Testimony before the House Committee on Foreign Affairs, Washington, DC, 2 June 2011.

19. See The White House, "Statement by President Obama on Burma," Bali, 18 November 2011.

20. See US Department of State, "Press Briefing by Secretary Clinton in Rangoon," 2 December 2011.

21. US Department of State, "Remarks," Hillary R. Clinton, Washington, DC, 13 January 2012, www.state.gov/secretary/rm/2012/01/180667.htm.

22. Joseph Yun, "U.S. Policy Toward Burma," Testimony before the Senate Committee on Foreign Relations, Subcommittee on East Asian and Pacific Affairs, Washington, DC, 26 April 2012.

23. US Department of State, "Recognizing and Supporting Burma's Democratic Reforms," Hillary Rodham Clinton, Washington, DC, 4 April 2012.

24. Also see The White House, "Statement by the President on Burma," 17 May 2012.

25. The president also signed a new executive order that allows the imposition of sanctions against those determined "to have engaged in acts that directly or indirectly threaten the peace, security, or stability of Burma, such as actions that have the purpose or effect of undermining or obstructing the political reform process or the peace process with ethnic minorities in Burma; to be responsible or complicit in, or responsible for ordering, controlling, or otherwise directing, or to have participated in, the commission of human rights abuses in Burma; to have, directly or indirectly, imported, exported, reexported, sold or supplied arms or related materiel from North Korea or the Government of North Korea to Burma or the Government of Burma; to be a senior official of an entity that has engaged in the foregoing acts."

26. The White House, "Remarks by President Obama at the University of Yangon," 19 November 2012.

27. Michael F. Martin, "U.S. Policy Towards Burma: Issues for the 113th Congress," Report R43035. (Washington, DC: Congressional Research Service, 12 March 2013).

28. USAID Press Office, "President Obama Announces US-Burma Partnership for Democracy, Peace and Prosperity," 19 November 2012.

29. Areas of emerging bilateral cooperation also extend to mine risk education. Washington has moreover funded training for better earthquake preparedness, helped explore potential partnership opportunities in the higher education sector, and agreed to initiate a Peace Corps program. The two sides also have been working on prisoner of war and missing in action (POW/MIA) issues (as approximately 730 Americans remain unaccounted for from World War II). The United States has also provided humanitarian assistance in Kachin State.

30. Daniel B. Baer, Statement to the hearing on "Rebalance to Asia: What Does It Mean for Democracy, Good Governance and Human Rights?" before the Subcommittee on East Asian and Pacific Affairs of the Committee on Foreign Relations of the United States Senate, 21 March 2013.

31. It was reported that Myanmar exports to the United States amounted to only US$1 million in the first quarter of 2013. See "Burma President Ends US Trip with Trade Deal," *VOA News,* 21 May 2013.

32. For a discussion of past IMET programs, see Mark S. Riley and Ravi A. Balaram, "The United States International Military Education and Training (IMET) Program with Burma/Myanmar: A Review of the 1980–1988 Programming and Prospects for the Future," *Asian Affairs: An American Review* 40, no. 3 (2013): 109–132.

33. Quoted in Tim McLaughlin, "US and Myanmar Up Military Engagement," *Myanmar Times*, 1 August 2013.

34. Lolita C. Baldor, "US Looking to Forge Military Ties with Burma," *Irrawaddy*, 2 June 2012.

35. In June 2013, the UK chief of defence staff General Sir David Richards visited Myanmar to focus on issues such as promoting human rights in the military, the role of the military in Myanmar's democratic transition, and security sector reform.

36. Murray Hiebert argued that "the United States has a narrow window of opportunity to establish a strategic foothold in Myanmar. Increasing military

engagement with Myanmar will give U.S. policymakers a more informed view of the military, its commander in chief and his closest advisers, and who is likely to succeed them." See Murray Hiebert and Phuong Nguyen, "Engaging Myanmar's Military: Carpe Diem Part II," *Commentary* (Washington, DC: Center for Strategic and International Studies, 5 September 2013).

37. Joseph Yun, "The FY 2014 Budget Request for the Bureau of East Asian and Pacific Affairs," Statement before the House Foreign Affairs Subcommittee on Asia and the Pacific, US Congress, Washington, DC, 16 May 2013.

38. See *US Congressional Record—Senate*, 1 August 2013, p. S6171

39. See *US Congressional Record—Senate*, 1 August 2013, p. S6172.

40. Tha Lun Zaung Htet, "We Will Work with Suu Kyi to Amend Constitution to 'Benefit State'—USDP," *Irrawaddy*, 16 May 2013.

41. The committee numbered 109 members, including 52 USDP members, 25 army representatives, and 7 NLD members. See Tha Lun Zaung Htet, "Burma's Constitutional Review to Stay Confidential Until Next Year," *Irrawaddy*, 28 August 2013.

42. Republic of the Union of Myanmar, *Pyidaungsu Hluttaw*, Notification 59/2013, 27 August 2013.

43. Anne Gearan, "Burma's Thein Sein Says Military 'Will Always Have a Special Place' in Government," *Washington Post*, 20 May 2013.

44. Lawi Weng, "In Naypyitaw, Suu Kyi Attends Armed Forces Day," *Irrawaddy*, 27 March 2013.

45. Soe Than Lynn, "A Tactical Retreat," *Myanmar Times*, 14 October 2013.

46. Kyaw Yin Hlaing, "Understanding Recent Political Changes in Myanmar," *Contemporary Southeast Asia* 34, no. 2 (2012): 211.

47. See Ye Tun, "How the USDP Can Avoid a Landslide Loss in 2015," *Myanmar Times*, 8 July 2013.

48. For analysis and discussion, see Chapter 8.

49. For details, see International Crisis Group, "A Tentative Peace in Myanmar's Kachin Conflict," *Asia Briefing* No. 140 (Brussels: ICG, 12 June 2013).

50. US Embassy Rangoon, "Press Release: Union Government-Kachin Independence Organization (KIO) Peace Talks," 31 May 2013.

51. For details, see, for instance, www.mmpeacemonitor.org

52. "US Ambassador Conveys Urgent Concern over Kachin," *Irrawaddy*, 9 January 2013.

53. US Embassy Rangoon, "Ongoing Conflict in Burma's Kachin State," 24 January 2013.

54. US Embassy Rangoon, "Ambassador Derek Mitchell Travels to Myitkina, Kachin State, October 24–26," 27 October 2013.

55. Samantha Michaels, "US Will 'Consider Seriously' Requests to Support Burma's Peace Process," *Irrawaddy*, 23 April 2014.

56. "Why Conflict Continues in Kachin State," *Eleven Myanmar*, 21 April 2014.

57. See, for instance, Khin Maung Saw, "The "Rohingyas"—Who Are They? The Origin of the Name 'Rohingya,'" in Uta Gärtner and Jens Lorenz, eds., *Tradition and Modernity in Myanmar* (Münster, Germany: Lit, 1994): 89–100; Maung Tha Hla, *Rohingya Hoax* (New York: Buddhist Rakhaing Cultural Association, 2009); Benjamin Zawacki, "Defining Myanmar's 'Rohingya Problem,'" *Human Rights Brief* 20, no. 2: 18–25.

58. Intercommunal tensions and violence have been a recurrent feature of the political history of both colonial and postindependence Burma.

59. See, for instance, Tom Fawthrop, "State Complicity in Myanmar Pogroms," *Asia Times*, 1 July 2013; also see Aung Zaw, "Dangerous Days for Burma's Age of Reforms," *Irrawaddy*, 25 June 2013.

60. US State Deparment, "Background Briefing on the Secretary's Meeting with Burmese President Thein Sein, New York," 26 September 2012.

61. W. Patrick Murphy, Testimony before the Tom Lantos Human Rights Commission, Washington, DC, 28 February 2013.

62. "Daily Press Briefing," US Department of State, 4 January 2013.

63. Bamar acronym for "Border Immigration Headquarter." When founded, NaSaKa was part of (the former) military intelligence apparatus.

64. See Jacques Leider, "The Muslims in Rakhine and the Political Project of the Rohingyas: Historical Background of an Unresolved Communal Conflict in Contemporary Myanmar," *Network Myanmar*, 18 October 2012, www.networkmyanmar.org/images/stories/PDF13/jl-18october2012.pdf.

65. See "Final Report of Inquiry Commission on Sectarian Violence in Rakhine State," 8 July 2013, 54.

66. International Crisis Group, "The Dark Side of Transition: Violence Against Muslims in Myanmar," *Asia Report* No. 251 (Brussels: ICG, 1 October 2013): 7. On Rakhaing Buddhist nationalism, also see Jacques Leider, "'Rohingya,' Rakhaing and the Recent Outbreak of Violence—A Note," *Network Myanmar*, 2012, www.networkmyanmar.org/images/stories/PDF15/Leider-Note.pdf.

67. See Matthew J. Walton, "Buddhism Turns Violent in Myanmar," *Asia Times*, 2 April 2013; Kyaw San Wai, "Myanmar's Religious Violence: A Buddhist 'Siege Mentality' at Work," *RSIS Commentary*, 20 February 2014; also see Maung Zarni, "Buddhist Nationalism in Burma," 26 March 2013.

68. Anjana Pasricha, "Aung San Suu Kyi Explains Silence on Rohingyas," *Voice of America*, 15 November 2012. In October 2013, Suu Kyi fell foul of some media commentators when she rejected flatly that what was happening in Rakhine State amounted to ethnic cleansing and also seemed to explain the use of violence by Buddhists against Muslims with reference to a "perception of global Muslim power."

69. Bureau of Democracy, Human Rights, and Labor, "Burma," *Country Reports on Human Rights Practices for 2013* (Washington, DC: US Department of State, 27 February 2014), 1.

70. See International Institute for Strategic Studies, *Preventing Nuclear Dangers in Southeast Asia and Australasia* (London: IISS, 2009), chapter 7.

71. Saw Yan Naing, "Shwe Mann Denies Nuclear Program," *Irrawaddy*, 7 December 2011.

72. Julian Borger, "Burma Suspected of Forming Nuclear Link with North Korea," *The Guardian*, 21 July 2009.

73. US Department of State, "Fact Sheet: Administration Eases Financial and Investment Sanctions on Burma," 11 July 2012.

74. Joseph Yun, "U.S. Policy Toward Burma." Testimony before the House Committee on Foreign Affairs, US Congress, Washington, DC, 26 April 2012.

75. Derek Mitchell, "Ambassador-Designate to Burma," Statement before the Senate Foreign Relations Committee, US Congress, Washington, DC, 27 June 2012.

76. Andrew Selth, "Burma and North Korea: Again? Still?" *The Interpreter*, 10 July 2013.

77. Marco Rubio, "Rubio Presses for Human Rights as Burma's President Visits U.S.," Press release, 20 May 2013.

78. See S.1885 (Burma Human Rights and Democracy Act of 2013), 20 December 2013.

79. Compare texts of H.R. 4377, Burma Human Rights and Democracy Act of 2014, introduced 2 April 2014, and H.R. 3889, Burma Human Rights and Democracy Act of 2014, introduced 15 January 2014.

80. H.Res. 418: Urging the Government of Burma to end the persecution of the Rohingya people and respect internationally recognized human rights for all ethnic and religious minority groups within Burma, 7 May 2014.

81. Derek Mitchell, Remarks at the Myanmar Institute of Strategic and International Studies, 27 May 2014.

82. See David I. Steinberg, "Japan and Myanmar: Relationship Redux," *Japan Chair Platform* (Washington, DC: Center for Strategic and International Studies, 15 October 2013).

83. See, for instance, Robert S. Ross, "US Grand Strategy, the Rise of China, and US National Security Strategy for East Asia," *Strategic Studies Quarterly* 7, no. 2 (Summer 2013): 20–40.

84. William C. Johnstone, *Burma's Foreign Policy: A Study in Neutralism* (Cambridge, MA: Harvard University Press, 1963); Chi-shad Liang, *Burma's Foreign Relations: Neutralism in Theory and Practice* (New York: Praeger, 1990).

85. For relevant works, see John Ciorciari, *The Limits of Alignment: Southeast Asia and the Great Powers Since 1975* (Washington, DC: Georgetown University Press, 2010); Jürgen Haacke, "The Nature and Management of Myanmar's Alignment with China: The SLORC/SPDC Years," *Journal of Current Southeast Asian Affairs* 30, no.2 (2011): 105–140. Also see Chapter 12 in this volume.

For further discussion, see Maung Aung Myoe, *In the Name of Pauk-Phaw: Myanmar's China Policy Since 1948* (Singapore: ISEAS, 2011), and David I. Steinberg and Hongwei Fan, *Modern China-Myanmar Relations: Dilemmas of Mutual Dependence* (Copenhagen: NIAS Press, 2012).

86.Thomas Donilon, "President Obama's Asia Policy and Upcoming Trip to the Region," Speech at CSIS, 15 November 2012.

87. Daniel R. Russel, Assistant Secretary-Designate, Statement before the Senate Foreign Relations Committee, 20 June 2013.

88. Barack Obama, Remarks at U.S. Military Academy–West Point, New York, 28 May 2014. My emphasis.

14

The Road Toward Change and Development

David I. Steinberg

In the preceding chapters we have explored a number of issues that the Republic of the Union of Myanmar will face over the next decade, and perhaps beyond. These are basic questions, rooted in the past, with ramifications in the present, and with future negative consequences if unaddressed. Progress in any society is subject to the vagaries of time, place, conditions, critical actors, and the international environment, and is likely to be uneven, with troughs and peaks unpredictable. Unintended consequences are likely to occur. Yet, recognition of potential problems is a necessary first step to mitigating them, and their amelioration is required if the complex of societies known as Myanmar is to progress.

This concluding chapter is neither a guide for the perplexed foreigner nor one for the concerned Myanmar citizen. It would be imprudent to speculate on potential progress in any specific sector, but it is safe to predict that all the factors addressed in this volume will interact in arcane ways and also will be affected by a wide variety of other forces that this volume could not address because of space and time, but which its authors acutely recognize. Burmese interpretations of their many cultures will no doubt affect politics, the functions of governance, issues of law and justice, social and economic roles, problems and potential solutions, and the explicit efforts to cope with multicultural issues; historical impedimenta matter. Starting *de novo* is not possible, even if the institutional memory of many states' official circles may be less than lucid. And, if institutional memories may be wanting, ethnic and personal memories linger and affect the future. So the lacunae and errors of the past and present remain relevant.

Burman culture and conditions are sui generis. Similarities do exist with other states that have a Buddhist tradition, experienced colonial occupation, attempted to resolve national identity with reified ethnic nationalism, are subjected to many geopolitical influences, and have experienced rapid modernization. These similarities may provide clues, although not models, for Myanmar has had a unique configuration of these forces historically and at a singular contemporary point that make rigid adherence to regional or ideal models more than questionable—perhaps even dangerous.[1] Yet there remains in many circles worldwide the search for simplistic formulas for developmental or political success, whatever these terms may connote. The realistic journey is thus without maps, but some guideposts are clear, some potholes evident.

Many of the issues are known to both domestic and foreign officials and observers, but recognition alone is not necessarily policy, and the forces for positive change in any society may be met with distinct and vigorous protestations, and with ambiguous outcomes. This has already become obvious in the three years since reform started in Myanmar, and these tensions are likely to increase in the near term with elections in the offing in 2015. The near term will also affect the "out years," as officials often refer to the future.

The dangers to progress in any field in Myanmar are apparent—well understood internally by many. Those expressed in the previous chapters need no explication or repetition here. The deficiencies of the state and its government and organs have been articulated by the government itself and its leaders. This concluding chapter, instead, addresses some of the potential issues that characterize assistance to Myanmar in its transition, and is based in part on experience from other developing states.

Underneath international goodwill and foreign assistance lurk a set of potential issues. Modern seasoned foreign observers have generally shed the bizarre anthropomorphic prejudices of many of their predecessors, who judged non-Western societies' value and progress as religiously and technologically interpreted—Christianity and mechanization were signs of civilization.[2] Yet a type of institutional anthropomorphism, a more subtle arrogance, has reasserted itself. Foreigners often prescribe the organizational configuration and policies that are to be the universal panacea for development and progress, but that may be in subtle or obvious conflict with local societal norms or political realities. Likely are also developmental "fads," where certain programs become fashionable whether or not relevant to the society under consideration. These externally designated criteria extend also to political and social institutions as well as those economic. This phenomenon is not limited to state or multilateral organizations, but has been apparent in the nonprofit sector as well. Aid organizations often demand institutional changes, theoretically the better to be effective, but also the easier to administer and monitor their programs.[3] These may have deleterious effects as well as structural advantages. They need to be carefully weighed, as historical evidence indicates.[4] Foreigners have the marbles, some of them say in effect, so they determine the rules of the game. In certain circumstances it may be better not to play. Too much assistance might be as much of a problem as too little; too many strings may be as destructive as too few.

The reform process will continue at a pace politically acceptable to the Myanmar government. How to anticipate, understand, and accommodate such a pace requires a deft understanding of the sociopolitical realities, likely shifting over time. The issues on which concerned foreigners need focus are the reforms that the Myanmar people and government have articulated they want to achieve, the stated goals that they have set, and how ignoring these vital issues will undermine attaining local ends, not necessarily what external organizations believe the country needs, which often reflect their own experiences. Many of these issues overlap, and agreement on some are easy—better education, improved health care, increased capacity in almost every field, and similar efforts—but others, such as peace with ethnic groups, require finesse and knowledge of Burmese realities.

Specialists agree that institutions in Myanmar are generally weak. In part this is because the *tatmadaw* over the years destroyed other organizations that might have assumed important roles and threatened their power, such as an independent judicial system or a vital legislature. Those resuscitated, such as a vibrant legislative system, need assistance; those planned, such as an independent judiciary, will need concentrated attention. Loyalty was considered more important than subject matter competence. But more fundamental is the personalization of power—a common characteristic of many developing societies. Concentration of authority in the hands of a single individual is not the product of military rule, although that characteristic has been accentuated under its domination. Personalized power was true historically, in the civilian period, and currently in the political party process.[5] This creates a dynamic that is difficult to overcome, partly because of the individual at the apex of any institution, but also because of the actions of subordinates who reinforce this tendency (and perhaps foreigners who contribute to this process). Despite this reality, because we focus on the future, this volume does not concentrate on the individuals of the moment: President Thein Sein, Speaker Thura Shwe Mann, Aung San Suu Kyi, former senior general Than Shwe, Commander-in-Chief General Min Aung Hlaing, or others. We should be watching the growth of new institutions, the resuscitation of old ones, and the emergence of new leaders who may attenuate the personalized problems of the past; as institutions are strengthened, loyalties may accrue to them rather than to their leaders. But personalities are likely to remain dominant for a considerable period.

As we look beyond the present and the immediate future, some domestic leaders and foreign observers and governments have called for amending the constitution, which requires approval by both three-quarters of the legislature and a national referendum. Many articles of the constitution, and not simply those on the role of the military or the requirements for the presidency, need review. But the deliberative process of review needs study, and the constitution adjusted to meet new requirements to make it germane—not simply a means for institutional domination, or an anachronistic ideal, or a fig leaf for public relations, internal or external. It need not be moribund or irrelevant. To completely dismiss it, as some have suggested, has twice occurred in Burma/Myanmar's relatively short independence period; dismissal would continue unfortunate precedents. As a distinguished Thai said to me many years ago as we passed the monument in Bangkok, "We only put up monuments to dead things." Myanmar does not need that quip in the future.

One constitutional issue in the period before the elections of 2015 is how much central authority to devolve to the various peripheries. Some form of "federalism" has been a demand of most ethnic groups and was an element in the National League for Democracy's political platform in 1989. Yet, since at least 1962 the military has regarded it, as General Ne Win said, as the first step toward secession—a concept inimical to the *tatmadaw*. This view has gradually changed under President Thein Sein, but its resolution is not yet in sight and will undoubtedly figure prominently in the coming years. This disagreement has been based on an absence of shared trust—so evidently lacking since independence. Yet some greater local authority is likely to emerge over time with the innovation of local legislatures as yet in their formative stage.

The question of federalism also evokes the conflict over which federalism was waged—a conflict that has left deep trauma and anger in many people. If the past is not forgotten, how does society achieve its resolution? This has been a primary question in the transitions from authoritarian rule to more plural political systems. In most cases, it has been exceedingly difficult. In other words, there may be a "rule of law" (with or without capital letters), but how does perceived justice differ from law? Can there be justice for those that have suffered at the hands of arbitrary rule? Calling for international and local courts to try those who have committed egregious acts in their official roles is foreclosed by current Myanmar law, and justice may elude many who should be held responsible. Yet attempting to impose the heavy hand of justice, should that even be possible, would likely jeopardize continued reforms and could lead to regression. Those who wielded power in the past still command directly and indirectly considerable influence and authority.[6] Although international models should generally be eschewed, perhaps the South African experience—a process devoted to truth and reconciliation through the exposition of multiple truths of many individuals—comes closest to a possible example.

We have omitted in this volume, but not ignored, a range of present problems that will extend into the future, and will to some degree unknown influence their resolution. How does the state, understandably determined to create a sense of national unity in a society that has exhibited highly centrifugal ethnic tendencies, develop an educational system that encourages unity but at the same time recognizes that divergent languages and cultures are the determining elements of ethnic identity and that these factors define their concepts of the legitimacy of the central government?[7] Educational diversity has been vigorously fought by the center and yet a national ethos is lacking. Although much attention will be placed on extending and improving primary and secondary education, and significant assistance is expected from a number of foreign donors, the problems are so pervasive that continued reforms are likely to be required for a decade or more. Two generations of Burmese youth have been badly educated.

How does Myanmar deal with its internally displaced persons and its external multifaceted diaspora? In the eastern portion of the country alone half a million have been uprooted. Others abound in the north and in the west. The diaspora is even more complex. Some two million Burmese workers in Thailand, mostly low skilled and exploited, have little incentive to return to Myanmar where jobs are lacking and fears persist. Another half million educated Burmese range over Asia, Europe, North America, and Australia. They have been invited back, and some high-profile, exceptionally skilled individuals have returned. But although Burmese from the previous military administrations have a constitutional provision protecting them from punishment from actions taken in their official positions, there is no equivalent legal protection for those who may have fled the country illegally or engaged in what once was considered inappropriate political activities. Will these long-standing animosities dissipate on their return, or will cleavages deepen over conflicting visions of Myanmar's future processes and prospects?

The push toward urban migration by the landless, those perceived under local threat, and those in search of higher standards of living has not been balanced by the pull of expanding urban, labor intensive employment opportunities, as has happened in so many Asian nations. How will this affect the role and status of women, family stability, urban crime, and political volatility?

How will an expanding extractive industry and the increased generation of electric power to meet rising demand have impacts on Myanmar's relatively pristine environment? In 1988, Thailand banned logging because of disastrous landslides killing hundreds of villagers near Myanmar, and then immediately signed agreements to clear-cut teak resources on the Myanmar side of the border. The former prime minister of Thailand publicly said in 2010 that if Thailand continues to ban environmentally deleterious industries and ventures, Thai firms could look to undertake such projects in Myanmar. Chinese companies often do not undertake appropriate environmental assessments.

Myanmar was known as the critical factor in the "Golden Triangle"—the production of opium transformed into heroin for the international market. It ceded first place to Afghanistan, and reached a low point in production in 2006, but since then it has increased production beyond the capacity of the state to control. Myanmar's periphery has also flooded regional markets with methamphetamines. Agriculturally based opium production at least provides subsistence for some minorities in mountainous regions, but methamphetamines are chemically derived, profiting only the middlemen and dealers. But both indicate an inability of the state to control its periphery, and one questions whether increased local governance will improve or exacerbate the problem.

The intensification of foreign concerns over ethnic rights and conditions is a product of increasing worldwide sensitivity, the growth of public and private agencies monitoring such developments, and the end of the Cold War during which many internal ethnic issues were intentionally sheltered from internal or external criticism or review in the interest of national "unity" in international politics. Ethnic violence and unrest in Myanmar have become the most important focal point of foreign concerns as reforms in other fields have progressed. Progress is evident but the needs are acute.

Opponents of military rule, and advocates of better human rights, have seized this quintessential national problem as a means to criticize the Burmese state in an effort to slow international support to the Thein Sein government. They are accurate in their assessment of the issue, but they neglect history, which the Burmese have a penchant for recalling. Not only is internal trust lacking among ethnic groups for varied and substantial reasons, but central government distrust of foreigners and their dealings with ethnic issues remains high. All the states (except Laos) surrounding Burma/Myanmar have at some time supported insurgencies or dissidents and provided safe havens for opposition groups. Some foreigners joined and supplied ethnic independence movements. The UK and the United States assisted some of those groups, ranging from the early days of independence when British elements supported the Karen and the United States clandestinely buoyed Chinese Nationalist (KMT) troops in Burma. China has supported the Burma Communist Party until its internal collapse in 1989. Well into the first Obama administration, the United States helped dissidents located in Thailand. Foreign Christian groups have helped ethnic coreligionists, as have Muslim organizations. No wonder, therefore, that key Burmese officials are concerned with foreign involvement in ethnic matters. The prime military mantra has been the protection of national unity. It is not irrelevant to recall that for a score of years US policy was for regime change in Myanmar, and there were palpable (obviously erroneous) fears of a United States–led invasion. Also, in the aftermath of Cyclone Nargis in 2008, an effort was made to apply the UN doctrine R2P (Responsibility to Protect; intervention to assist people without that state's approval), which many in the *tatmadaw* felt would be the excuse for regime change.

The question of the most appropriate and equitable manner of dealing with the various ethnic groups in the state—specifically, the sharing of power and resources in this series of complex societies—remains, as previously noted, the single most important issue facing the state since independence. Scholars have argued that colonial power brought ethnicity to the fore, when before the Europeans entered the scene identities were fluid and continuously changing with the social context; it simply was one of a number of local issues. However accurate that may be, the re-reification of ethnic identity and nationalism has paralleled the increase in Burman nationalism—that of the majority and its power structure. This has become apparent in the formation of a multitude of ethnic political parties; their roles are likely to increase.

But how is ethnicity defined among culturally plural and interlocking populations? This is likely to be an unresolved problem in the 2014 census. Although this issue is relevant in other countries in Southeast Asia, in Myanmar it has been particularly acute, and unpleasant memories are not simply residual. A former head of state, Senior General Saw Maung (1988–1992), said that a million people had been killed in internecine political and ethnic strife since independence in 1948. Burma/Myanmar had the longest insurrection in the modern world (the Karen, 1949–2012). In addition to two communist rebellions that persisted for some score and a half years, over seventeen ethnic insurgencies of varying size and intensity led to a situation that deprived the people and their state from development.

These memories of mistrust, rapacious military offensives, and civilian atrocities will not be quickly erased—indeed, some analysts argue that the recent surge in sectarian violence may be linked with increased and unequally distributed resources flooding into the state; from this perspective, massive development assistance may exacerbate tensions.[8] The Thein Sein administration has attempted in late 2013 to create a national cease-fire for the first time since independence, but cease-fires are not peace treaties, and some equitable (*Myanmar-lo,* in a Burmese manner), solution to the local-national authority nexus and financial distribution of assets has yet to be negotiated. This looms large into the future. As Martin Smith wrote in the last sentence of his monumental ethnic study, "It is to be hoped, then, that this will be the generation that finally achieves solutions—and a real and lasting peace."[9]

A tendency to ignore the Rohingya, a Muslim minority on the Bangladesh border, is evident in any discussion within Myanmar of the ethnic issues facing the state. In part this is because this group is not legally and popularly considered citizens, but rather Bengali interlopers, and even the term *Rohingya* is abhorred in state documents and in the media, and is considered a foreign, even an American, term.[10] Yet this is the singular minority problem in Myanmar on which international attention is now focused. How Myanmar will be judged in certain Western circles will to some considerable degree be determined by the government's handling of this most explosive humanitarian issue. Although the Muslim dilemma is explored in Chapter 6, and mentioned in the discussion of ethnic issues in

Chapter 7, this issue transcends both the general Muslim and ethnic questions facing the state.

The Rohingya are probably the most deprived people in East Asia. No evident solution to this problem has been forthcoming from the government, in part because of the strong anti-Rohingya and anti-Muslim prejudice in Burman (Bamar) society exacerbated by the forthcoming 2015 elections, for politicians of all stripes recognize the strength of this sentiment. During the 2014 census, 135 "ethnic" groups were identified, but the term *Rohingya* was not allowed even under the 136th category—"other" (nonindigenous ethnic nationalities). Even strong Burmese proponents of democracy regard the Rohingya as foreigners. Bangladesh refuses to consider them as its responsibility and will not negotiate their status or allow them legal residency.

Muslims have lived in the Rakhine (Arakan) region for a number of centuries, but their numbers have grown and their history is more than complex. Since British Burma was governed as a province of India until 1937, India-to-Burma migration was open and not an obviously controversial issue in Arakan at that time. Conflicts in the frontier area during World War II, however, exacerbated the dilemma, and various Rakhine, Muslim "Mujahid," and communist insurgencies followed the British departure in 1948.[11] Opposition then revived following General Ne Win's 1962 military coup, with many Muslim leaders (although not all) promoting the ethnic nationality Rohingya term of identity for Muslim communities in the north of the territory—a designation that the post-1962 government as well as most Rakhines rejected. Under the 1982 Citizenship Law, full citizenship rights were denied to those who could not prove family ancestry in the country before the first British annexation in 1824,[12] and government military and police sweeps into the northern borderlands in 1978 and 1991–1992 led to over 200,000 refugees fleeing into Bangladesh on each occasion, most of whom were later repatriated under UN auspices.

The exact number of Rohingya are not known, but popular estimates center around some 800,000 in the border townships near Bangladesh. In an exodus that is still continuing, many thousands have fled by boat in recent years to Thailand and Malaysia in an unprecedented attempt to escape their poverty, degradation, and oppression. Since the Thein Sein government assumed office, around 140,000 civilians have been internally displaced (mostly Muslims) and over 250 persons (also predominantly Muslims) have been reportedly killed in a Buddhist-Muslim crisis that has spread from its Rohingya roots to several parts of the country, including Meiktila and Lashio.[13] Furthermore, Western humanitarian and medical aid efforts to mitigate their conditions have led Rakhine Buddhists, who also perceive themselves as a neglected minority, to complain about discrimination against Buddhists, fueling anti-Muslim sentiment more generally.[14] Amid tight border security, a low level (mostly very low) Rohingya insurgency has continued until the present day—as well as small-armed opposition among Rakhine-based groups. But because of geographic isolation, the community disruption and potential outbreaks of conflict do not internally threaten the power of the state, as do relations with other armed ethnic groups, but they do sustain humanitarian crisis and materially affect international relations with the West. Equally important, ethnic and religious instability in the borderlands with Bangladesh and the continuing outflow of Muslim refugees to Thailand, Malaysia, and other Asian countries remind that this crisis has greater international importance.

If there is not significant mitigation of the plight of the Rohingya, the Myanmar government will be subject to severe condemnation in spite of the multitude of reforms already implemented and even should there be a national cease-fire with all the armed ethnic groups, of which the Rohingya are not included. A dilemma for foreign states is that the more complaints against the Burmese state are focused on this problem, the less credibility such governments have in suggesting other reforms. In a sense, there are two "imagined communities." To the Burmese, the Rohingya are all recent interlopers, but to the Rohingya advocates, they are centuries-old residents of the region. Both characterizations are inaccurate, and inflame mutual resentments.

In conflict resolution terms, too, the issue of anti-Muslim prejudice and violence will remain singularly difficult to resolve. Unlike conflicts between the state and ethnic armed groups, anti-Muslim violence is a product of deep-rooted prejudice across many sectors of Myanmar society, including ordinary Burmese citizens. Even during the present time of political change, it has continued to be expressed in intracommunal riots and violence. As experience elsewhere in the world has shown, this kind of conflict is less amenable to intra-elite political negotiation than are the country's ongoing ethnic insurgencies, which in principle could be resolved through political negotiations.

The more fundamental issue that should not be ignored, however, is the enduring popular anti-Indian (all those from the subcontinent) prejudice, as distinct from various positive government-to-government relations, that now focuses on Muslims (since Hindus do not attempt to convert others) who are popularly charged with attempts to subvert Burman culture and convert Buddhist women. Changing such attitudes will require a generation of strong, liberalized government in Naypyitaw to address the cultural aspects. The problem will fester and affect the next generation of leaders if ameliorating actions are not taken.

Myanmar is in transition—from a socialist to a market economy, from authoritarian to pluralistic rule, from a single party and then junta domination to a multiparty political system, from military control to shared civilian governance, from a unitary state to one less centralized, from single ethnic domination to a more pluralistic multicultural society, and from traditional rural-based poverty toward urban industrial growth and rural improvements. Evidence worldwide is that these transitions are never easy; asynchronous and uneven progress is likely, temporary regression in some areas probable. Change is disturbing to many, and fraught with difficulties. This should neither deter internal renovations nor foreign assistance. The realities, however, need to be addressed by all concerned.

Foreign assistance has been proffered by a wide range of institutions: multilateral, bilateral, and nongovernmental. The World Bank, the Asian Development Bank, the International Monetary Fund, the European Union, the United States, India, Japan, the Republic of Korea, Australia, as well as China and a number of smaller states, have all been delivering development assistance and promoting foreign investment. Each state pursues its national interests in Myanmar, but not often with altruistic motives. India is concerned over Chinese penetration, its access to the Bay of Bengal, and the fragility of relations with its northeast Indian population bordering Myanmar. China has considered Myanmar within its traditional sphere of interest, and access is integral to its national and Yunnan provincial goals, as well as partly obviating any possible blockage of the Straits of Malacca. It views any improvement of US relations with Myanmar as part of a second US attempt to "contain" China's rise. The primary policy rationale and driving force for US concerns about Burma/Myanmar were human rights and democracy, prompted by an effective lobby and the figure of Aung San Suu Kyi as the harassed avatar of democracy. Japan has concerns over extensive Chinese influence there, and has emotional and economic reasons for greater engagement. South Korea sees itself as a potential economic model for Myanmar and desires to gain market share and balance Japanese and any potential North Korean influence. ASEAN, previously embarrassed by Myanmar's human rights record, urges reform for the benefit of the regional community. Thailand especially sees major economic opportunities, and remains ambivalent about its potential loss of a low-cost labor force should Burmese return to Myanmar. Given the limited management capacities of the Myanmar government, too much assistance may be engendered too soon with problems for the state.[15]

Myanmar will continue to have close and friendly relations with China—a necessary condition of present international relations. China would do well to temper its often demonstrated cultural arrogance in negotiations with the Burmese, and the United States must be careful to avoid similar problems, but Myanmar will likely attempt to reinvent its Cold War neutralism reinterpreted to fit contemporary conditions; this appears to be in its national interests. US support to Myanmar's development will in part depend on how the Myanmar government continues its reform process.

Although the Chinese leadership independently may pursue a Myanmar policy, the US policy is in large part determined by its internal political considerations, and the Burma/Myanmar lobby is strong and active, and is likely to remain so if there are "backslidings" in Myanmar's reform process. It may be tempered by rising internal US business interests.

Specific policy recommendations for foreign assistance or internal reform for the years ahead are not feasible because of likely near-term internal changes and external priorities. Yet it is worthwhile to caution the purveyors of concepts and cash, wherever located, to recognize realities that should form the foundation of support to change. Whatever the field, sensitivities to Burmese history and national sentiment will remain the critical backdrop in any program or activity. Often treated with condescension by foreign powers, both Western and Asian, the Burman population is acutely aware of snubs and implicit insults, as are the ethnic groups in their relations with the majority Burmans.[16] A former Burmese foreign minister said that the Burmese were not donkeys—carrots and sticks were an insulting analogy.

Change and progress must be seen as internally derived no matter if implementation may financially be assisted from abroad. This has been true since independence and is not simply, as some might claim, a product of military pride, although the *tatmadaw* has been more vociferous in its statements.[17] Technical capacity and the acceptance of objective inquiry, destroyed for a half-century in the search for political conformity, needs resuscitation in an atmosphere that encourages open and analytical review. This will be especially difficult when Burmese core norms and values are subjected to internal scrutiny, as they will be by some elements of the population. With the newly articulated openness, the Burmese themselves will be exploring their own traditions and raising questions of social and intellectual change.

Foreign hortatory support to particular political systems, parties, or individuals—a predilection of militarily and economically strong and ideologically driven states and one that has been a hallmark of Western thinking and policy toward Burma/Myanmar since 1988—often results in simple slogans or even creates in this nationalistic environment adverse reactions often deleterious to the very goals such foreign public support is designed to advance, as it would if national fortunes were reversed. Political terms such as *federalism* or *democracy* as defined abroad may cause blowback, as different interpretations and definitions abound based on national cultural experiences or misunderstanding, whether they are known as "discipline-flourishing," "guided," "people's," or otherwise. The West's judgments have subjected Myanmar to far higher standards of governance than that of many of its neighbors. Many educated Burmese surely want more freedoms, but the subtleties of democratic processes and systems may be less understood since reading about such matters has been neglected, even prohibited, for half a century.

Foreign organizations, governmental and private, should be cautious in attributing progress to their own activities—taking credit for positive change. Although organizations generally must justify their activities to their sponsors and evaluation entities, the temptation to take credit should be resisted, as this too is a form of arrogance, intimating that the Burmese were incapable of understanding and acting to ameliorate their own dilemmas. Many foreigners still consider the reforms of 2011 and beyond as a direct result of their actions—sanctions or engagement. Both are likely to be erroneous. Such hubris is not only inaccurate, but it undercuts and diminishes the roles of those Burmese who have worked for reform. Even in the most dire times when candid public analyses were impossible, there were those, as demonstrated by the irreverent colonel cited in the introduction to this volume, who understood the problems but whose views were suppressed. Many more like him were forced to remain silent.

Diplomats often end dialogues stating that they are "cautiously optimistic." For half a century little if any intimations of optimism were heard about Myanmar. Yet since 2011, overtures have been made, opportunities for dialogue at high levels continue, good intentions from official and unofficial foreign observers are evident, the beginnings of a sense of movement, of increasing space between the state and the individual, dialogue among ethnic groups, and a sense of social and economic hope all are present. Few states have proceeded to invoke such extensive reforms so quickly without an overt revolution from below. Myanmar has made remarkable advances. Continued internal vigilance is essential, external support important. The momentum for progress is highly appreciated and, indeed, contagious. A feeling of progress achieved is not misplaced; a sense of cautious optimism is not amiss.

Notes

1. The reverse is sometimes true: some point to political reforms in Myanmar as a potential model for North Korea. This is more than unlikely. See David I. Steinberg, "Transforming 'Outposts of Tyranny'? Lessons and Cautions." Paper presented at the ASAN Institute conference on "Myanmar's Liberalization and North Korea," Seoul, March 2013.

2. Michael Adas, *Machines as the Measure of Man: Science, Technology, and the Ideology of Western Domination* (Ithaca: Cornell University Press, 1989).

3. This was recognized as a problem by the World Bank. See "World Bank Civil Society Engagement: Review of Fiscal Years 2005 and 2006," World Bank, 2006.

4. See Lant Prichett, "Looking Like a State: Techniques of Persistent Failure in State Capability for Implementation," *Journal of Development Studies* 49, no. 1 (2013): 1–18.

5. David I. Steinberg. "Legitimacy in Burma: Concepts and Implications." In N. Gamesan and Kyaw Yin Hlaing, eds., *Myanmar: State, Society and Ethnicity* (Singapore: The Hiroshima Peace Institute and the Institute for Southeast Asian Studies, 2007).

6. The evidence is apparent. After the opposition won the May 1990 elections, the spokesman for the National League for Democracy said there would be no Nuremberg Trials, but this so raised fears among the military that the elections were never recognized. Aung San Suu Kyi has eschewed retribution in her public statements.

7. This may be changing. "Mon State to Allow Ethnic [Mon] Language Classes in Govt Schools," *Irrawaddy*, 10 April 2014.

8. See Elliott Prasse-Freeman, "The Futile and Violent Search for Authenticity in Burma," *Democratic Voice of Burma*, 12 July 2013.

9. Martin Smith, *Burma: Insurgency and the Politics of Ethnicity,* 2nd edition (London: Zed Books, 1999), 453.

10. Personal interview with demonstrators for democracy. The official Rakhine inquiry commission report never uses *Rohingya* but only *Bengali*. "The Report of the Commission of Inquiry on the Sectarian Violence in Rakhine State," The Republic of the Union of Myanmar, 22 April 2013. The term *Rohingya* remains a subject of controversy. For reference to different studies and histories, see "Rohingya/Muslim Issues," www.networkmyanmar.org/index.php/rohingyamuslim-issues.

11. See, for example, Smith, *Burma* (1991 and 1999).

12. For a recent analysis, see Transnational Institute, "Ethnicity Without Meaning, Data Without Context: The 2014 Census, Identity and Citizenship in Burma/Myanmar," *Burma Policy Briefing* No. 13 (Amsterdam: Transnational Institute–Burma Centre Netherlands, February 2014).

13. See, e.g., "The Dark Side of Transition: Violence Against Muslims in Myanmar," *Asia Report* No. 251 (Brussels: International Crisis Group, 1 October 2013); "Policies of Persecution: Ending Abusive State Policies Against Rohingya Muslims in Myanmar," *Fortify Rights,* February 2014.

14. International Crisis Group, "Counting the Costs: Myanmar's Problematic Census," *Update Briefing, Asia Briefing* No. 14 (Brussels: ICG, 15 May 2014); Michel Gabaudan and Melanie Teff, "Myanmar: Act Immediately to Protect Displaced People's Rights," Refugees International, 17 March 2014.

15. See Lex Rieffel and James W. Fox, *Too Much, Too Soon? The Dilemma of Foreign Aid to Myanmar/Burma* (Arlington, VA: Nathan Associates, March 2013)

16. For a perceptive analogy, see Matthew Walton, "The Wages of Burmanness: Ethnicity and Burman Privilege in Contemporary Myanmar," *Journal of Contemporary Asia* 43, no. 1 (2013): 1–27. For cautions on antiforeign sentiment, see David I. Steinberg, "Myanmar: The Fire Next Time," *YaleGlobal Online,* February 2014, http://yaleglobal.yale.edu.

17. Since independence, the various Burmese governments have rejected making formal, public requests for assistance, although they may be made privately and/or informally. Such requests are perceived as humiliating and a subversion of national sovereignty.

Acronyms

AAPP	Assistance Association for Political Prisoners
ABMA	All Burma Monks Alliance
ADB	Asian Development Bank
AEC	ASEAN Economic Community
AFAFIST	ASEAN Framework Agreement on Facilitation of Inter-State Transport
AFAMT	ASEAN Framework Agreement on Multimodal Transport
AFPFL	Anti-Fascist People's Freedom League
AMRDP	All Mon Regions Democracy Party
ASEAN	Association of Southeast Asian Nations
ASEAN-BAC	ASEAN Business Advisory Council
ASW	ASEAN Single Window
ATIGA	ASEAN Trade in Goods Agreement
ATM	automatic teller machine
BCP	Burmese Communist Party
BGFs	Border Guard Forces
BSPP	Burma Socialist Programme Party
CBM	Central Bank of Myanmar
CBO	community-based organization
CESD	Center for Economic and Social Development
CinC	commander-in-chief
CNP	Chin National Party
CPP	Chin Progressive Party
CRPPFMS	Committee for Reform of the People's Police Force Management System
CSOs	civil society organizations
CSW	commercial sex workers
DDI	Directorate of Defense Industries
DIILS	Defense Institute for International Legal Studies
DP(M)	Democratic Party (Myanmar)
DPRK	Democratic People's Republic of Korea
DSA	Defence Services Academy
EAG	ethnic armed group
EFTPOS	Electronic Funds Transfer at Point of Sale
EITI	Extractive Industries Transparency Initiative
ERIA	Economic Research Institute for ASEAN and East Asia
EU	European Union

FDI	foreign direct investment
FESR	Framework for Economic and Social Reforms
FUP	Federal Union Party
FY	fiscal year
GUB	Government of the Union of Burma
HIV/AIDS	human immunodeficiency virus infection/acquired immunodeficiency syndrome
IDU	intravenous drug user
IMET	International Military Education Training
IMF	International Monetary Fund
INDP	Inn National Development Party
INTERPOL	International Criminal Police Organization
JADE	Junta's Anti-Democratic Efforts
KIA	Kachin Independence Army
KIO	Kachin Independence Organisation
KMT	Kuomintang
KNP	Kayan National Party
KNPP	Karenni National Progressive Party
KNU	Karen National Union
KPP	Kayin People's Party
KSDPP	Kayin State Democracy and Development Party
KTA	Knappen Tippetts Abbett (engineering firm that worked on the Pyidawtha Plan)
LNDP	Lahu National Development Party
MCDV	Myanmar Comprehensive Development Vision
MDRI	Myanmar Development Resource Institute
MESAP	Myanmar Economic Structural Adjustment Program
MIC	Myanmar Investment Commission
MMK	Myanmar kyat
MNCs	multinational corporations
MOB	Myanmar Oriental Bank
MP	Member of Parliament
MPC	Myanmar Peace Center
MPF	Myanmar Police Force
MPSI	Myanmar Peace Support Initiative
NBF	Nationalities Brotherhood Federation
NCCT	Nationwide Cease-Fire Coordination Team
NCDP	National Comprehensive Development Plan
NDF	National Democratic Force
NDPD	National Democratic Party for Development
NDSC	National Defense and Security Council
NESAC	National Economic and Social Advisory Council
NGOs	nongovernmental organizations
NLD	National League for Democracy
NMSP	New Mon State Party
NPED	National Planning and Economic Development (ministry)

NSAG	nonstate armed group
NUP	National Unity Party
OCMSA	Office of the Chief of Military Security Affairs
OFAC	Office of Foreign Assets Control
PLAN	Chinese People's Liberation Army Navy
PNO	Pa'O National Organization
PPF	People's Police Force
PPP	public-private partnership
PSDP	Phalon-Sawaw Democratic Party
R2P	Responsibility to Protect
RCSS	Restoration Council of the Shan State
RNDP	Rakhine Nationalities Development Party
RoL	rule of law
RUMFCCI	Republic of the Union of Myanmar Federation of Chambers and Commerce and Industry
SEZ	special economic zone
SLORC	State Law and Order Restoration Council
SMEs	small and medium enterprises
SNDP	Shan Nationalities Democratic Party
SNLD	Shan Nationalities League for Democracy
SOE	state-owned enterprise
SPDC	State Peace and Development Council
SSA-N	Shan State Army–North
SSMNC	State Sangha Maha Nayaka Council
TNI	Tentara Nasional Indonesia
TNLA	Taaung (Palaung) National Liberation Army
TPNP	Taaung (Palaung) National Party
UDPKS	Unity and Democracy Party (Kachin State)
UEC	Union Election Commission
UNA	United Nationalities Alliance
UNFC	United Nationalities Federal Council
UPWC	Union Peacemaking Work Committee
USAID	US Agency for International Development
USDA	Union Solidarity and Development Association
USDP	Union Solidarity and Development Party
UWSA	United Wa State Army
VPA	Vietnam People's Army
WA	ward administrator
WDP	Wa Democratic Party
YMCA	Young Men's Christian Association

Appendix A: Economic and Social Data

Essential data on key economic and social indicators are often lacking or have been manipulated for political purposes. All such estimates should be treated with a degree of caution.

The Myanmar fiscal year is April 1–March 31.

Country size 676,578 sq km[1]

Population Population estimates have varied from 49 to 60 million. Officially released figures from the 2014 census indicate that the total population is 51.4 million.[2]

Religion[3]

Buddhist	89.5%
Baptist	3.2%
Catholic	1.0%
Other Christian	0.7%
Hindu	0.5%
Muslim	3.9% (3.8% are Sunni)
Animist	1.1%

Ethnicity The state officially has 135 "races," "nationalities," or "ethnic groups." (The Burmese term *lu-myo*, literally person-type, may be differentially translated and often creates confusion among foreign observers. These 135 categorizations are based on linguistic dialect distinctions established in the colonial era.) In this volume, we typically use "ethnic groups" when discussing these diverse peoples. There are seven "states" (provinces) for major indigenous ethnic groups and six additional geographic subdivisions for some others; a significant number of smaller recognized identities are scattered throughout the country. The Rohingya of northwestern Rakhine State, not included in the list below,[4] are considered as stateless by the government. Known in official circles as Bengalis, they are excluded from citizenship based on the 1982 citizenship law.

Burman (Burmese)	69.0%
Kachin	1.4%
Kayah	0.4%
Karen	6.2%
Chin	2.2%
Mon	2.4%
Rakhine	4.5%
Shan	8.5%
Other indigenous	0.1%
Foreign and "mixed"	5.3%

Size of military 350,000 (estimated)

Size of police 72,000 (estimated)

Size of *sangha* (2012 estimate)[5]

Monks	265,204
Novices	291,293
Nuns	45,353

Economic data (2012-2013 estimates)[6]

Exchange rate (June 2014)	MMK952=US$1.00
Gross domestic product (GDP) (% change)	7.3%[7]
Consumer price index period average (% change)	2.8%
Consolidated public sector revenue (% of GDP)	23%
Consolidated public sector expenditure (% of GDP)	27.2%
Domestic public debt (% of GDP)	22.5%
Exports (% of GDP)	18.6%
Imports (% of GDP)	–22.4%
Trade balance (% of GDP)	–3.8%
Current account balance (% of GDP)	–4.4%
Gross official reserves	US$4.591 billion
Gross official reserves, in months of total imports	3.6
External debt	US$13.5 billion
GDP	US$55.8 billion
GDP per capita	US$876
Foreign exchange reserves	US$3.08 billion[8]
Foreign direct investment (% of GDP)	5%

Social and Development Indicators

Population living in urban areas	33.9%[9]
Population below poverty line	25.6%[10]
School life expectancy (primary to tertiary)	7 years[11]
Education expenditures (% of GDP)	1.6%
Defense expenditures (% of GDP)	4.4%
Human Development Index rank	149 of 186 countries

Notes

1. Central Intelligence Agency, "Myanmar," *World Factbook*, www.cia.gov/library/publications/the-world-factbook/geos/bm.html. (accessed 5 October 2013), under "Geography."
2. World Bank, *East Asia and Pacific Economic Update* (Washington: The World Bank, October 2013), 104.
3. *Burma 1983 Population Census*. (Rangoon: Ministry of Home and Religious Affairs, Immigration and Manpower Department, June 1983). A new census was conducted in March-April 2014. Its results will be available in 2015.
4. Ibid. Listed as "Race" in original publication.
5. Ministry of Information.
6. Unless otherwise stated, all economic data from International Monetary Fund, "Second Review Under the Staff-Monitored Program," *IMF Country Report* No. 14/91 (March 2014).
7. Staff estimate.
8. 31 December 2012 estimate.
9. 2010 estimate. Asian Development Bank, "Myanmar in Transition: Opportunities and Challenges" (Philippines: Asian Development Bank, 2012), 2.
10. 2010 estimate. Ibid.
11. Central Intelligence Agency. *World Factbook*.

Appendix B: Geographic Name Changes

Old Name	New Name
Akyab	Sittwe (city)
Arakan	Rakhine (state)
Chindwin	Chindwinn (river)
Irrawaddy	Ayeyarwady (region, river)
Karen	Kayin (state, ethnic group)
Magwe	Magway (region)
Maymyo	Pyin-U-Lwin (city)
Mergui	Myeik (city, archipelago)
Moulmein	Mawlamyine (city)
Pagan	Bagan (old capital)
Prome	Pyay (city)
Rangoon	Yangon (city, region)
Salween	Thanlwin (river)
Sandaway	Thandwe (city)
Tavoy	Dawei (city)
Tenasserim	Thanintharyi (region, river)

Bibliography

Adas, Michael. *Machines as the Measure of Man: Science, Technology, and the Ideology of Western Domination* (Ithaca: Cornell University Press, 1989).
Agaben, Giorgio. *State of Exception*. Chicago: Chicago University Press, 2004.
Alagappa, Muthiah. *Political Legitimacy in Southeast Asia: The Quest for Moral Authority.* Stanford, CA: Stanford University Press, 1995.
Albright, Madeleine. *Madam Secretary: A Memoir.* New York: Pan Books, 2003.
Anderson, Benedict. "The Javanese Idea of Power." In *Language and Power: Exploring Political Cultures in Indonesia.* Ithaca, NY: Cornell University Press, 1990.
Aolain, Fionnuala Ni, and Michael Hamilton. "Gender and the Rule of Law in Transitional Societies." *Minnesota Journal of International Law* 18 (2009).
Arter, David. "Introduction: Comparing the Legislative Performance of Legislatures." *Journal of Legislative Studies* 12, no. 3/4 (2006): 245–257.
Asian Development Bank. *Myanmar: Energy Sector Initial Assessment.* Manilla, Philippines: Asian Development Bank, October 2012.
Asian Development Bank–Accenture. *New Energy Architecture: Myanmar.* Manilla, Philippines: Asian Development Bank, June 2013.
Asian Human Rights Commission. "Burma's Cheap Muscle." Hong Kong: Asian Human Rights Commission, 13 March 2009.
———. "Burma/Myanmar: Courts, Cops, Cronies—The Three C's Driving Farmers to Ruin, and Jail." Hong Kong: Asian Human Rights Commission, 13 May 2014.
Aung, Hti La. "Burma and Democracy." *Ottama Journal,* no. 2 (January 2007).
"Aung San Suu Kyi—Remarks to Hawaii Community Leaders." Talk given 25 January 2013. Published 28 January 2013. Available at http://www.youtube.com/watch?v=6fvtItKzCBk.
Aung, Shwe. "Land Seized by Crony Companies to be Returned to Locals." *Democratic Voice of Burma (DVB).* 25 June 2013.
Aung-Thwin, Michael, and Maitrii Aung-Thwin. *A History of Myanmar Since Ancient Times: Traditions and Transformations.* London: Reaktion Books, 2012.
Baer, Daniel B. Statement to the hearing on "Rebalance to Asia: What Does It Mean for Democracy, Good Governance and Human Rights?" before the Subcommittee on East Asian and Pacific Affairs of the Committee on Foreign Relations of the United States Senate. 21 March 2013.

Bagshawe, L. E., translator. *Rajadhammasangaha*. Online Burma/Myanmar Library, 2004.

Baldor, Lolita C. "US Looking to Forge Military Ties with Burma." *Irrawaddy.* 2 June 2012.

Barkan, Joel D., ed. "African Legislatures and the Third Waves of Democratization." In Joel D. Barkan, ed., *Legislative Power in Emerging African Democracies,* 1–31. Boulder, CO: Lynne Rienner, 2009.

———. *Legislative Power in Emerging African Democracies.* Boulder, CO: Lynne Rienner, 2009.

Bayley, D. H. "The Police and Political Change in Comparative Perspective." *Law and Society Review* 6, no. 1 (August 1971): 91–112.

Bell, Derrick. "On the Jewish Question." Available at www.marxists.org /archive/marx/works/1844/jewish-question/.

———. *Race, Racism, and American Law*, 3rd edition. Boston: Little, Brown, 1992.

Benjamin, Walter. "Critique of Violence." In E. Jephcott, trans., *Reflections*. New York: Shocken Books, 1978.

Benjamin, Walter. "Theses on the Philosophy of History" (1940).

Benshoof, Janet. "Burma's New Threat to Global Security." *Democratic Voice of Burma.* 6 October 2011.

———. "It's Time for the International Community to Address Burma's Constitution." *Democratic Voice of Burma.* 20 February 2012.

"Big Shift to Dawei Predicted." Welcome to Dawei Sea Port website, 2013.

Borger, Julian. "Burma Suspected of Forming Nuclear Link with North Korea." *The Guardian*. 21 July 2009.

Brunk, Conrad. "Shaping a Vision—the Nature of Peace Studies." In Larry Fisk and John Schellenberg, eds., *Patterns of Conflict, Paths to Peace,* 11–33. Toronto: Broadview Press and University of Toronto Press, 2000.

Brunson, Rod K., and Jody Miller. "Young Black Men and Urban Policing." *British Journal of Criminal Justice* 46, no. 4 (2006): 46, 613–640.

Buchanan, John, Tom Kramer, and Kevin Woods. "Developing Disparity: Regional Investment in Burma's Borderlands." Amsterdam: Transnational Institute-Burma Centre Netherlands, February 2013.

Bünte, Marco. "Burma's Transition to Quasi-military Rule: From Rulers to Guardians." *Armed Forces and Society*. 5 July 2013.

Bureau of Democracy, Human Rights, and Labor. "Burma." *Country Reports on Human Rights Practices for 2012.* Washington, DC: US State Department, 2013.

———. "Burma." *Country Reports on Human Rights Practices for 2013.* Washington, DC: US State Department, 27 February 2014.

"Burma: Junta Moves to Control Rift in Police, Former Soldiers Shed Uniforms." *BBC Monitoring International Reports.* 3 January 2002.

Burma Director of Information. *Is Trust Vindicated? A Chronicle of a Trust, Striving,and Triumph. Being an Account of the Accomplishments of the Government of the Union of Burma, November 1, 1958–February 1, 1960.* Rangoon: Government of the Union of Burma, 1960.

"Burma Forms New Intelligence Unit." *Irrawaddy*, 3 May 2011.

Burma News International. *Deciphering Myanmar's Peace Process: A Reference Guide 2013.* Chiang Mai:Wanida Press, 2013.

"Burma President Ends US Trip with Trade Deal." *VOA News*, 21 May 2013.

"Burma to Launch Tourist Police Force." *Irrawaddy*, 26 March 2013.

Callahan, Mary P.. *Making Enemies: War and State-Building in Burma*. Ithaca, NY: Cornell University Press, 2004.

——— "On Time Warps and Warped Time: Lessons from Burma's Democratic Era." In Robert Rotberg, ed., *Burma: Prospects for a Democratic Future*, 49–67. Washington, DC: Brookings Institution Press, 1998.

———. "The Opening in Burma: The Generals Loosen Their Grip." *Journal of Democracy* 23, no. 4 (2012): 120–131.

———. *Political Authority in Burma's Ethnic Minority States: Devolution, Occupation, and Coexistence*. Washington, DC: East-West Center, 2007.

Carothers, Thomas. "The Rule-of-Law Revival." In Thomas Carothers, ed., *Promoting the Rule of Law Abroad: In Search of Knowledge.* Washington, DC: Carnegie Endowment for Peace, 2006.

Chambers, Paul. "Where Agency Meets Structure: Understanding Civil-Military Relations in Contemporary Thailand." *Asian Journal of Political Science,* 19, no. 3 (December 2011).

Chatterjee, Partha. *Politics of the Governed.* New York: Columbia University Press, 2004.

Cheesman, Nick. "Policing Burma." Unpublished background research paper no. 2. Canberra: Australian National University, 24 February 2009.

———. "The Politics of Law and Order in Myanmar." Ph.D. thesis. Canberra: Australian National University, June 2012.

———. . "Thin Rule of Law or Un-Rule of Law in Myanmar?" *Pacific Affairs* 82, no. 4 (Winter 2009/2010): 597–613.

Chen, Yangyong. "The Creation of Jiang Zemin's 'Going Out' Strategy and Its Importance." *Ren Min Wang,* 10 November 2008.

Cheng, Ruisheng. "The Strong Virility of the Five Principles of Peaceful Coexistence Shown in the Sino-Myanmar Friendship." *People's Daily.* 19 September 2009.

"China Now No.1 Investor in Burma." *Mizzima News*. 18 January 2012.

"Chinese Economic Aid to Myanmar." *Gold Phoenix*. 4 January 2013.

Chiva, Cristina. "The Institutionalisation of Post-communist Parliaments: Hungary and Romania in Comparative Perspective," *Parliamentary Affairs* 60, no 2 (2007): 187–211.

Chomsky, Noam. *Hegemony or Survival.* New York: Metropolitan Books, 2003.

Ciorciari, John. *The Limits of Alignment: Southeast Asia and the Great Powers Since 1975.* Washington, DC: Georgetown University Press, 2010.

Clapp, Priscilla. "Prospects for Rapprochement Between the United States and Myanmar." *Contemporary Southeast Asia* 32, no. 3 (December 2010): 409–426.

Collier, Paul (with Anke Hoeffler) "Resource Rents, Governance, and Conflict," *Journal of Conflict Resolution* 49, no. 4, (2005): 625–633.

Colton, Timothy J. "The Constituency Nexus in the Russian and other Post-Soviet Parliaments." In Jeffrey W. Hahn, ed., *Democratization in Russia: The Development of Legislative Institutions.* Armonk, NY: M. E. Sharpe, 1996, 49–82.

Constitution of the Republic of the Union of Myanmar (2008). [S.l.]: Print. Naypyitaw: Pub. Enterprise, Ministry of Information, 2008.

Comaroff, John, and Jean Comaroff. "Law and Disorder in the Postcolony." *Social Anthropology* 15, no. 2, 2007: 133–152.

"Conflicting Realities: Reform, Repression and Human Rights in Burma." Report of the Standing Committee on Foreign Affairs and International Development,

Subcommittee on International Human Rights, House of Commons, Canada, 41st Parliament, June 2013.

Corben, Ron. "US Senators Signal Conditional Support for Lifting Burma Sanctions." *Voice of America*. 20 January 2012.

Dallmayr, Fred. *Border Crossings: Toward a Comparative Political Theory*. Lanham, MD: Lexington Books, 1999.

Dapice, David. *Creating a Future: Using Natural Resources for New Federalism and Unity.* Boston: Ash Center for Democratic Governance and Innovation, Harvard Kennedy School, July 2013.

Davison, Jill. "Rights-Claiming in a Rule of Law Vacuum." *Democratic Voice of Burma.* 11 March 2013.

De, Gokuldas. *Democracy in Early Buddhist Sangha*. Calcutta: Calcutta University, 1955.

Deininger, Klaus. "Land Policies for Growth and Poverty Reduction." *World Bank Policy Research Report.* Oxford: World Bank and Oxford University Press, June 2003.

Desposato, Scott W. "Legislative Politics in Authoritarian Brazil." *Legislative Studies Quarterly* 26, no. 2 (2001): 287–317.

Donilon, Thomas. "President Obama's Asia Policy and Upcoming Trip to the Region." Speech at CSIS, 15 November 2012.

Duffield, Mark R. *Global Governance and the New Wars: The Merging of Development and Security*. London: Zed Books, 2001.

———. "On the Edge of 'No Man's Land': Chronic Emergency in Myanmar." Working Paper 1, Independent report commissioned by the Office of the UN RC/HC, Yangon and UNOCHA, New York. Bristol, UK: Centre for Governance and International Affairs, University of Bristol, 2008.

Dun, General Smith. "Memoirs of the Four Foot Colonel." *Southeast Asia Data Paper* No. 113. Ithaca, NY: Cornell University Southeast Asia Program Publications, 1980.

Dworkin, Ronald. *Taking Rights Seriously*. Cambridge, MA: Harvard University Press, 1977–1978.

Eckert, Julia, Brian Donahoe, Christian Strümpell, and Zerrin Özlem Biner, eds. *Law Against the State: Ethnographic Forays into Law's Transformations*. Cambridge and New York: Cambridge University Press, 2012.

Egreteau, Renaud. "The Continuing Political Salience of the Military in Post-junta Myanmar." In N. Cheesman, N. Farrelly, and T. Wilson, eds., *Debating Democratisation in Myanmar.* Singapore: ISEAS Publications, 2014, 259–284.

———. *Histoire de la Birmanie Contemporaine: Le pays des prétoriens*. Paris: Fayard, 2010.

———. "Patterns of Military Behavior in Myanmar's New Legislature," *Asia Pacific Bulletin* No. 233, Washington, DC: East-West Center, 2013.

———. "Soldiers as Lawmakers: Assessing the Legislative Role of the Burmese Armed Forces in the Post-SPDC Era." In Renaud Egreteau and François Robinne, eds., *Burma/Myanmar: A Country in Transition.* Singapore: NUS Press, forthcoming.

Egreteau, Renaud, and Larry Jagan. *Soldiers and Diplomacy in Myanmar. Understanding the Foreign Relations of the Burmese Praetorian State*. Singapore: NUS Press, 2013.

Englehart, Neil A. "Two Cheers for Burma's Rigged Elections." *Asian Survey* 52, no. 4 (2012): 666–686.

Ethnic Community Development Forum (ECDF). *Biofuel by Decree: Unmasking Burma's Bio-energy Fiasco*. Yangon: ECDF, 2008.

Euben, Roxanne. *Enemy in the Mirror: Islamic Fundamentalism and the Limits of Modern Rationalism*. Princeton, NJ: Princeton University Press, 1999.

Euro-Burma Office. "Analysis of the UNFC Position." Brussels: Euro-Burma Office Briefing Paper, August 2013.

———. "The Tatmadaw: Does the Government Control the Tatmadaw?" Brussels: Euro-Burma Office Briefing Paper, March 2013.

"Eviction Order for Burma Monk Shwe Nya War Sayadaw." *BBC News*. 15 December 2011.

Fan, Hongwei. 2012. "China-Burma Geopolitical Relations in the Cold War." *Journal of Current Southeast Asian Affairs* 31 (January 2012): 7–27.

Fawthrop, Tom. "State Complicity in Myanmar Pogroms." *Asia Times*. 1 July 2013.

Ferguson, James. *The Anti-Politics Machine: "Development," Depoliticization, and Bureaucratic Power in Lesotho*. Minneapolis: University of Minnesota Press, 1994.

Filipovic, Jill. "Is the US the Only Country Where More Men Are Raped Than Women?" *The Guardian*. 21 February 2012.

"Final Report of Inquiry Commission on Sectarian Violence in Rakhine State." 8 July 2013.

Fineman, Martha. "Feminist Legal Theory." *Journal of Gender, Social Policy & the Law* 13, no. 1 (2005).

Finer, Samuel E. *The Man on Horseback: The Role of the Military in Politics*. Boulder, CO: Westview Press, 1998.

Fish, M. Steven. "Stronger Legislatures, Stronger Democracies," *Journal of Democracy* 17, no. 1 (2006): 5–20.

Friedman, George. "The End of the Chinese Economic Miracle." *Forbes*. 23 July 2013.

Fujita, Koichi, and Ikuko Okamoto. "Agricultural Policies and Development of Myanmar." *Discussion Paper* 63. Institute of Developing Economies, Japan External Trade Organization (JETRO), 2006.

Furnivall, John. *Colonial Policy and Practice: A Comparative Study of Burma and Netherlands India*. Cambridge, UK: Cambridge University Press, 1948.

Galtung, Johan. *A Theory of Peace*. Transcend Press, 2010.

Gearan, Anne. "Burma's Thein Sein Says Military 'Will Always Have a Special Place' in Government." *Washington Post*. 20 May 2013.

Geertz, Clifford. *Negara: The Theatre State in Nineteenth-Century Bali*. Princeton, NJ: Princeton University Press, 1980.

Godrej, Farah. "Toward a Cosmopolitan Political Thought: Non-Western Texts and the Methodology of Comparative Political Theory." Ph.D. dissertation. Washington, DC: Georgetown University, 2006.

Goh, Evelyn. *The Struggle for Order: Hegemony, Hierarchy, and Transition in Post–Cold War East Asia*. Oxford: Oxford University Press, 2013.

Green, Michael J., and Bates Gill, eds. *Asia's New Multilateralism: Cooperation, Competition, and the Search for Community*. New York: Columbia University Press, 2009.

Green, Michael, and Derek Mitchell. "Asia's Forgotten Crisis: A New Approach to Burma." *Foreign Affairs* 86, no. 6 (November/December 2007): 147–158.

Gronholt-Pedersen, Jacob. "Chinese Investment in Myanmar Falls Sharply." *Wall Street Journal*. 4 June 2013.

Guha, Ranajit, ed. *Subaltern Studies, Vol. 1: Writings on South Asian History and Society*. Delhi/New York: Oxford University Press, 1982.

Gyi, Maung Maung. *Burmese Political Values: The Socio-Political Roots of Authoritarianism*. New York: Praeger, 1983.

Haacke, Jürgen. *Myanmar's Foreign Policy: Domestic Influences and International Implications*. Abingdon: Routledge for IISS, 2006.

———. "The Myanmar Imbroglio and ASEAN: Heading Towards the 2010 Elections." *International Affairs* 86, no. 1 (January 2010): 153–174.

———. "The Nature and Management of Myanmar's Alignment with China: The SLORC/SPDC Years." *Journal of Current Southeast Asian Affairs* 30, no. 2 (2011): 105–140.

Habermas, Jürgen. *The Inclusion of the Other: Studies in Political Theory.* Ciaran Cronin, and Pablo De Greiff, eds., Cambridge, MA: MIT Press, 1998.

"The Handling of Sino-Burma Border Issue." Zhou Enlai Studies Association, 25 November 2011. Available at www.zelyj.com/jpwz/html/?4579.html.

Hardin, Harry. 1990. "The Impact of Tiananmen on China's Foreign Policy." *NBR Analysis* (December). Seattle, WA: National Bureau of Asian and Soviet Research.

Hiebert, Murray, and Phuong Nguyen. "Engaging Myanmar's Military: Carpe Diem Part II." *Commentary.* Washington, DC: Center for Strategic and International Studies (CSIS), 5 September 2013.

Hindstrom, Hannah. "Burma Disbands Notorious NaSaKa Border Guard Force." *Democratic Voice of Burma*. 15 July 2013.

Hla, Maung Tha. *Rohingya Hoax*. New York: Buddhist Rakhaing Cultural Association, 2009.

Hlaing, Kyaw Yin. "Understanding Recent Political Changes in Myanmar." *Contemporary Southeast Asia* 34, no. 2 (2012): 197–216.

Hopkins, Raymond F. "The Role of the M.P. in Tanzania." *American Political Science Review* 64, no. 3 (1970): 754–771.

Horsey, Richard. *Ending Forced Labour in Myanmar: Engaging a Pariah Regime*. Hoboken, NJ: Taylor & Francis, 2011.

———. "The Initial Functioning of Myanmar Legislatures." Conflict Prevention and Peace Forum Briefing. New York: Social Science Research Council, 17 May 2011.

———. "Outcome of the Myanmar Elections." Conflict Prevention and Peace Forum Briefing. New York: Social Science Research Council, 17 November 2010.

Houtman, Gustaaf. "Mental Culture in Burmese Crisis Politics: Aung San Suu Kyi and the National League for Democracy." *Monograph Series* 33. Tokyo: Tokyo University of Foreign Studies, Institute for the Study of Languages and Cultures of Asia and Africa, 1999.

Htet, Tha Lun Zaung. "Burma's Constitutional Review to Stay Confidential until Next Year." *Irrawaddy*. 28 August 2013.

———. "We Will Work with Suu Kyi to Amend Constitution to 'Benefit State'—USDP." *Irrawaddy*. 16 May 2013.

Hudson-Rodd, Nancy, Myo Nyunt, Saw Thamain Tun, and Sein Htay. *The Impact of the Confiscation of Land, Labor, Capital Assets and Forced Relocation in Burma by the Military Regime.* NCUB/FTUB Discussion Paper 2003.

Human Rights Watch (HRW). *"The Government Could Have Stopped This": Sectarian Violence and Ensuing Abuses in Burma's Arakan State*. New York: HRW, 2012.

———. "Untold Miseries: Wartime Abuses and Forced Displacement in Burma's Kachin State." New York: HRW, 2012.

Huntington, Samuel P. "Political Development and Political Decay." *World Politics* 17, no. 3 (1965): 383–430.

Huxley, Andrew. "Burma: It Works, but Is It Law?" *Journal of Family Law* (1988–1989).

———. "Pre-colonial Burmese Law: Conical Hat and Shoulder Bag." *International Institute for Asian Studies Newsletter,* no. 25 (2001). Available at www.iias.nl/iiasn/25/theme/25T7.html.

Immigration and Refugee Board of Canada Research Directorate. "Myanmar (Burma): Whether the Military Intelligence Force in Myanmar Has Been Fully or Partially Disbanded and Who Is Carrying Out Their Duties (2004–February 2008)." Ottawa: Immigration and Refugee Board of Canada, 25 February 2008.

International Bar Association. "The Rule of Law in Myanmar: Challenges and Prospects: Report of the International Bar Association's Human Rights Institute (IBAHRI)." London: International Bar Association, December 2012.

International Center for Transitional Justice (ICTJ). *Impunity Prolonged: Burma and Its 2008 Constitution*. New York: ICTJ, 2009.

International Crisis Group (ICG). "Counting the Costs: Myanmar's Problematic Census." *Update Briefing, Asia Briefing* No. 14. Brussels: ICG, 15 May 2014.

———. "The Dark Side of Transition: Violence Against Muslims in Myanmar." *Asia Report* No. 251. Brussels: ICG, 1 October 2013.

———. "Myanmar's Post-Election Landscape." *Asia Briefing* No. 118. Brussels: ICG, 2011.

———. "Reform in Myanmar: One Year On." *Asia Briefing* No. 136. Brussels: ICG, 2012.

———. "A Tentative Peace in Myanmar's Kachin Conflict." *Asia Briefing* No. 140. Brussels: ICG, 12 June 2013.

International Institute for Strategic Studies. *Preventing Nuclear Dangers in Southeast Asia and Australasia*. London: International Institute for Strategic Studies, 2009.

International Monetary Fund. "Myanmar: 2013 Article IV Consultation and First Review Under Staff Monitored Program." *IMF Country Report* 13/250, August 2013.

INTERPOL. "Myanmar." Available at http://www.interpol.int/Member-countries/Asia-South-Pacific/Myanmar.

Jackson, Peter A. "Thai-Buddhist Identity: Debates on the *Traiphum Phra Ruang*." In Craig J. Reynold, ed., *National Identity and Its Defenders: Thailand Today.* Chiang Mai, Thailand: Silkworm Books, 2002.

Janowitz, Morris. *The Military in the Political Development of New Nations: An Essay in Comparative Analysis*. Chicago: University of Chicago Press, 1964.

Jenco, Leigh. "'What Does Heaven Ever Say?' A Methods-Centered Approach to Cross-Cultural Engagement." *American Political Science Review* 101, no. 4 (2007): 741–755.

Johnstone, William C. *Burma's Foreign Policy: A Study in Neutralism*. Cambridge, MA: Harvard University Press, 1963.

Jolliffe, Kim. "People's War: People's Peace—How Can International Peacebuilders Facilitate Reconciliation of the KNU Conflict and Address Local Security Concerns?" London: King's College War Studies Department, 2013.

———. "US Myanmar Eye Military Links." *Asia Times Online*. 26 June 2012.

Jordt, Ingrid. 2007. *Burma's Mass Lay Meditation Movement: Buddhism and the Cultural Construction of Power*. Athens: Ohio University Press.

Karen Human Rights Group (KHRG). *Development by Decree: The Politics of Poverty and Control in Karen State*. Thailand: KHRG, 2007.

———. "Losing Ground: Land Conflicts and Collective Action in Eastern Myanmar." Report No. 2013-01. Thailand: KHRG. March 2013.

Kasuya, Yuko, ed. 2013. *Presidents, Assemblies and Policy-making in Asia*, New York: Palgrave Macmillan.

Kean, Thomas. "Burma's Biggest Win: Its Legislature." *The Diplomat.* 1 February 2013.

———. "Myanmar's Parliament: From Scorn to Significance." In N. Cheesman, N. Farrelly, and T. Wilson, eds., *Debating Democratisation in Myanmar,* 43–74. Singapore: ISEAS Publications, 2014.

———. "Pro-poor Land Program Unveiled." *Myanmar Times*. 2–8 July 2012.

Keen, David. *Complex Emergencies*. Cambridge, UK: Polity Press, 2008.

Keenan, Paul. "The UNFC and the Peace Process." *Burma Centre for Ethnic Studies Briefing Paper* No. 16, August 2013.

Kennedy, David. "The 'Rule of Law,' Political Choices, and Development of Common Sense." In David M. Trubek and Alvaro Santos, eds., *The New Law and Economic Development: A Critical Appraisal*. Cambridge, UK: Cambridge University Press, 2006.

Kinetz, Erika. "US to Boost Military, Trade Ties to Burma." *Irrawaddy*. 26 April 2013.

Kleinfeld, Rachel. *Advancing the Rule of Law Abroad*. Washington, DC: Carnegie Endowment for International Peace, 2012.

Kramer, Tom. "The United Wa State Party: Narco-Army or Ethnic Nationalist Party?" *Policy Studies* 38. Washington, DC: East-West Center, 2007.

Kramer, Tom, and Kevin Woods. *Financing Dispossession: China's Opium Substitution Program in Northern Burma*. Amsterdam: Transnational Institute, February 2012.

Kurlantzick, Joshua, and D. T. Stewart. "Burma's Reforms and Regional Cooperation in East Asia." New York: Carnegie Council for Ethics in International Affairs, Summer 2013.

Kyi, Aung San Suu. *Freedom from Fear: And Other Writings*. New York: Penguin Books, 1991.

———. *Letters from Burma*. London and New York: Penguin Books, 1997.

Laba, Ashin. "Golden Democratization." *Ottama Journal,* no. 4 (September 2008): 40.

Lall, Marie, and Ashley South. "Comparing Models of Non-state Ethnic Education in Myanmar: The Mon and Karen National Education Regimes." *Journal of Contemporary Asia* 2 (2013): 1–24.

"Laos, Myanmar Begin Bridge." *Bangkok Post*. 18 February 2013.

Latt, Win Ko Ko. "Rep Tells of Land Grabs in Nay Pyi Taw." *Myanmar Times*. 20 August 2012.

Leckie, Scott. "Bridging the HLP Gap—The Need to Effectively Address Housing, Land and Property Rights During Peace Negotiations and in the Context of Refugee/IDP Return: Preliminary Recommendations to the Government of Myanmar, Ethnic Actors and the International Community." Report for Displacement Solutions, Geneva, June 2013.

Leckie, Scott, and Ezekiel Simperingham. *Housing, Land and Property Rights in*

Burma: The Current Legal Framework. Geneva: Displacement Solutions and the HLP Institute, 2009.

Lee, Jeong Seok. "Hedging Against Uncertain Future: The Response of East Asian Secondary Powers to Rising China." Paper prepared for the International Political Science Association XXII World Congress of Political Science, 8–12 July 2012.

Leider, Jacques. "The Muslims in Rakhine and the Political Project of the Rohingyas: Historical Background of an Unresolved Communal Conflict in Contemporary Myanmar." *Network Myanmar.* 18 October 2012.

———. "'Rohingya,' Rakhaing and the Recent Outbreak of Violence—A Note." *Network Myanmar* (2012).

Liang, Chi-shad. *Burma's Foreign Relations: Neutralism in Theory and Practice.* New York: Praeger, 1990.

Liang, Jinwen. "Security Impact of Armed Conflicts on China After the Sino-Burma Border Demarcation." *Yunnan Police Academy Journal* 1 (2013).

Lijphart, Arend. *Patterns of Democracy: Government and Performance in Thirty-Six Countries,* 2nd edition. New Haven, CT: Yale University Press, 2012.

Lin, Bwa. "Burma." In *Burma Speaks: A Collection of Broadcast Talks from the Burma Broadcasting Station.* Rangoon: Government Printing and Stationery, 1950.

Lin, Sanay. "Govt to Compensate 90 Farmers Affected by Thilawa SEZ." *Irrawaddy.* 11 June 2013.

Lin, Zaw Naung, and Thant Zin Oo. "At Opening of Buddhist University, Sitagu Sayadaw Exhorts Political, Religious, and Social Organizations to Be United." *The Messenger.* 30 June 2011.

Linn, Zin. "Burma Army's Boss Calls for Stronger Armed Forces." *AsianCorrespondent.com.* 28 March 2013.

Lintner, Bertil. *Outrage: Burma's Struggle for Democracy.* London: White Lotus, 1995.

Lissak, Moshe. *Military Roles in Modernization. Civil-Military Relations in Thailand and Burma.* London: Sage Publications, 1976.

"Lt-Gen Khin Nyunt Accuses Police." *New Light of Myanmar.* 14 March 1994.

Lwin, Ei Ei Toe. "One Year On, No Respite for Peace March Organizers." *Myanmar Times.* 15 September 2013.

Lynn, Soe Than. "The *Hluttaws* Flexes Its Muscles." *Myanmar Times.* 21–27 May 2012.

———. "Hluttaw Refuses Human Rights Body Budget." *Myanmar Times.* 26 March–1 April 2012.

———. "Man of the House," *Myanmar Times,* 21–27 November 2011.

———. "A Tactical Retreat." *Myanmar Times.* 14 October 2013.

Macdonald, A. P. "From Military Rule to Electoral Authoritarianism: The Reconfiguration of Power in Myanmar and Its Future." *Asian Affairs: An American Review* 40, no. 1 (2013): 20–36.

———. "The Tatmadaw's New Position in Myanmar Politics." *East Asia Forum.* 1 May 2013.

Mann, Michael. "Autonomous Power of the State: Its Origins, Mechanisms, and Results," *European Journal of Sociology* 25 (1984).

Mann, Zarni. "Only Fraction of Land Seized by Military Will Be Returned: Minister." *Irrawaddy.* 18 July 2013.

"Marine Police Established in Myanmar." *Eleven Myanmar.* 9 August 2012.

Martin, Michael F. "U.S. Policy Towards Burma: Issues for the 113th Congress."

Report R43035. Washington, DC: Congressional Research Service, 12 March 2013.

———. "U.S. Sanctions on Burma." Report R41336. Washington, DC: Congressional Research Service, 2012.

Mattei, Ugo, and Laura Nader. *Plunder: When the Rule of Law Is Illegal.* Malden, MA: Blackwell, 2008.

Maung Htin. *Yaw Mingyi U Hpo Hlaing's Biography and "Rajadhammasangahagyan."* Yangon: Unity Publishing House, 2002.

Maung, Min Maung. *The Tatmadaw and Its Leadership Role in National Politics.* Yangon: News and Periodicals Enterprises, 1993.

McCarthy, Stephen. "The Buddhist Political Rhetoric of Aung San Suu Kyi." *Contemporary Buddhism* 5, no. 2 (2004): 67–81.

———. "Burma and ASEAN: Estranged Bedfellows." *Asian Survey* 48, no. 6 (2008): 911–935.

McLaughlin, Tim. "US and Myanmar Up Military Engagement." *Myanmar Times.* 1 August 2013.

Mezey, Michael L. "The Functions of Legislatures in the Third World." *Legislative Studies Quarterly* 8, no. 4 (1983): 511–550.

Mietzner, Marcus. "The Political Marginalization of the Military in Indonesia." In Marcus Mietzner, ed., *The Political Resurgence of the Military in Southeast Asia: Conflict and Leadership.* London: Routledge, 2011, 126–147.

Min, Aung, and Toshihiro Kudo. "New Government's Initiatives for Industrial Development in Myanmar." In Hank Lim and Yasuhiro Yamada, eds., *Economic Reforms in Myanmar: Pathways and Prospects.* Report No. 10. Chiba, Japan: Bangkok Research Center, 2013.

Ministry of Commerce of the People's Republic of China. "Chinese Chamber of Commerce Hosted New Year's Reception in Mandalay." 3 January 2013.

Ministry of Foreign Affairs of the People's Republic of China. Chinese Embassy in Myanmar. "Premier Zhou Enlai's Nine Visits of Myanmar."

Mitchell, Derek. "Ambassador-Designate to Burma." Statement before the Senate Foreign Relations Committee, US Congress, Washington, DC, 27 June 2012.

Moe, Maung Aung. "The Soldier and the State: The Tatmadaw and Political Liberalisation in Myanmar Since 2011." *South East Asia Research* 22, no. 2 (2014): 233–249.

Moe, Wai. "Tatmadaw Commanders Discuss Recent Ethnic Conflicts." *Irrawaddy.* 29 June 2011.

Montera, Celeste. "EU Restoration of Myanmar Preferential Trade Regime: Neglect of Human Rights Concerns?" *EU-Asia at a Glance.* Brussels: European Institute for Asian Studies, August 2013.

Munoz, Carlo. "US Opens Door to Military Ties with Burma." *The Hill.* 15 October 2012.

Murphy, W. Patrick. Testimony before the Tom Lantos Human Rights Commission, US Congress, Washington, DC, 28 February 2013.

"Myanmar (Burma): 41st Anniversary of Myanmar Police Force Observed." *Asia Africa Intelligence Wire.* 13 October 2005.

"Myanmar Farmers Call for Amendments to Land Law." *Radio Free Asia.* 20 August 2013. Available at www.rfa.org/english/news/myanmar/farmers-08202013180804.html.

"Myanmar Police Slow to Adjust to Unfamiliar Role of Peacekeepers." *Japan Times.* 12 April 2013.

"Myanmar Police to Receive Assistance in Setting Up Cyber-Crime Division." *Eleven*. 27 March 2013.

"Myanmar Police to Study Abroad." *Eleven*. 28 November 2012.

"Myanmar Police Urged to Implement Three Main Tasks." *Xinhua*. 20 June 1998.

"Myanmar to Beef Up Anti-Riot Forces." *Global Times*. 4 July 2013.

Myint-U, Thant. *The River of Lost Footsteps*. New York: Farrar, Straus and Giroux, 2006.

Myoe, Maung Aung. *In the Name of Pauk-Phaw: Myanmar's China Policy Since 1948*. Singapore: ISEAS, 2011.

———. "Military Doctrine and Strategy in Myanmar: A Historical Perspective." Working Paper No. 339. Canberra: Australian National University, Strategic and Defence Studies Centre, 1999.

———. "The Soldier and the State: The Tatmadaw and Political Liberalization in Myanmar Since 2011." Paper presented at the Burma Update conference. Canberra, 2013.

———. "The Soldier and the State: The Tatmadaw and Political Liberalization in Myanmar Since 2011." *South East Asia Research* 22, no. 2 (June 2014): 233–249.

———. "The Tatamadaw in Myanmar Since 1988: An Interim Assessment." Working Paper No. 342. Canberra: Australian National University, Strategic and Defence Studies Centre, 1999.

Na, Saw Eh. "Karen Health Workers Push for Recognition." *Karen News*, 3 October 2013.

Naing, Saw Yan. "Shwe Mann Denies Nuclear Program." *Irrawaddy*. 7 December 2011.

Naing, Saw Yan, and A. D. Kaspar. "UK to Renew Military Ties with Burma." *Irrawaddy*. 16 July 2013.

Nakanishi, Yoshihiro. *Strong Soldiers, Failed Revolution: The State and the Military in Burma, 1962–88*. Singapore: National University of Singapore Press, 2013.

"New Police Force to Patrol Myanmar." *Wanderlust*. 4 April 2013.

Nilsen, Marte, and Stein Tønnesson. "Can Myanmar's 2008 Constitution Be Made to Satisfy Ethnic Aspirations?" Policy Brief No. 11. Oslo: Peace Research Institute Oslo, 2012.

Norton, Philip, ed., *Legislatures*. Oxford: Oxford University Press, 1990.

Oberndorf, Robert B. *Legal Review of Recently Enacted Farmland Law and Vacant, Fallow and Virgin Lands Management Law.* Yangon: Food Security Working Group's Land Core Group, November 2012.

O'Brien, Kevin J., and Laura M. Luehrmann. "Institutionalizing Chinese Legislatures: Trade-Offs Between Autonomy and Capacity." *Legislative Studies Quarterly* 23, no. 1 (1998): 91–108.

O'Brien, Kevin J., and Lianjiang Li. *Rightful Resistance in Rural China*. Cambridge, UK: Cambridge University Press, 2006.

"Old Problems Resurface on Myanmar's Road to Freedom." *The Nation*. 6 August 2013.

Olson, David M. *Democratic Legislative Institutions: A Comparative View*. Armonk, NY: M. E. Sharpe, 1994.

Oo, Tin Htut. "New Agricultural Strategy to Enhance Myanmar's Rural Economy." In Nick Cheesman, Monique Skidmore, and Trevor Wilson, eds., *Myanmar's Transition: Openings, Obstacles, and Opportunities*. Singapore: Institute of Southeast Asian Studies, 2012.

Oppel, Richard A., Jr. "Sentencing Shift Gives New Leverage to Prosecutors." *New York Times*. 25 September 2011.

Organisation for Economic Cooperation and Development (OECD). *Multi-dimensional Review of Myanmar, Volume 1, Initial Assessment* (Paris: OECD, 2013).

Paing, May Sitt. "Buddhist Committee's 969 Prohibitions Prompts Meeting of Movement Backers." *Irrawaddy*. 10 September 2013.

Parks, Thomas, Nat Colletta, and Ben Oppenheim. "The Contested Corners of Asia: Subnational Conflict and International Development Assistance." Bangkok: The Asia Foundation, 2013.

The Parliaments of Myanmar. Yangon: MCM Book Publishing, 2013.

Pasricha, Anjana. 2012. "Aung San Suu Kyi Explains Silence on Rohingyas." *Voice of America*. 15 November.

Pedersen, Morten B. 2008. *Promoting Human Rights in Burma: A Critique of Western Sanctions Policy*. Lanham, MD: Rowman & Littlefield.

Pittman, Todd. "In Myanmar, Internal Spy Network Lives On." *The Hindu.* 30 July 2013.

Ponnudurai, Parameswaran. "Is Reform Stalling in Burma?" *Radio Free Asia*, 4 December 2010.

Povinelli, Elizabeth. *Economies of Abandonment: Social Belonging and Endurance in Late Liberalism.* Durham, NC: Duke, 2011.

Powell, Colin L. "It's Time to Turn the Tables on Burma's Thugs." *Wall Street Journal*. 12 June 2003.

Power, Timothy J. "Elites and Institutions in Conservative Transitions to Democracy: Ex-Authoritarians in the Brazilian National Congress." *Studies in Comparative International Development* 31, no. 3 (1996): 56–84.

Prasse-Freeman, Elliott. "Animating Reform from Within." *Democratic Voice of Burma*, 24 January 2012.

———. "Power, Civil Society, and an Inchoate Politics of the Daily in Burma/Myanmar." *Journal of Asian Studies* 71, no. 2 (May 2012): 371–397.

Prichett, Lant. "Looking Like a State: Techniques of Persistent Failure in State Capability for Implementation." *Journal of Development Studies* 49, no. 1 (2013): 1–18.

"A Public Address by Daw Aung San Suu Kyi." Harvard Institute of Politics, published 28 September 2012. Available at www.youtube.com/watch?v=-QnBE5Xsx74&noredirect=1.

Pye, Lucian. *Politics, Personality, and Nation Building.* New Haven, CT: Yale University Press, 1962.

Rahman, Taiabur. *Parliamentary Control and Government Accountability in South Asia: A Comparative Analysis of Bangladesh, India and Sri Lanka.* London: Routledge, 2008.

Rajagopal, B. *International Law from Below; Development, Social Movements, and Third World Resistance.* Cambridge, UK: Cambridge University Press, 2003.

Rajan, Raghuram, and Arvind Subramanian. "Aid, Dutch Disease and Manufacturing Growth." *Journal of Development Economics* 94, no. 1 (January 2011): 106–118.

Ranciere, Jacques. *Dissensus; On Politics and Aesthetics.* Translated by Steven Corcoran. New York: Continuum, 2010.

———."Who Is the Subject of the Rights of Man?" *South Atlantic Quarterly* 103, no. 2/3 (Spring/Summer 2004).

Remington, Thomas F., ed. *Parliaments in Transition: The New Legislative Politics in the Former USSR and Eastern Europe.* Boulder, CO: Westview Press, 1994.

Republic of the Union of Myanmar. *Pyidaungsu Hluttaw,* Notification 59/2013. 27 August 2013.

"Retired Police Officers Criticise Current Police Force." *Mizzima News*. 28 August 2013.

"Retrospection of Sino-Burma Border Demarcation—Losing 5 Million Chinese." *Sina Blog*. 12 April 2013. Available at http://blog.sina.com.cn/s/blog_9008489d010199jh.html.

"Rice Names 'Outposts of Tyranny.'" *BBC News*. 19 January 2005. Available at news.bbc.co.uk/1/hi/world/americas/4186241.stm.

Richmond, Oliver. *The Transformation of Peace*. Basingstoke: Palgrave Macmillan, 2007.

Rieffel, Lex, and Jaleswari Pramodhawardani. *Out of Business and on Budget. The Challenge of Military Financing in Indonesia*. Washington, DC: Brookings Institution, 2007.

Rieffel, Lex, and James W. Fox. *Too Much Too Soon? The Dilemma of Foreign Aid to Myanmar*. Arlington, VA: Nathan Associates, 2013.

Riley, Mark S., and Ravi A. Balaram. "The United States International Military Education and Training (IMET) Program with Burma/Myanmar: A Review of the 1980–1988 Programming and Prospects for the Future." *Asian Affairs: An American Review* 40, no. 3, (2013): 109–132.

Roberts, Christopher. 2010. *ASEAN's Myanmar Crisis: Challenges to the Pursuit of a Security Community*. Singapore: ISEAS.

Robinson, Gwen. "Britain Revives Links with Myanmar's Military Establishment." *Financial Times*. 6 June 2013.

———. "EU and US Seek Closer Ties with Myanmar." *Financial Times*, 19 October 2012.

———. "The Contenders." *Foreign Policy*. 12 July 2013.

Rodrik, Dani. "Understanding Economic Policy Reform." *Journal of Economic Literature* 32, no. 1 (March 1996): 9–41.

Ross, Robert S. "US Grand Strategy, the Rise of China, and US National Security Strategy for East Asia." *Strategic Studies Quarterly* 7, no. 2 (Summer 2013): 20–40.

Rubio, Marco. "Rubio Presses for Human Rights as Burma's President Visits U.S." Press Release. 20 May 2013.

Rüland, Jürgen, and Maria-Gabriela Manea. "The Legislature and Military Reform in Indonesia." In Jürgen Rüland, Maria-Gabriela Manea, Hans Born, eds., *The Politics of Military Reform: Experiences from Indonesia and Nigeria*. Heidelberg: Springer-Verlag, 2013, 123–145.

Rüland, Jürgen, C. Jurgenmeyer, M. H. Nelson, and P. Ziegenhain. *Parliaments and Political Change in Asia*. Singapore: ISEAS Publications, 2005.

Russel, Daniel R. Assistant Secretary-Designate, Statement before the Senate Foreign Relations Committee, US Congress, 20 June 2013.

San, Aung. *Burma's Challenge*. Rangoon: self-published, 1946. Cited in Maung Maung, *Burma's Constitution*. The Hague: Martinus Nijhoff, 1959.

Sarkisyanz, Manuel. *Buddhist Backgrounds of the Burmese Revolution*. The Hague: M. Nijhoff, 1965.

Saw, Khin Maung. "The 'Rohingyas,' Who Are They? The Origin of the Name 'Rohingya.'" In Uta Gärtner and Jens Lorenz, eds., *Tradition and Modernity in Myanmar*. Münster, Germany: Lit, 1994.

Sayadaw, Sitagu. "On the Day of the Exalted Buddha's Enlightenment, Buddha's Ten Perfect Messages." *7 Day News*, 30 June 2011.

Schaffer, Teresita C. "India's Sagging Economy: Strategic Consequences." Washington, DC: Brookings Institution, 23 September 2013.

Scobell, Andrew. 2000. "Going Out of Business: Divesting the Commercial Interests of Asia's Socialist Soldiers." *Occasional Papers* No. 3, January. Washington, DC: East-West Center.

Scott, James C. *The Art of Not Being Governed.* New Haven, CT: Yale University Press, 2009.

———. *Domination and the Arts of Resistance: Hidden Transcripts.* New Haven: Yale University Press, 1990.

Sein, Daw Mya. "The Women of Burma." *Atlantic*, 1 February 1958.

Sein, Thein. "Myanmar's Complex Transformation: Prospects and Challenges," Transcript of President Thein Sein's Speech, London, 15 July 2013.

Selth, Andrew. "Burma and North Korea: Again? Still?" *The Interpreter*. 10 July 2013.

———. *Burma's Armed Forces: Power Without Glory.* Norwalk, CT: EastBridge, 2002.

———. "Burma's Intelligence Apparatus." *Intelligence and National Security* 13, no. 4 (Winter 1988): 42–44, 54.

———. "Burma's Police: The Long Road to Reform," *The Interpreter*. 13 December 2012.

———. "Burma's Police Forces: Continuities and Contradictions." *Regional Outlook* No. 32. Brisbane: Griffith Asia Institute, 2011.

———. "Burma's Police Forces: Society, State and Sovereignty," forthcoming.

———. "Burma's 'Saffron Revolution' and the Limits of International Influence." *Australian Journal of International Affairs* 62, no. 3 (September 2008).

———. "Even Paranoids Have Enemies: Cyclone Nargis and Burma's Fears of Invasion." *Contemporary Southeast Asia* 30, no.1 (December 2008): 379–402.

———. "Known Knowns and Known Unknowns: Measuring Myanmar's Military Capabilities." *Contemporary Southeast Asia* 31, no. 2 (August 2009): 272–295.

———."Police Reform in Burma (Myanmar): Aims, Obstacles and Outcomes." *Regional Outlook* No. 44. Brisbane: Griffith Asia Institute, 2013.

———. "West Reaches Out to Burma's Security Sector." *The Interpreter.* 26 July 2013.

Shan Herald Agency for News. "Naypyitaw: Nationwide Ceasefire in October." 3 September 2013.

Shan Herald Agency for News. "Ethnic Ceasefire Draft Accepted 'In Principle.'" 9 September 2013.

Shan Herald Agency for News. "Ethnic Working Group Presents Draft Framework for Political Negotiations." 20 June 2013.

Sherlock, Stephen. *Struggling to Change: The Indonesian Parliament in an Era of Reformasi.* Canberra: Center for Democratic Institutions, 2003.

Shin, Sanda. "Our Desire." *Ottama Journal,* no. 5 (January 2009).

Shissler, Matt. "Changing Dynamics of Forced Labour: The International Labour Organization and Local Responses to Abuse in Eastern Myanmar." Masters dissertation. Oxford: Oxford University, 2013.

Smith, Martin. *Burma: Insurgency and the Politics of Ethnicity.* 2nd edition. London: Zed Books, 1999.

South, Ashley. "Burma: The Changing Nature of Displacement Crises." *Working Paper* No. 39. Oxford: Refugee Studies Centre, Oxford University, 2007.

———. "Burma's Longest War: Anatomy of the Karen Conflict." Amsterdam: Transnational Institute/Burma Centre Netherlands, 2011.

———. *Ethnic Politics in Burma: States of Conflict.* London: Routledge, 2010.

———. "Prospects for Peace in Myanmar: Opportunities and Threats." Working Paper, December. Oslo: Peace Research Institute, 2012.

South, Ashley, with Malin Perhult and Nils Carstensen. "Conflict and Survival: Self-Protection in Southeast Burma." *Asia Programme Paper* ASP PP 2010/04. London: Chatham House/Royal Institute of International Affairs, September 2010.

"Speech Delivered by the Chief of Police at the 49th Anniversary of Myanmar Police Force." Ministry of Home Affairs, Myanmar Police Force. 1 October 2013.

Steinberg, David I. "Aung San Suu Kyi and U.S. Policy Toward Burma/Myanmar." *Journal of Current Southeast Asian Affairs,* no. 3 (2010): 36–37.

———. *Burma: The State of Myanmar*. Washington, DC: Georgetown University Press, 2001.

———. "Burma/Myanmar: The Role of the Military in the Economy." *Burma Economic Watch* (August 2005).{

———."Japan and Myanmar: Relationship Redux." *Japan Chair Platform*. Washington, DC: Center for Strategic and International Studies (CSIS). 15 October 2013.

———. "Legitimacy in Burma: Concepts and Implications." In N. Gamesan and Kyaw Yin Hlaing, eds., *Myanmar: State, Society and Ethnicity.* Singapore: The Hiroshima Peace Institute and the Institute for Southeast Asian Studies, 2007.

———. "Moving Myanmar: The Future of Military Prominence." *Kyoto Journal of Southeast Asian Studies* 14 (2013).

———. "The Problem of Democracy in the Republic of the Union of Myanmar: Neither Nation-State nor State-Nation?" *Southeast Asian Affairs* (2012): 220–237.

———. "The Significance of Burma/Myanmar's By-Elections." *Asia Pacific Bulletin* No. 156. Washington, DC: East-West Center, 2012.

———. Testimony before Senate Foreign Relations Committee, Subcommittee on Asian and Pacific Affairs, US Congress, 26 April 2012.

———. "Transforming 'Outposts of Tyranny'? Lessons and Cautions." Paper presented at ASAN Institute conference, Seoul, Korea, 26 March 2013.

———. *Turmoil in Burma: Contested Legitimacies in Myanmar*. Norwalk, CT: EastBridge, 2006.

———. "The United States and Its Allies: The Problem of Burma/Myanmar Policy," *Contemporary Southeast Asia* 29, no. 2 (August 2007): 219–237.

Steinberg, David I., and Hongwei Fan. *Modern China-Myanmar Relations: Dilemmas of Mutual Dependence.* Copenhagen: NIAS Press, 2012.

Sun, Yun. "China's Strategic Misjudgment on Myanmar." *Journal of Current Southeast Asian Affairs* 31, no. 1 (January 2012): 73–96.

Syed, Murtaza, and James P. Walsh. "The Tiger and the Dragon." *Finance and Development* 49, no. 3 (September 2012).

Tamanaha, Brian Z. *On the Rule of Law History, Politics, Theory* (Cambridge, UK: Cambridge University Press, 2004).

Taylor, Robert H. "Elections in Burma/Myanmar: For Whom and Why?" In Robert H. Taylor, ed., *The Politics of Elections in Southeast Asia.* Washington, DC: Woodrow Wilson Center Press, 1996, 164–183.

———."Myanmar in 2012: *Mhyaw ta lin lin* or Great Expectations." *Southeast Asian Affairs* (2013): 189–203.

———. *The State in Burma*. Honolulu: University of Hawaii Press, 1998.

———. *The State in Myanmar.* London: Hurst, 2009.

Thailand Burma Border Consortium (TBBC) "Program Report 2012: January to June." Bangkok, 2012.

———. *Internal Displacement in Eastern Burma: 2006 Survey.* Bangkok: TBBC, 2006.

Than, Tin Maung Maung. "Myanmar: Preoccupation with Regime Survival, National Unity, and Stability." In Muthiah Alagappa, ed., *Asian Security Practice: Material and Ideational Influences,* 390–417. Stanford, CA: Stanford University Press, 1998.

———."Myanmar's 2010 Elections: Continuity and Change." *Southeast Asian Affairs* (2011): 190–207.

———. "Myanmar's 2012 By-Elections: Return of NLD." *Southeast Asian Affairs* (2013): 204–219.

———. *State Dominance in Myanmar: The Political Economy of Industrialization.* Singapore: Institute of Southeast Asian Studies, 2007.

Thawnghmung, Ardeth Maung. *Behind the Teak Curtain: Authoritarianism, Agricultural Policies and Political Legitimacy in Rural Burma/Myanmar.* London: Kegan Paul, 2004.

———. *The "Other" Karen in Myanmar: Ethnic Minorities and the Struggle Without Arms.* Lanham, MD: Lexington Books, 2012.

Thayer, Carlyle A. "The Political Role of the Vietnam People's Army: Corporate Interests and Military Professionalism." Paper presented to the annual Association for Asian Studies meeting, Toronto 15–18 March 2012.

Thēpwisutthimēthī, Phra, and Donald K. Swearer. 1989. *Me and Mine: Selected Essays of Bhikkhu Buddhadāsa.* Albany: State University of New York Press.

Thittila, Ashin. *Essential Themes of Buddhist Lectures.* Rangoon: Department of Religious Affairs, 1987.

Thu, Myat Kyaw. "Burma Has First Woman Cabinet Member in over 60 Years." *Mizzima.* 10 September 2012.

Tinker, Hugh. *The Union of Burma: A Study of the First Years of Independence.* London: Oxford University Press, 1961.

Tomkin, Derek. "The 'Rohingya' Identity-British Experience in Arakan 1826–1948." *Network Myanmar.* 9 April 2014.

Trager, Frank N. *Burma: From Kingdom to Republic.* New York: Fredrick A. Praeger, 1966.

"Training Activities." Central Institute of Civil Service, Union Civil Service Board, Phaunggyi. Available at www.ucsb.gov.mm/about%20ucsb/Central%20Institute%20of%20Civil%20Service%20(Phaung%20Gyi)/details.asp?submenuid=33&id=502.

Transnational Institute. *Access Denied: Land Rights and Ethnic Conflict in Burma.* Amsterdam: Transnational Institute–Burma Centre Netherlands, May 2013.

———."Burma at the Crossroads: Maintaining the Momentum for Reform." *Burma Policy Briefing* No. 9. Amsterdam: Transnational Institute–Burma Centre Netherlands, 2012.

———. "Burma's Ethnic Challenge: From Aspirations to Solutions." *Burma Policy Briefing* No. 12. Amsterdam: Transnational Institute–Burma Centre Netherlands, October 2013.

———. "Ethnicity Without Meaning, Data Without Context: The 2014 Census, Identity and Citizenship in Burma/Myanmar." *Burma Policy Briefing* No. 13. Amsterdam: Transnational Institute–Burma Centre Netherlands, February 2014.

———. "Ethnic Politics in Burma; the Time for Solutions." *Burma Policy Briefing* No. 5. Amsterdam: Transnational Institute–Burma Centre Netherlands, February 2011.

———. "The Kachin Crisis: Peace Must Prevail." *Burma Policy Briefing* No. 10. Amsterdam: Transnational Institute–Burma Centre Netherlands, March 2013.

Tun, Thet. "A Critique of Louis J. Walinsky's Economic Development in Burma, 1951–1969." *Journal of the Burma Research Society* 47, no. 1 (1964): 179.

Tun, Ye. "How the USDP Can Avoid a Landslide Loss in 2015." *Myanmar Times*. 8 July 2013.

Turnell, Sean. "Finding Dollars and Sense: Burma's Economy in 2010." In Susan L. Levenstein, ed., *Finding Dollars, Sense, and Legitimacy in Burma,* 30–31. Woodrow Wilson Center for Scholars, November 2010.

———. "The Glass Has Water: A Stock-Take of Myanmar's Economic Reforms: Exchange Rate, Financial System, Investment, and Sectoral Policies." In N. Cheesman, N. Farrelly, and T. Wilson, eds., *Debating Democratization in Myanmar.* Singapore: Institute of Southeast Asian Studies, 2014.

UN Department of Public Information. "Security Council Fails to Adopt Draft Resolution on Myanmar Owning to Negative Votes by China, Russia Federation." 12 January 2007.

UN Habitat. *Human Settlements Sector Review, Union of Myanmar*. Nairobi: United Nations, 1991.

UN Human Rights Council. *Guiding Principles on Business and Human Rights*. Endorsed by the UN Human Rights Council. New York and Geneva: UN Office of the High Commissioner for Human Rights, June 2011.

Unger, Roberto. "The Critical Legal Studies Movement." *Harvard Law Review* 96, no. 3 (January 1983): 561–675.

United Nationalities Federal Council (UNFC). "Riposte to Article in EBO Briefing Paper No. 8, dated August 2013," 15 August 2013.

United Nations Development Program (UNDP). *Myanmar Agricultural Sector Review and Investment Strategy*. Volume 1, Sector Review. Yangon: UNDP 2004.

United States. Tom Lantos Block Burmese JADE (Junta's Anti-Democratic Efforts) Act of 2008. Washington, DC: US Government Printing Office. Available at www.govtrack.us/congress/bills/110/hr3890/text.

"US: Federal Statistics Show Widespread Prison Rape," *Human Rights Watch*. 16 December 2007.

USAID. *Property Rights and Resource Governance*. Washington, DC. 2013.

USAID Burma, Michigan State University, and the Myanmar Development Resource Institute's Center for Social and Economic Development. "Strategic Choices for the Future of Agriculture in Myanmar: A Summary Paper." July 2013.

USAID Press Office. "President Obama Announces US-Burma Partnership for Democracy, Peace and Prosperity." 19 November 2012.

"US Ambassador Conveys Urgent Concern over Kachin." *Irrawaddy*. 9 January 2013.

"US Begins 'Calibrated' Defence Engagement with Myanmar." *ZeeNews.Com*. 26 April 2013.

US Congress. 2012. H.R. 6431, 112th Congress, 2nd Session, September.

US Department of State, "Background Briefing on the Secretary's Meeting with Burmese President Thein Sein, New York." US State Department. 26 September 2012.

———. "Daily Press Briefing." US Department of State. 4 January 2013.

———. "Fact Sheet: Administration Eases Financial and Investment Sanctions on Burma." 11 July 2012.

———. "Press Briefing by Secretary Clinton in Rangoon." 2 December 2011.

———. "Recognizing and Supporting Burma's Democratic Reforms," Hillary R. Clinton. Washington, DC, 4 April 2012.

———. "Remarks." Hillary R. Clinton. Washington, DC, 13 January 2012. Available at www.state.gov/secretary/rm/2012/01/180667.htm.

———. "Remarks at United Nations After P-5+1 Meeting." Hillary R. Clinton. New York, 23 September 2009.

US Embassy Rangoon. "Ambassador Derek Mitchell Travels to Myitkina, Kachin State, October 24–26." 27 October 2013.

———. "Ongoing Conflict in Burma's Kachin State." 24 January 2013.

———. "Press Release: Union Government–Kachin Independence Organization (KIO) Peace Talks." 31 May 2013.

"US-Myanmar Military Engagement: A Step to Counter China?" *Daily Star*. 1 December 2012.

Vitikiotis, Michael. "Lessons for Cairo from Jakarta, Manila and Elsewhere." *International Herald Tribune*. 9 July 2013.

Wacquant, Loic. "Deadly Symbiosis: When Ghetto and Prison Meet and Mesh." *Punishment and Society* 3, no. 1 (2001): 95–134.

Walinsky, Louis. *Economic Development in Burma, 1951–1960*. New York: Twentieth Century Fund, 1962.

Walton, Matthew J. "Buddhism Turns Violent in Myanmar." *Asia Times*. 2 April 2013. Available at www.atimes.com/atimes/Southeast_Asia/SEA-01-020413.html.

———. "Ethnicity, Conflict, and History in Burma: The Myths of Panglong." *Asian Survey* 48, no.6 (2008): 889–910.

———. "Myanmar Needs a New Nationalism." *Asia Times Online*. 20 May 2013.

———. "Politics in the Moral Universe: Burmese Buddhist Political Thought." Ph.D. dissertation. Seattle: Department of Political Science, University of Washington, 2012.

———. "The Wages of Burman-ness: Ethnicity and Burman Privilege in Contemporary Myanmar." *Journal of Contemporary Asia* 43, no. 1 (2013): 1–27.

Weiser, Benjamin. 2011. "Jury Nullification Advocate Is Indicted." *New York Times*. 25 February.

Weng, Lawi. "Army MP Halts Talks on Military Land Grabs in Burma's Parliament," *Irrawaddy*. 16 August 2013. Available at http://www.irrawaddy.org/burma/army-mp-halts-talks-on-military-land-grabs-in-burmas-parliament.html.

———. "In Naypyitaw, Suu Kyi Attends Armed Forces Day." *Irrawaddy*. 27 March 2013.

———. "Stop Protests Against Copper Mine, Suu Kyi Tells Communities." *Irrawaddy*. 13 March 2013. Available at www.irrawaddy.org/burma/stop-protests-against-copper-mine-suu-kyi-tells-communities.html.

Weng, Lawi, and Saw Yan Naing. "Government-Backed Militias Clash with Kachin, Karen Rebels." *Irrawaddy*. 19 August 2013. Available at www.irrawaddy.org/karen/govt-backed-militias-clash-with-kachin-karen-rebels.html.

"What Does the Rule of Law Have to Do with Democratization (in Myanmar)?" Paper for Myanmar (Burma) Update 2013, Canberra, Australia, 15–16 March 2013.

The White House. "Remarks by President Obama at the University of Yangon." Office of the Press Secretary. 19 November 2012.

———. "Statement by President Obama on Burma." Office of the Press Secretary. Bali, 18 November 2011.

———. "Statement by President Obama on Burma's November 7 Elections." Office of the Press Secretary. 7 November 2010.

———."Statement by the President on Burma." Office of the Press Secretary. 17 May 2012.

Win, Mya. *Tatmadaw's Traditional Role in National Politics*. Yangon: News and Periodicals Enterprises, 1992.

Win, Swe. "Kristallnacht in Myanmar." *International Herald Tribune*. 29 March 2013.

Woods, Kevin. *Agribusiness Investments in Myanmar: Opportunities and Challenges for Poverty Reduction.* Kunming: Yunnan University Press, 2013.

Woods, Kevin, and Kerstin Canby. *Baseline Study 4, Myanmar: Overview of Forest Law Enforcement, Governance, and Trade*. Washington, DC: Forest Trends, 2011. Available at www.forest-trends.org/documents/files/doc_3159.pdf.

World Bank. "Development Indicators." 2012. Available at http://data.worldbank .org/country/myanmar.

Xu, Yan. "The Rise and Fall of the Burmese Communist Party." *Wen Shi Can Kao*. 13 September 2010. Available at www.people.com.cn/GB/198221/198819 /198859/12706724.html.

"Yangon: Regime Pours Funds into Army and Intelligence to Block Web Protests." *AsiaNews.it*. 3 September 2011.

Yun, Joseph. "The FY 2014 Budget Request for the Bureau of East Asian and Pacific Affairs." Statement before the House Foreign Affairs Subcommittee on Asia and the Pacific, US Congress, Washington, DC, 16 May 2013.

———. Testimony before the House Committee on Foreign Affairs, US Congress, Washington, DC, 2 June 2011.

———. "U.S. Policy Toward Burma." Testimony before the Senate Committee on Foreign Relations, Subcommittee on East Asian and Pacific Affairs, US Congress, Washington, DC, 26 April 2012.

Zan, Myint. "Judicial Independence in Burma: No March Backwards Towards the Past." *Asian-Pacific Law & Policy Journal* 1, no. 5 (2000).

———. "Legal Education in Burma Since the 1960s." *Journal of Burma Studies* no. 12 (2008): 63–107.

———. "Position of Power and Notions of Empowerment: Comparing the Views of Lee Kuan Yew and Aung San Suu Kyi on Human Rights and Democratic Governance." *Newcastle Law Review* 2, no. 1 (1997).

Zarni, Maung. "Buddhist Nationalism in Burma." 26 March 2013. Available at www.rohingyablogger.com/2013/03/buddhist-nationalism-in-burma.html.

Zaw, Aung. "Burmese Spy Reveals MI's Dirty Deeds." *Irrawaddy*. 24 April 2006.

———. "Dangerous Days for Burma's Age of Reforms." *Irrawaddy*. 25 June 2013.

———. "The Great Game over Burma." *Irrawaddy*. 11 April 2013.

Zaw, Htet Naing, and Aye Kyawt Khaing. "Military Involved in Massive Land Grabs: Parliamentary Report." *Irrawaddy*. 15 March 2013.

Zawacki, Benjamin. "Defining Myanmar's 'Rohingya Problem.'" *Human Rights Brief* 20, no. 2 (2013): 18–25.

Ziegenhain, Patrick. *The Indonesian Parliament and Democratization*. Singapore: ISEAS Publications, 2008.

The Contributors

Renaud Egreteau is research associate with the Centre for International Studies and Research (CERI) at Sciences Po Paris, France.

Christina Fink is a professor of practice of international affairs at the Elliott School of International Affairs, George Washington University.

Jürgen Haacke is associate professor in the Department of International Relations, London School of Economics and Political Science.

Elliott Prasse-Freeman is associate fellow at the Carr Center for Human Rights, Harvard University.

Lex Rieffel is nonresident senior fellow in the Global Economy and Development Program at the Brookings Institution and visiting professor at the Johns Hopkins University School of Advanced International Studies.

Andrew Selth is adjunct associate professor at the Griffith Asia Institute, Griffith University, Australia.

Martin Smith is senior advisor to the Transnational Institute and an analyst on ethnic nationality and Burma/Myanmar affairs.

Ashley South is research associate at the School of Oriental and African Studies, University of London, and research fellow at Chiangmai University, Thailand

David I. Steinberg is Distinguished Professor of Asian Studies Emeritus, Georgetown University and visiting scholar in Southeast Asian Studies at the Johns Hopkins University School of Advanced International Studies.

Yun Sun is fellow at Henry L. Stimson Center and visiting fellow at Brookings Institution.

Tin Maung Maung Than is senior research fellow at the Institute of Southeast Asian Studies (ISEAS), Singapore.

Moe Thuzar is fellow at the Institute of Southeast Asian Studies, Singapore, and a member of its Myanmar Studies Programme.

Matthew Walton is Aung San Suu Kyi Senior Research Fellow in Modern Burmese Studies at St. Antony's College, University of Oxford.

Index

Page references followed by *t* indicate table. Page references followed by *fig* indicate figure.

About the Book

What issues will Myanmar need to address as it moves beyond the immediate complexities of a transition from an authoritarian state to a more pluralistic polity? How will the new government navigate the challenges—some new, some old—of increasing public participation, persistent coercive forces, economic transformation, ethnic tensions, varying conceptions of the role of law, and more? The authors of this forward-looking volume offer a careful, timely analysis of the kaleidoscopic array of changes occurring in Myanmar and consider the potential long-term impact of those changes for both the country and the region.

David I. Steinberg is Distinguished Professor of Asian Studies Emeritus at Georgetown University and visiting scholar at the Johns Hopkins University School of Advanced International Studies. His recent publications include *Burma/Myanmar: What Everyone Needs to Know*.